EXPLORING THE WORD

~ Daily Inspirational Studies ~

"Enjoy Reading Through The Bible In One Year."

Volume II

July 1 – December 31

Author: Rev. Rodney E. Whittle

EXPLORING THE WORD Volume II
Daily Inspirational Studies
by Rodney E. Whittle

Printed in the United States of America

ISBN 9781615792566

www.xulonpress.com

July 1

O. T. Bible Reading: Job 21-22   **Our Focus: Job 22:21**

ACQUAINT THYSELF WITH GOD

Worship is the real expression of our thoughts as to who God is. It is, therefore, of vital importance that we get to know God in a most perfect way. This is possible only through the Word of God in which we have the clearest portrait of God. Our thoughts of Him are as vital to worship as was the foundation to the mighty Temple.

It is essential that we possess a heart knowledge of God based strictly upon the revelation of Him in the Word of God. Without this we will substitute a head knowledge of God based upon our moral conduct and ideals. It is for this reason that it can accurately be said that a man's theology is determined by his morality. Man will attempt to bring God *down* to his own level, but God's way is to bring man *up* through regeneration into fellowship with Himself.

Nothing is easier than to think. However, nothing is more difficult than to think correctly. It is for this reason that we must be transformed by the renewing of our mind (Rom. 12:2). Our minds are too complex, and His fullness too vast for us to take in such heights and depths at any single time. This requires many an encounter and much time in His Word. We must live in the atmosphere of His presence until we absorb His very life and nature.

Thought For Today

He became what we are to make us what He Is!

July 1

N. T. Bible Reading: Acts 10:1-23   **Our Focus: Acts 10:20**

DOUBTING NOTHING

God never changes, but His dealings with men certainly do. Acts chapter 10 seems to mark an official landmark, as a glorious Gospel dispensation is extended to the Gentiles. How like the Lord to grant a special Divine visitation to Peter, to prepare and instruct him as to one of the most momentous events in the history of Christianity. There is little doubt that Peter struggled with this problem to the very end. It is very difficult for those who have been greatly used of God to adjust when God makes another significant move.

The temporary cutting off of the nation of Israel and the grafting in of the Gentiles is a twin mystery of the New Testament. The opening of this great fact must come by revelation, and becomes yet another key to understanding the Scriptures (Rom. 11:17, 25).

This is indeed a great drama: one man praying, three men traveling, and the risen Lord continuing the work He began during His earthly ministry. The sequel is most exciting. Seven Jewish men and three Gentile men walk to the north for some 20 miles (I wonder what they talked about for five hours). All of this is a beautiful unfolding of a Divine method; the urging of the Spirit, the Divine commission or vision of duty, and the certain knock or appeal of providential circumstances.

God works by fixed and eternal principles. An ear of corn will always have even rows of 8-10-12-14-16 (even 24), but never ever an odd number. A farmer counted rows of corn ears for 27 years without ever finding one exception.

Thought For Today

Those who yield to God's appeal never lack excitement!

July 2

O. T. Bible Reading: Job 23-25   **Our Focus: Job 23:10**

TRIALS THAT PURIFY

"… when he hath tried me, I shall come forth as gold."

The same sunlight which melts the ice also bakes the clay. The key is not what happens _to_ us, but what happens _in_ us. Not every trial will end in triumph: not every adversity will lead it to amenity. The peaceable (conflict ending) fruit of righteousness is the gracious reward of those who have graduated from the school of hard knocks with a Christ-like spirit. It is our reaction which determines the results. Many people become bitter survivors from life's battering: others become better saints from God's bruising.

Much of the problem lies in the perspective. The 10 spies viewed the Promised Land through natural eyes. The inevitable result was that they magnified the obstacles and the enemy. They became grasshoppers standing before mighty giants. Joshua and Caleb saw the land through the eyes of faith. The inspiring result was that they magnified the promises of God, and fixed their focus on the Almighty God who has never lost a battle. _They_ became Giants energized by supernatural strength skipping triumphantly over the 9 foot grasshoppers under their feet.

Thought For Today

Giants are grasshoppers when viewed correctly!

July 2

N. T. Bible Reading: Acts 10:24-48 **Our Focus: Acts 10:34**

NO RESPECT OF PERSONS

God is no respecter of race, rank, or reason. Pride lodges in the branches of human nature, and bears ugly fruit: pride of race, pride of face, and pride of grace. We find ourselves enmeshed and fettered by prejudice, pride, and pretense. Only a miracle could ever emancipate such abject slavery. The true gospel message is God's miracle-working formula for freedom, forgiveness, and fruitfulness.

The dynamic power of the Word of God delivers us from the dominion of sin, the delusions of self, and the deceptions of Satan. The experience of genuine salvation involves the very nature of God entering a mortal being. In my humble opinion the very heart of the Lord Jesus begins to throb again in a human vessel. The purifying and energizing flow of His life and power begins the glorious miracle of regeneration.

The great liberator of Calvary does not coddle our opinions nor does He nurse our prejudices. He blasts them, brings them to the searchlight of heaven, and if we will allow Him, buries them in the mighty flow from Calvary. This process, and indeed it is a process, will liberate us from the old ways. It will so transform our life-style that we will become a marvel even to ourselves. He will wean us from every weakening thing until we reach the heights from which we no longer seek His blessings, but only the living Lord Himself. Let us never settle for a flimsy substitute when the song of saints on higher ground beckons us heavenward.

Thought For Today

Leave the disease-laden marshes ... seek the mountain peaks yonder!

<u>July 3</u>

O. T. Bible Reading: Job 26-28   **Our Focus: Job 28:7**

THE PATH

My childhood was spent on a farm in a remote area, and I spent many days walking on paths. There were no paved roads, no blacktop, not even gravel roads, and no sidewalks, but there were hundreds of paths. We called them trails. There were cow trails, deer trails, rabbit trails, and even school-kids trails through the snow to the school several miles away. Perhaps all of this has made the Scriptures which speak of paths very suggestive and challenging to my mind. We have space here to barely touch on two of those passages.

The above Scripture speaks volumes to me. The many trails which were so much a part of my childhood in so many ways were not blazed (that is marked off) and were in many cases hidden to the uninitiated. The way of the Lord is a path which the unclean will not even detect. There is a broad well-travelled and well paved (with good intentions) way which leads to destruction (Matt. 7:13). Jesus also said that this way (to me a pathway or trail) must first be found before any can walk on it. Only those who have a keen well-trained eye would ever discover the leaf covered trails of yesterday; and only the honest, seeking, hungry heart will find the way of life.

On numerous occasions the Bible speaks of "their ways", "thy ways" and "my ways." Jeremiah added "… the old paths …" (Jer. 6:16) which is the right (good) way. There is indeed a confusing proliferation of religious groups in our time, but there is a sure guide and an accurate map which God has provided for our safety. His Word is a lamp unto our feet and an illuminating light to enable us to find the path (Ps. 119:105); and the precious Holy Spirit will direct us to Him who is our life.

<u>Thought For Today</u>

The path of life has room for only two … Jesus and you!

<u>July 3</u>

N. T. Bible Reading: Acts 11   **Our Focus: Acts 11:19-20**

WITNESSES

The key word in the book of Acts is "witness." It occurs 21 times, but the idea of it fills the entire book. We are distinctly told that, "And with great power gave the apostles witness ..." (Acts 4:33). It is significant that the word "great" occurs 6 times in the Gospel of John and 39 times in the book of Acts. Everything takes on great proportions when the Holy Ghost is operating: great power, great grace, great joy, and great fear.

The apostles are very prominent in the book of Acts. It is interesting that 75 individuals are named in this book and most of them only once. The name of Peter is used 58 times, and we read of Paul 130 times. Some of us would be very happy if our name might just be included in such a great move of God. The apostles are collectively referred to 23 times. The subject of their witness is one key to the book.

The death and resurrection of Christ were the primary points of emphasis in the early church. Every Sunday was Easter; the day of the resurrection, and for them, the day to proclaim the resurrection. The great crowning fact of all time is that "He Is Risen" (Matt. 28:6). The echo of that one super-victory was heard in the vacated tomb and resounds through the ages. Oh, that we too might know Him in the power of His resurrection (Phil. 3:10).

<u>Thought For Today</u>

The tomb is empty ... therefore, our hearts are full!

July 4

O. T. Bible Reading: Job 29-30   **Our Focus: Job 30:17**

THE NIGHT SEASON

The Bible clearly says "And we *know* that *all* things work together for good to them that love God …" (Rom. 8:28). At one time or another every saint of God in adversity would modify the certainty and the inclusiveness of this great promise. However, it is not only true; it is also a great key to an apparent mystery, "why do Christians suffer?" William Cowper's couplet also helps …
Behind a frowning Providence, God hides a smiling face.

Behind all the sufferings and nights of weeping for the Godly, unseen by the tear-drenched eyes, and unheard amid the sobs of sorrow, there is a higher purpose of God. This will not in this vale of tears … the school of faith … be fully understood and thoroughly explained. If it were we would have no need of living and walking by faith. The certainty of knowing that God is still in control, when at least our world seems virtually out of control, will help cope with the uncertainty of an apparently sinking vessel.

> How easy when sailing the sea at a calm,
> To trust in the strength of Jehovah's right arm;
> But somehow I find when the waves swamp the boat,
> It takes some believing to keep things afloat!

Another sweet portion with the bitter herbs is the "afterwards." After the storm comes there are clear skies and a bright shining sun. After our night season of deep sorrow and bitter tears comes the promised enrichment of our inner man.

Thought For Today

The eye of faith frames what the hand of faith claims!

July 4

N. T. Bible Reading: Acts 12   **Our Focus: Acts 12:7**

THE ANGEL

The Scriptures clearly tell us that the Lord went with the disciples confirming the Word with signs following. The book of Acts traces this exciting mission for the next 33 years. When heaven moves, then all of heaven moves. The Angels are mentioned 18 times in the book of Acts. Their direct involvement in the ministry of the early church was crucial.

The Sadducees of old did not believe in Angels nor did they believe in the resurrection. One is left to wonder if the ancient sect has survived the centuries when we hear little or nothing said about Angels from the modern pulpits. The Bible is by no means silent; Angels are spoken of nearly 300 times throughout the Scriptures. The fact is that only a handful of the books of the Bible fail to mention Angels. Jesus himself spoke openly of their personal existence, their sinless condition, their being immortal creatures, and of their vast numbers.

The record of the prison escape of Peter gives us just a glimpse into the amazing work and activity of these mighty creatures. They operate only as precisely directed; transcend natural barriers, perform supernatural assignments, are able to converse and communicate with human beings, and are "… ministering spirits, sent forth to minister for them who shall be heirs of salvation" (Heb. 1:14). Let us thank God for so great a salvation, and for the vast resources He has placed at our disposal.

Thought For Today

Speeders beware! Angels retire at 65!

July 5

O. T. Bible Reading: Job 31-32   **Our Focus: Job 32:1**

SELF-RIGHTEOUSNESS

The book of Job is not a special favorite to most of us. You will experience the full range of emotions as you read it: shock, sympathy, disgust, pity, disbelief, boredom, amazement, excitement (at the end), bewilderment … they're all there! You may even develop a spiritual headache from sheer fatigue … you will scratch your head, shake your head, turn your head, nod your head, and in the end _bow_ your head as did Job.

The central problem which evaded Job's comforters, and which all too easily evades each of us, was self-vindication. In the grand conclusion Job could easily say "I abhor myself", but during the grueling ordeal he heatedly defended himself. He was given a genuine revelation of God which caused him for the very first time to say, "… now mine eye seeth thee" (Job 42:5). It was then, and only then, that he could triumphantly say, "Wherefore I abhor myself, and repent …" (Job 42:6). This was no morbid introspection. It was a glorious deliverance, a release from a barren prison cell of captivity, and the bright dawning of a new day of freedom and fruitfulness.

The ugly beast of self must die. We are to be self-less disciples of the most unselfish Man who ever lived. The natural life is not sinful, but it is selfish; and, therefore, it is subtle and destructive to genuine spirituality. This nature will not and cannot be removed, but it must die and be transformed through rugged and determined obedience (Gal. 5:24).

Thought For Today

The world awaits the Bible bound in shoe leather!

July 5

N. T. Bible Reading: Acts 13:1-23   **Our Focus: Acts 13:2, 4**

THE HOLY GHOST

The promise of Acts 1:8 becomes the outline of the book. The mighty witness to the risen Savior must begin in Jerusalem, and the first seven chapters of Acts are the record of this. In Acts chapters 8-12 the outreach extends to Judea and Samaria, and finally in chapter 13 begins the witness to "the uttermost part of the earth."

We never read about the resolutions of the apostles, but we are all thrilled by the acts of the apostles. It is not so much an account of words but of actions. It is the "doings" of individuals anointed and led by the Holy Ghost. There are 261 references to the Holy Spirit in the New Testament, and 57 of them are in the book of Acts. The spiritual key to the power and effectiveness of that early church is the expression in Acts "... through the Holy Ghost ..." (Acts 1:2).

We are told in Acts 13:2 that "As they ministered to the Lord, and fasted, the Holy Ghost said, Separate me Barnabas and Saul ..."; these men were sent forth not by a Mission Board, nor by a missionary Society, but by the Holy Ghost (Acts 13:4). We do not know precisely how this Divine commission was communicated to the praying band, but it was both clear and conclusive. We are also told "For as many as are *led* by the Spirit of God, they are the sons of God" (Rom. 8:14). It is our privilege and responsibility to be directed in our lives and activities by the precious Holy Spirit; let us not live below our privileges.

Thought For Today

It is as we obey that we hear Him most clearly!

<u>July 6</u>

O. T. Bible Reading: Job 33-34   **Our Focus: Job 34:31**

SUFFERING

Those who lack the facts will always fail in judgment. The book of Job makes clear that Job was not meant to know the facts which would clarify the mystery of his suffering. The truth is that the all-wise God is as infinitely wise in His reservations as He is in His revelations. It was vitally important to the outcome that Job not know all the facts of the case. The very revealing of the facts would thwart the design of God for the good of Job and for the glory of God.

The hopeless and futile dogmatic theories of Job's friends is a mighty exposure of the perils of jumping to conclusions with little or no clear understanding of all the evidence. To venture a solution to some hypothetical circumstance is an adventure in futility. The wise will avoid the trap. The very core of our relationship with the Lord is faith. Without faith it is impossible to please God (Heb. 11:6). With all, or even most of the facts, there is neither room nor need for faith. The great message of the ancient Book is clear: there is a Divine purpose for our ultimate good and God's greater glory in everything we experience. The only right conclusion to the whole subject must justify the ways of God. Imperfect knowledge results in imperfect conclusions. The subject of the book of Job should not be taken to be the final and full answer to the mystery of suffering. It is rather a beautiful unveiling of a loving and caring God overruling and controlling the most complex human elements for the Godly pilgrims. For us the temporary revelation is that suffering fulfills a Divine purpose and exercises a gracious ministry in us. We justify God by faith, and we await the rest of the story at the final unveiling.

<u>Thought For Today</u>

We must face today's problems with tomorrow's promises!

July 6

N. T. Bible Reading: Acts 13:24-52   **Our Focus: Acts 13:52**

JOY

The empty promise of the world says "happiness is …", and they add an unending list of wishful fantasies. None will fulfill the promise. Happiness depends upon happenings, and with the turn of events it takes wings and forsakes the grasping heart. The joy of the Lord is entirely different. It springs from a different source, and flows through a different channel. The full tide of joy is never experienced until we are weaned from every earthly and natural crutch. It is not found in vibrant health, not in material success and prosperity, not even in singularly blessed service for the Lord. It is realized only in a perfect understanding of God and His ways, and in the resulting communion with Him in sharing His eternal purposes.

All that God has done for us is but the threshold of a vast treasure house. He wants to lure us into the banquet room and fill us with the transforming reality of Himself. We will emerge from this blessed encounter, "… like pillars of smoke, perfumed with myrrh and frankincense, with all powders of the merchant" (Song of Sol. 3:6).

Strange are the ways of the Lord to the natural mind of man. We artfully try to avoid the very things which will enrich our lives spiritually. It is from the wine-press that the stimulant flows. The heavy load, the crushing burden, the sorrows and the heartaches, and the heartbreaks are many times the tools which God uses to squeeze out the wine of joy. Jesus said, "… My meat is to do the will of him that sent me …" (John 4:34).

Thought For Today

Give all He asks so you can claim all He promises!

July 7

O. T. Bible Reading: Job 35-37   **Our Focus: Job 37:22**

MAJESTY

The word "majesty" denotes greatness and dignity. There seems to be a very special sense of thrilling exultation whenever we sing of His exaltation and His Majesty. The song of Moses in Deuteronomy chapter 32 was inspired and became somewhat like our national anthem. It begins by exalting the name of the Lord, and by "… ascribe ye greatness unto our God" (Deut. 32:3). In this song he used the word "rock" seven times. The original word is more inclusive than our English translation: it infers a mass of rock. The first thing that suggests to our minds is a mountain or to others simply, The Rockies. The greatest single impression made when an individual first views the mighty mountains is that they are so "majestic." It is simply amazing how many Bible events are associated with some mountain:

1.   On Ararat the new world began.
2.   On Moriah the faith of Abraham was perfected.
3.   On Sinai the law was given.
4.   On Horeb the Tabernacle was designed.
5.   On Nebo the land of promise was unveiled.
6.   On Zion the capital of Judah was fixed.
7.   On Moriah the temple was reared.
8.   On Carmel Israel was called to their covenant God.
9.   On Hattin Jesus preached a sermon.
10. On Hermon He was transfigured.
11. On Calvary He died.
12. On Olivet He ascended.

Thought For Today

What the light reveals the blood will cleanse!

July 7

N. T. Bible Reading: Acts 14   **Our Focus: Acts 14:5**

PERSECUTION

Jesus, we know, was a man of sorrows and acquainted with grief (Isa. 53:3). He forewarned His disciples that in the world they would experience tribulation (John 16:33). Paul also declared that all that would live godly in Christ Jesus would suffer persecution (II Tim. 3:12). It is most interesting that the root of the word "witness" is "martus" from which is derived the English word "martyr."

The Apostle Paul declared his credentials were threefold:

1.   His call and conduct.
2.   His sufferings.
3.   His vision and message.

He enumerates some although we know there were others after this unusual catalog. Many of the sad lists of sufferings for the heroes of faith in Hebrews chapter 11 were tragic, and very likely of fairly brief duration; but Paul's stretched over a 30 year period of time. The Lord had prepared him at the time of his conversion: "For I will shew him how great things he must suffer for my name's sake" (Acts 9:16).

The ministry of Paul was a living martyrdom. They plotted to kill him in Damascus as well as in Jerusalem. He was driven out of Antioch. The angry mob attempted to stone him in Iconium. He *was* stoned in Lystra. He was beaten with rods and thrown into prison at Philippi. He was mobbed at Thessalonica. He was driven out of Berea. They plotted to kill him in Corinth. Another angry mob nearly ended his life at Ephesus. Besides all of this he was beaten with 39 stripes five times. He was shipwrecked three times. It seems to me that we have it pretty easy! The most difficult part of our calling may not be to *die* for Him, but to truly *live* for Him.

Thought For Today

The mighty Apostle of Christ was an enemy to the religious leaders!

July 8

O. T. Bible Reading: Job 38-39   **Our Focus: Job 38:4**

GOD'S QUESTIONS

The first recorded communication of God with man after the fall was a question: "… Where art thou?" (Gen. 3:9). We are told that Jesus asked 150 questions in the record we have of His words in the Gospels. God enters the scene of Job's lengthy dialogue by asking 59 unanswered questions. It seems that the speech of Elihu had stirred up quite a storm. "Then the Lord answered Job out of the whirlwind …" (Job 38:1). How many times this has been repeated through the centuries; out of a storm or tempest of trouble and distress the precious voice of the Lord reaches our troubled heart.

The method of the Lord is that of the Supreme Teacher. An effective teacher will always begin where the student is and will proceed to where he should be. In the above passage nature is raging with a violent storm. God breaks in as the Creator; the One who not only was there, but the very One who designed and carried out the work of creation. Someone said that they like to read the dictionary because the stories are so short. Job had darkened counsel by many words, but without knowledge. If silence is golden, then Job and his friends really failed.

It is a surprise to many that God offers Job no explanation for his mysterious sufferings. Job is being led to see that there is a God who not only controls but also cares. He is also being wisely drawn to the place of absolute trust; a place where he will rest peacefully in God Himself, apart from any explanations.

Thought For Today

Sometimes God's questions are revelations!

July 8

N. T. Bible Reading: Acts 15:1-21 **Our Focus: Acts 15:12**

THE GENTILES

There are three broad definitions of mankind as God views them: Jews, Gentiles, and the Church of God (I Cor. 10:32). The Jewish nation generally is thought of as the covenant people through Abraham, Isaac, and Jacob. Strictly speaking the Jews were the descendants of Judah. The Israelites were descendants of Jacob whose name was changed to Israel. Hebrew is the linguistic designation; Israelite is the national designation; Jew is the religious designation which came to be used quite broadly.

The Gentiles in the most inclusive sense are all nations outside of the nation of Israel. From the very outset God made it clear that the Gentiles were included in His plan. The covenant made with Abraham stated: "... in thee shall all families of the earth be blessed" (Gen. 12:3). Isaiah's prophecy reached out to the entire world, "And the Gentiles shall come to thy light ..." (Isa. 60:3). There are many other Old Testament Scriptures which clearly include the Gentiles in God's great plan of redemption.

The Old Testament is replete with examples of Gentiles being blessed of God: Melchizedek, Jethro, Rahab and Ruth, Naaman and many others. The most amazing thing of all is that His great love included each one of us in the offer of salvation. The Gospel Truth continues to ring out its glorious message: "... whosoever will, let him take the water of life freely" (Rev. 22:17).

Thought For Today

The Revealer of God is the Redeemer of men!

July 9

O. T. Bible Reading: Job 40-42   **Our Focus: Job 42:10**

JOB'S DOUBLE PORTION

What a happy ending to a sad story! The proverb of Solomon takes on real meaning, "Better is the end of a thing than the beginning thereof: and the patient in spirit is better than the proud in spirit" (Eccl. 7:8). The glad ring of final victory gives expression to a common proverb even down to our time, "... the patience of Job ..." (Jam. 5:11).

Many unfair comments have been critically made by shallow thinkers concerning Job. May I humbly offer a few thoughts in his defense? The lengthy speeches of Job are not so much answers to Eliphaz, Bildad, and Zophar as they are the agonizing sob of a desolate soul to a God who could not be found, from a self which could not be escaped, through an anguish which could not be explained.

There is a threefold aspect to the grand conclusion of this ancient story which rings with a familiar sound. First, there is a personal transformation. God turned his captivity and in the process transformed his character, and he does come forth as "... gold tried in the fire ..." (Rev. 3:18). Second, there is vindication. God calls Job his servant, makes him a priest to his friends, and has him pray on their behalf. Third, there is restoration. Job is given a double portion of the Divine blessing (Job 42:10).

Thought For Today

If we saw the desired end we would smile at the process!

<u>July 9</u>

N. T. Bible Reading: Acts 15:22-41   **Our Focus: Acts 15:22**

BARNABAS

The name of Barnabas occurs 24 times in the book of Acts, but never after chapter 15. His original name was Joses. He was a Levite, and his home was in Cyprus. He later moved to Jerusalem and acquired property there which he sold and put the money into the Common Fund of the Apostles. The church in Antioch, by the direction of the Spirit, sent Paul and Barnabas on what is known as Paul's first missionary journey which covered a period of about two years. They also took with them John Mark, a cousin of Barnabas, who withdrew from them in Perga. The two men had known each other for 10 years, and had lived and served together for about 6 of those years.

Paul prepared to begin his second missionary journey, and Barnabas wished to take his cousin again. Paul, however, steadfastly refused, and they parted company. This was a sad turn of events. We know very little about the sharp contention, but subsequent history may tell us a great deal. We do know that things were reconciled with Paul and Mark.

There is a reference in Galatians 2:13 which tells us that when Peter withdrew from the Gentile brethren, Barnabas joined in with the dissimulation. This Paul quickly and publicly condemned. There seems little doubt that Barnabas took a carnal stand with flesh and blood and lost out in his ministry because of it. This is one more sobering reminder of the weakness of the flesh. Rare indeed are the souls who will stand with God and with His Word against their own flesh and blood.

<u>Thought For Today</u>

To stand against wrong, even in close natural ties, is true spirituality!

July 10

O. T. Bible Reading: Psalms 1-3   **Our Focus: Psalms 1:1**

THE BLESSED MAN

God wants to bless His people. When He spoke to Abraham He emphatically told him, "... I will bless thee ..." (Gen. 12:2). Jesus opened the great Sermon on the Mount with the word "blessed" repeated 9 times. The expression, "blessed is the man" is used 14 times in the Scriptures. It behooves us to know the conditions God has laid down which put us in a position from which He will bless us.

We are told that a river went out of Eden, and was parted and became four streams (Gen. 2:10). The name of the first river meant freedom. Jesus is the great emancipator who sets us free from every fetter which may have held us in bondage. The name of the second river meant fullness. It is God's purpose for all to enjoy the fullness of the Lord Himself (Eph. 3:19). The name of the third river means power. This is the exact provision which the Lord has made for this dispensation: "... ye shall receive power, after that the Holy Ghost is come upon you ..." (Acts 1:8). The fourth name means fruitfulness. Jesus said, "... I have chosen you ... that ye should go and bring forth fruit, and that your fruit should remain ..." (John 15:16).

The cleansed leper of Leviticus chapter 14 is a type of the forgiven sinner. After the significant application of the blood and oil to his ears, hands, and feet "... the rest of the oil ..." (Lev. 14:17, 29) was to be poured upon his head. This was a copious shower of abundance and overflow. May it be ours in a very special way this very day.

Thought For Today

The out-flow of the overflow depends upon the in-flow!

July 10

N. T. Bible Reading: Acts 16:1-15   **Our Focus: Acts 16:6-7**

CLOSED DOORS

The steps and the stops of a good man are ordered of the Lord (Ps. 37:23). Paul was certainly a Spirit-led man, and he was Divinely directed as to what to do as well as what not to do. One is as much a supernatural directive as the other. One morning I was approaching a long two-lane bridge into Omaha, Nebraska. Something within seemed to say, "stop here and eat." I continued on for a short distance and then an even more insistent command: "stop now, pull in and eat." Almost alarmed by the unexpected interruption I stopped, and went into the truck stop to order breakfast. My food had not yet been served when the air was filled with wailing sirens. A drunken driver from the other side of the river had slammed into a car on the bridge and three people were dead. I thanked the Lord over and over for causing me to stop. You may say that really wasn't a stop … it was only a delay. Well, whatever it was, it saved my life and I thank God for His goodness!

God was preparing to make a new move. He would send the glorious Gospel message to Europe. The Spirit forbade them to go south into the province of Asia. The Spirit of God also stopped them from going north into Bithynia. Paul had just come from the east. There was only one direction left and that was west across the Aegean Sea into Europe. It was at this point that the great Apostle was given a vision in the night, and the man of Macedonia said, "… Come over into Macedonia, and help us" (Acts 16:9). God is an on-time God!

Thought For Today

If we knew the future we would never question the present!

July 11

O. T. Bible Reading: Psalms 4-6   **Our Focus: Psalms 4:1**

ENLARGEMENT

The narrow way to the flesh is the way of enlargement and expansion to the spirit. The Psalmist said he would quit dragging his feet (my version) when the Lord had enlarged his heart (Ps. 119:32). It is so refreshing to find individuals who have a heart for God. They would rather talk about the Lord, the word of God, and the things of the Lord than any other subject. These rare souls have had an enlargement of their heart creating a great capacity and hunger for spiritual things. This is not something that is inherited; it is something which is imparted by the Lord. "Blessed are they which do hunger and thirst after righteousness: for they shall be filled" (Matt. 5:6).

Great spiritual transactions and operations transpire in the most unlikely circumstances. There is a recounting of the experience of Joseph in Egypt in Psalm 105, verse 18 simply states the fact that, "Whose feet they hurt with fetters: he was laid in iron." The margin throws an entirely different light on the whole experience. It states that, "his soul came into iron." The first statement describes the scene as men viewed it. The margin gives an insight into what God was doing in the heart of Joseph through the awful ordeal. God was preparing His vessel. An awesome responsibility lay ahead for Joseph and God was putting metal into his character. It is this culture of the soul which is precious to the Lord, and so utterly essential for the leader in training.

Thought For Today

Enlargement is a process accomplished through quiet resignation!

July 11

N. T. Bible Reading: Acts 16:16-40   **Our Focus: Acts 16:25-26**

MIDNIGHT MIRACLE

This is an amazing demonstration of miraculous and supernatural intervention. There was supernatural grace and strength given to the beaten and bleeding disciples. There was a supernatural convulsion of nature. Nature is at God's disposal, and will respond to His command. This was not just a 6.5 tremor on the Richter scale. It was a direct divine intervention accompanied by a natural phenomenon with supernatural results. No earthquake of whatever magnitude would unlock the shackles as well as unlock and unlatch the prison doors and leave them wide open. It has always been interesting to me that amid this unbelievable manifestation of miraculous power the wounds of the flogged disciples were not instantly healed. It was left for the now converted jailer to bathe their still bleeding lacerations. Beware of concluding that if a certain phenomenon was really of God then this or that would certainly also happen. You could be entirely wrong!

The rapid-fire sequence of events here seemed to me to have a very real symbolic value. The nature of the message these men preached would shake, shock, and shame the guilty sinner. It seems safe to conclude that the thunder from the modern pulpits would not crumble stonewalls – it would scarcely ripple a pup-tent! The ancient message proclaimed deliverance to the captives, the opening of the prison doors to all who were chained, and the setting at liberty of those who were bound. It would be refreshing to witness another midnight miracle of this magnitude.

Thought For Today

When the fire leaves the pulpit the smoke will fill the pews!

July 12

O. T. Bible Reading: Psalms 7-9   **Our Focus: Psalms 9:9**

A REFUGE

"The name of Lord is a strong tower: the righteous runneth into it, and is safe" (Prov. 18:10). The final words of Moses reminded Israel that, "The eternal God is thy refuge, and underneath are the everlasting arms ..." (Deut. 33:27). The Psalmist painted a most beautiful picture for God's people, "He that dwelleth in the secret place of the most High shall abide under the shadow of the Almighty" (Ps. 91:1). One of the great anthems of the Reformation was Luther's song: "A Mighty Fortress Is Our God." When the Israelites came into the land of Canaan there were 6 cities designated as "cities of refuge" to which any person guilty of death by accident might flee. The 3 cities, which lay on the west of Jordan, were each set upon a hill. Forty-eight cities were assigned to the Levites, and these 6 cities were selected from them.

Many profitable applications have been made from this interesting type. The names of the cities are most suggestive. The first mentioned was "Kadesh" which means consecrated or a sacred place. This is full of meaning. It may be applied to the Lord Himself for after all He alone is the refuge for our souls. We must be careful not to look to anyone, nor to anything to provide our true and certain resting place. The second city was "Shechem", the city of 80 springs. All of our springs are in Him, and He is our most glorious hiding place.

Thought For Today

Christ is present in all of His people, but pre-eminent in very few!

<u>July 12</u>

N. T. Bible Reading: Acts 17:1-15   **Our Focus: Acts 17:12**

CONVERTED

Those who seriously read and study the Word of God will experience supernatural results. These of Berea were convinced, convicted and converted. There is both a crisis and a process involved in this great transaction. It involves the total person … intellect, emotions, and will. The basic root meaning of the word convert is *to turn*. This involves a reversal of direction: a turning *from* and a turning *to*. It is a Divine visitation which brings about a new relationship with God. The primary elements (although certainly not the only ones) are repentance, faith, and a grand deliverance; "… ye turned to God from idols to serve the living and true God … which delivered us …" (I Thess. 1:9-10).

The preaching of Paul made Bible students of them all. What a worthy and productive exercise: they "examined daily", that is, from top to bottom, up and down as in a legal research. We will only act upon that which we, by examination, are convinced is truth. It is just here that the precious Holy Spirit brings the strength of Divine persuasion and produces genuine conviction; this results in a new creation (II Cor. 5:17). It is significant that in the account of creation in the book of Genesis the words "let" and "God" are very prominent. The word "let" occurs 14 times and the word "God" is used 35 times for a combined total of 49. Seven is the number of Divine completeness (seven sevens equals forty nine). The key to both the old and the new creation is to "let God" have His perfect way.

<u>Thought For Today</u>

The measure in which we turn from determines the degree we turn to!

July 13

O. T. Bible Reading: Psalms 10-12   **Our Focus: Psalms 10:2**

THE WICKED

The tragic plight of those classified in Scripture as "the wicked" needs to be thoughtfully considered. The word in one form or another is used about 500 times in the Word of God. It occurs in the reading for today, and a total of 109 times in the Psalms. The first use of the word is in Genesis 6:5, "And God saw that the wickedness of man was great in the earth, and that every imagination of the thoughts of his heart was only evil continually." The last mention is in I John 5:19, "And we know that we are of God, and the whole world lieth in wickedness."

The root meaning of the word wicked is "morally wrong" as well as "lawless." The term is used broadly to contrast the ungodly from the righteous. We are clearly warned by the prophetic Scriptures that, "Many shall be purified, and made white, and tried; but the wicked shall do wickedly …" (Dan. 12:10). Paul also warned that, "… evil men and seducers shall wax worse and worse, deceiving, and being deceived" (II Tim. 3:13).

There can be little or no doubt in the minds of serious and thoughtful souls that we are living in the last days. Every fiber of this world is permeated with what is morally wrong, and is lawless in nature. The spirit of this age is to promote these elements and to create the mind-set that it is just normal living. In the very midst of this profusion of evil *many* shall be purified, and made white. What a challenge … what an opportunity!

Thought For Today

The springs of character fill the streams of conduct!

July 13

N. T. Bible Reading: Acts 17:16-34   **Our Focus: Acts 17:31**

APPOINTMENTS

There are some things in life which are open to negotiation and others which are non-negotiable. It is well for us to realize that this applies most significantly in the spiritual realm. What God has appointed cannot be annulled and should not be appealed. Real life will require the making of many appointments; some are kept and others are not. The appointments which God has made will be kept without rescheduling. Some appointments spoken of in the Scripture are obvious and hopefully recognized and accepted by all of God's people. There are some others which are much less apparent and not so readily accepted. Paul told the Thessalonians believers that there were some afflictions which God had arranged in their appointment book (I Thess. 3:3). Peter says the same thing using a little different language in I Peter 3:9. God has called us (or appointed us) to encounter contrary circumstances, but we are to act and react as ambassadors of heaven.

The circumstances God allows usually come at an unannounced time and are delivered in some very unattractive packages. Many of us could more easily keep the appointments if we could choose the delivery man. Someone has pointed out that Jesus has invited us to a great banquet and not to a picnic. When we understand that the same God who arranged the circumstances also included the instruments. The key to victory is to see God and not the people. He is still in control and intends only our best good for His eternal glory.

Thought For Today

When I smile at the storm He rebukes the wind!

July 14

O. T. Bible Reading: Psalms 13-16   **Our Focus: Psalms 16:11**

THE PATH OF LIFE

Psalms chapter 16 has been called, "David's Jewel." The title is Michtam of David: the Hebrew word can mean the revelation of the blessed mystery. This seems consistent with the triumphant conclusion of the Psalm, "Thou wilt shew me the path of life ..." (Ps. 16:11). It would be a major discovery to be directed to the path which leads to life. The flaming sword of Eden which kept or guarded the way to the tree of life has become a neon arrow pointing the way to "paradise restored" in Christ.

There are many paths and many ways which criss-cross on their dubious courses. It is not the beauty, the attractiveness, the appeal, the challenge nor even the pleasantness of the path that really matters; it is "where does it lead to?" We are warned that, "There is a way which seemeth right unto a man, but the end thereof are the ways of death" (Prov. 14:12, 16:25). The path of life is in the singular: there is but one way and Jesus is the way, the truth, and the life (John 14:6). The ways of death are many as Jeremiah enjoined us to, "... Stand ye in the ways, and see, and ask for the old paths, where is the good way, and walk therein, and ye shall find rest for your souls ..." (Jer. 6:16).

The Word of God provides abundant direction to seeking souls. It speaks of "the word of life", "the bread of life", "the light of life" and "the ways of life." The book of Revelation concludes the pursuit by finding "the tree of life", "the water of life", "the spirit of life" and victoriously "the crown of life."

Thought For Today

The path of life winds upward to ever higher ground!

July 14

N. T. Bible Reading: Acts 18   **Our Focus: Acts 18:5**

PRESSED IN THE SPIRIT

The highest privilege afforded to mortal creatures is to be led or directed by the Spirit of God. The Psalmist refers to "… the man of the earth …" (Ps. 10:18). No doubt this stands in sharp contrast to "the man of God", which is used for seven men in the Old Testament, and of one man in the New Testament. It is of special interest that the prophet Elisha is so designated 29 times. However, there is another very specialized dimension for the very few who will be men and women of the Spirit. It is one of the most glorious and most miraculous facts of all time that a God who is a Spirit can and does communicate to the spirit of man.

The Psalmist declared, "Blessed is the people that know the joyful sound: they shall walk, O Lord, in the light of thy countenance" (Ps. 89:15). Jesus was, without question, the most spiritual person ever to live on this earth. We are told that this giant of the Spirit was, "driven by the Spirit", "rejoiced in spirit", "groaned in spirit" and He "was troubled in spirit." There are some distinctive features which characterize the Divine activities in the life of a child of God. There is always a lift in the spirit. Other pressures will come and always the direction is downward, outward or inward, but never upward. They come with the shroud of death and defeat. The blessed heavenly impact is always upward and brings with it the hope of life and the shout of victory.

Thought For Today

Any Divine impulse always vibrates with heaven's music!

July 15

O. T. Bible Reading: Psalms 17-18   **Our Focus: Psalms 18:2**

THE LORD IS

Today is the test for the lessons of yesterday, and the foundation for the uncertainties of tomorrow. Most of us tend to live in the past, or to be obsessed with the ghosts of the future. This is a very unhealthy condition. The word of God is a primary source of help: that the emphasis in the Scriptures is on a present tense relationship with the Lord is beyond question. The singularly significant statement, "the Lord is" occurs over 90 times … 34 times in the Psalms. When Moses was told to lead the nation of Israel out of Egypt he asked the Lord what he should say as to the name of the God who had sent him. The answer was swift and emphatic: "… I Am That I Am …" (Ex. 3:14). He is the eternally self-existent One.

Faith operates in the realm of the present: unbelief will focus on the failures of yesterday or the impossible issues of tomorrow. The words of a very old hymn have been a favorite of mine through many a fierce battle:

> Before the battle lines are spread,
> Before the boasting foe is dead,
> I win the fight tho' not begun,
> I'll trust and shout, still marching on,
> Jesus saves me now.

The Lord is everything I need at this very moment. It is not so much that "He was" or "He has been" or "He will be", but a refreshing and reassuring "He is." This is the voice of faith which dispels the clouds of doubt and fear. Let us live today in such a way that we tell the world: "The Lord *IS*."

Thought For Today

Just as I see "HE IS" in that measure I also say "I CAN!"

July 15

N. T. Bible Reading: Acts 19:1-20   **Our Focus: Acts 19:17**

MAGNIFY THE LORD

The Psalmist invited us to, "… magnify the Lord with me, and let us exalt his name together" (Ps. 34:3). This is a very high honor, and a rare privilege. We realize, of course, that He is infinite and therefore cannot really be made greater. The point is that His name grows in manifested glory in our minds as we focus upon Him and His majesty. This is why it is so important for us to meditate on the Lord and upon the Word of God. Only Divine inspiration can summon us to such lofty heights of thought and devotion. We can magnify Him only in proportion as we know Him. The knowledge of God is more essential to all of us than the knowledge of anything else … indeed, of all things put together.

It is incumbent upon us to exalt, magnify, glorify and worship the Lord. We are admonished in the song of Moses to "… ascribe ye greatness unto our God" (Deut. 32:3). The Prophet Isaiah said, "… his name shall be called Wonderful …" (Isa. 9:6). The adjective which means "marvelous", "astonishing", becomes a noun … and the name for Messiah. Jesus, our Savior, the Son of God is a wonder! Everything about Him is Wonderful. His birth was wonderful; the only baby born into this world who did not have a human father. His teaching was wonderful. Those who heard Him sat spellbound as He taught and they said, "… Never man spoke like this man" (John 7:46). His character was wonderful. He was "… holy, harmless, undefiled, separate from sinners, and made higher than the heavens" (Heb. 7:26). His death and resurrection were wonderful. The empty tomb echoes with the shout of victory, "He is not here: for he is risen …" (Matt. 28:6).

Thought For Today

To magnify the Lord is to modify all else!

July 16

O. T. Bible Reading: Psalms 19-21   **Our Focus: Psalms 19:1**

GOD REVEALED

Those who can read may discover God in three books. The first, the Book of Nature is a revelation of God as to His glory (Ps. 19:1). The heavens do not tell of God's will, His mercy, nor of His love; but they incessantly and universally show forth His Majesty, power, wisdom, and His goodness. Those who study the stars estimate that the Milky Way, the galaxy to which our earth and solar system belong, contains many thousands of suns, and most of them immensely larger than our sun, which is a million and a half times larger than the earth. The Milky Way stretches like a thin watch band, its diameter from rim to rim being 200,000 light years: a light year is the distance that light travels in a year at the rate of 186,000 miles per second. They maintain that there are at least 100,000 galaxies like the Milky Way, some of them millions of light years away. How *great* is our God!

The second Book, which reveals God, is the Scriptures (Ps. 19:7-14). There are 6 titles used here to describe the Word of God, and 6 attributes ascribed to the law of the Lord, also 6 which the precious truth of God has upon those who explore its pages. Thirdly, it is left to the Book of the Human Heart to witness to the glorious personal experience all of this revelation makes so real to each individual. To know God is to know His creative power in a transforming new creation. This power purifies the heart, protects the mind, prepares the soul for righteousness, and will present the faithful pilgrim into everlasting habitations and the eternal glory.

Thought For Today

When we behold we believe ... when we wonder we worship!

July 16

N. T. Bible Reading: Acts 19:21-41   **Our Focus: Acts: 19:35**

EPHESUS

One of the Seven Wonders of the World was the temple dedicated to the Asiatic goddess, Diana in Ephesus. The month of May was called the Artemisian, because it was the month in which they celebrated with great gatherings dedicated to Artemis or Diana. These conventions were attended by vast crowds and were called the Ephesia. The theater here described was capable of seating 25,000-30,000 people. The magnificent temple according to one authority was 418 feet long by 239 feet wide and had 127 columns, each 60 feet high.

Paul visited Ephesus at least 3 times, and ministered there from 2 to 3 years … more time than he spent in any other city. Paul wrote the Epistle to the church at Ephesus. It has been called, "the Alps of the New Testament" by one writer, and by Dr. Pierson, "Paul's third heaven Epistle." One of the seven letters to the churches of Asia Minor was written to the church at Ephesus. Timothy also ministered at Ephesus, and the apostle John is believed to have spent his last years there.

The word Ephesus means "to relax" or "let go" and aptly describes the tragic condition which led to ruin and decay. They had left their first love. The warning of Revelation 2:5 has been fulfilled: the candlestick has been removed, the church is gone, and the proud city reduced to ruins. The busy harbor is now a reedy pool surrounded by malaria infested marshes. This sad scene has been repeated in thousands of lives. We must maintain that bright flame of devotion in our daily lives. It is the *secret* and the *source* of personal victory.

Thought For Today

Where the flame glows the life flourishes!

July 17

O. T. Bible Reading: Psalms 22-24   **Our Focus: Psalms 24:6**

THE GENERATION

The dictionary definition for the word *generation* is: "a bringing into being, the act of begetting." We are very familiar with the genealogies of certain men introduced with the words: "these are the generations of …." The prophet Isaiah lamented concerning the then future and unmarried Messiah: "… and who shall declare his generation? for he was cut off out of the land of the living …" (Isa. 53:8). The prophetic designations given by Isaiah for the Virgin born Immanuel included: "… The everlasting Father …" (Isa. 7:14, 9:6). The great mystery of the new birth, the new creation, and an holy nation is brought into early focus. He is to have many sons (Heb. 2:10), and as a new creation in Christ He would give them everlasting life (John 3:16, 36).

The law of reproduction and the preservation of species is forever settled by the words, "after his kind" repeated 10 times in Genesis chapter 1. This law carries over into the spiritual realm as well. Jesus will have a posterity by the miracle of the new birth, who will supernaturally be transformed into the very nature of Christ by the process of regeneration. His royal blood will flow in their veins and they may claim their inheritance as children of *the King*! The Psalmist declared, "A seed (a remnant) shall serve him; it shall be accounted to the Lord for a generation" (Ps. 22:30). This fact must be kept clearly in our minds. We are by Divine decree a minority group. This makes us both pilgrims and strangers with our permanent home in an eternal city, which has foundations whose builder and maker is God (Heb. 11:10, 13).

Thought For Today

Our regeneration has made us a chosen generation!

July 17

N. T. Bible Reading: Acts 20:1-16   **Our Focus: Acts 20:6**

TRIUMPH AT TROAS

The Apostle Paul was in Troas three times. Acts chapter 20 is the record of his last visit there. There is no record of what he did during the one week of this stay. It is of the last day we are given a very vivid account by Luke. The names of the small company of friends of Paul are listed who gathered with the little band of disciples in Troas. Luke was there on Sunday, the first day of the week, for the breaking of bread. What a service they had. Many a preacher has taken unwarranted license from what transpired. Some have even boasted that they were better preachers than Paul. He preached until midnight to put one person to sleep, and they usually have at least half a dozen dozing in 45 minutes. Others justify an hours-long rambling of boredom, as Apostolic succession. The results here are much more important than the circumstances involved.

Eutychus fell from the open window, and Dr. Luke pronounced him "dead." Paul went down to him and presented him alive to the very relieved audience. He then continued his discourse even 'till the break of day (Acts 20:11). What a preacher! What a Congregation! It would seem safe to say that any preacher who could raise the dead would not lack for a congregation who would hear him gladly through a 12 hour sermon. However, we are left to wonder where we might find honest and open hearts with that kind of a thirst to hear the Word of God.

Thought For Today

Those who pray before they sleep will awaken refreshed!

<u>July 18</u>

O. T. Bible Reading: Psalms 25-27   **Our Focus: Psalms 25:9**

THE MEEK

Jesus plainly said that He was meek and lowly in heart (Matt. 11:29). He also said, "… All power is given unto me in heaven and in earth" (Matt. 28:18). This great attribute of the Mighty Creator is the fruit of power. The infinite resources of omnipotence produced a beautiful and blessed balance of spirit in the Lord Jesus. He was neither elated nor cast down, neither exuberant nor depressed, simply because He was self-less (not occupied with self at all). The thundering Niagara Falls draws millions of awe-struck tourists but does little or nothing to irrigate the land. It is the tiny streams, the 10,000 creeks and rivers that glide unseen and unheard throughout the earth which imparts life, healthy growth, and abundant harvests.

It has always seemed to me that most of the attempts to define "meekness" fall infinitely short. The reason for this may not be too difficult to find. Most attempt to relate this rare quality to some human or natural trait: this spells failure. Meekness is the product of direct Divine impartation. It is heavenly in origin, and therefore transcends any human definition. It is a temper of spirit, supernaturally derived, from sustained and direct contact with the living Christ. It is an attitude of the heart which bows reverently in submission before the Almighty God: it accepts His word as final, it recognizes His Lordship as complete, and it honors Him in every practical way without resisting, disputing, limiting, or even questioning. No wonder Jesus said, "*Blessed* are the meek" (Matt. 5:5).

<u>Thought For Today</u>

Meekness in the creature is closeness to the Creator!

July 18

N. T. Bible Reading: Acts 20:17-38   **Our Focus: Acts 20:28**

TAKE HEED

The admonition of Paul to the elders of the church in Ephesus includes the idea of watchfulness. One translation says, "keep a watchful eye on yourselves." The word is used in three senses:

1. To watch in order to guard.
2. To watch, meaning to look for.
3. A watch in the night.

The context pretty clearly indicates the first meaning: they were to guard themselves first, and then the church for which they were responsible.

Hebrews 2:1 begins by saying, "Therefore we ought to give the more earnest heed to the things which we have heard, lest (as Williams translates it) we should drift to one side." None are exempt from these two Divine directives. It has been wisely said, "unguarded strength is double weakness."

When a farmer begins plowing in a field he must be on guard not to swerve or drift from a straight line. As a youth this was a real challenge to me. The most effective way was to set up two or three flagged stakes in a direct line. By keeping these lined up, you will not deviate to the right or to the left, and the furrow will be a thing of beauty.

There is a great lesson here for every child of God. If we are to run in a straight line we must set up a near stake and a distant one. We should have a goal for today, but we must have a clear and final goal and purpose for which we live, and toward which we consistently move.

Thought For Today

Without a clear purpose we will leave a crooked track!

July 19

O. T. Bible Reading: Psalms 28-30   **Our Focus: Psalms 29:11**

THE PEACE OF GOD

The Psalmist promised, "… the Lord will bless his people with peace" (Ps. 29:11). Jesus declared, "Peace I leave with you, my peace I give unto you …" (John 14:27). Paul taught, "And the peace of God, which passeth all understanding, shall keep your hearts and minds through Christ Jesus" (Phil. 4:7). The word "peace" in one form or another occurs about 300 times in the Bible, and in every book of the New Testament except I John. The basic thought is that of harmony and calm. People in many areas of this troubled world are crying for "peace at any price." What they have in mind, of course, is a cessation of hostilities. There may well be a false sense of calm without any harmony, which is only a disguised time-bomb. It was for this reason Jesus said, "… I came not to send peace, but a sword" (Matt. 10:34). Any tranquility which is not based on a personal relationship with the Prince of Peace must be given the sword.

We must first experience peace _with_ God before we can ever know anything about the peace _of_ God. Doubts, anxieties, frustrations, and confusion abound any time we lose our focus on the Lord Jesus. He is the Prince of Peace: as we look into His peace-filled face we are transformed into children of peace. It is His peace which is transmitted to our very lives. Transmitted and reflected peace is proof that we are in contact with the Lord and there is nothing between to deflect it. Any impediment causes us to turn our minds to ourselves and to our problems. It is our responsibility to keep the line clear: it is His promise to fortify our very beings with the peace of God.

Thought For Today

Spiritual growth ceases where disobedience begins!

July 19

N. T. Bible Reading: Acts 21:1-14　　　　　　　　　**Our Focus: Acts 21:14**

THY WILL BE DONE

Jesus taught His disciples to pray, "… Thy will be done in earth, as it is in heaven" (Matt. 6:10). The Bible says of Him, "… Lo, I come to do thy will, O God" (Heb. 10:7, 9). The single most important thing that any man will ever do is to find and do the will of God. Nothing else really matters, and all else is but the vegetation on the branches: it is the fruit that counts and not the leaves.

The basic issue in the Garden of Eden was that of two wills. God's will was made very clear and very plain, but man must choose. The sovereignty of God is most clearly seen in the free will of man. This faculty of free moral agency is no threat to God, but it is the ultimate key to the salvation of man. For any person to say, "thy will be done" from the heart involves a total surrender to the Lordship of Christ. God does not crush our will into submission, He does not force us to submit, He simply waits for us to *yield* to Him, to His Word, and to His will.

The real crisis in every life is just at this very point. It is not a question of decision; it is an issue of rebellion. This is a matter of the will. When once that battle is won, and the heart bows in absolute surrender, the triumphant reign of Christ begins in the experience of the yielded life. When this is done, all is done, and this battle will never need to be re-fought. Then, and only then, we too can say victoriously, "I *delight* to do thy will …" (Ps. 40:8).

Thought For Today

The paradox of the spiritual life is that we conquer only where we yield!

July 20

O. T. Bible Reading: Psalms 31-33   **Our Focus: Psalms 31:20**

THE SECRET PLACE

We *are* in public what we *do* in private. It is in the hidden, concealed, and unseen areas of life that the real person is fashioned. "For as he thinketh in his heart, so is he …" (Prov. 23:7). We may not be what we think we are, but what we *think* we actually are. It is for this reason that this great salvation activates and energizes the very spirit of our minds, and causes the imaginations of the thoughts of the heart to be renewed and riveted on the Lord and on spiritual things. This is a miracle, and an ongoing transformation; a glorious reality made possible by the Spirit of Holiness filling our lives and our thoughts (Rom. 1:4, 12:2).

There is a place which is hidden, concealed, and unseen by a careless and ungodly world, which is opened to a chosen few, where they dwell in the secret place of the Most High (Ps. 91:1). They are thus described by the Psalmist as, "… thy hidden ones" (Ps. 83:3). Truly a secret society! There is a dwelling place where our lives are hid with Christ in God (Col. 3:3). They are to be ushered into the innermost part of His tent (Ps. 31:20). Could this suggest, into the very Holy of Holies? He said He would "keep" them there, and certainly this means Divine protection. And it also seems to me to include the idea of continuity. It is this *dwelling* or *remaining habitually* which seems to agree with what Jesus meant when He spoke of our need to abide in Him.

Thought For Today

When we cannot trace we can confidently trust!

<u>July 20</u>

N. T. Bible Reading: Acts 21:15-40   **Our Focus: Acts 21:20**

EMPHASIS

The temptation among men is to put a barrel of emphasis on an ounce of truth. We tend to major on minors and to minor on majors. It would seem to be wisdom on our part to consider carefully what the Word of God emphasizes. The two and three-quarters chapters from Luke 21:17 to Luke 23:30 covers only 12 days. It is not without significance that the same author, Dr. Luke, devotes nine and a half of his 24 chapters in the Gospel of Luke to the last week of our Lord's life. The captivities (imprisonments) of the Apostle Paul cover five years of time: seven and a half of the 28 chapters of Acts are dedicated to this period. The book represents a span of 33 years, and one-quarter of it deals with only five years.

There are intervals of time in the history of the church when God is making a major move, and it is a crucial time of transition. Transition is a time of change, and it is fraught with great danger. By the very nature of things, to go through a change is to experience something quite new. By definition it means to alter, to shift, or to make different. This is a delicate act which requires great diligence. Policy and procedure which involve preferences and prejudices can be altered without sacrificing principle.

The Scripture reading for today is a focal point in church history. The Mosaic day is at eventide, the sun is rising on the church age of New Testament Christianity. Thousands believed, but were zealous for the Law of Moses. Fanaticism (of the Jews) stemmed from prejudice which resorted to lying and violence, and was based upon a false supposition. "… they supposed …" (Acts 21:29); a supposition is a very weak framework woven together by threads of unproven gossip yet it has broken countless hearts, ruined families, split churches, and shaken the very foundation of nations.

<u>Thought For Today</u>

To walk we must take action, but we need not stumble!

July 21

O. T. Bible Reading: Psalms 34-35   **Our Focus: Psalms 34:11**

THE FEAR OF THE LORD

The Scriptures declare, "The fear of the Lord is the beginning of knowledge …" (Prov. 1:7). "The fear of the Lord is the beginning of wisdom …" (Prov. 9:10). The expression is used 30 times in the Word of God, and 14 times in the book of Proverbs. We are told that, "… fear hath torment …" also that, "… perfect love casteth out fear …" (I John 4:18); it is quite obvious even to a first-time reader that there must be different kinds of fear.

"The fear of man bringeth a snare …" (Prov. 29:25). This kind of fear demoralizes men, robs them of courage and hope, and makes a coward out of a giant. It is the dread of the opinions of our neighbors which makes us cowards to declare our faith. This is an unhealthy fear which must be overcome.

The fear of the Lord may be said to consist of a healthy respect or reverence for the Lord. It is not a doleful dread nor is it a slavish state of mind: it is a blessed attitude with a supreme desire to please the Lord in everything and to offend Him in nothing. The fear of the Lord includes the *way* of the Lord: His principles, His eternal methods and fixed laws, His plan and His eternal purposes. It is not something which may be taught in a single lesson nor learned in a single day. It is a vast subject which requires a very keen student, a very able teacher, a very protracted lesson time, and a vast treasure of teaching materials. The fear of the Lord does not mean that we are afraid of Him; it means rather that we have learned to love Him dearly and our greatest desire is to please Him in all that we say and do.

Thought For Today

The Almighty God satisfies the weakness of man!

July 21

N. T. Bible Reading: Acts 22   **Our Focus: Acts 22:28**

FREEDOM

The river which flowed out of the Garden of Eden was parted into four streams. The first of which was "Pison" which some have said means freedom (Gen. 2:10-11). The cry of the human heart world-wide is for liberty or freedom. There are 86 nations in the world where the people are free, but 46 nations where the word is never used. Patrick Henry spoke to the Virginia Convention on March 23, 1775, at which time he made a now famous statement:

- "Is life so dear, or peace so sweet, as to be purchased at a price of chains and slavery? Forbid it, Almighty God! I know not what course others may take, but as for me, give me liberty, or give me death!"

Jesus declared, "If the Son therefore shall make you free, ye shall be free indeed" (John 8:36). He had previously said to the Jewish believers, "And ye shall know the truth, and the truth shall make you free" (John 8:32). Paul rejoiced, "For the law of the Spirit of life in Christ Jesus hath made me free from the law of sin and death" (Rom. 8:2).

There were three memorials especially celebrated by the nation of Israel. Twelve stones were deposited in Jordan, and twelve were erected on the land ... the very stones crying out, "This land is His!" The rite of circumcision was a seal and a sign of the covenant proclaiming to all: "This man is His!" The Passover feast was celebrated nationally to tell all other nations, "These people are His!" There is a seal, a sign, a memorial which we should celebrate today; "... The Lord knoweth them that are his. And, let everyone that nameth the name of Christ depart from iniquity" (II Tim. 2:19). The miracle of a transformed life is a memorial tribute to the mighty power of the risen Savior: "This life is His!"

Thought For Today

Spiritual freedom is freedom to fully do the will of God!

July 22

O. T. Bible Reading: Psalms 36-37   **Our Focus: Psalms 37:3**

NATURAL OR SPIRITUAL

The plain lesson of history is a revelation as to Israel. The election of Israel relates to past history. The rejection of Israel relates to their past and present history. The restoration and conversion of Israel relates to their future history. There are many promises in the Word of God which relate to a natural people and to their natural and physical blessings. God promised earthly and material blessings to an earthly people. The cutting off of Israel and the grafting in of the Gentiles is one of the mysteries of the New Testament. The unfolding of this previously veiled truth clearly reveals that the rejection of Israel was not total, neither was it final. The Bible uses the phrase, "in the land" approximately 40 times, and it refers to the land of Canaan and to the nation of Israel.

The great emphasis of the New Covenant is not natural but spiritual. Paul longed to see the Romans, "… that I may impart unto you some spiritual gift, to the end ye may be established" (Rom. 1:11). He said to the church in Ephesus, "Blessed be the God and Father of our Lord Jesus Christ, who hath blessed us with all spiritual blessings in heavenly places in Christ" (Eph. 1:3). Those who promote and emphasize material and physical prosperity miss the whole thrust of the New Testament. We are now to "… seek ye first the kingdom of God, and his righteousness; and all these things shall be added unto you" (Matt. 6:33). The natural, material, and physical blessings (and they are many) are not an end in themselves; they are benefits which automatically flow from a right relationship with Christ. Our inheritance is not in Minnesota, not in the USA, not in the land of Israel, but "in Christ." He has blessed us as spiritual people, in a spiritual realm, with a spiritual experience, called with a heavenly calling, to an eternal reward.

Thought For Today

Our treasures are in heaven … our problems are on earth!

July 22

N. T. Bible Reading: Acts 23:1-11   **Our Focus: Acts 23:11**

THE NIGHT FOLLOWING

The focus of the flesh is always on "me" and "now." The focus of faith is on "Him" and "then." The Word of God fills us with hope because there is always an "afterward" in God's reckoning for us. "Now no chastening for the present seemeth to be joyous, but grievous: nevertheless afterward it yieldeth the peaceable fruit of righteousness unto them which are exercised thereby" (Heb. 12:11). "For I know the thoughts that I think toward you, saith the Lord, thoughts of peace, and not of evil, to give you an expected end" (Jer. 29:11).

Any deep trial or fierce spiritual battle takes on extremely exaggerated proportions while the storm is raging. It seems overwhelming in terms of the intensity: it seems forever in terms of the duration. However, the Word of God weighs it in eternal scales and from God's perspective. He calls it, "… our *light* affliction, which is but for a *moment*, worketh for us a far more exceeding and eternal weight of glory" (II Cor. 4:17); to us it appears to be a near tragedy of crushing proportions with no real purpose but to overwhelm us if not to completely destroy us.

We must be tried before we can triumph. The night of weeping comes before the joyful morning. Calvary precedes Pentecost. There must first be a death before there can be a resurrection. "And the Lord said unto Abram, *after* …" (Gen. 13:14); "*After* these things the word of Lord came unto Abram …" (Gen. 15:1). Jesus remained on the cross only until He was dead. Our trials and tests are meant to bring us to an utter end of ourselves. When we die to ourselves, our ambitions, and our views the Lord will remove the cross. It has fulfilled its purpose. "The end may come, and that tomorrow … when God has wrought His will in me."

Thought For Today

The promises for tomorrow lighten the trials of today!

July 23

O. T. Bible Reading: Psalms 38-40   **Our Focus: Psalms 40:1**

PATIENCE

> Patience is a virtue: possess it if you can,
> Seldom in a woman: never in any man.

Usually when a statement is anonymous it is also open to question. The above lines have been repeated millions of times, but that does not mean they are entirely true. Patience may be called a virtue because it is certainly a moral excellence: it may also be defined as a principle because it is a moral rule or element of conduct. The first or primary meaning of the word is, "to abide under." This clearly is the key to the meaning of the word in Scripture. It is primarily a New Testament word: it is used only three times in the Old Testament, in the above Scripture, in Psalms 37:7, and in Ecclesiastes 7:8.

Patience is born of God (Rom. 15:5), germinates in conflict (Jam. 1:3), and matures in tribulation (Rom. 5:3). That would be enough to close the book on it for many people. Who needs or wants all of that? If this isn't enough to frighten the faint of heart the root of "tribulation" is from the Latin word, "Tribulum." For your encouragement we are told it alludes to a heavy piece of timber with spikes, used anciently to thrash grain, it was drawn over the grain to separate the straw and the chaff. This may discourage many from praying for patience. However, it is associated with faith, and is a vital element of hope. We are commanded to be patient (Jam. 5:7-8), and there can be no doubt, from the very lack of it, that we all need it!

Thought For Today

Patience germinates in conflict and matures in tribulation!

July 23

N. T. Bible Reading: Acts 23:12-35   **Our Focus: Acts 23:12**

AND

The word "and" is a conjunctive which connects phrases or clauses. In the Scriptures it often is more than that. It is an affirmation of an ongoing series of events linked together by the overruling providence of a Master Planner. Nothing happens by chance for God's people, and "all is right that seems most wrong if it be his sweet will": "behind a frowning providence He hides a smiling face." The word "and" is the first word in eleven of the 23 verses in today's Bible reading; it is also the first word in fourteen of the 27 chapters of the book of Acts. The second chapter of Acts describes the day of Pentecost and the first five verses begin with "and." There is a rapid-fire sequence of events, but they are by no means unrelated nor are they out of control.

The last words of the Bible reading for yesterday included the reassuring words of the risen Savior still in control of the governor, the magistrate, the 40 assassination plotters, and of the prison itself: "be of good cheer." Paul, be strong, be brave, be courageous: I am standing by not as an idle spectator but as the Supreme Commander: I am in control of every situation, and you can rest in that confidence. The casual inclusion of the youthful nephew and the incidental (or so it might seem) overhearing of a plot to kill the Apostle was no accident: it was the overruling Lord, and unseen but mighty presence, working through the commonplace to produce the ultimate deliverance.

Thought For Today

Nothing is common when God is in it!

July 24

O. T. Bible Reading: Psalms 41-43   **Our Focus: Psalms 42:2**

THIRSTING FOR GOD

The Psalmist said, "My soul thirsteth for God, for the living God ...", and repeated the statement three times (Ps. 42:2, 63:1, 143:6). The great prophet Isaiah promised, "For I will pour water upon him that is thirsty, and floods upon the dry ground: I will pour my spirit upon thy seed, and my blessing upon thine offspring" (Isa. 44:3). Jesus pronounced a special blessedness or happiness to those who "... do hunger and thirst after righteousness: for they shall be filled" (Matt. 5:6).

Thirst is said to be the strongest of the natural appetites, and even more demanding than hunger. Everyone has this natural craving, and everyone regularly slakes their thirst. Very few experience the deep craving after God which the Scriptures describe. It is very rare. What is spoken of is a strong and intense driving desire after spiritual reality. It is the most urgent of all other desires. It is a longing for Him who is the living God. It is also an Holy discontent with all that is unlike Him.

Jesus told the woman of Samaria, "... whosoever drinketh of the water that I shall give him shall never thirst; but the water that I shall give him shall be in him a well of water springing up into everlasting life" (John 4:14). Once this blessed water of life has been tasted, the thirst for all else ceases, but the heart cries out, "Lord, evermore give me this water." May the Lord increase the tribe of "the thirsty ones!"

Thought For Today

Thirsting for God means forsaking all else!

July 24

N. T. Bible Reading: Acts 24   **Our Focus: Acts 24:16**

A GOOD CONSCIENCE

God placed within man at the time of his creation a unique faculty which we call conscience. Animals were created with instincts; man was created with something much higher and loftier than mere animal instincts. Because man was created in the image of God there was built into his very nature a Divinely imparted capacity which would both guard and direct his thinking, his attitudes, and his conduct. It would be the eye of the soul. The word conscience essentially means, "co-knowledge." It is an inner principle of right, a built in gauge of right or wrong, a monitor within (which agrees with and witnesses to) the appeal of law and order from without. It is the law of God written in the heart.

The Fall of Man forever distorted and diminished this grand creation, but it did not destroy it. It has been said, "control the conscience and you control the life", and it could also be said, "destroy the conscience and you destroy the life." Is this not the very soul and goal of godless humanism?

There is a Divine remedy. We may now become new creatures in Christ Jesus. The imparting of this new life quickens this inner faculty into vibrant activity. It is awakened, and now must be educated, taught, and trained by the Word of God to be directed and empowered by the Holy Spirit. When the conscience has been cleansed by the precious blood of the Lord Jesus Christ it is made responsive to all of the claims of Christ. It may become seared by consistent disobedience and rebellion. It may become clear through obedience and consistent behavior. It may be called "pure" when it is void of offense toward God, and toward men (Acts 24:16; I Tim. 3:9).

Thought For Today

When the conscience is purified the life is sanctified!

July 25

N. T. Bible Reading: Psalms 44-46   **Our Focus: Psalms 46:7, 11**

GOD WITH US

We are told that John Wesley on his deathbed scarcely able to speak mustered all strength possible and raised his hand and waving it in triumph exclaimed: "the best of all is, God is with us!" Psalm chapter 46 was the favorite of the great reformer, Martin Luther. When under fierce attack and beset by impossible odds he would say to his friend Melanchthon, "come, Philip, let us sing the 46th Psalm." No doubt he had this Psalm in mind when he wrote the great reformation hymn, "A Mighty Fortress Is Our God." Twice the Psalmist repeats the identical words, "The Lord of hosts is with us; the God of Jacob is our refuge" (Ps. 46:7, 11).

Self-consciousness if allowed to persist will be an insidiously slow process leading to self-pity, and self-pity is a one-way street to defeat. On the other hand God-consciousness is the sweet awareness of His presence. His presence is manifest by His very life: the proofs of His presence are the manifestations of life. The glory of the presence of the Lord will one day literally cause "… the desert (to) rejoice, and blossom as the rose … And the parched ground shall become a pool, and the thirsty land springs of water …" (Isa. 35:1, 7). It can now become a blessed spiritual reality to every child of God. By His presence we are made confident even amid discouragement: we are made patient even amid the most trying of circumstances: we are made strong amid grave danger: we are made calm and peaceful even amid bitter conflict: we are made to have joy even amid great sorrows. His presence shall go with us, as promised, and always there is added, "… and I will give thee (you) …" (Ex. 33:14) just everything we need! It is well for us to remember that the Times of Refreshing come from the presence of the Lord (Acts 3:19).

Thought For Today

Omnipotence is terrible to crush, but Almighty to protect!

July 25

N. T. Bible Reading: Acts 25   **Our Focus: Acts 25:4**

BUT FESTUS

Acts chapter 25 is a running account of the doings of some Roman officials who weighed heavily on the scales of political importance. The Apostle Paul was face-to-face with the central authority of the world. Festus was the host. Agrippa was a vassal of Rome and Festus was representing the imperial purple. The chief captains were present; they were the heads of the military in that region. The prominent civil rulers were also gathered with great pomp.

Agrippa the second was the last of the Herod's. It was his great-grandfather who ordered the murder of the innocent less than two years of age at the time of Jesus' birth. His grand-uncle had ordered John the Baptist beheaded. James had been executed by his father. Each of these had died or in humiliation were disgraced soon after the events mentioned. Just 16 years earlier his father had been Divinely judged as worms devoured his flesh in a tragic death. From every human aspect this was an *august* occasion. The story unfolds with recurring phrases: "But Festus ..." (Acts 25:4, 9), "Then Festus ..." (Acts 25:12), "Then Agrippa ..." (Acts 25:22, 26:1, 28) etc. It reads as though these dignitaries were doing as they pleased in the way they pleased and when they pleased.

We must dig a bit deeper to get the true picture. At the time of his conversion the Lord told the disciple Ananias to tell Paul that he would bear His name before the Gentiles, and *kings*, and the children of Israel (Acts 9:15); the Lord stood by Paul and informed him, "... so must thou bear witness also at Rome" (Acts 23:11). Had all of this not transpired we would not have the books of Ephesians, Philippians, Colossians, Philemon, and the pastoral Epistles of First and Second Timothy and Titus. It is good to know that there is a mighty God who sits on His Royal Throne and is the One who is really in control ... even in adversity!

Thought For Today

God still rules even in the kingdoms of men!

July 26

O. T. Bible Reading: Psalms 47-49   **Our Focus: Psalms 49:14**

IN THE MORNING

The phrase, "in the morning" is repeated scores of times in the Word of God. Another very challenging aspect is introduced by adding the word "early." The words "early in the morning" occur about 38 times in the scriptures. It has always seemed to me that you lose the very best part of the day if you miss the early morning. The thought of morning expresses the most necessary philosophy of life and attitude of mind.

Today is not the last and final word on the calendar. There will be another sunrise, and in saying that, there is the anticipation of hope and the expectation of faith. The events of today: its clouds, its trials, its heartaches, its disappointments, even its sunshine and its blessings are but for a day ... they too "came to pass." It is reassuring that the Scriptures say that "... faith, hope, charity ..." are all elements of the morning: they will abide and remain (I Cor. 13:13).

One of the many things promised and prophesied for the morning is joy; "... weeping may endure for a night, but joy cometh in the morning" (Ps. 30:5). Those who live for today have their reward in whatever the day may bring of good or of evil. Those who live for God have a blessed hope which reassures them that all is not lost at the setting of the sun. There is an eternal home which gives us both confidence and patience. What I get from today may well disappear with the darkness of the night, what I get from God springs from an eternal source and becomes a vital part of the "... eternal weight of glory" (II Cor. 4:17) which is reserved beyond the reach of rust and decay for us "in the morning."

Thought For Today

Those who live for today only must always dread of the sunset!

July 26

N. T. Bible Reading: Acts 26   **Our Focus: Acts 26:16**

A WITNESS

The Apostle Paul was called to be an apostle, a preacher, and a teacher (I Tim. 2:7). This Divine ordination was clear, positive, and very compelling. It was a very lofty ministry into which he had been launched. It was in many ways unique. However, his great office notwithstanding, it is of primary interest to everyone that he was very specifically also ordained to be a witness. There is nothing as convincing as a testimony of personal experience. It seems to me that we have here the strongest possible proof that office, argument, and lecture without the element of personal experience falls far short of the intended pattern. In this model defense before Agrippa, the Apostle Paul used the personal pronoun "some" 36 times. A profound message without personal experience may be a pronounced failure. The miracle of Divine intervention and transformation in an individual life has no equal in the ears of any congregation.

Each one of us has a personal responsibility to also be a witness. People are quick to claim Acts 1:8 as a promise of power, and certainly it is; however, it is primarily the power to be a witness. Only "a witness" is allowed to speak in court. It must be something which the individuals saw, heard, or with which they have had some personal experience. The greatest miracle of all time is the miracle of a transformed life. We must be very careful not to glamorize or in any way advertise the former life, but in the simplest way to state the tragic fact. We must focus on the mighty power of God which has made us a new creature and on the person of the resurrected Jesus who died for our offenses, and was raised again for our justification (Rom. 4:25).

Please allow me to insert right here my own testimony. It is because He has so completely transformed my life, satisfied my deepest needs, and filled my life with His blessing and glory that I can recommend Him without hesitation as the fairest of ten thousand.

Thought For Today

What God has wrought cannot effectively be fought!

July 27

O. T. Bible Reading: Psalms 50-52   **Our Focus: Psalms 51:6**

THE INWARD PARTS

The shallow nature is just that, very shallow, light, and frivolous feeding on impulses, impressions, and to a large extent on its surroundings. The appeal of God does not function on that level. "God is a Spirit: and they that worship him must worship him in spirit and in truth" (John 4:24). Truth is profound and makes no appeal to a chaffy nature. There are dimensions in the spirit realm which are both infinite and heavenly. The woman of Samaria spoke far more accurately than she ever imagined, "… Sir, thou hast nothing to draw with, and the well is deep …" (John 4:11).

It is the Spirit that searches the deep things of God (I Cor. 2:10). The carnal mind of man is left far behind helplessly floundering on the shoals that abound near the shore. The Psalmist revealed that God's thoughts are *very* deep (Ps. 42:7). The foolish may feed on folly and trivia (Prov. 15:14), and Ephraim who is a "… a silly dove without heart …" (Hos. 7:11) may feed on ashes and every trendy wind that blows (Hos. 12:1; Isa. 44:20), but the "hidden ones" are driving to the very heart of God. One reason given for the good seed not bringing forth fruit was because there was no depth in the life of the person involved (Mark 4:5-6).

It is in the innermost recesses of our being that God desires to see the image of His Son. The Christ-likeness is miraculously wrought in the hidden man of the heart by His very presence and transforming power. These are the rare souls who in their ever-ascending pursuit of God discover His ways in the secret places of the stairs (Song of Sol. 2:14).

Thought For Today

There is no shout of a king in a self-ruled life!

53

July 27

N. T. Bible Reading: Acts 27:1-25   **Our Focus: Acts 27:22**

BE CHEERFUL

The great Apostle Paul has never appeared more apostolic than on this occasion. A swirling tempest rages on in unabated fury, and all hope of survival is gone (Acts 27:20). For 14 days they ... all 276 of them ... had been battered by a raging sea; much of the ship's equipment was already lost, all of them seemed to have been violently seasick, and they were in imminent danger of being drowned. A more dire set of circumstances, a more likely scene of disaster, and a more frantic and desperate crew cannot be imagined. In the midst of these horrific conditions Paul admonishes all not just to not fear, not just to have courage and be brave, but amazingly to be cheerful. What an unlikely turn of events!

A short time earlier in his life when it appeared the angry Jewish mob would prevail to end his life the Lord again revealed Himself to Paul in the night and spoke these very words "... Be of good cheer, Paul ..." (Acts 23:11). The Word of the Lord is creative. Paul would never forget the miracle those words produced in his heart. A great calmness, a triumphant confidence, and an absolute assurance of ultimate victory flooded his entire being. The angel of God who visited Paul in that tempestuous night may have said that very same thing ... we do not know. At any rate, that same blessed tranquility gripped his heart and mind as he admonished this frightened crowd to "... be of good cheer ..." (Acts 27:22).

Paul could easily say now, "... I believe God, that it shall be even as it was told me" (Acts 27:25). The Word of the Lord through Paul was like magic. "Then were they all of good cheer, and they also took some meat" (Acts 27:36). What a testimony! What a victory! What a mighty Savior!

Thought For Today

God-given faith rejoices where human fear cringes!

July 28

O. T. Bible Reading: Psalms 53-55   **Our Focus: Psalms 55:22**

HE SUSTAINS

The word sustain seems to have two primary meanings: first, to keep from falling or sinking; second, to nourish or keep alive. One translation appears to give the true meaning of Psalms 55:22: "commit your problems to the Lord, and He will uphold you." That is, you roll the whole package (yourself and the burden you are carrying) upon the Lord. This is not an escape hatch: it is a supernatural provision for an inescapable condition. We are not to fling off our burden, but we are to ease over more closely to Him and to lean heavily upon Him so that He sustains us and the burden. The burden here is not the burden of sin, of transgression, nor of doubt and fear. It is the burden the Lord has given us to bear (Gal. 6:5).

He will not allow the righteous to be overthrown. They will not flounder and sink; they will not be uprooted and swept away. They may and will sway like the boughs of a tree in a mighty storm, they may and will have some huge wave splash over the entire deck, but they will survive to sail on and into the safe harbor beyond. This great reassurance quickens this heavily burdened man to cry out in faith, "... I will trust ..." (Ps. 55:23). There is a burden of responsibility to *try* us, a duty to be shouldered to *test* us, and a promise made to *sustain* us. The Lord is a very present help in trouble because He is our refuge and strength (Ps. 46:1). We could never know and experience this without some test or trial.

Thought For Today

Difficulties are the tools of the heavenly architect!

July 28

N. T. Bible Reading: Acts 27:26-44   **Our Focus: Acts 27:35**

HE GAVE THANKS

The circumstances were far from favorable; the wind was fierce, the waves were boisterous and threatening, and there was the frightening awareness that this ship was about to sink. In spite of and in the midst of all of this the Apostle Paul gave thanks.

It was this very same apostle who gave the 22 Commandments to the Thessalonians in which he said, "In everything give thanks: for this is the will of God in Christ Jesus concerning you" (I Thess. 5:18). We are instructed to "give thanks" some 37 times in the Scriptures. To *give thanks is to obey*. It is an act of the will. It is one sacrifice in New Testament times with which He is well pleased (Heb. 13:15-16). It is generally connected to the preposition "for." You can only really "give thanks" for some specific thing. We know that all things must work together for good (Rom. 8:28), that God loves us and designs only our spiritual best and highest, that He is on the throne, and that every condition and person must submit to His authority. There is so much for which we should give thanks.

To give thanks is to take the first step upward and into the Royal Palace of communion with God. The British author Isaac Walton said, "God has two dwellings: one is in heaven, the other in a meek and thankful heart." To give thanks is to cultivate a grateful spirit which issues in an outpouring of thanksgiving and quickens the spirit of praise which opens the inner sanctuary of genuine worship. The Bible never mentions the word "smile." We give thanks even when we cannot even smile. It is then that it is truly a sacrifice. The root meaning of the word is "to extend the hand"; surely a fitting posture for the humble pilgrim before the Almighty God.

Thought For Today

To give thanks is to unlock the door of communion!

July 29

O. T. Bible Reading: Psalms 56-58   **Our Focus: Psalms 56:3**

FEAR

There is a first-class section, "… I will trust, and not be afraid …" (Isa. 12:2): and a second-class section, "What time I am afraid, I will trust in thee" (Ps. 56:3). The first is more costly, but by far and away much more comfortable and enjoyable. Fear is a basic natural human emotion of foreboding, dread, or danger. It is a feeling of anxiety and agitation caused by the presence or nearness of danger, evil, or pain. The Word of God gives us a much broader concept. There is a normal and healthy fear which is a God-given faculty:

1.   A good healthy respectful attitude called by many a "filial" fear.
2.   A normal emotion essential to the preservation of life.
3.   A healthy reaction to sudden alarm.

There is also a fear which is evil and which has torments:

1.   Fear of want or poverty.
2.   Fear of serious illness or death.
3.   Fear of penalty or judgment.

We know from the Scriptures that "… God hath not given us the spirit of fear …" (II Tim. 1:7). The key to conquering the tormenting paralyzing dread which will attack God's people is clearly outlined in two Scriptures: "… for _he_ hath said, I will never leave thee, nor forsake thee. So that _we_ may boldly say, The Lord is my helper, and I will not fear …" (Heb. 13:5-6). We focus on what God has said, laugh at impossibilities, and cry "it shall, it shall be done!" "There is no fear in love; but perfect love casteth out fear …" (I John 4:18).

The Word of God creates a very real personal awareness of the awesome majesty of God which gives us a calm reverential attitude toward God. It also fills us with a strong personal love for our great Redeemer which casts out the fears which have torment.

Thought For Today

One cannot fear while filled with trust and confidence!

July 29

N. T. Bible Reading: Acts 28:1-15   **Our Focus: Acts 28:14**

WE WENT

The book of Acts is the only record we have of the first century activities, ministry, and mission of the New Testament church. One way to judge the relative importance of anything is to consider "what would we do without it?" The long list of individual names and seemingly endless names of places may in themselves seem unimportant if not a little boring. They take on a very different significance when we see them as the individuals who were responsible for writing the first chapter in the exciting record of the church which Jesus said He would build. The book of Acts covers about 33 years of time, approximately the same as that covered by the four Gospels. It is the bridge between the vital Gospel record and the rest of the New Testament.

A thoughtful study of the great Apostle Paul is a veritable revelation of the meaning of the word witness. Here we have a God-called and Holy Ghost anointed Apostle to the Gentiles exposed to every vicissitude of life. He is stoned, he is beaten, he is thrown into prison, he is bitten by a scorpion, he is shipwrecked, and he suffers beyond any other person except the Lord Himself. We are not called to be a centerpiece in an elaborate showroom. We are called to be so united to the blessed Savior that we lose all self-consciousness and self-importance and become absorbed in Him. Luke says, "… we went toward Rome" (Acts 28:14); however, what we see is a glowing example of men who lose their identity in their mission to carry out His purposes in and through them. They are but vessels and instruments utterly at His disposal to pour forth one unceasing, uncompromising, and unbridled devotion to Jesus Christ their Lord and Master.

Thought For Today

When His greatness eclipses our importance we begin to witness!

July 30

O. T. Bible Reading: Psalms 59-61   **Our Focus: Psalms 60:4**

A BANNER

The first major battle which the nation of Israel fought was against Amalek, and when victory was secured "… Moses built an altar, and called the name of it Jehovah-nissi (the Lord my banner)" (Ex. 17:15). The lessons learned by God's people at Rephidim were vital to their future, and remain foundation truths for the saints of God for all time.

Moses, Aaron, and Hur went to the top of the hill, and Moses held out the rod of God in his hand as Israel prevailed in the battlefield below. When his weary hands were lowered Amalek prevailed. Aaron and Hur then held the hands of Moses aloft until final victory was won. The great and supreme lesson was clear, obvious, and emphatic. It was a repeat of David's prophetic words to Goliath the Philistine of Gath, "And all this assembly shall know that the Lord saveth not with sword and spear: for the battle is the Lord's …" (I Sam. 17:47).

The Psalmist encouraged himself in the Lord by the thoughtful reminder that the Almighty God has given a banner to be displayed because of His unchangeable faithfulness and unlimited power (Ps. 60:4). The banner (ensign) was, and still is, a great uniting and rallying point which carries with it the pledge of strength and safety. It is a visible proof of the Army's common heritage, and a waving signal of certain victory. The *Lord* is our banner! His victory assures ours as well.

Thought For Today

To raise the banner is to signal defeat to our enemies!

July 30

N. T. Bible Reading: Acts 28:16-31   **Our Focus: Acts 28:30-31**

CONTINUED

Many a clever captivating article leaves the excited reader dangling between suspense and disgust with the concluding words, "to be continued." I have written these very words after verse 31 in my study Bible. The book of Acts certainly seems to close abruptly and to the minds of many prematurely. This also seems to be by design. The first words of the book, "The former treatise (the Gospel of Luke) have I made, O Theophilus, of all that Jesus *began* both to do and teach" (Acts 1:1), ended not with a period but with a comma. The words which follow (the book of Acts), will be a continuation of what Jesus began both to do and to teach. In exactly the same way, to my mind, the great book of Acts closes with a clear message, "to be continued." The nearly 2,000 years since then have added many more chapters to the history (His story) of the church He came to build. The last chapter has not yet been written.

Our names may also be included in the ever expanding "roll-call" of those who followed the Lamb "... whithersoever he goeth ..." (Rev. 14:4). The pattern has forever been made and clearly marked, the great mother church has been identified, and the New Testament model has been cast in silver (the symbol of redemption) and stained with martyrs' blood. What a great honor to follow in the train of such a holy band. What a challenge to live after the pattern shown to us in the Scriptures and not to conform to some compromising copy if not an outright counterfeit of the original.

Thought For Today

Substitutes can be more deadly than flame or sword!

July 31

O. T. Bible Reading: Psalms 62-64   **Our Focus: Psalms 62:1, 5**

WAIT UPON GOD

The only thing more difficult than to "wait" on the Lord is to "… wait patiently …" for Him (Ps. 37:7). Waiting on the Lord is hope, confidence, and trust extended. To wait is to obey the last command, to continue steadfastly in the path of duty, to eagerly expect and anticipate His further direction and intervention, and to "keep silent" (some give this translation) until He moves. We are not to keep silent in prayer to God, but we are to refrain from murmuring, carnal reasoning, and fleshly appeals for sympathy by complaining to men.

One of the most frustrating times of my life was a period of time when the only thing I could get from the Lord was the single word, "wait" … the last thing I wanted to hear or to do. Someone has well said, "The waiting time, my brother, is the hardest time of all." Indeed it is! Rush is always wrong. Speech is silver, but silence is golden.

The directives which the Lord gives are clear, concise, and compelling, but never abstract and unrelated to practical life and personal experience. This idea, "… walk before me …" (Gen. 17:1) is very simple, but amazingly profound. To walk is to perform the most elementary exercise, but here God is instructing Abraham to alter his entire lifestyle. His every action, his very manner of living, his conduct, and his daily behavior were to express a God-controlled example of the supernatural. To wait upon God is not a brief stage of experience; it is a lifelong attitude of eager anticipation.

Thought For Today

He who waits upon the Lord loses no time!

July 31

N. T. Bible Reading: Romans 1   **Our Focus: Romans 1:7**

CALLED TO BE SAINTS

Many people have their ears tuned to hear God's call to be a great teacher, a powerful preacher, a mighty apostle, or some other highly visible kind of office. It is doubtful that there would be any response at all to the invitation to come forward and answer the call to become saints. The first part of the problem is that most people would have no idea what they were getting into. A young boy volunteered to answer the teacher's question, "what is a saint?" His answer was, "a saint is a dead Christian." At that rate we should have an overflow crowd.

The root meaning is generally agreed to be "holy" or "holy ones." That should be enough to scare most people off at the very start! It is variously used in the Scriptures, but in the above verse it very certainly refers to the people of God, His redeemed. We are Divinely called to be saints. It is the plan and purpose of God that His children will be decent, devout, dedicated, and delivered individuals who are miraculously different in their thinking, in their manner of life, and in their behavior. Ours is a high and a holy calling (Phil. 3:14; II Tim. 1:9). It is not an ecclesiastical appointment, but a Divine intention. May our lives reflect the Godly design, and our behavior becomes a consistent testimony to the transforming power of the Gospel.

Thought For Today

Saints are not dead Christians but living Epistles!

August 1

O. T. Bible Reading: Psalms 65-67   **Our Focus: Psalms 67:4**

THOU SHALT ... GOVERN

Prophecy is defined by Scripture as, "sure" words (II Pet. 1:19): that is, certain of fulfillment. The Psalmist joins the great chorus of Old Testament prophets who project their vision to a yet future day when literally *He* shall govern on this very earth. The prophet Isaiah beamed in on this coming millennial reign also when he proclaimed, "... and the government shall be upon his shoulder ... Of the increase of *his* government and peace there shall be no end ..." (Isa. 9:6-7). The pronouncement of the vast throng of voices in heaven at the sounding of the seventh trumpet have echoed and re-echoed through the centuries, "... The kingdoms of this world are become the kingdoms of our Lord, and of his Christ; and *he shall reign* forever and ever" (Rev. 11:15). It is such prophetic promises which give us hope. It is "this hope" which is both blessed and purifying (I John 3:3).

The greatest single mystery of the prophetic Word is the time-gap between the promises and the fulfillment. The prophet sees the peaks of prophetic events, but is not given to see the stretch of time covered by the valleys between. All of this has an amazing parallel in the experience of each of us. When the Lord gives us some precious promise, the fulfillment seems as immediate as the Word was real. However, time will prove that "... the vision is yet for an appointed time ... though it tarry, wait for it ..." (Hab. 2:3), and wait we will. It is in the testing time that we prove our faithfulness and loyalty to His Word.

Thought For Today

The greatest test of faith is the delay in fulfillment!

<u>August 1</u>

N. T. Bible Reading: Romans 2   **Our Focus: Romans 2:7**

PATIENT CONTINUANCE

To continue is to persist and indicates an uninterrupted succession of consistent behavior. Too many people "go steady by jerks." Someone has well said, "oh, consistency, thou art a jewel!" The words "patient continuance" sounds poetic if not musical. At least the thought suggested certainly sounds like music to my ears.

There's a great difference between dedication to a principle or to a cause and dedication to a person. Many people pursue their creeds with abandon, and God has to blast them out of their prejudices before He can unite them in a loving betrothal to the Lord Jesus Himself. To be committed to a cause issues the dogged demand of duty which can very easily become a fetish. An individual commitment to the person of Christ produces a delightful dedicated demonstration of devotion. It flows from a heart of love, thrills with the overflow of living communion, and continues steadfastly toward an exciting goal.

It is much easier to be a short-term enthusiast than to be just a long-term faithful servant. Perhaps the most humbling thing any person will ever do is to maintain a steadfast and unflinching loyalty to the Lord Jesus Christ. This relationship results in the creation of a hunger and a longing after God on the part of others, and an awareness of having been with Jesus. Patient continuance will yield a bountiful harvest both here and hereafter.

<u>Thought For Today</u>

Consistency is a diamond that glows after sundown!

August 2

O. T. Bible Reading: Psalms 68-69   **Our Focus: Psalms 68:4**

JAH

The study of the many names and titles of God which are used in the Scriptures is fascinating and rewarding. In Psalm 68:4 He is referred to as "Jah." The same original Hebrew word occurs 40 times in Isaiah, the Psalms, and in Exodus, but is translated "The Lord" in our English Bible. Pronounced "Ya" the name signifies "He is." One way in which we get to know God is by understanding His names, for in Scripture, a name is symbolic of the nature or character. God has chosen to reveal Himself to the human family in a progressive manner, and as occasion demands. In creation He shows Himself as "Elohim" which is used 35 times in the first two chapters of Genesis and 26 times in Psalm 68. He is the Great Creator, the Majestic Ruler, and the All-powerful One who controls all that He creates. When God gave the unlikely promise of a son to the aged Abraham and Sarah He revealed Himself as the Almighty God (Gen. 17:1).

Moses asked the name of the God who had commissioned him to lead the children of Israel out of Egypt, and was told, "… *I AM* hath sent me unto you" (Ex. 3:14). It is also well for *us* to realize that "*He is*": not that He was or that He will be, but the present tense reality is that He who *is* will continue to be *what* He is. One of the final words of the Old Testament declares, "For I am the Lord, I change not …" (Mal. 3:6). It is because He is "… the same yesterday, and today, and forever" (Heb. 13:8) and that we can trust Him implicitly, without any reservations. Faith in God's Word is absolute faith in God against all that challenges or seems to contradict Him. It is just here that we must remain true to God's character regardless of circumstances. The most complete expression of faith in the entire Bible is, "Though he slay me, yet will I trust in him …" (Job 13:15).

Thought For Today

When we know that Who is we also know that He will!

August 2

N. T. Bible Reading: Romans 3   **Our Focus: Romans 3:24**

JUSTIFIED

The book of Romans is profound, philosophical, comprehensive, relative, and practical. All of this is impossible in one package apart from inspiration and revelation. Coleridge said, "the Book of Romans is the most profound writing extant." It is our purpose here to squeeze as much juice from the great document as possible. In as simple a way as possible let it be said that to condemn is to pronounce guilty, to justify is to pronounce righteous.

Paul argues that Abraham "... believed God, and it was counted unto him for righteousness" (Rom. 4:3). He then adds a most vital truth, "... he believed, even God, who quickeneth the dead ..." (Rom. 4:17). It is this infusion of Divine life which transforms a mere profession into a miraculous participation. It is not an imitation of Christ; it is an impartation of Christ. It is "... Christ in you, the hope of glory" (Col. 1:27). This Divine revelation spells the difference between defeat and victory, between dead formalism and living reality, and between barren failure and abundant fruitless. Jesus told His disciples on the last night of His earthly sojourn, "At that day ye shall know that I am in my Father, and ye in me, and *I in you*" (John 14:20). This truth, as most truths, comes to us over a period of time as a progressive insight. Paul added, "That Christ may dwell in your hearts by faith ..." (Eph. 3:17). When we grasp the liberating truth that "... Christ is all, and in all" (Col. 3:11), our Christian experience is totally transformed. From henceforth, it is "... not I, but Christ liveth in me ..." (Gal. 2:20). "Let in the Overcomer, and He will conquer thee!"

Thought For Today

"Christ in you" is God's formula for our victory and His fullness!

August 3

O. T. Bible Reading: Psalms 70-72   **Our Focus: Psalms 72:19**

AMEN

Nearly everyone has used the word "Amen" at least once, and most have used it hundreds of times without ever being certain of the meaning. It is a Hebrew word, and is transliterated into Greek and English as well as many other languages. The meaning becomes clear by the way in which it is used in the Scriptures. Isaiah 65:16 in some translations would read, "... May the God of truth and faithfulness (the amen) ...." This seems to give us the root meaning of true and faithful. Revelation says, "... These things saith the Amen, the faithful and true witness ..." (Rev. 3:14). This indicates that when the word "Amen" is used with reference to God it means "it is and it shall be so", and when used by men "so let it be."

It is quite interesting that the Lord Jesus often used the word at the beginning of a statement to introduce a new revelation of the mind of God. It has been translated "verily, verily" 25 times, and only in the Gospel of John. It is properly used after a discourse or prayer by the speaker when those in attendance sanction what has been said or make the substance of what has been said their very own. Jerome spoke of the united response of the congregation after a message or public prayer as being "like the roar of a waterfall or the noise of thunder." Surely we live in much calmer times, but I'm not at all convinced that this "silence is golden!"

"For all the promises of God in him are yea, and in him Amen ..." (II Cor. 1:20). When we add our hearty "Amen" to His every word (His yea) our lives will be much more familiar with His glory (II Cor. 1:20).

Thought For Today

When we lose our Amen we may have lost His witness!

August 3

N. T. Bible Reading: Romans 4   **Our Focus: Romans 4:5**

JUSTIFYING FAITH

The statement "... the just shall live by his faith" is first recorded in Habakkuk 2:4, repeated in Romans 1:17, and emphasized throughout the New Testament. It was the golden text of the great Protestant reformation. Martin Luther proclaimed this primary truth after receiving a Divine revelation which restored a very basic truth to the church. It is as relevant today as it was in the 16th century.

The fundamental aspects of this doctrine are very clear in the Scriptures: it is an act of God whereby He not only forgives the sinner on the merits of Christ's death but also imputes to the believing sinner the perfect righteousness of Christ. The basis of this miracle of the new birth is our faith in what Christ has accomplished for us at Calvary. It cannot be accomplished by rituals and ceremonies, nor can it be realized by the keeping of the law. The Old Testament prophecy in Jeremiah 23:5-6 becomes a joyful reality as the forgiven soul discovers, "... The Lord Our Righteousness." It is a glorious personal thrill to learn that our righteousness is not *something* but *someone*, even that One who is "... declared to be the Son of God with power ... by the resurrection from the dead" (Rom. 1:4).

The experience of forgiveness and salvation is always accompanied by a new mind-set. This transformation involves a new creation, a new pattern of behavior, a new code of conduct, a new love for God, and a new love for the word of God. It also produces a new love for the church, a new joy in worship, and a great hunger to know Him more deeply. There is also a new and keen desire to make Him known to a sin-sick world. Let us justify our justification by our consistently living justly (Mic. 6:8; I Thess. 2:10).

Thought For Today

The Spirit witnesses to what the blood has cleansed!

<u>August 4</u>

O. T. Bible Reading: Psalms 73-74   **Our Focus: Psalms 73:1**

GOD IS GOOD

What a great conclusion! Many of the Psalms begin with bursts of praise or of some profound conclusion. No less than 16 times the Scriptures declare that "God (or the Lord) is good." The lips and lives of God's true people throughout the ages have repeated the same words millions of times. There have been times when it may have been said in a hushed voice muted by some distressing condition, but always with a firm faith in His unchanging faithfulness to His Word and covenant.

In Psalms 73, as in other Psalms, the writer is perplexed by an age-long problem: why do the wicked prosper and the godly suffer? There are many problems which the probing mind can never solve, but which the worshiping heart in communion with God will resolve to the vindication of the Lord, and at least to the satisfaction of the trusting heart. The fact is that all of the wicked do not prosper, and all of the godly do not suffer. The real problem lies in the fact that some wicked people do prosper, and some good people do suffer. The solution lies in the fact that the consideration of this present life cannot be separated from the anticipation of the future life.

There is a Divine intent for _good_ in every circumstance we encounter. _All_ things must and will "… work together for _good_ to them that love God, to them who are the called according to his purpose" (Rom. 8:28). The really important thing is not the severity of the pain, nor the heat of the flame, but the purity of the refined gold and the maturity of the tested saint. It is the end result and not the process we must keep in focus. There is an expected end in whatever God allows in our lives.

<u>Thought For Today</u>

The vision of tomorrow hallows the tears of today!

August 4

N. T. Bible Reading: Romans 5   **Our Focus: Romans 5:9**

MUCH MORE

The Lord Jesus stated the superiority of God's way over man's ways by three words, "... how much more ..." (Matt. 7:11). The writer of the book of Hebrews declares the new and living way to be "better" (repeated 13 times) in every way. In Romans chapter 5 Paul reinforces both claims by setting this great plan of salvation by faith in another realm by itself which he rejoicingly labels "much more" (used 5 times in 21 verses).

This new life discovered in this new way is the expression of a new nature imparted to a new creature thus producing a new man. This leaves no room for "less" and no excuse for failure. We are not to prevail "somehow", but, rather, to come through triumphantly by His grace and through His power (II Cor. 2:14). We are not simply to be victors, but, amazingly, we are to be super-victors. "Nay, _in_ all these things we are more than conquerors through him that loved us" (Rom. 8:37).

Our perspective must never be "the best we can do" nor should it be "as near the highest as possible": it should rather be _the_ highest for _the_ prize (Phil. 3:13-14). This is God's point of view, and when it becomes ours we will bid farewell forever to the lowlands of mediocrity and defeat. We will have fallen in step with Him to march forward victoriously in the train of His triumph. The victor has taken us prisoner, and we are His bond-slaves sharing joyfully in His victory over every circumstance and condition. It is this blessed union which makes real in our experience the promised "much more."

Thought For Today

When we enjoy the "much more" we avoid the "much less!"

August 5

O. T. Bible Reading: Psalms 75-77   **Our Focus: Psalms 77:11**

FAITH'S MEMORY

Faith enables us to remember: unbelief causes us to forget. The greatest contribution to unbelief is a poor memory. The surest remedy for doubt is to call to mind the multitude of God's unceasing mercies and blessings. When faith encounters seven years of famine, she opens wide her overflowing storehouses from seven years of bounty and blessing. It is most significant that the Psalmist declares in chapter 77 verse 10 that he will remember "… the *years* of the right hand of the most High." Not the fleeting moments, not the flying hours, not even the tenuous days; but oh glory, the unnumbered *years* of His right hand.

We must honestly affirm that God has not forgotten to be gracious (Ps. 77:9). It is the infirmity of the forgetful heart to question the Providences of the Lord. It can never be said that God forgot. We are the ones who forget the manifold and unmerited abundance of His dealings in our lives.

The empty howl of the hound, when he has lost the scent, will be instantly replaced by the keen anxious bark of pursuit when he has retraced his steps to the very spot where he missed the trail. All of God's bounties of the past are most wonderful. They are the manifestation of His wonders! Every phase and aspect of our salvation is nothing short of a Divine wonder. How wonderful that God should ever reach out in love to redeem and to restore! Let faith rejoice in all such memories!

Thought For Today

Seven years of famine will cause faith to open her storage bins!

<u>August 5</u>

N. T. Bible Reading: Romans 6   **Our Focus: Romans 6:6**

KNOWING THIS

One aspect of "knowing" in the Bible sense of the term is not just the mental apprehension of a fact or truth, but also the personal participation or the personal experimental reality. The unique and exciting appeal of the Gospel message is that it is very personal and individual in its application and outworking. The appeal which Jesus made was, "… If any _man_ …" (Matt. 16:24), not if any group or community.

Paul argues that there must be a particular and personal signing off on our own death certificate. We come to an ID crisis. His point here is that we know from personal experience that our old man is crucified with Christ. Most Christians don't know this at all, and would be horrified if they were so informed. If the question with which he opens the chapter, "… Shall we continue in sin …" (Rom. 6:1), is to be answered at all, it can only be answered by and through our identification with Christ. It is when we recognize His Almighty and omnipotent power that we realize and experience that same power in our personal lives.

There is as much difference between the revelation of Redemption and the experience of salvation as there is between reading about the Island of Tobago and actually being on the Island. When the reality of our being united with Christ in His death and in His resurrection becomes a living bright reality we are then introduced to the supernatural. We cease to measure God's ability by our past failures, but our faith rejoices in His resurrection power.

<u>Thought For Today</u>

Our death with Christ guarantees our resurrection with Him!

August 6

O. T. Bible Reading: Psalms 78   **Our Focus: Psalms 78:8**

STEDFAST

The dictionary spelling of this great word is "steadfast." However, the meaning is the same. It means to be firmly loyal, steady, and fixed. It has to do with a moral state of strength and dependable continuity. It is indeed a great word, and an even greater quality of character. The word conveys the total opposite of anything which is fickle or easily moved.

The apostle Paul urged the Corinthian Saints to "... be ye steadfast, unmovable, always abounding in the work of the Lord ..." (I Cor. 15:58). The word used comes from a root which means "a seat" or "be settled." This gives us yet another key principle of godly conduct. He is admonishing them to thoroughly grasp and confidently rest in the great fact of the resurrection. They were to personally and deliberately take a seat on this blessed and firm foundation of Divine revelation. You may sit down with all confidence in the seat which you know is solid, firm, and safe; and where you and many others have reposed without anxiety or fear. It is such unwavering confidence in the Word of God which produces unchangeable consistency in daily conduct.

The Psalmist begins by saying that he would declare deep truths of old (Ps. 78:2). Lord Bacon said: "old wood is best to burn; old books are best to read; and old friends are best to trust." There is no book more reliable, there is no foundation for faith more certain, because the Bible is _the_ Word of God. We are to confidently be seated on the reality of His faithfulness. It is this unqualified trust which instills a moral fiber of trustworthiness and unflinching loyalty. The more certain our confidence in Him, the more consistent our conduct before men.

Thought For Today

Those are the most steadfast who rest on His faithfulness!

August 6

N. T. Bible Reading: Romans 7   **Our Focus: Romans 7:6**

NEWNESS

Many have observed that there is no mention of the Holy Spirit in Romans chapters 6 and 7, and that there are 18 such references in the victorious 8th chapter. This is apparently correct, and gives emphasis to a wonderful and liberating truth. There is neither life nor liberty to be found in the law alone (law is used 20 times in Romans 7). However, it seems to me at least, that the word "spirit" in verse 6 could have a capital "S." Whether that is correct or not it certainly is correct to say that there is no newness apart from the Holy Spirit. When and only when, we are quickened by the Spirit is there any new quality or manner of life.

That which is new is fresh and recent. It is not old, used, nor worn out. The Gospel gives promise of a New Covenant, a new commandment, a new creative act, a new creation, and of a new man. We are also assured in the Scripture of a new name, a new song, a new heaven and the new birth, the New Jerusalem, and finally all things are to be made new (Rev. 21:5).

There is also the promise of a renewing or a rejuvenating for the child of God. This speaks of being made new or of being made the young, fresh, and vigorous. There is a beautiful challenge in all of this. We must not allow our experience in God to become stale, old, or threadbare. God is not the God of the dead, but of the living (Matt. 22:32). He is not to be found in the leftovers from yesterday, the memories of past blessings, nor in the archives of ancient history. All of these when used of God or of His actions only give faith and confidence for today. It is now that we need and must have His quickening, life-giving, and renewing presence and power. Whenever we really meet Him there is always something living and fresh which is communicated to us.

Thought For Today

Those who enjoy new life abide with the Great Renewer!

August 7

O. T. Bible Reading: Psalms 79-81   **Our Focus: Psalms 81:16**

HONEY

God is great and God is good. He is mighty and He is merciful. He is crowned with majesty and He is confirmed in His magnificence. He desires to manifest His greatness to an obedient people. Jesus declared that the pure in heart would see God; and, indeed, they do (Matt. 5:8). It may also be said, blessed are the obedient for they shall experience His glory (Ex. 40:33-34). He desires to manifest His strength to those who know Him and work with Him (II Chron. 16:9). To the faithful the very joys of heaven begin right here on the earth. This spring of the eternal summer has already begun. The flowers bloom, the birds sing, the long winter is over and there is rejoicing in the camp.

He feeds His children with "... the finest of wheat ..." (Ps. 81:16) not just wheat, that is good; but with the fat of the wheat. Others may eat the bran, but these shall enjoy the very best portion. Benjamin's portion was 5 times that of his brothers (Gen. 43:34). In addition they will be treated with "... honey out of the rock ..."; luxuries as well as necessities (Ps. 81:16).

It is common in Palestine, in the summer, for bees to store honey in the hollows of the trees and in the crevices of the rocks. The land may be parched and barren, but sweet honey trickles in shiny drops down the face of the rocks. God extracts honey from the flinty Rocks ... the sweetest springs and refreshings will flow from the very most difficult circumstances. From the bitterness and the agony of Calvary flash the tongues of fire and the mighty river of life. We must not cringe from the cross for it is out of death that life will flow. Ahijah (brother of Jehovah), the prophet, received a cruise of honey from king Jeroboam's wife (I Ki. 14:3). Honey is symbolic of sweetness. Let us, this very day, taste and see that the Lord is good (Ps. 34:8).

Thought For Today

The supreme sweetness is reserved for the super-dedicated!

<u>August 7</u>

N. T. Bible Reading: Romans 8:1-18   **Our Focus: Romans 8:1**

NOW

The voice of the Lord is "*now*." The voice of the procrastinator is "*later.*" The voice of the sluggard is "*another time*." The voice of unbelief is "*not for you*" and "*not now*." The voice of the Holy Spirit is "*today*" and "*you*." One of the simplest and surest words of the spiritual vocabulary is "*now*." It is a great key to consistent and continuous victory.

We sing about the sweet by and by, but we groan in the nasty now and now. We brood over the bumps and bruises of yesterday, and we fret over the ghosts of tomorrow. What is past is history, and is left to memory and to the records. What is future is uncertain: we may plan for it, dream about it, and anticipate it, but we must wait for it to unfold to experience it. Today is the tomorrow which we longed for yesterday. It is only here and now that we live and move and have our being (Acts 17:28). It is the world of reality. There is mercy for yesterday and earnest prayers for tomorrow, but there is Divine grace only for today. It is for this reason that many suffer severe depression or are overwhelmed by anxiety and fear. The God of all grace (I Pet. 5:10) is not the God of the dead, but of the living. Therefore, He giveth more grace (Jam. 4:6), but only as the realities of life require it.

There is a very fulfilling sense in which it is the process which is the end as God sees it. We tend to project everything toward an ultimate end or goal. We only get to know God, and experience His grace and strength, in the real world of right now. When we rise above the turmoil and confusion, and calmly walk with God right through the conflict in victory, we have just realized the very end and purpose of God. It is thus that we glorify God, and it is thus that we learn the great secrets of overcoming.

<u>Thought For Today</u>

God has trained, prepared, and equipped us for today!

August 8

O. T. Bible Reading: Psalms 82-84   **Our Focus: Psalms 83:3**

THY HIDDEN ONES

The limelight, the spotlight, and the floodlight will often obscure the true light. The flesh basks in the lunacy of the luster and lure of the luxuriant. The soul thrives in the soothing solitude of His presence. In these days of mass media mesmerism it is well for us to keep in mind that we are not here to revel in our own coronation, but to learn to know God, and to learn how to walk with God. These vital lessons are not taught by the princes of this world nor are they learned among the glittering lights of Main Street. The secrets of the Lord will not be published in the headlines nor will the ways of the Lord be discovered on some website.

Solitude is the very soul of saintliness. Saints are not produced by decrees; they are fashioned in the closet of communion, and forged in the flames of trials and tests and then only by degrees. The Lord of harvest has long patience, waiting for the precious fruit of the earth (Jam. 5:7). The flesh demands satisfaction and that right now. Those who wait on the Lord must learn to do just that … to wait (Isa. 40:31). In this world of push and bustle there is an unexplored continent of secret and hidden riches reserved for the pioneers of prayer and faith.

Our life (that is our spiritual life), says the Apostle Paul, "… is hid with Christ in God" (Col. 3:3). It is to these that there is a promise of hidden manna, as well as a white stone with a secret name (Rev. 2:17). The real strength and power of the Christian life flows from the secret springs of deep communion and unbroken fellowship (Ps. 87:7). We know God only in the measure in which we have found Him in the solitude of devotion, meditation, and worship. It is there that we behold His transforming glory (Song of Sol. 3:4, 2:4).

Thought For Today

The secret of the Lord is revealed to His hidden ones!

August 8

N. T. Bible Reading: Romans 8:19-39   **Our Focus: Romans 8:21**

FROM – INTO

There are times when very small words define huge issues. An example is in Romans 8:21, and the terse statement, "… shall be delivered *from* … *into* the glorious liberty of the children of God." These very words could be appended to and applied to the lives and the experiences of all of God's children many times and in many different circumstances. Always, however, they declare an eternal truth; every encounter with God, at whatever level, will involve a supernatural change. It will be what the Scripture describes as a transformation. The word from the dictionary definition involves changing markedly in appearance or form and to change in nature or condition. Genuine conversion includes both.

Paul uses an even more graphic word in Colossians 1:13: "Who hath delivered us *from* the power of darkness, and hath translated us *into* the kingdom of his dear Son." This involves a miracle. It is to remove from one condition, to place in an entirely different condition, and to supernaturally cause to stand and walk in the realm of this new environment. The Bible calls this a new creation (II Cor. 5:17). We call it salvation. The world calls it fanaticism, but whatever you call it we all need it. Burdens are lifted at Calvary, shackles are broken at the cross, lives are changed and a whole new creature emerges to walk in newness of life and spirit (Rom. 6:4, 7:6).

Many times it can be said that we realize only what we anticipate. It can also be said that we anticipate only what we understand. If these great truths are taught and preached, people will know and expect that these are the things which accompany the new birth (Heb. 6:9). Ignorance revolves in darkness, and produces confusion and frustration. It is the light which emancipates. Let us look back only long enough to see what we have been delivered from.

Thought For Today

There is neither from nor into in any graveyard!

<u>August 9</u>

O. T. Bible Reading: Psalms 85-87   **Our Focus: Psalms 85:8**

I WILL HEAR

The order, as recorded in Scripture, is first the hearing ear and then the seeing eye (Prov. 20:12). The Pharisees, Sadducees, and religious leaders certainly saw the mighty miracles which Jesus performed, but their ears were dull and never heard His liberating message. Jesus repeated these words eight times in the Gospel record: "he that hath an ear let him hear." The plural form is repeated 8 times in the letters to the 7 churches of Revelation: "he that hath ears to hear let him hear."

Many believe the eye is the window of the soul, but few have considered that the ear may well be the door to the heart (the word heart is simply hear with a "t" added). It is *the door* which must be opened. Jesus said that he would stand at the door and knock (Rev. 3:20). It is then that we encounter yet another *if*; "… if any man hear my voice, and open the door, I will come in to him, and will sup with him, and he with me" (Rev. 3:20). It is well to know that the Lord directed amputation for the offending hand, foot, and eye, yet spared the ear (Mark 9:43-47). If you lose your ear you have lost all hope of salvation. He plainly said that such a one might enter into life maimed of hand, foot, or eye; however, if there is no ear to hear the truth of the way, there will not be even one foot to enter into life. The way into the house is by the door, not but by the window; that is why He knocks at the door instead of tapping on the window.

A sound and healthy spiritual ear, as Bernard has said, is "an ear which willingly hears what is taught, wisely understands what it hears, and obediently practices what it has heard and understood." Blessed indeed is such an ear. There are conflicting and confusing sounds in abundance. There is one unique wavelength on which the voice of the Lord is communicated to the soul. The inner ear must be Divinely touched and tuned to that frequency. Others may hear nothing but the din of discordant sounds, but such an ear will hear what God the Lord is saying.

<u>Thought For Today</u>

The sense of hearing is one thing which is very personal!

August 9

N. T. Bible Reading: Romans 9   **Our Focus: Romans 9:33**

A STUMBLING STONE

It is the Lord's doing, and it will be found to be one of His ways. An obstacle against which any person may dash his foot and stumble is defined as a stumbling stone, or as we more commonly would say, a stumbling block. It is a rock which will prove to be a hindrance; some barrier which gets in the way, delays progress, or causes to get hung up on. This seems strange, but it is the very truth of God. He has seen fit to surround some of His most precious realities with a barbed wire fence. Many get hung up on the barbs, and never reach the prize.

These barbs or rocks of offence may come in a great variety of ways. Sometimes they are people; or they may be peculiar or strange manifestations. But always they are something or someone which distracts our focus and we are offended. To be offended is to get hung up on the barbs of the fence. That which is offensive is something which is disagreeable to the natural senses and especially our culturally refined senses. It causes anger, resentment, or affront. When that happens you are stuck or hung up, and have stumbled, and are unlikely to recover. Only God can help us over these barriers. A deep heart-hunger will help us overlook these offending rocks and press on to the prize which they surround.

Perhaps this is one way in which it can be said that, "It is the glory of God to conceal a thing: but the honour of kings is to search out a matter" (Prov. 25:2). God seems to hide His secrets behind some very prickly briers. Our natural senses will halt us right there, and deny us the concealed treasure. To recognize the problem is to discover the solution. Very few would allow any person, a strange or peculiar manifestation, or any other offensive condition to deny them some rich treasure once they saw what they were doing. No wonder Jesus said, "And blessed is he, whosoever shall not be offended in me" (Matt. 11:6).

Thought For Today

Those who step over the offences discover concealed treasures!

August 10

O. T. Bible Reading: Psalms 88-89   **Our Focus: Psalms 89:1**

THY FAITHFULNESS

The Psalmist speaks of "thy faithfulness" four times in Psalm 89, and twice the Lord responds by speaking of "My faithfulness." The book of Revelation deals with the conclusion in many ways and it is conclusive in defining the Lord. He is called: "The Faithful and True" (Rev. 19:11), "The Faithful Witness" (Rev. 1:5), "The Faithful and True Witness" (Rev. 3:14), and "He that is True" (Rev. 3:7). It will be found that His faithfulness is anchored to His character and to His eternal principles as declared in His word. Jesus was not only faithful to the truth at all times, and also faithful in the application of truth, He was in His very nature the personification of truth.

John declares Him to be "The Faithful Witness", and the book of Acts reminds us that we are to be His witnesses (Acts 1:8). What is a true witness? The Scriptures have much to say about false witnesses; those whose testimony is not consistent and, therefore, it is not truthful and is false. These individuals are guilty of perjury, they lie in the evidence they give. The Greek word for witness is a "martyr"; one who gives testimony to the truth and will not compromise if it costs him his life. John uses this word in his writings no less than 72 times.

There are several things which go into the making of a true and faithful witness. They must be consistent. Any deviation or inconsistency in testimony discredits and in some cases even disqualifies an otherwise vital witness ... even more so in the spiritual realm. Any daily life which is not consistent with the Bible standard is a reproach to the Gospel. A witness must also be positive and confident. Hesitation or uncertainty will be interpreted as weakness and will cause the testimony to be doubted and questioned. Life and lips must ring true. Jesus spoke "... as one having authority, and not as the scribes" (Matt. 7:29). Behind His gracious words was a faithful and consistent life. When these elements are clearly present there will also be a kind of contagious courage and boldness.

Thought For Today

Faithfulness is required, and can only be acquired!

August 10

N. T. Bible Reading: Romans 10   **Our Focus: Romans 10:11**

NOT ASHAMED

Those who put their trust in the Lord will never need to suffer the pain of embarrassment or disappointment. He is absolutely trustworthy, and He simply cannot fail. Paul quotes here from Isaiah 28:16 "Therefore thus saith the Lord God, Behold, I lay in Zion for a foundation a stone, a tried stone, a precious cornerstone, a sure foundation: he that believeth shall not make haste." It might seem that Paul changes the quotation, but this is not the case. The word from which "confound" (or ashamed) is taken is the very same as for "make haste." In the simplest possible way it means to flee because of fear. We will never need to beat a hasty retreat when we put our confidence in the God of battles. The only time we should be on the run is when we are fleeing from youthful lusts (II Tim. 2:22). This must be followed by patiently and steadily walking forward in pursuit of righteousness, faith, charity, and peace in company with the pure in heart (II Tim. 2:22).

The Apostle Paul also declared confidently that he would never be confounded or put to any embarrassment by the Gospel (Rom. 1:16). It is Divine Energy from a supernatural source. There is no limit to the supply, there is no lingering in the delivery, and there is neither lack nor loss in the transmission of power. It is the Divine "dunamis" which is heavenly dynamite. "Awake, awake; put on thy strength, O Zion ..." (Isa. 52:1).

"The words of the Lord are pure words ... purified seven times" (Ps. 12:6). The process of purifying silver involves being refined seven times. When God speaks to men He uses human language which we can understand. He gives them a higher meaning, a new meaning, and above all a personal meaning. Thus they are pure words with a crystal clear meaning and with a perfect (the number seven) application to us and to our particular needs. They are *quickened* words which both bring and produce life.

Thought For Today

The voice of the Lord imparts both strength and confidence!

August 11

O. T. Bible Reading: Psalms 90-92   **Our Focus: Psalms 91:9**

BECAUSE

The word "because" indicates that there is a specific reason or cause for certain conditions. Things do not just happen; there are laws which are fixed, firm, and final which God has decreed; "... the curse causeless shall not come" (Prov. 26:2). The law of cause and effect cuts across all borders and functions unhindered in every life. We cannot escape these eternal fiats and principles. The life of every person only proves them true in a positive way or in a negative way.

Three times in this brief Psalm the word "because" (Ps. 91:9, 14) peals out the message of sowing and reaping. Their echo rings through the entire world like the church bells sounding in a local neighborhood. Approximately 1,100 times this word is used throughout the Bible. If they flashed like diamonds or were made to glow like fire nearly every page of your Bible would be illuminated. Anything which is repeated so frequently should not be carelessly overlooked. At the very least we should consider seriously that here we have an inexorable and non-negotiable eternally fixed law. It is like a spider's web which can be found even in kings' palaces (Prov. 30:28).

There is a sure and certain "because" and a consequent "therefore" in the iron hand of the law. There is also a very blessed and precious "because" and "therefore" in the glad tidings of the Good News. It is for this precise reason that the individual who, with intense single-hearted purpose and commitment, has set or fixed his love on the Lord that he is to be blessed and rewarded. The heart that is genuinely involved in positive spiritual transactions will always be richly rewarded. The half-hearted are half-defeated before they begin. The name "Enoch" means dedicated. We are told that he pleased God, and that he walked with God. It must be that others were doing neither. Only the wholehearted enjoy these great spiritual benefits.

Thought For Today

God's greatest benefits accrue to those who invest their all!

August 11

N. T. Bible Reading: Romans 11:1-21   **Our Focus: Romans 11:5**

A REMNANT

A remnant is what is left over; it is what remains. Isaiah prophesied that, "For though thy people Israel be as the sand of the sea, yet (only) a remnant of them shall return ..." (Isa. 10:22). Paul quotes from this Scripture in Romans 9:27: "... a remnant shall be saved." The Psalmist takes up this principle in Psalm 22:30: "A seed shall serve him; it shall be accounted to the Lord for a generation." It is estimated that there were at least one million people on the earth at the time of the flood. Only eight souls were in the Ark, and they alone survived that great deluge. Certainly, that would qualify as a remnant.

Isaiah was instructed by the Lord to take his son, Shear-Jashub (the remnant shall return) to meet Ahaz (Isa. 7:3). This was meant to carry a special message to the king to encourage him to turn to the Lord, and to warn him that if he refused God's invitation he would have no part in the restored remnant. It is a fact of history that when Ezra returned from captivity in Babylon there were a mere 49,677 brave souls who ventured to the call to restore and to rebuild (Ezra 2:64-65). The 4 month trek across the pitiless desert was undertaken by a very small remnant (Ezra 3:8).

The prophet Joel assures us that: "... in mount Zion and in Jerusalem shall be deliverance, as the Lord hath said, and in the remnant whom the Lord shall call" (Joel 2:32). This very encouraging and hopeful Scripture is given a clear time-frame by the words of Joel 2:28: "And it shall come to pass *afterward* ..."; there is a pattern in all of this. God does not have nor does He need a "majority" to accomplish His purposes. Jesus said: "Fear not, *little* flock; for it is your Father's good pleasure to give you the kingdom" (Luke 12:32). The majority report caused one entire generation of Israel to miss the Promised Land, and to bleach their bones in the barren desert.

Thought For Today

It is the faithful few who inherit the promises!

August 12

O. T. Bible Reading: Psalms 93-95   **Our Focus: Psalms 95:3**

ABOVE ALL

Those who think of lofty thoughts also live lofty lives. Ours is not a culture designed to produce thinkers. If anything, all of the gadgets and gimmicks seemed determined to rob people of the capacity to think at all. The dictionary defines thinking as a process which involves: to consider, to ponder (or carefully weigh), to reason, to remember, to visualize or imagine. The Scriptures teach: "For as he thinketh in his heart, so is he ..." (Prov. 23:7). Many times we interpret that as to *what* he thinks, but more accurately it is *as* he thinks, that is, the quality of his thought patterns. The Word of God is a discerner of the thoughts and intentions of the heart (Heb. 4:12), and it is also a great stimulator of thoughts to the renewing of the mind.

Jeremiah complained that the pastors had sunk to the level of animal thinking (Jer. 10:21). Animals are not famous for profound thinking. They think about the present only as it relates to their enjoyment and preservation. This Psalmist pictured the thoughts of God as being very deep (Ps. 92:5). The faithful Jeremiah again stated that the prophets had caused the people to err by their lightness or lack of depth (Jer. 23:32). The wisdom which will build the enduring house with seven pillars will also appeal to the highest levels of the city (Prov. 9:1). Surely that is not physical or geographic levels, but must include the highest peaks of thought and mind (Prov. 9:3). Every recorded call of God in Scriptures is to higher ground; "... and the first voice which I heard ... which said, Come up hither, and I will shew thee ..." (Rev. 4:1). So it is always the clearest vision, and the broadest view is from the highest elevations. Jesus was to be called: "The Son of the Highest" (Luke 1:32). God is spoken of as "The Most High" 37 times in the Word of God. Jesus taught that His followers would be the children of The Highest (Luke 6:35). He is high and lifted up (Isa. 6:1), and His people must also live their lives on the highest possible plain.

Thought For Today

The scope of our thoughts defines the scale of our experience!

August 12

N. T. Bible Reading: Romans 11:22-36   **Our Focus: Romans 11:22**

BEHOLD

Behold is a stronger word than see or look. It involves greater intensity, greater vividness, greater earnestness, and greater contemplation. All of this adds up to greater perception, greater discovery, and a greater vision. It clearly marks the difference between the careless and superficial glance, and the concentrated gaze which involves much more focus and much more effort. It is closely related to the word "know."

This was vividly pictured at the empty tomb (John 20). Peter and John hurried to the tomb. John outran Peter, came to the sepulcher, stooped down, and looking in, saw the grave clothes, "… yet went he not in" (John 20:4-5). He took a hurried peek, a brief look, a mere glance. Peter, at the time, was more thorough and more intense. He went into the tomb and seeth the linen clothes etc., but the word used is "theoreo" which is to behold or to view with great intensity and concentration. Then John viewed the scene with more perception, and he *knew*, and believed (John 20:8). Peter had perhaps the better sight, but John had the better insight. However, this illustrates a very vital principle. To behold, in the Scriptural sense, will lead to a perceptive comprehension, which produces certainty and assurance. Perhaps this may be one reason why John loved and used the word "know." In the epistle of I John he uses the word "know" 36 times in 105 verses. It requires the blessed Holy Spirit to take the things pertaining to Christ and make them reality to us personally; "… for he shall receive of mine, and shall shew it unto you" (John 16:14-15).

There is a most appropriate prayer recorded in Psalm 119:18 "Open thou mine eyes, that I may behold wondrous things out of thy law." The careful and intense gazing into the Word of God gives us the necessary time, waiting on the Lord, for Him to quicken us with life-changing insights. We have been told of the pause that refreshes; there is also the pause that renews and restores.

Thought For Today

Those who pause to behold will also know how to behave!

August 13

O. T. Bible Reading: Psalms 96-98   **Our Focus: Psalms 96:1**

UNTO THE LORD

Three very simple words spell the difference between failure and success in the long road of Christian service and ministry. Those who labor and sacrifice as "… unto the Lord …" (Ps. 96:1) endure criticism, disregard neglect, tolerate coldness and indifference, and press joyfully on as sweet as honey and as happy as a termite in a lumberyard. Others stumble and fail utterly in much more inviting circumstances and in a much more encouraging atmosphere. The key is the blessed commitment to an enduring and loving relationship to the person and lordship of Jesus Christ. This simple but profound discovery involves an attachment as well as a liberating detachment.

The attachment is not an artificial or humanly designed scheme which would harness or control the life and actions of an individual. It is really the automatic outflow of the overflow. Service is the human side of a Divine relationship. It is the super-abounding flow of devotion and a genuine expression of true love. It is what turns sacrifice into fulfilling service and transforms duty into a rewarding delight. To serve God is the deliberate expression of a vital and transforming relationship. It is what men see of an unseen love affair. It is a heart filled with the joy of the Lord, and manifesting itself in joyful and loyal devotion and service. The issues are response, recognition, and reward. The difference is rejoicing vs. reacting. Paul found and used this key to convert tribulation and trouble into experiences of transforming triumph.

The detachment is as real as the air we breathe, and may be as elusive as the tormenting mosquito. When we live and serve as "unto the Lord" there is a liberating release which frees us from the prison of praise. There is a blissful disregard of human responses. Praise does not elevate the level of emotion; and criticism, no recognition, and no appreciation do not crush and destroy. Those who serve for lesser reasons have their reward here and now. Those who truly serve for eternal values are oblivious to earthly accolades.

Thought For Today

What is "unto the Lord" is highly esteemed underline{by} the Lord!

August 13

N. T. Bible Reading: Romans 12   **Our Focus: Romans 12:9**

CLEAVE TO GOOD

Some words tend to lose their original meaning. In the dictionary listings for "cleave" there are two exact opposite meanings. One meaning is to split or divide; and the other it is to adhere to or to stick closely to. Jesus quoted the words which God had given to Adam and Eve in the beginning: "Therefore shall a man leave his father and his mother, and shall cleave unto his wife ..." (Gen. 2:24; Matt. 19:5). Some appear to reverse the order: they cleave to father and mother and leave their wife or husband. Statistics indicate that many have confused the meaning of the word and have split up and divided the home and those in it. The tragic fact is that most entirely disregard what the Bible teaches on this or any other subject.

Our focus for today emphasizes a vital principle of godly living. We are instructed to abhor that which is evil, and cleave to that which is good (Rom. 12:9). Both are strong words, and allow for no half-hearted neutrality. To abhor is to detest or to loathe; to cleave to includes the thought of clinging to or of grasping firmly and holding tenaciously. It is said of the Lord Jesus: "Thou hast loved righteousness, and hated iniquity; therefore God, even thy God, hath anointed thee with the oil of gladness above thy fellows" (Heb. 1:9). This clearly explains this much desired two-fold quality.

We are called upon to manifest our hatred for evil by expressing our convictions in word and in action. It is not always wise to verbalize our abhorrence of evil, but it is always right for us to express it by our attitude toward it and most emphatically by avoiding it entirely. Our moral fiber must have some muscle in it if it is the product of genuine salvation. This is a part of the power promised to those who experience the infilling of the Holy Spirit. There is no greater witness for the Lord than the clean life lived apart from the corrupting influences of the world.

Thought For Today

The power to cleave to good excludes any other grasp!

August 14

O. T. Bible Reading: Psalms 99-102   **Our Focus: Psalms 101**

NEW LIFE RESOLUTIONS

A New Year's resolution is almost a modern acronym for futility. A new life resolution in modern religion would be like the deserted sparrow alone on the house top or the D. P. (displaced Pelican) in the waterless desert (Ps. 102:6-7). Call it what you may, Psalms 101 contains 6 declarations of dedication. The word "dedication" and the word "commitment" are avoided by moderns as if they each contained exploding cells of the Bubonic Plague. Both are traits of transformation from the very spirit of the man after God's own heart (I Sam. 13:14). The previous Psalms 100 is commonly known as "the Psalm of praise." It is both fitting and significant that it should be followed by a "Psalm of practice."

The ancients called Psalms 101 "the Psalm of pious resolutions." That would be enough to put it on "the most neglected" list of most ministers. It is incumbent upon us to formulate an express purpose of more fervent and steadfast obedience proportionate to the advantages and favors His mercy has granted us. The badge of the ship in which Paul sailed was "Castor and Pollux" who were, we are told, semi-deities and twin brothers. The signs of the great ship of Zion are faith and obedience. To divorce these is to uproot the family of faith. They are united over and over again in the Word of God just as they are in the life of a true child of God.

Saving faith is a heaven-born confidence which results in an earth-expressed yieldedness and submission which is called obedience. This is the only faith which really counts; and that which really *counts* is usually that which also really *costs*. Such implicit trust which relishes the responsibility of obedience yields a thousand benefits. A habitual life of continual obedience brings vistas of ever-expanding insights and spiritual vision. Obedience is the eye of the Spirit. Failure to obey, results in spiritual astigmatism. The by-product of obedience to the Lord is a deep inner understanding, and a joy which is unspeakable and full of glory (I Pet. 1:8).

Thought For Today

Faith that really counts yields an obedience which really works!

August 14

N. T. Bible Reading: Romans 13   **Our Focus: Romans 13:12**

LIGHT

The first recorded words which God spoke are found in Genesis 1:3, "And God said, Let there be light: and there was light." The words "let there be" occur 10 times in chapter 3. Perhaps we could say that these are the 10 Commandments of creation. It would seem clear from this record that the very first thing which God created was light. It seems significant also that first, "... the Spirit of God moved ..." (Gen. 1:2). This was the order in the original record of creation, and it is also true in the new creation. Light is of no significance to the person who has no sight. Therefore, "The hearing ear, and the seeing eye (note the present tense), the Lord hath made even both of them" (Prov. 20:12). First, the Lord must move on us to give us eyes to see; then, the Word of the Lord comes to bring light.

We do not often think of light as any kind of armour or as part of our spiritual defenses, but it is. Paul says in Romans 13:12, today's reading: "... and let us put on the armour of light." In II Corinthians 6:7 he speaks of "... the armour of righteousness on the right hand and on the left." There is a great prophecy which is yet to be fully realized for Jerusalem and the inhabitants of Mount Zion: "... for upon all the glory shall be a defense" (Isa. 4:5). The idea is framed in a military setting: when the bugle sounds the wake-up morning reveille, it is time to put off the night-gear, and to put on the garments of the day (light) appropriate and necessary for spiritual warfare. Just 2 verses later in Romans 13:14 Paul clarifies the issue by saying: "But put ye on the Lord Jesus Christ, and make not provision for the flesh, to fulfil the lusts thereof." The beautiful secret of putting off is putting on: the key to emptying the heart of evil is to fill it with righteousness.

Thought For Today

True Biblical armor is genuine Christian character!

<u>August 15</u>

O. T. Bible Reading: Psalms 103-104   **Our Focus: Psalms 103:1**

BLESS THE LORD

Psalms 103 is truly a Psalm of praise. There is not a single prayer nor is there a petition found in it. David touches every chord there was on his harp until the whole vibrated with the purest of praise and adoration. The number of verses in Psalm 103 is equal to the total number of letters in the Hebrew alphabet. "The Lord" is used 11 times; and the first 2 verses as well as the final 3 verses call upon the whole/all of creation to "*bless* the Lord." "All thy works shall praise thee, O Lord; and thy saints shall *bless* thee" (Ps. 145:10). There can be no silencing the voice of nature and of the creation of God. But, alas, we ourselves can mute "The Hallelujah Chorus" of worship and of praise. Others may keep silent and refrain their voices, but let us, and *all* that is within us, bless and magnify His Mighty Name (Ps. 103:1). Let every faculty, every emotion, every capacity, and every element of our regenerated beings unite together in the great harmonious chorus of blessing and honor to the Lord, our Great Redeemer. Little children may well praise the Lord for His goodness and mercy, but let the mature fathers in deep humility magnify His spotless purity and His Divine holiness.

Talk is cheap. Words come easily. Mere words can very well be just that; merely words. If all that is meant is simply to render lip service, then the tongue alone is sufficient; but to bless the Lord is more, much more. The entire being, which involves the heart, the spirit, the will, the affections, the mind, and the understanding are all quickened to this high and elevated honor to *bless* the Lord. Let our conscience "*bless* the Lord" by steadfast and consistently faithful behavior. Let our minds and judgment *bless* Him with pure and holy thoughts and imaginations. Let our affections magnify Him by loving what He loves, and with the same intensity, and by hating what He hates. Let our daily conversation and manner of life *bless* His holy Name by choosing His highest and His very best. Yea, "all that is within me bless His Mighty Name!"

<u>Thought For Today</u>

He who gave His all <u>for</u> us also demands our all <u>from</u> us!

August 15

N. T. Bible Reading: Romans 14   **Our Focus: Romans 14:9**

LORD

One of the most common names and titles of Jesus is "Lord" which occurs approximately 650 times in the New Testament. That would be an average of nearly twice on every page. The same title is used about 6,000 times in the Old Testament alone. It is the name used by doubting Thomas, and by all who have a real and personal revelation of the risen Savior: "… My Lord and my God" (John 20:28). When He returns triumphantly in power and great glory (Matt. 24:30; Luke 21:27) He will then be recognized as "King of Kings, and Lord of Lords" (Rev. 17:14, 19:16). Peter pointed out to the listeners on the day of Pentecost that God had exalted Jesus to now be recognized as "… both Lord and Christ" (Acts 2:36). Perhaps we might be helped in our grasp of this significant title by considering the following:

1.   *Jesus* = suggests His mission and message as the Great Prophet teaching and delivering the truth of God.
2.   *Christ* = suggests His anointed office as our exalted High Priest making atonement for our sins.
3.   *Lord* = suggests His saving power and His kingly right to rule and to reign over men and nations.

It is just at this very point we must humbly bow at His crucified feet and own Him as our Lord and our Master. Hudson Taylor made famous the expression: "if He is not Lord of all, He is not Lord at all." The early church proclaimed this great fact, and lived accordingly: "… he is *Lord* of all" (Acts 10:36). The term "master" is used 52 times in the four gospels alone, and defines a vital, but very much neglected, relationship to the Lord.

All personal and Christian responsibility and accountability whether of a corporate, individual, or social character is directly connected to the reality of knowing Christ as *Lord*. The very title glows with His exaltation and majesty, and of our recognition and glad submission to His right to own, govern, control, and to direct our lives. The primary meaning of the Greek word "kurios" (Lord) is *owner* and clearly implies authority and Lordship.

Thought For Today

"Jesus is either Lord of all or He is not Lord at all!"

August 16

O. T. Bible Reading: Psalms 105-106   **Our Focus: Psalms 105:2**

SING UNTO HIM

Many of the Psalms are addressed to the chief musician (55 of them). Song, music, and praises are prominent. In the Hebrew Bible the Psalms are called "Sepher Tehillim", the Book of Praises. The various forms of the word "sing" occur 74 times; and just the word "song" is used another 48 times, 31 of them in the Psalm titles. Music and singing are, and always have been, a very vital part of the Christian faith. Singers are spoken of over 60 times in the Bible, and singing is mentioned over 100 times.

Many times we are instructed to sing unto the Lord. This would seem to say, "bring your very highest thoughts and express them in the highest possible language and with the highest possible sounds." We are told that the first 15 verses of Psalm 105 were written on the occasion of the bringing up of the Ark (I Chron. 16). Any token of the Divine presence will always bring with it the highest expressions of worship. It may be possible to worship the Lord without music, but many of us have found it much easier and more fulfilling to worship while singing. The songs we sing should be *unto* the Lord: He must be the theme, and when they are *of* Him then they will also be *unto* Him. We have often felt that prevailing prayer is a cycle. It begins with the heart of God, the pulse of heaven, a Divine intention. It is then transmitted by the faithful Holy Spirit to some obedient child of God. The intercessor, directed by the Spirit, offers the petition to our Great High Priest through the merits of and in the name of the Lord Jesus Christ. Jesus presents the earnest prayer back to the Father where it actually began. Can such a prayer go unanswered? I believe the very same can be said of genuine praise. The spirit of the worshipping saint somehow seems to cautiously tip-toe into the very portals of heaven. The high praises which echo and re-echo in that Holy Place fills and thrills the human heart and the worshipping soul. If there is any greater joy than this it has never been found on earth. If there is any greater fulfillment than this it could only be found among the angels of heaven. Let us learn the song, and cherish such a melody.

Thought For Today

To sing in the Spirit is to worship in the highest!

August 16

N. T. Bible Reading: Romans 15:1-20   **Our Focus: Romans 15:13**

THE GOD OF HOPE

Hope is earnest expectation. God is the only source or reason for the great expectations and anticipations of God's children. If we lose hope we have lost everything. While there is life there is hope, and where there is no hope there is no life, nor reason for living. Hope is one of the three anchors of the faith: faith, hope, and charity (I Cor. 13:13). It is said that hope springs eternal. The real truth is that hope in its highest form springs from Him who is eternal. Thomas Jefferson explained his philosophy of life to his friend John Adams in this way: "… I steer my bark with hope in the head, leaving fear astern." Hope which is built upon the word of God insures the very progress which it predicts.

The clearer our understanding of God's Word and of His plan, the brighter and more consistent will be our hope. There are several phrases used in the Word of God which give expression both to the nature and to the vastness of our hope: "the hope and resurrection of the dead" (Acts 23:6), "the hope of the promise made unto the fathers" (Acts 26:6), "the hope of righteousness" (Gal. 5:5), "the hope of the Gospel" (Col. 1:23), "the hope of the glory of God" (Rom. 5:2), "the hope of salvation" (I Thess. 5:8), "the hope of his calling" (Eph. 1:18), "the hope of your calling" (Eph. 4:4), "the hope of eternal life" (Tit. 1:2, 3:7), "the hope of Israel" (Acts 28:20). It is not difficult to see why Paul described the condition of the Gentiles apart from Christ and "the hope of the Gospel" as being "without God and without hope" (Eph. 2:12). Certainly, that is a lost condition.

Hope is defined in the New Testament by three adjectives: "good hope" (II Thess. 2:16), "blessed hope" (Tit. 2:13), and "lively hope" (I Pet. 1:3); and we may add a confident chorus to the great song of hope: it is truly "a better hope" (Heb. 7:19). We get an honest picture of the frustrated and disheartened disciples in their confessions, that they *had* trusted (or hoped) (Luke 24:21). We must keep our hope in the present tense. If we fail to do so, we lose "… an anchor of the soul …" (Heb. 6:19). How rich is our heritage of hope.

Thought For Today

The fullness of hope is the harbor of the obedient heart!

August 17

O. T. Bible Reading: Psalms 107-108   **Our Focus: Psalms 107:2**

THE RESPONSE OF THE REDEEMED

Our responses reveal our reservoirs. What we have stored up in our hearts eventually finds expression from our lips. It is "… out of the abundance of the heart the mouth speaketh" (Matt. 12:34). Those thoughts which have filled our idle moments and built up a reservoir of feelings, ideas, imaginations, and inclinations in a certain direction, will express themselves later in words and actions. When Christ is the center, the circumference is automatically a beautiful garden of heavenly attributes and holy aromas. One of the sweetest refrains from heaven is that which was composed on earth: "… for thou wast slain, and hast redeemed us to God by thy blood out of every kindred, and tongue, and people, and nation; And hast made us unto our God kings and priests: and we shall reign on the earth" (Rev. 5:9-10).

The Ark must be pitched within and without before it could ever weather the storm and survive the great flood (Gen. 6:14). Those who have experienced this unique redemption are under a unique obligation to render unique praises. The Redeemer is so glorious, the price of the ransom so huge, and the redemption so far beyond human language to explain, that we are under a seven-fold obligation to give thanks unto the Lord, and to do our very best to enlist others in the great choir of "singing saints" living on "thanksgiving avenue." The gushing stream of gratitude flows from the fountain of love and devotion. The inner being simply overflows with the enriching and ennobling revelation that "… he is good (all the time) …", and that "… his mercy endureth forever" (Ps. 107:1). The heart that begins with these great truths and fills the inner life with them will also end as this great Psalm ends: "Whoso is wise, and will observe these things, even they shall understand the loving kindness of the Lord" (Ps. 107:43). He has provided abundant reasons for us to worship Him, but only we can fill our reservoirs with thoughts of gratitude for His overwhelming goodness and loving mercy.

Thought For Today

A heart full of gratitude produces a life full of praise!

95

August 17

N. T. Bible Reading: Romans 15:21-33   **Our Focus: Romans 15:29**

FULLNESS

Those who excel are the rare individuals who discover the secret of functioning at full capacity. They are referred to as over-achievers, but that is only as compared to others or to the average. The grim reality is that most fail to put everything they have into their efforts. Such output is called half-hearted, mediocre, or to use another figure of speech, lukewarm. These are repulsive terms which no one would cherish as describing their life or their conduct. However, few do what is necessary to avoid any such designation. Intensity, enthusiasm, and endurance are the anatomy of excellence.

The very word "fullness" is a challenge. It could not exist if there were no other categories. The optimist may say it is half-full, and a pessimist may insist that it is half-empty; but all must agree it simply is not full.

For the child of God there is no lack in the supply. John gives us an interesting insight in John 1:16: "And of his fullness have all we received …"; His resources are unlimited. The qualifier is on our part not on His part. The tiny preposition "of" puts the onus squarely on us. That portion of His vastness which we experience depends not upon a limited supply but rather upon a partial appropriation. The amazing prayer of the Apostle Paul for the Ephesians believers is refreshing and relevant: "… that ye might be filled with all the fullness of God" (Eph. 3:19).

To be filled with God, is truly a great thing; to be filled with the *fullness* of God, is an even greater thing; and to be filled with *all* the fullness of God absolutely boggles the mind, staggers the imagination, but excites the child of faith. One thing is sure there would be no room for anything else in such a life. This is the answer to the tragic lack among God's people. We can only overcome evil as we are filled with His grace, strength, and power.

Thought For Today

His fullness is the glorious solution to our sad lack!

August 18

O. T. Bible Reading: Psalms 109-111   **Our Focus: Psalms 111:3**

HIS WORK

There are 22 Scriptures which use the words "His works." This Psalmist declares that all His works are done in truth (Ps. 33:4). He also stated that "All thy works shall praise thee ..." (Ps. 145:10). Some elements of His creation praise Him by their very existence. The vastness and immensity of His creation project and magnify His omnipotence. The intricate details and exquisite beauty display His omniscience, His eternal love, and His infinite goodness. The voice of nature and creation alone leave men without excuse. The combined chorus of mountains, oceans, rivers, vegetation, flowers, stones, and humanity itself sing aloud the praises of Him who made them. How tragic that some have never heard their harmonious melody.

In addition there is "His work ..." (Ps. 111:3) in the singular. It is but one; the amazing and mighty plan of redemption (Ps. 111:9). This is progressive, ongoing, complete, unlimited, and life-long. He has "begun" a good and an awesome process of salvation in the lives of the redeemed (Phil. 1:6). He is a Faithful Creator, and will stay with the task until it is completed (Phil. 1:6; I Pet. 4:19). His work is not temporary, it is not superficial, it is not partial; but it is total, complete, and eternal. We, as humans with limited vision, fail many times to recognize the grand design, while we are in the grinding withering process. At best we may conclude that the frowning providences are useful lessons, but they are really designed to be turned into a transformed character. Even the precious mountain-top encounters are not primarily designed to *teach* us anything, but they are meant to *make* us something.

Isaiah spoke of another work, "... his strange work ..." (Isa. 28:21). We must never imagine this to be anything bizarre, odd, or foolish. He does not bless a mess! God is not the author of confusion and nonsense (I Cor. 14:33). His *strange* work is what He is compelled, by human rebellion and disobedience, to do in wrath and in judgment. God is love, and punishment is contrary to His very nature.

Thought For Today

The fulfillment of God's will is the completion of His work!

August 18

N. T. Bible Reading: Romans 16   **Our Focus: Romans 16:26**

THE OBEDIENCE OF FAITH

Obedience is not an option; it is a vital element of faith. This kind of saving faith is not some intellectual understanding; it is a deliberate commitment to a person. It involves unconditional surrender which issues in absolute loyalty to Him. Loyalty to my ideas or to my conclusions means that I must analyze, scrutinize, and rationalize at the shrine of my own intelligence. Loyalty to the Lord Jesus means that many times I must step out where I cannot trace. It is not foolish, fanatical, and irresponsible action. It is rather infinite directions from Supreme Wisdom, directing an obedient child into paths and ways he knows not of. This process cuts across the will of the natural man, and will bring self-pity to a partially yielded vessel. The process of death to the flesh is both disagreeable and uncomfortable. One may exult victoriously in the furnace, but only in the measure of the enthusiasm we know in letting the life of the Son of God manifest itself in us. This is a mystery which requires a revelation to comprehend.

The last word of Jesus to a disciple is not *believe*, it is *abandon*. Unfaithfulness is infidelity. The sure cure for infidelity is obedience to the Word of God and to the Holy Spirit. We fail to see that obedience is a vital human part of the recreating power of His redemption. God does not *force* nor does He *insist* that we obey. He simply *asks* for our devotion. He is not a taskmaster nor is he a slave-driver. He is the mighty emancipator. The clearest evidence of my growth in grace is the attitude I have toward obedience. Obedience, as the Bible defines it, is the relationship between a father and his son, not between a master and his servant. It is a relationship of kinship and of the bond of family love and loyalty. It is the genuine reality of seeing and experiencing His creative life within us which illuminates the inner eye of faith to recognize His right of absolute authority over us. This is a beautiful and rewarding love relationship. It is the end of legalism and the glorious beginning of true freedom and liberty. Duty now becomes a delight and obedience a way of *life*.

Thought For Today

Obedience is a great joy when we experience His Almighty presence!

<u>August 19</u>

O. T. Bible Reading: Psalms 112-115   **Our Focus: Psalms 112:1**

PRAISE THE LORD

The words "praise the Lord" are used 45 times in the Word of God. They are repeated thousands of times on a daily basis by those who walk with God and know His fullness. The cup cannot run over unless it is full. The spontaneous outbursts of praise to the Lord are foreign to the lukewarm and half-hearted. There are 9 Psalms which begin with the words, "praise the Lord." A literal rendering of the original words would simply be one word, "Hallelujah." A word which we are told is the same in every language; the universal expression of praise and worship. The very word is repeated four times in Revelation 19. There it is the key-note in the doxology of the triumphant redeemed host in heaven. They are sure to praise God best who know Him and love Him most. The Almighty God has so closely woven His own glory and our blessedness together that at the same time we advance the one we also promote the other.

The word praise in one form or another is used 186 times in the book of Psalms. Psalms 113-118 are termed the "Hallel" or the praise group. In the nation of Israel at the family celebration of the Passover, Psalms 113 and 114 were sung before the emptying of the second cup before the meal, and 115-118 after the meal, and the filling of the fourth cup. It is generally thought also that this was the "hymn" which the Lord and His apostles sang after the Passover, and just before they left the Upper Room to go to the garden of Gethsemane.

Praise is to be directed to the Lord. He alone is worthy of our praises. One clear reason He is to be praised is that He is supremely "above" all that is human (Ps. 113:4), and all that is in this world or the world to come (Eph. 1:21). The wonder and awe of His Majesty evokes the high praises of God from all true worshipers. The wonder of it all is that there are so few who really do.

<u>Thought For Today</u>

Praise is to salvation what light is to the sun!

August 19

N. T. Bible Reading: I Corinthians 1   **Our Focus: I Corinthians 1:20**

FOOLISH

The dictionary defines "foolish" as: lacking good sense or judgment, unwise, absurd or ridiculous. Let no one ever even imagine that God, His glorious Gospel, or His wise-hearted and Spirit taught messengers could (in any sense) be thus defined. The simplest way to state what Paul is saying in I Corinthians chapter 1, is that man can be too big for God to use, but never too little. We must keep the facts clearly and humbly in mind that God can use us, but that He does not need us. There is a powerful eternal and uniform principle being manifest in this Divinely chosen process; "That no flesh should glory in his presence" (I Cor. 1:29).

Let the humble people be ever grateful and thankful, and let the affluent and privileged be humble and respectful. The social, ethnic, and institutional distinctions which are so big among men are nothing with God. We must be careful not to in any way despise or discount any of God's children, for in so doing we despise the Divine method and indirectly the One who has chosen them. If we take our rightful place humbly at His feet we will be less inclined to feel qualified to instruct Him in His eternal purposes. The One who reached _down_ and called us in spite of all our sinfulness can also use us in spite of our puny and feeble condition … if we will only yield to Him and allow Him to work.

The genuine and honest awareness of being unworthy may be more of a supernaturally adjusted attitude than a Christian attribute. Some have been spared in mercy by the letter "m." If He had said not _any,_ that would have closed the door completely. An arrogant and exalted youthful University graduate approached a former close childhood friend who was wearing the Salvation Army uniform. His haughty remark to her was: "That's all old-fashioned and outdated. We are more educated now and know better, why, if it came to it, do you know I could say the Lord's Prayer in five languages." She humbly replied: "Well, I certainly cannot say the Lord's Prayer in five languages; but, thank God, I can say _I am saved_ in English!"

Thought For Today

Those who see who He really is know what they really are!

August 20

O. T. Bible Reading: Psalms 116-118   **Our Focus: Psalms 118:24**

THIS DAY

The expression, "this day" is found over 100 times in the Word of God. Add to this the fact that the word, "now" may be found over 200 times and you begin to get the picture. God is not the God of the dead, but of the living (Mark 12:27); neither is He the God of yesterday nor of tomorrow. It is *today* in which He speaks, and the voice of all Holy Spirit is *now* (Heb. 3:7, 13; II Cor. 6:2). We so easily use the thought of tomorrow, or another time, as Felix foolishly sought for "... a convenient season ..." (Acts 24:25). It is easy for us to see from the record that season never came. It never does. I like to add one simple word to a familiar Scripture to make a point: "And this is life eternal, that they might know thee (*now*) ..." (John 17:3). When quickened by the Holy Ghost everything seems to settle down into one amazing and glorious "this day."

One primary element in learning to walk with God is that His grace is personal and immediate. There is always a special measure of grace for any special assignment, as well as for every severe test. One of the 37 "greats" in the book of Acts was "... great grace ..." (Acts 4:33). It is ever so. The present tense salvation always results in the present tense manifestation of the supernatural. Faith and prayer are the human arms which reach out and draw on or appropriate the grace of God *now*. Prayer is not the reflex action of devotion it is the present tense practical reality of communion and experience. It is this flow of supernatural provision and Divine life which transforms the distressed and humiliated disciple into a marvel of transforming grace ... *a saint*!

Delay brings defeat; procrastination is disobedience in slow motion. When God deals with the human heart we must take action at once or in most cases we will do nothing. Every moral or Divine call has an "ought" in the very middle of it. Our carnal thinking persuades us that our dreams of success are the very end or goal of God's purpose for us. It is not so. What we call the process is, in fact, what God calls the end.

Thought For Today

We know God in the measure in which we experience His grace now!

August 20

N. T. Bible Reading: I Corinthians 2   **Our Focus: I Corinthians 2:4**

POWER

The New Testament church was formed with the specific *promise* of power (Acts 1:8). It was launched by the *manifestation* of supernatural phenomena (Acts 2:1-4). It ministered with great Divine power and energy (Acts 6:8). It may be helpful and a little embarrassing to look at a few of the things which are involved in this Holy Ghost power:

- It is power to live a godly life.
- It is power to get along with others.
- It is power to manifest the Spirit of Christ.
- It is power to be honest and truthful.
- It is power to be peaceful in the storm.
- It is power to obey the Word of God.
- It is power to live in victory.
- It is power to love my enemies.
- It is power to overcome the flesh.
- It is power to pray effectively.
- It is power to discipline my tongue.
- It is power to make me sweet and pleasant.
- It is power to return good for evil.
- It is power to control my temper.
- It is power to resist temptation.
- It is power to witness and win.
- It is power to be calm amid confusion.
- It is power to bear long and do good.
- It is power to have a Christ-like spirit.

Thought For Today

It takes a revelation to see what the "fullness" really is!

August 21

O. T. Bible Reading: Psalms 119:1-48   **Our Focus: Psalms 119:1**

UNDEFILED

It is no marvel that the undefiled are described as "blessed." To be undefiled is to be free from corruption; it is in a positive way to be chaste, clean, unspotted, and unspoiled. These rare souls are said to be "… in the way …" (Ps. 119:1), and that is most challenging. They are not in another realm nor are they in glorified bodies. They are in the way, the right way, the way of the Lord; they keep rank and walk with holy carefulness washing their feet daily lest they to be spotted by the world and the flesh.

Jesus began the great Sermon on the Mount (Matt. 5) with the words "blessed" … repeated nine times. The book of Psalms begins with the very same word (Ps. 1:1). This lengthy Psalm (Ps. 119) of 176 verses also begins with the word "blessed." The blessed condition here spoken of is the actual realization in personal experience of the blessedness which we come to know through faith in Christ.

There are some obvious reasons why it is the will of God for His children to be undefiled. He has chosen us to be His disciples, His witnesses, His servants, His Temple, and His bride. Therefore, if we see our calling, and our privileges, it behooves us to consistently and conscientiously avoid all defilement (II Cor. 7:1). This is in no sense of the word legalism nor is it bondage: it is glorious freedom and a triumphant personal walk with God. This means to walk in His ways, and not the ways of the world: can anyone walk on hot coals of fire and not be burned?

The way of blessedness is *the way*; it is the King's Highway, the high road of separation, the way *of* and *to* life. Some may choose an easier way, a more modern way, a way convenient to the flesh; but the voice of the Lord is always "… Come *up* hither …" (Rev. 4:1, 11:12). Why should we opt for any other way when this glorious reality is just a *choice* away?

Thought For Today

Those who are truly "blessed" will never be "wretched!"

August 21

N. T. Bible Reading: I Corinthians 3   **Our Focus: I Corinthians 3:1**

SPIRITUAL OR CARNAL

Every child of God is either spiritual or carnal. Some are much more deeply spiritual than others. There are broad ranges in both categories. These vastly different segments of people will be found in every church. The $64 question is what makes for these extremes, and how can the dilemma be solved? The answer is as simple as it is complex: "… Walk in the Spirit, and ye shall not fulfil the lust of the flesh" (Gal. 5:16). That is the cure, but the condition persists. The problem is that either people are unaware of their condition or they simply will not take the medicine that would cure them.

Each group can easily be identified. Those who are carnal and walk after the flesh are manifest; that is, exposed to view (Gal. 5:19). Can anyone hide a full moon on a clear night? The more subtle forms, the pastel hues, the corruptions of the spirit (II Cor. 7:1) are as apparent to the Lord and to those who walk in the Spirit. There is a discernment which will discover even the hidden things of darkness (I Cor. 4:2).

The fruit of the Spirit is as obvious, and so much more pleasant and refreshing (Gal. 5:22-25). It is a matter of value and importance that God's people should be fruit inspectors. They must have enough spiritual insight to recognize the most spiritual and to enjoy true fellowship on the highest level.

The beautiful cluster of fruit-bearing attributes of a Spirit-filled child of God all have to do with character and behavior. We must keep clearly in mind that the "fruit of the Spirit" has always been and will always be that rare but fragrant Christ-likeness of character.

Thought For Today

All things are manifestly exposed to the All-seeing eye!

August 22

O. T. Bible Reading: Psalms 119:49-104   **Our Focus: Psalms 119:89**

THY WORD

Psalms 119 is an amazing passage of Scripture. It has 22 divisions, each beginning with a letter of the Hebrew alphabet in its proper order (there are 22 letters in the Hebrew alphabet). It is the longest of the Psalms, just as Psalms 17 is the shortest. There are exactly 8 verses in each of the 22 stanzas.

The number 8 is a significant number in Scripture. The Hebrew word is sh'moneh, from shaman, to make fat, to super-abound. Seven is considered to be the number of Divine completeness. Eight, of course, is 7 + 1; thus going beyond seven, and marking the beginning of a new series, era, or order. It is the number which speaks of resurrection. Jesus arose from the dead on "... the first day of the week ..." (Matt. 28:1), which was the eighth day, Saturday being the seventh or the Jewish Sabbath.

The superabundance of the Word of God is easily seen as the focus of this Psalm. Every single verse gives some reference to it except three verses ... there are 173 references in 176 verses. There are 152 references to God, and 325 personal references to himself. There is no doubt that he made a vital connection between the two. It is also interesting that he says "I have" upwards of 50 times, and "I will" or "I shall" approximately 40 times. This great Psalm has encouraged the downcast, instructed the searching, refreshed those who were weary, and at least in one instance saved the life of a condemned saint. George Wishart, when upon the scaffold, availed himself of the custom of the times, which allowed the condemned to choose and sing a Psalm before his execution. He shrewdly selected Psalms 119, and before he was two-thirds of the way through, a pardon arrived, and he was spared. He, for the first time, must have been truly thankful that his mother insisted he memorize this Psalm as a youth.

Thought For Today

To magnify the Word of God is to honor the Lord of the Word!

August 22

N. T. Bible Reading: I Corinthians 4   **Our Focus: I Corinthians 4:6**

PUFFED UP

Paul uses the expression "puffed up" six times, and three of them in I Corinthians chapter 4. To be puffed up is to have an exalted spirit. The basic thought relates to a pair of bellows. Everyone gets the picture. Bellows are instruments for producing strong currents of air to increase the draft and to fan the flames of a fire. Self-conceit, or just old-fashioned pride, behaves in this manner. The guilty individual is just manufacturing hot air and is fanning the flames of conceit and arrogance. It could accurately be said, "he is full of hot air." It puts no strain on the mind to find an apt illustration or a living example. They are in abundance. Such is a very noisy demonstration of emptiness and non-productive talk.

The same Apostle Paul said later to the same Corinthian church, "... Knowledge puffeth up, but charity edifieth" (I Cor. 8:1). This is a very simple but accurate test for any teacher or preacher. When the air settles down, and the individual finally quits talking, do you feel wind-blown or does your inner man feel nourished, fed, and strengthened in God and in His Word? The test is whether it fed your mind or touched your heart. What comes from the mind can and will only reach the mind; what comes from the heart goes much deeper and reaches the inner man of the listeners. Moses heard from God, and knew God; that is why he was called, "... Moses the man of God ..." (Deut. 33:1). When he spoke to the people he was a messenger of God, and their hearts were touched. "And Moses gathered all the congregation ... and said unto them ... And they came, every one whose heart stirred him up, and every one whom his spirit made willing ..." (Ex. 35:1, 21). One can talk, and merely beat the air; or one can talk and minister to the hearts of those who hunger for God. This is *soul food* and ministers life and not just logic.

Thought For Today

The true Prophet hears __from__ God and speaks to men __for__ God!

August 23

O. T. Bible Reading: Psalms 119:105-176   **Our Focus: Psalms 119:125**

UNDERSTANDING

The intended fruit of knowledge is understanding, and the product of understanding is wisdom. To understand is to perceive or comprehend both the nature and the significance of an event; it is to know thoroughly by close contact and long experience. It is not just to grasp; it is also to comprehend. It is to get the big picture, and to have a full view. It is the eagle's-eye view. It is the panoramic sweep of the entire scene.

The skilled and able craftsman, Bezaleel, was filled "... with the spirit of God, in wisdom, and in understanding, and in knowledge, and in all manner of workmanship" (Ex. 31:3). He was assigned the primary responsibility to make or to build all the items and furnishings of the Tabernacle. He was not to parade his gift, nor was he to advertise his calling and ability. We do not read of him saying anything nor claiming any gift or glory. He simply went to work, and began to build. We hear much hooting and ado about some great gift or title; what is needed is an energetic exercising (better known as hard work) of a gift to build. The real test of any gift is by no means the great claims, but the beauty of the finished product. Paul did not tell Timothy to proclaim and boast in the gift of an evangelist. He quite simply, and very wisely, told him to do the work of an evangelist (II Tim. 4:5). Good advice!

Bezaleel was the great grandson of Caleb; his name means, "in the shadow of God"; what a precious hiding place. Perhaps it was the understanding which the Lord gave him that made him so successful and productive. The words of Proverbs 8:5 echo through the corridors of time, "O ye simple, understand wisdom: and, ye fools, be ye of an understanding heart." One of the fruits of the Spirit is meekness (Gal. 5:23). Perhaps this rare faculty or quality may include the true meaning of an understanding heart.

Thought For Today

An appropriate prayer, "the Lord give thee understanding!"

August 23

N. T. Bible Reading: I Corinthians 5   **Our Focus: I Corinthians 5:7**

PURGE

The word "purge" as used in Scripture means to cleanse thoroughly or completely. The reference is to Exodus 12:18-20, 13:6-7; the Jewish household was instructed to remove all leaven from their homes in preparation for the feast of Passover. It was to symbolize their total break with their old life in Egypt. Paul used that familiar ceremony to summon the church in Corinth to remove the moral reproach caused by the guilty members' unclean actions. An Assembly must be kept and maintained in all purity to preserve the new life, and to respond consistently and decisively to the Holy calling into which they have entered. This standard of conduct must first be realized personally before it can be maintained in the corporate body. But both are clearly required by the Word of God.

It is no coincidence that chapter 5 comes before chapter 13. Those who would attempt to make love a cover-up or an excuse to condone unclean or ungodly living, are simply twisting or distorting Scripture to their own condemnation. The wisdom which is from above is first pure (Jam. 3:17). Purity, by any definition, is a condition free from defilement, it means to be chaste, and unspotted by the world. To maintain any such condition requires a genuine purging.

Those who are God's children are also possessors of the Spirit and nature of God. This beautiful new nature will and must express itself in a Godly manner of life. It is the transformation of life and character which proclaims to an unbelieving world that Jesus is alive, salvation is real, and it really works.

Thought For Today

Those who would be filled must first be purged!

August 24

O. T. Bible Reading: Psalms 120-123   **Our Focus: Psalms 121:5**

THY KEEPER

We are assured in scripture of the lively hope unto an inheritance reserved in heaven for us "Who are kept by the power of God ..." (I Pet. 1:5). We are urged amid troubles and sufferings to "... commit the keeping of their souls to him in well doing, as unto a faithful Creator" (I Pet. 4:19). In the complexities of human life there is much to guard or keep: our physical life, our minds and our thoughts, our health and happiness, our homes and possessions and so much more. However, all of these put together could not begin to compare to the keeping or guarding of the soul. Man failed to keep the garden which God had committed to him, but God will not fail to keep the life which is genuinely committed it to Him.

The compound names of Jehovah are a treasure-house of knowledge and of almost infinite application. In Psalms 23:1 God is revealed as *Jehovah-Rohi* which means, "The Lord is my shepherd." In Exodus 17:15 we are told that "... Moses built an altar, and called the name of it Jehovah-Nissi" meaning, "Jehovah, my Banner." Because He is our Great and Good Shepherd we can lift the victorious banner, and all because of Jehovah-Shammah (Ezek. 48:35). The great Jehovah is there. We can surely say with David, "... I shall not want ..." (Ps. 23:1).

The very same God who is promised to the individual in Psalms 121:3 will also protect the corporate body (Israel in this case). He is on a 24 hour vigil, and requires no rest. Not only does He protect and guard by day and by night, but He also is our shade by day and night. Sun-stroke was very common in that area and He will cover them in their forward march. The moon by night had great meaning to them. There were ancient ideas which held that the rays of the moon were very dangerous to the mind. Hence the term "lunatic" (luna, the moon) arose from that belief. At any rate, this great Psalm, along with many other passages of Scripture, should generate faith and confidence in every tested pilgrim. There is good reason why we are told, "fear not."

Thought For Today

His keeping power is unlimited for those who remain on the ship!

August 24

N. T. Bible Reading: I Corinthians 6   **Our Focus: I Corinthians 6:3**

KNOW YE NOT

Corinth was corrupt. The city, 50 miles west of Athens, was the capital of Achaia. It was a flourishing city of Commerce and was made up of a very cosmopolitan population. It was characterized, at the time of Paul, by wealth and wickedness, and the two were closely tied together. Impurity was rampant, and morals were rare. Chrysostom labeled Corinth, "a city the most licentious of all that are or ever have been." It was a huge quagmire of depravity and gross sensualism. There is no description of human sin and depravity more awful than the first chapter of Romans, and it was written from Corinth.

Environment is no excuse for evil. There is not one Gospel for Corinth and another for Jerusalem. The faithful, but heart sickened Apostle, must energetically begin the long and demanding process of instruction in righteousness, of correction in behavior, and of direction in doctrine according to godliness (II Tim. 3:16; I Tim. 6:3). For this reason Paul says, "know ye not" six times in I Corinthians chapter 6. These young converts from heathenism and from an environment of shocking corruption must learn at once that the true gospel cannot tolerate compromise. There must be a clean and total break with the past. When evil is tolerated under the guise of charity, then charity becomes a vice.

The final appeal of I Corinthians 6:19-20 is powerful, profound, and most practical. Our bodies are the temple, or dwelling place, of the Holy Ghost. Our body belongs to God, and is now the very temple of God; therefore, to allow that body to be used in an unclean manner is taking from Christ what is His very property and giving it to a harlot. It still is. The word *clean* is closely associated with the *Holy* Spirit. The unclean vessel is unfit. We are called with a high and holy calling. Let us by our thoughts, words, and daily conduct hold high the royal banner of holiness.

Thought For Today

He who calls us does not condescend to our condition!

August 25

O. T. Bible Reading: Psalms 124-127   **Our Focus: Psalms 127:2**

HE GIVETH

God is a giving God. It has been so from the very beginning of time. In the beautiful garden, after the creation of Adam and Eve, God communed with them and twice repeated the words, "… I have given …" (Gen. 1:29-30). It will be so to the very end. In the very last chapter of the great book of Revelation we are told, "And there shall be no night there; and they need no candle, neither light of the sun; for the *Lord God giveth* them light: and they shall reign forever and ever" (Rev. 22:5). It is so now and in the fullness of time, "For God so loved the world, that *he gave* his only begotten Son, that whosoever believeth in him should not perish, but have everlasting life" (John 3:16).

We are not to imagine that His giving is in the past tense, and is over and completed. It is present progressive. He is giving at this very moment. Troubled soul, reach out to Him in your distress. "But he giveth *more* grace …" (Jam. 4:6), that is, more grace that you received yesterday; more grace than you were given in calmer waters. There is a new need. The skies are black with threatening clouds, the raging storm is upon you, and the angry billows splash over your frail bark. It is now you need supernatural intervention. He knows your need and He dispenses His Divine energies accordingly. What we need is not a greater supply, but a greater capacity to receive and to contain the mighty provision.

What a precious promise, "… he giveth his beloved sleep" (Ps. 127:2). Some have translated it, "in sleep"; it is true either way. There are times when the Lord will make His will known or deliver a personal message to instruct "… in the night seasons" (Ps. 16:7). It is just what is needed, and just when it is needed, and in whatever way He chooses. The on-time God!

Thought For Today

The resources of the giver define the value of the gift!

August 25

N. T. Bible Reading: I Corinthians 7:1-24   **Our Focus: I Corinthians 7:15**

PEACE

The common greeting in Israel is "shalom." It is more than just peace; it is wholeness or completeness. The title, "the God of peace", is used many times in the New Testament. Peace is also listed as a fruit of the Spirit. Jesus promised a very unique and special kind of peace, "Peace I leave with you, my peace I give unto you ..." (John 14:27). This was a peculiar quality which He possessed in a special manner and to a special degree. It was to be an imparted ingredient in accordance with His very nature. It is the bestowal of a holy affection, the tranquility of a firm and settled purpose, and it is the sunshine of unclouded communion and fellowship with God.

The peace of which Jesus spoke was something apart from and superior to anything this world has to offer (John 14:27). The manner in which the world offers peace is superficial, temporary, and evasive at best. It cannot give what it does not have; and the Word of God declares, "There is no peace, saith my God, to the wicked" (Isa. 57:21). Jesus was announced to be "... The Prince of Peace" (Isa. 9:6), and the peace which he imparts has been procured for His redeemed children at the supreme sacrifice of His atoning death. The content of this Divine essence is not just a peace of conscience, but goes far beyond that as a confident rest and composure in the will of God. It is not a morbid resignation, but a rejoicing delight in Him and in all of His dealings.

In Philippians 4:9 He is said to be "... the God of peace ..." and He is the only source from which genuine peace can flow. He bestows peace through His Word, and by the Spirit. He imparts it first in the life and conscience of His children, and then in the harmonious relationships they maintain. Their experience and enjoyment of that peace depends upon their obedience to the Word of God.

Thought For Today

His peace reigns in the heart which is ruled by His Word!

August 26

O. T. Bible Reading: Psalms 128-131   **Our Focus: Psalms 130:5**

I HOPE

Only those who have a genuine hope will also wait. He who has no hope will not and cannot wait. No one ever has waited for that for which they have no hope. The attitude of patient waiting is a great part of the discipline of faith. It is an exercise which will give strength and stamina to patience. It is a vital element in the culture of the soul which prepares the vessel for deeper insights and richer fields of usefulness to the Lord. We must learn, in this great school of spiritual refinement, not to wait so much for any special event, but to wait for the Lord of that event. We must wait *for* and *on* the Lord *in* the event. It must be His Word which prompts our efforts, and which will achieve the desired end.   Such hope contains no element of uncertainty burdened with the possibility of disappointment. It is certain of fulfillment.

There are three adjectives which are used to define the hope of the New Testament:

1.   II Thessalonians 2:16 "... good hope ..." – This is said of the hope of the final resurrection which was well grounded and worthy of their full trust.
2.   I Peter 1:3 "... a lively hope ..." – The sad and dejected disciples said they had hoped, but all hope had died with their master when he expired on the cross. In His triumphant resurrection they and we were begotten again unto a lively hope.
3.   Titus 2:13 "Looking for that blessed hope ..." – Happy are the people who share the bright and sure prospect of the glories of life eternal.

The prophecy of Hosea 2:15, "And I will give her her vineyards from thence, and the valley of Achor for a door of hope ..." is primarily a yet future promise for the nation of Israel. However, there is honey in the rock, and we can extract some beautiful lessons from it by applying the principles to our own personal experience. The valley of Achor is literally the valley of trouble. God is able to turn the valley of defeat into the valley of victory when we, as Israel, deal with sin in the camp. This is a fundamental law of the spiritual realm. You must deal with sin before you can experience victory; when you do, a door of opportunity and blessing is opened to you, and this is a door of hope.

Thought For Today

Hope is both an anchor and a bright shining star!

August 26

N. T. Bible Reading: I Corinthians 7:25-40   **Our Focus: I Corinthians 7:31**

USING OR ABUSING

Anything of value may be distorted and abused. Even the very Word of God may be, and is, twisted and distorted; "... which, unhappy, ill informed and unbalanced people distort ..." (II Pet. 3:16, Phillips' translation). To use something is to exercise it in the proper manner so as to accomplish the end for which it was designed. To abuse a thing is to swerve it aside from this design and employ it for personal or other distorted purposes. Those who have some personal agenda or some idea or doctrine to defend will torture (twist) the Scriptures to make them say what was never originally intended.

We are admonished to use this world for exactly what God originally intended, but to discreetly avoid being tainted and influenced by it. We must develop the fine art of skillfully passing through the world of the temporal in such a manner as not to lose or sacrifice anything which is eternal. This is walking a tightrope. It will require more than human skills; it will demand Divine assistance and supernatural strength.

Alexander the Great, we are told by historians, overcame the known world, and then "sat down and wept because there were no more worlds to conquer": how totally wrong! The pitiful slave of alcohol and lust died prematurely in a drunken debauchery when only 33 years of age.

Jesus, by contrast, accurately and honestly proclaimed at the end of his life, also at 33, "... I have overcome the world" (John 16:33). He had conquered the world of moral and spiritual evil, and when seen with spiritually enlightened eyes, we crown Him as the greatest conqueror in history. "The world", in a spiritual sense, so far as we as individuals are concerned, is anything which separates us from God, and blocks our communion with Him. This is a good litmus test for any issue, does it hinder my fellowship with God, and does it break my communion with Him? This world, in that sense, is as alluring and attractive as it is deceptive and destructive. He overcame, and so may we; "... greater is he that is in you, than he that is in the world" (I John 4:4).

Thought For Today

To live above the world is to enjoy His very life!

114

August 27

O. T. Bible Reading: Psalms 132-135   **Our Focus: Psalms 133:1**

UNITY

Jesus prayed in John 17:21 "That they all may be one; as thou, Father, art in me, and I in thee, that they also may be one in us ..."; that prayer would seem to have been answered, at least in part, on the day of Pentecost. "And when the day of Pentecost was fully come, they were all with one accord in one place" (Acts 2:1). Paul admonished the church at Ephesus to "... keep the unity of the Spirit in the bond of peace" (Eph. 4:3). The word he used for unity was "henotes" the root of which means "one." The measure in which this is accomplished may be the measure in which the blessing of the Lord is experienced. It is there that the Lord _commands_ the blessing. When we live in peace, then the God of peace manifests His presence among us (II Cor. 13:11). Even the very prospect of such an experience is both good and pleasant.

It is most unpleasant to any member of any home where there is division or disagreement. God decreed in the beginning that "... they shall be one ..." (Gen. 2:24). When this is realized, then just in that measure, there is sweet fellowship and pleasant harmony. This cannot be fully realized until there is a definite personal fellowship and communion established with the Lord on the part of both husband and wife. His presence brings the very fragrance of the atmosphere of heaven into any life, any home, and into any fellowship. What a pleasant experience to learn to walk with Him.

Dew is the noiseless unseen distilling of heavens' condensation in the calm and quietness of the night. It will not fall in stormy or windy conditions. The dew of Herman was copious with pristine freshness. Mount Hermon rises to a height of nearly 10,000 feet and at its peak is crowned with snow the year round. The almost tropical rays of the day-time sun melts the snowy sides of the lower slopes, which creates a run-off of melted snow, and a vapor cloud of humidity is precipitated in the night seasons into the heaviest dew most people have ever experienced. It penetrates and distills everywhere until everything it reaches is saturated. Such is the picture which the Lord uses to describe the beautiful and blessed results of the experience of unity. This is indeed an ointment most precious. It is most significant that for ancient Israel the manna fell on the dew (Num. 11:9) ... so also it does today!

Thought For Today

Where unity is achieved the glory lingers ever near!

August 27

N. T. Bible Reading: I Corinthians 8   **Our Focus: I Corinthians 8:1**

CHARITY

Charity is love in action; it is the Divine impulse expressing itself in reaching out to help, bless, or minister to anyone in need. It is not just the "glow" of love; it is the practical and genuine "flow" of love which actually reaches out and touches those are around us. It is the _proof_ of discipleship, and the _evidence_ of genuine salvation. "By this shall all men _know_ that ye are my disciples, _if_ ye have love one _to_ another" (John 13:35). It is in this issue of delivering love that reality is clearly identified, and sham and pretense are exposed. Charity, in the Bible sense, is the missing link in the confused world of counterfeit Christianity; but it is the badge of the genuine. It is I Corinthians 13 expressed in this and every other day of any year. It is one ingredient for which the enemy has no counterfeit, and for which men can find no substitute. The scriptures tell us that "... Knowledge puffeth up ..." (I Cor. 8:1), that is, it blows up or inflates. It produces an exalted spirit, an inflated attitude, an arrogant feeling, and a demanding manner. Charity, we are told, edifies (I Cor. 8:1); that is, it builds up, stabilizes, strengthens, inspires, and lifts. It is a very positive virtue which expresses itself in a very positive way. The first, knowledge, is what the mind has absorbed; the latter, charity, is what the heart has experienced.

Natural love is as different than Divine love, as a candle is different than the sun. Both produce light and heat, but in utterly different degrees. Human love is like honey; it will sour under stress and in time. It is the impartation and the expression of the very _love of God_ which makes all the difference; "... the love of God is shed abroad in our hearts by the Holy Ghost which is given unto us" (Rom. 5:5). The mercy of God extended to the unworthy sinner is justified only in the transformation of that life. The mighty miracle of redemption is that God turns the sinner, the unholy one, into the very standard of Himself, _The Holy One,_ by imparting a whole new disposition, the very nature and spirit of the Lord Jesus Christ.

Thought For Today

Charity is a rare virtue in an uncharitable world!

August 28

O. T. Bible Reading: Psalms 136-138   **Our Focus: Psalms 136:1**

HIS MERCY

The Psalmist repeats his appeal 4 times, "O give thanks", and gives us a special reason for doing so 26 times, "for his mercy endureth forever." That is the jubilant refrain at the conclusion of every single verse of this Psalm. The Pharisaical attitude is betrayed by making any expression of thanksgiving to revolve around and to terminate in some person, virtue, or personal goodness; "… God, I thank thee, that I am (or am not) …" (Luke 18:11). It is easy to see why the Scriptures tell us that he prayed *with himself*. Such praying would never go beyond the ceiling of the room in which it was prayed. The true worshipper, by contrast, centers all thanksgiving in Him and to the glory of God. The phrase, "for his mercy endureth forever", is the theme song of David (I Chron. 16:34), the wonder of Moses, the sum of revelation, the hope of mankind, and the song of the soul set free.

The human scene is very different from the heavenly. On earth people are very short on their long-suffering, very meager and miserly with their mercy, and very harsh and severe in their actions, showing little or no gentleness. We are depleted by deployment, diminished by distribution, and depressed by every deposit. His mercy knows no end, suffers no interruption, is never exhausted, and remains constant and concentrated forever. The mercy of His wonderful plan is the amazingly wonderful plan of His mercy; and this He graciously continues to do from generation to generation because "… he delighteth in mercy" (Mic. 7:18). He is slow to anger, and judgment is His strange work: His abundant mercy extends itself on into eternity, and to everlasting, and if one everlasting is not convincing enough, there is a chorus of 26 everlastings in this one Psalm.

The Psalms speak of "thy mercy" 24 times: the first of which is Psalm 5:7 "… I will come into thy house in the multitude of thy mercy …." He is good: therefore, we are to give thanks unto the Lord. We must render unto him the calves of our lips (Hos. 14:2), for we have by personal experience seen, proved, and have tasted that He is good. He is the source of good, the sustainer of good, the perfecter of good, and the rewarder of good.

Thought For Today

His love is our theme: His mercy is our plea!

August 28

N. T. Bible Reading: I Corinthians 9   **Our Focus: I Corinthians 9:19**

SERVANT

To serve is to minister: to minister is to serve. Some would associate ministering with recognition, regalia, respect, and rewards. The Scriptures paint a very different picture: sacrifice, solitude, self denial, and suffering. The marvel of love is the magnitude of love: the satellite of love is sacrifice: the sentiment of love is service. The universal proclamation of the pouring forth of the alabaster box of ointment carries with it the awesome fragrance of love and service beyond the call of duty (Matt. 26:7). This act was very pleasing to the Lord, and it was given His highest praise. He said she had wrought a good work, and it was an expression of great value to Him. Jesus saw to it that this pouring forth of love, in utter abandon and with great sacrifice, would be recorded, remembered, and universally heralded. It was eternally of more value than the rare and costly spices. Mary of Bethany produced in the heart of the Lord what can only be reproduced by the same depth of love manifest in sacrificial service. Those who offer unto the Lord of that which is convenient have not learned the first principles of ministering unto the Lord.

The apostle Paul clearly grasped this vision of being a minister of the Gospel which Jesus pioneered. Jesus said, "... I am among you as he that serveth" (Luke 22:27). Paul echoed the same sentiment when he affirmed, "For we preach not ourselves, but Christ Jesus the Lord; and ourselves your servants for Jesus' sake" (II Cor. 4:5). In this New Testament sense we get a new revelation of love in action. To be a spiritual leader is not to be seen or recognized as superior, but to be known as a sacrificial servant.

The love of God is poured forth in our hearts by the Holy Ghost (Rom. 5:5), and that very love will pour forth through us to others. His love in us will enable us to identify ourselves deliberately and consistently with the Lord Jesus' interests in other people. We lay down or pour forth our love in devoted service for and to Him; this is sweet, precious, and eternally rewarded service.

Thought For Today

The ability to minister is the agility to serve!

August 29

O. T. Bible Reading: Psalms 139-141   **Our Focus: Psalms 139:22**

PERFECT HATRED

Perfect hatred is like anything else which is perfect: it is rare and of supreme value. This is the only time these words are used together in the entire Bible, and the frame of mind which is portrayed is perhaps as solitary and singular as this unique text. There is another rare Scripture in Ezekiel 35:5 which the Lord used to condemn Mt. Seir "... thou hast a perpetual hatred ..."; their hatred was ancient, adamant, and advertised. Everyone knew it: it was a by-word or a proverb of the time.

We can accurately define these words by the context and by the main body of truth taught and depicted by the Scriptures. David had already clearly stated, "Do not I hate them, O Lord, that hate thee? and am not I grieved with those that rise up against thee?" (Ps. 139:21). He adds later, "... I count them mine enemies" (Ps. 139:22). It is quite evident that he is expressing more than an emotion; he is defining a principle. It is a very personal thing with him. There is no sham neutrality here. He erases every question mark, and adds his own personal exclamation mark. He is whole-hearted, intense, complete, and energetic in his hatred of wickedness, vice, and vicious evil. David here makes an open declaration of war against every evil work and way. These wicked individuals are doing despite to God, they are flouting His laws, and they are rejecting in open rebellion, the principles of truth and righteousness. Any godly person must contend with those who contend with God.

It is the positive which justifies the negative. Moses hated sin and rebellion, but he prayed for those who were guilty. Jesus loved righteousness, and hated iniquity. God is angry with the wicked everyday (Ps. 7:11), and yet He loved the world enough to sacrifice His Son, our blessed Savior, for its' redemption. This is another, and perhaps the only, perfect example of perfect hatred.

Thought For Today

Those who stand for the right will always stand against the wrong!

August 29

N. T. Bible Reading: I Corinthians 10:1-13   **Our Focus: I Corinthians 10:3**

SPIRITUAL MEAT

The children of Israel ate the same spiritual meat; that is, what was Divinely supplied. It was called, "manna." Paul calls it spiritual meat because it was supernaturally supplied directly from heaven (angels' food, Ps. 78:25), and because it was a type of the Lord Jesus Christ. Jesus Himself, made this clear in John 6:48-50, "I am that bread of life. Your fathers did eat manna in the wilderness, and are dead. This is the bread (the real meat) which cometh down from heaven, that a man may eat thereof, and not die."

Jesus was the meat, and He also was the Water of Life. He was the complete meal. They tested the patience of the Lord (I Cor. 10:9) by their murmuring and rebellion. He was The Rock from which came the water in the wilderness, and His unfailing presence accompanied their every move. It was this Divine presence which God promised to Moses, and it never failed (Ex. 33:14).

The promise of His presence as well as His power is even more essential in our pilgrim journey (Matt. 28:20; Mark 16:20). We need the manna, and the ever-flowing and refreshing Water of Life as our daily portion. The eternal truth for both the Old Testament and the New Testament is, "… Man shall not live by bread alone, but by every (quickened) word that proceedeth out of the mouth of God" (Matt. 4:4; Deut. 8:3). We need "soul food", the Spirit-quickened Word of God, to maintain our spiritual strength.

We cannot live and maintain our vim, vigor, and vitality, without nourishment and refreshing; and that on a regular and ongoing basis. Where there is no "feasting on the Lord" there certainly will be no banquet or bounty. At the very best it will be picking the left-over bones from former days of feasting. "Give us *this* day our *daily* bread" (Matt. 6:11).

Thought For Today

There is none so thirsty as he who has left the stream!

August 30

O. T. Bible Reading: Psalms 142-144　　　　　　**Our Focus: Psalms 144:15**

HAPPY

The word most used by the happy family of God is "*blessed*." The world uses and exploits the word "happy." Happiness to them is the ultimate expression of pleasure and personal enjoyment. The root of the word (hap) has to do primarily with luck. Happiness, then, depends on happenings, and happenings to the world are the spin of chance or luck. The word does occur about 26 times in the Bible; however, the word "blessed" in its various forms (bless-blessing) is used approximately 600 times. It is the preferred word, and by far the more meaningful and expressive to the child of God. It involves the thought of Divine favor, and the focus is on the heavenly involvement. It becomes a much more appropriate expression for God's children to include the favor and mercy of God, more than the flip of the coin, when we speak of our surroundings and circumstances; "... the Lord gave, and the Lord hath taken away; blessed be the name of the Lord" (Job 1:21).

The gold of heaven far exceeds the silver of earth in true value to the child of God. We certainly appreciate material and temporal blessings, but we do not set our hearts upon them (Col. 3:2). They are benefits, and not life-time goals. The enjoyment they bring is brief and limited. They are of the earth, earthly; and will quickly vanish and "... are to perish with the using ..." (Col. 2:22). We are to seek first the things of God (Matt. 6:33). Our focus is on the spiritual and the eternal. It is from these we enjoy the most satisfying fulfillment.

Those who worship the happy God become and are a happy people. Rotherham translates I Timothy 1:11, "according to the glad message of the glory of the happy God." The balance is in focus when Solomon pointed out: "... in her left hand riches and honour" (Prov. 3:16), but most important and most essential "Length of days (or fullness of days) is in her right hand ..." (Prov. 3:16). The primary element of real Joy is to find the print of the hand of God even in temporal benefits, and then to praise and glorify Him in the right use of them.

Thought For Today

It is blessed to <u>know</u> Him: it is unspeakable joy to <u>serve</u> Him!

August 30

N. T. Bible Reading: I Corinthians 10:14-33   **Our Focus: I Corinthians 10:17**

ONE BREAD

There is but one loaf of bread, and Jesus is that loaf. Anything or anyone who is represented as the central element on which any particular religious group feasts is an impostor, or a dangerous substitute. The Lord Jesus Christ is the head of the body of Christ. He is "Far above all principality, and power, and might, and dominion, and every name that is named, not only in this world, but also in that which is to come" (Eph. 1:21). The bread which was used in the feast of the Passover could only be _unleavened_ bread. Jesus fulfilled that feast. He was our Passover Lamb (I Cor. 5:7). There was no leaven (or sin) found in Him, neither did guile ever defile His mouth (I Pet. 2:22). We are instructed to feast on Him, but we must beware of the constant danger of adding our own leaven. For this very reason Paul urged these New Testament believers to "… flee from idolatry" (I Cor. 10:14). An idol is anything or anyone put in the place of Christ.

God will always make a way of escape from temptation (I Cor. 10:13). More times than not that way will be the King's Highway, and a good pair of running shoes. Too many times people are like the little boy in the pantry. His mother was alerted when she heard him take down the cookie jar. She quickly asked, "Johnny, where are you?" He answered that he was in the pantry. She further asked, "and what are you doing in there?" He answered, "I'm fighting temptation!" The pantry was not the place to fight temptation. To walk away from it would have produced much better results.

We sing, "bread of heaven, feed me 'till I want no more", and this is Scriptural. Psalms 78:23 declares that God commanded the clouds, opened the doors of heaven, rained down upon them the corn of heaven, and men ate angels' food, or as the margin says, "the bread of the mighty." He was the delight of the Fathers' heart before He became the source of life and sustenance for lost humanity.

Thought For Today

When we feast on Jesus we are _one_ with all others who do the same!

August 31

O. T. Bible Reading: Psalms 145-147   **Our Focus: Psalms 145:1**

EXTOL

The seldom used word "extol" is found in Isaiah 52:13, "Behold, my servant shall deal prudently, he shall be exalted and extolled, and be very high." This prophetic verse describes the Lord Jesus, and accurately defines the word "extol." The word means to praise highly. It is a word which is meant to encourage worship at its highest level. His royalty should arouse our loyalty, and our quickened spirit should be moved to magnify His majesty. Worship, at this level, is rarely experienced. Few are truly *moved* in their highest and most spiritual faculties to adore the altogether Lovely One. The sad fact is that very few are moved in any way to do anything. There are, it seems, too many Peters who follow him but from afar off, sitting with the wrong crowd; and warming at the wrong fire (Mark 14:54). May the Lord increase the Johns (no wonder he is described as the disciple whom Jesus loved, John 19:26) who, sensing the gravity of the moment, leaned upon Jesus bosom (John 21:20).

This is both a pleasant plan and a plain pledge. "I will extol thee ..." (Ps. 145:1), indicating that it was a present tense activity, and stating emphatically this is exactly what I intend to continue to do. A Psalm is the praise of God accompanied by song; it consists of songs containing the praise of God. There could be praise which is not of God; and, therefore, is not a Psalm. When there is praise of God which is not sung, that is not a Psalm. There must be a trio, not of voices, but of conditions: true praise, and that the praise of God, and, thirdly, there must be singing.

To extol is to set preeminently on high; to exalt far above all others. Those who enjoy this kind of depth in worship because of their high opinion and honor of the King will not go very far without sharing their experience to magnify the object of such praise. He is now, and one day shall be universally crowned, king of kings and Lord of Lords. He is The King in truth and verity; all others are only pretenders in vanity.

Thought For Today

We can only extol His Majesty by our unqualified devotion and loyalty!

August 31

N. T. Bible Reading: I Corinthians 11:1-15   **Our Focus: I Corinthians 11:3**

THE HEAD

It is a principle of Scripture that God has ordained authority for the sake of order, to avoid confusion. This, as all other Biblical principles, applies to everyone and to every situation. Specifically it has immediate application to the Christian church and to the Christian home. The problem expresses itself in a two-fold way in our time. The first, and most obvious, is that there is a general disregard for, if not outright antagonism to any authority, because it involves responsibility. The second problem which we face is that there is a universal shirking of responsibility because it involves initiative. A very real part of growing "… in grace, and in the knowledge of our Lord and Saviour Jesus Christ …" (II Pet. 3:18) will be to learn this great principle. It will take much more than one short lesson. This must be repeatedly explained and responsibly demonstrated by consistent example.

A common objection heard from the play-room of growing siblings is, "but you're not the boss." And even more common attitude expressed in the market place is, "let George do it." Perhaps this is one reason why there is a decreasing number of babies given the name of George: who wants to overwhelm their own child with such an awesome load!

The law of nature is that the unworthy will discredit, attack, and reject that which is worthy, and particularly that which is supremely worthy. Those who join in adoration of the finally triumphant Lord Jesus have a common chorus they sing: "thou art worthy" (repeated three times in Revelation). These words, and more importantly, this attitude which recognizes and gladly owns His Lordship and right to rule is one major reason they are with the Lamb in His kingdom and glory. When that within me which is unworthy rejects and rebels against His right to rule over me with absolute authority I immediately begin the tragic retreat from the recreating power of His redemption. The revelation of the order of God, and His structure of authority, is one of the most life-transforming insights we will ever receive from the true gospel.

Thought For Today

Those who crown Him Lord of all begin to share His glory <u>even now</u>!

September 1

O. T. Bible Reading: Psalms 148-150   **Our Focus: Psalms 150:1**

HIS SANCTUARY

The word "sanctuary" occurs over 100 times in the Scriptures, only four times in the New Testament, and all four are in the book of Hebrews (Heb. 8:2, 9:1, 9:2, 13:11). Any definition, and there are several, will always include the words holy or sacred. As expected, when used in the Bible, it nearly always has reference to the Tabernacle in the wilderness or to the inner part of the Temple in Jerusalem, the Holy of Holies. The dictionary definition suggests a sacred *place*, or a *place* of *refuge*.

The word is first used in Exodus 15:17 in the passage which records what is commonly known as The Song of Moses. They are the words of praise and worship from Moses on the occasion of the miraculous Red Sea deliverance. He there projects the purpose of God to bring the nation of Israel into the land of promise, into the mountain of His inheritance, and into the very place where He could *dwell* among His people. He clearly stated repeatedly that His intent was to "... *dwell* among the children of Israel, and will be their God" (Ex. 29:45), "and let them make me a sanctuary; that I may dwell among them" (Ex. 25:8).

The glory and the mystery of the New Testament revelation is that God no longer seeks any building as the place of His dwelling. He now seeks for dedicated, devoted, and devout hearts and lives through whom He can manifest His power, presence, and His very person. It is now, "To whom God would make known what is the riches of the glory of *this mystery* among the Gentiles; which is *Christ in you*, the hope of glory" (Col. 1:27). The *full* Gospel is to know Christ *for* me; Christ *in* me; and Christ *through* me. Dr. F. B. Meyer is given credit for the saying, "in all His people Christ is *present*: in some He is *prominent*: in a few He is *preeminent*." Those few rare souls are the "hidden ones" who feast on the riches of His fulness.

Thought For Today

God possesses only what is fully yielded to Him!

September 1

N. T. Bible Reading: I Corinthians 11:16-34   **Our Focus: I Corinthians 11:29**

DISCERNING

It is strange and sad that divisive interpretations of Scripture revolve around some of the most precious statements in The Word of God. This certainly is one of those passages. It would be presumptuous to attempt to resolve these differences on a single sheet of paper. However, if we could just lay aside all the various interpretations perhaps we could find honey in the carcass (Jud. 14:8-9), and the living water at the common well (John 4:10).

Two of Jesus' disciples were walking on the road to Emmaus which was 7½ miles from Jerusalem. They were at their lowest; downcast, disappointed, disillusioned, dejected, and defeated. Jesus was dead and buried and so were their hopes and dreams. The risen Savior joined them, and an amazing and revealing experience followed; "… he expounded unto them in all the scriptures the things concerning himself" (Luke 24:27). They constrained Him to spend the night with them as it was now late and the road was dangerous to travel when dark. They still had not recognized Him. It was later, as they prepared to eat "… he took bread, and blessed it, and brake, and gave to them" (Luke 24:30), when their eyes were opened and they saw and knew that it was *Jesus Himself*. He *revealed Himself* to them.

This is reality, and it revived, restored, renewed, and revolutionized those two disciples. What could have been a mere formality; or worse, a religious ritual, was gloriously quickened into a personal encounter with the mighty risen and victorious Savior Himself. So it should be in our every observance and spiritual exercise. Jesus Himself must not only be present, but He must reveal Himself to each one personally. It is not a symbol, it is not a ritual, it is not a formality; it is a transforming encounter with Jesus Himself! It is *discernment* which produces *reality*.

Thought For Today

"They knew Him", but only when He revealed Himself to them!

September 2

O. T. Bible Reading: Proverbs 1-2   **Our Focus: Proverbs 1:2**

WISDOM

The clear theme of the book of Proverbs is wisdom. The word "wisdom" will be found 54 times in these 31 chapters, and the basic word "wise" 66 times. There are many definitions to be found for wisdom; it is important to know what it is, as defined by the Scriptures. The most basic idea is the right use of the mind, and as a practical matter, the ability to use knowledge correctly. This suggests a very vital fact; it is possible to have knowledge without wisdom, but it is impossible to have wisdom without knowledge. Knowledge is not to be limited to academic training. It is the familiarity, awareness, or understanding gained through experience, and includes the whole spectrum of what has been perceived, discovered, or learned. Thus, an individual may be very knowledgeable without "lettered" credentials as were the early apostles (Acts 4:13).

The Proverbs are a collection of concentrated cogitations relating to conduct. It is a cafeteria of wisdom in capsule form. The book requires special attention. It must be read carefully, thoughtfully, lingeringly, and meditatively. It is not suitable material for a speed-reading test. The warning sign at a railroad crossing in by-gone days read: "stop, look, listen." Perhaps a fitting caption to the book of Proverbs would be: "pause, think deeply, meditate prayerfully, the well is deep!!"

The Proverbs are not just a collection of pithy expressions; they are "*applied*" precepts. That is, they are related to real life and go far beyond the realm of theory; they reach the work-a-day world where we all live. It is significant that wisdom is linked to instruction. To instruct is to teach or impart in the atmosphere or in the environment of discipline. A disciple is a disciplined follower of Christ. He is a learner with the emphasis not just on accumulated facts, but rather on endeavor and an applied relationship.

Thought For Today

Those who think deeply should also live accordingly!

September 2

N. T. Bible Reading: I Corinthians 12　　　　**Our Focus: I Corinthians 12:28**

MIRACLES

I Corinthians chapter 12 is dealing with the supernatural. It is life on an entirely different level. The church is not a human institution; it is meant to be a Divinely directed organism. It is, as defined in Scripture, a work of the Holy Spirit, not the product of human abilities or activities. The generating force is Divine "dunamis" (heavenly energy); it is not human genius, talents, and abilities. Paul is dealing here with a strictly spiritual element (I Cor. 12:1). Anything which is so stamped of God must of necessity include the supernatural.

Miracles are as much a part of the functioning New Testament church as is teaching and preaching. The problem is that preaching and teaching can both be carried out on a purely human level, and sadly, in most cases they are. The work of miracles separates the supernatural from the human. Peter declared that they (the apostles) ministered "… the gospel unto you with the Holy Ghost sent down from heaven; which things the angels desire to look into" (I Pet. 1:12). In I Corinthians chapter 12 the apostle Paul speaks of miracles three times:

1.　　"… the workings of miracles …" – I Corinthians 12:10.
2.　　"… God hath set some … miracles …" I Corinthians 12:28.
3.　　"… workers of miracles." – I Corinthians 12:29.

The reason for this is that he is dealing with the subject of the gifts of the Holy Spirit in the church, and that must, by the very nature of it, include miracles and the manifestation of the supernatural. If we are to exclude miracles, as some contend, then why not also exclude pastors, teachers, and evangelists?

A miracle by dictionary definition is, "an event inexplicable by the laws of nature and so held to be supernatural in origin or an act of God." It is something which could not be produced by natural agents and means. It is God in action. Many of us can testify to just such experiences in our own lives. We serve a God of might and miracle. He is still on His throne of glory. His Almighty power has never been diminished nor has it been exhausted. Those who praise and worship Him for who He is, will not fail to experience the miracles of which Paul speaks.

Thought For Today

Without miracles, we operate on the human level only!

September 3

O. T. Bible Reading: Proverbs 3-4   **Our Focus: Proverbs 3:26**

CONFIDENCE

Any definition of confidence will include trust and faith. Those who possess it express it in boldness and assurance. Those who lack it manifest timidity and fear because of insecurity and uncertainty. It is a basic element in the experience of salvation. The book of Acts closes with the witness of the Apostle Paul who continued "Preaching the kingdom of God, and teaching those things which concern the Lord Jesus Christ, with all *confidence*, no man forbidding him" (Acts 28:31).

Psalms 65:5 expresses the same truth, "… O God of our salvation; who art the confidence of all the ends of the earth …"; Proverbs continues the theme, "In the fear of the Lord is *strong* confidence: and his children shall have a place of refuge" (Prov. 14:26). Isaiah added, "… In returning and rest shall ye be saved; in quietness and in confidence shall be your strength …" (Isa. 30:15). Hebrews 10:35 concludes, "Cast not away therefore your confidence, which hath great recompense of reward."

It seems accurate to say that confidence is a product and not an inherent attribute. It is produced either by knowledge or by experience, and it is much stronger where both are included in the formula. The Bible states that faith *comes* by hearing, and hearing by the Word of God (Rom. 10:17). It also explains that experience *produces* hope which in turn causes one not to be ashamed (Rom. 5:4-5).

You can only have confidence in that of which you have a clear understanding or by experience have proven it to be absolutely trustworthy. The more thoroughly we study and understand the Word of God, the stronger will be our faith and trust. By getting to know God and learning to walk with Him we prove His faithfulness to us and to His Word on a daily basis. It is when certain conditions combine that the coveted ingredient of confidence is produced, "… *then* have we confidence …" (I John 3:21).

Thought For Today

Those who know their God have strong faith and confidence!

September 3

N. T. Bible Reading: I Corinthians 13   **Our Focus: I Corinthians 13:1**

CHARITY

The word translated charity here is agape, a noun; the verb is agapao. It is love, but love on the very highest possible plane. The Bible declares that "... God is love" (I John 4:8, 16). This is a unique view of the Divine nature, and there are no equivalent statements as to other qualities. Love is the highest characteristic of God, and it is the single attribute in which all others harmoniously unite and function. The clearest picture of God's love is seen in the plan of salvation, and the miraculous provisions of redemption. Luther spoke of this great truth as "the shortest and longest Divinity" (food for thought).

The Lord Jesus Christ was the ultimate and perfect expression of the love of God among men. We could not and would not have comprehended God's love except as we saw it pictured in the amazing revelation of redemption in and through Christ's birth, death, and resurrection. Paul seems to reach for words which would be adequate to describe this mystery of all mysteries, "... that ye ... May be able to comprehend with all saints what is the breadth, and length, and depth, and height; And to know (or experience) the love of Christ, which passeth knowledge, that ye might be filled with all the fulness of God" (Eph. 3:17-19).

Love is the fruit of the Spirit (Gal. 5:22). Each quality listed in the cluster given, is but another expression of that love. This love, which is none other than the very love of God Himself, "... is shed abroad in our hearts by the Holy Ghost which is given unto us" (Rom. 5:5). It cannot be duplicated, it cannot be manufactured, and it cannot be equaled. It is the miraculous, and humanly impossible, manifestation of God Himself in His redeemed children. This Divine attribute cannot be generated by any human effort. It is spontaneous or it is spurious. It must flow or it is not flowing. Out of the innermost being shall *flow* rivers of living water (John 7:38). The source and the springs are *in God*, not *in* any human instrument. It is like ointment hid in the hand ... it betrayeth itself (Prov. 27:16). If it is there, it will spontaneously overflow at the most unexpected times, and in the most unexpected ways, and always for *His* eternal glory.

Thought For Today

Love is the truest expression of heaven, which we have on the earth!

September 4

O. T. Bible Reading: Proverbs 5-6   **Our Focus: Proverbs 6:23**

THE WAY

Much is said in the Word of God about "The Way." The Book of Proverbs uses the expression at least 19 times. It makes a most challenging and enlightening study in the Scriptures. It is appended by the preposition "of" which gives it a more defining expression. To mention just a *few* of those used in the Bible:

- The way of his saints (Prov. 2:8).
- The way of the evil (Prov. 2:12).
- The way of the wicked (Prov. 4:19).
- The way of life (Prov. 6:23, 15:24).
- The way of a fool (Prov. 12:15).

It is obvious that all of these many qualifiers are dealing with something much more than theories, doctrines, or philosophies. It might be helpful to add the word "*path*" before the word "way." It is a path on which we *walk*, not a subject about which we *talk*. It is not fine words which express it; it is the walk which *tells* it as it is. Some may not understand exactly what I say, but everyone can clearly see how I walk.

It is for this reason that the Bible declares, "... the *path* of the just is as the shining light, that shineth more and more unto the perfect day" (Prov. 4:18), and then quickly adds, "The way of the wicked is as darkness: they know not at what they stumble" (Prov. 4:19). The walk of His saints is in the element of light, and it illuminates a pathway which all can see. However, it also is "... a path which no fowl knoweth, and which the vulture's eye hath not seen" (Job 28:7).

Jesus settled the issue once and for all when He said, "... I am *the way*, the truth, and the life: no man cometh unto the Father, but by me" (John 14:6). If the pathway on which we walk does not cause us to walk in His steps, it is not the right way. If it does not lead us to the truths which He taught and practiced, it is the way of error. If it does not produce spiritual life, and the very nature of Christ manifested through us, it is the wrong way. Only those who walk this path can say with Eleazar of old, "... I being *in the way*, the Lord led me ..." (Gen. 24:27).

Thought For Today

*The ways of mankind are *many* ... the way of God is but *one*!*

September 4

N. T. Bible Reading: I Corinthians 14:1-20   **Our Focus: I Corinthians 14:4**

EDIFY

The word "edify" is repeated five times in the 20 verses of today's Bible reading. Repetition in Scripture indicates a point of emphasis. What is emphasized in the Word of God should not be neglected by those who study it. The most basic meaning of the word edify is *to build*. The primary thrust of what Paul is teaching here is as stated in I Corinthians 14:5 and 14:12, "… that *the church* may receive edifying" and "… the edifying of *the church*." Something is to be done or said which will, in a positive way, contribute to the construction of or the reinforcing of the local assembly of believers. This simple test alone would eliminate a lot of clutter which local assemblies encounter both from their own members and from visitors.

Paul exhorts the Corinthians to "… *seek* that ye may *excel* to the edifying of the church" (I Cor. 14:12). To seek is to search diligently, with earnest effort, and with a very specific purpose. No thought is given here to entertainment, personal aggrandizement, or self-centered promotions. It would be profitable and practical if all local assemblies were diligently taught how to edify and build when they participate in any public way in the church. Many years ago I was strongly impressed to make a list of "my personal goals when ministering." They consist of 12 Scriptural ideals and principles which seem vital to the specific purpose of building or assisting those Divinely chosen to build the church on a local level. They included 11 positives and one negative … there are some things to be *avoided* also.

Another aspect of this subject is to define who and what is *a builder*. Not everyone has the qualities and abilities required to actively participate in the construction and erection of any edifice. We are clearly directed to make it a matter of personal concern and intent that everything we do or say will be at least one more building block in the local assembly. Paul said a bit later, "… Let *all* things be done unto edifying" (I Cor. 14:26). This would seem to include the truth that *all* do have something to contribute, and that some provision should be made for just that.

Thought For Today

No skills or gifts are required by those who tear down and destroy!

September 5

O. T. Bible Reading: Proverbs 7-8　　　　　　**Our Focus: Proverbs 8:19**

MY FRUIT

Proverbs chapter 8 gives us some unique insights into the construction, content, and conclusion of wisdom; verse 7 speaks of "my mouth"; verse 10 adds "my instruction"; verse 31 gives a challenging aspect both of wisdom and the personification of wisdom, the Lord Jesus Christ, "my delights." Inevitably all of this will include, "my ways" (Prov. 8:32); and the very vital consideration, and our focus for today, "my fruit" (Prov. 8:19).

How rich are the fertile fields of wisdom, and of the Word of God. Wisdom incarnate is to be found only in the person of our blessed Lord and Savior, *The Living Word*. The instructions and directions of wisdom are to be found in the *written word* of God, our precious Bible. It is here that the *secrets* of the Lord are made known, and the *hidden* things are revealed to honest and seeking souls. It should be noted that what has been stored there by inspiration are, "excellent things" (Prov. 8:6), "right things" (Prov. 8:6), what is the only absolute "truth" (Prov. 8:7). They declare and define "righteousness" (Prov. 8:8), they are both "plain" and "right" (Prov. 8:9) to him who finds wisdom, and the fruits of wisdom are better than gold bullion or refined silver (Prov. 8:19) for they give understanding and impart strength (Prov. 8:14). How essential then that we search the Scriptures daily (Acts 17:11), hide God's word in our heart (Ps. 119:11) by meditation and memorization, and faithfully "Study to shew thyself approved unto God, a workman that needeth not to be ashamed ..." (II Tim. 2:15).

"... Wisdom is justified of (or by) her children" (Matt. 11:19; Luke 7:35), but "... a fool layeth open (or exposes) his folly" (Prov. 13:16). Some early manuscripts, we are told, have the word "works" in Matthew 11:19. This seems to agree with the context, for in every instance he appealed to their works. It is certainly true also of each one of us. It is by our behavior and conduct of life that we reflect the measure of wisdom which we possess. Thus faithfully by our transformed behavior we adorn or decorate the great gospel story with our bouquets of beautiful thoughts and actions (Tit. 2:10).

Thought For Today

Those who lack wisdom are as obvious as those who possess it!

September 5

N. T. Bible Reading: I Corinthians 14:21-40   **Our Focus: I Corinthians 14:40**

IN ORDER

There is a Divine order for everything which pertains to God and to the worship of God. Earlier, Paul said in I Corinthians 14:33, "For God is not the author of confusion, but of peace, as in all churches of the saints." The amazing symmetry and correlation of the vast universe illustrates the beauty of the function of God's order. Each unit functions and operates as an entity, and in harmony with every other element. There is a delicate and Divinely established balance in the creation of God. The constitution of the air we breathe, the precise balance of water and land, the constant speed and cycle of the rotating earth on which we live, the exact timing and duration of the seasons, the location, direction, and energy of the sun, and a thousand more intricate, but defining synergisms, only prove and demonstrate the government and administration of His handiwork. Should the eloquent but muted voice of creation be clearer than the functioning of another Divine institution, the church?

The Scriptures state that the vast universe exists by and through the government of *His word*: "By the word of the Lord were the heavens made; and all the host of them by the breath of his mouth ... For he spake, and it was done; he commanded, and it stood fast" (Ps. 33:6, 9). When the ark of God was being returned to the camp of Israel they ignored God's directions and death followed. It was later explained "... the Lord our God made a breach upon us, for that we sought him not after the *due order*" (I Chron. 15:13). The error was corrected and the Ark was victoriously returned and according to the Word of the Lord "... the children of the Levites bare the ark of God upon their shoulders ..." (I Chron. 15:15).

When men attempt to control and govern what was meant to be left in the hands of the Lord, the results are always the same; complication, confusion, concoctions, conflicts, and consternation. Where He rules there is peace and precision, as our thought for today states. The government of and in the local Assembly, and in the Body corporate, was Divinely arranged to be upon His shoulders (Isa. 9:6-7). When and where it remains upon His shoulders it always brings peace and unity for "... The zeal of the Lord of hosts will perform this" (Isa. 9:7). One translation reads, "this is going to happen because the Lord of heaven's armies has dedicated Himself to do it."

Thought For Today

What His word has created, His word also is able to manage!

<u>**September 6**</u>

O. T. Bible Reading: Proverbs 9-10   **Our Focus: Proverbs 10:20**

THE TONGUE

The tongue and the lips, both having to do with speech, are referred to 61 times in the book of Proverbs. If Proverbs is the book of wisdom, as we know it is, then the tongue and the lips have a great deal to do with the expressions of wisdom. It is of great significance that the symbol of Pentecost was "... tongues like as of fire, and it sat upon each of them" (Acts 2:3). The result was both immediate and revolutionizing for they fulfilled the promise and prophecy of Mark 16:17 "... they shall speak with new tongues." Those who receive the promised Divine enduement will certainly do the same.

James accurately said, "And the tongue is a fire, a world of iniquity ... the tongue can no man tame; it is an unruly evil, full of deadly poison" (Jam. 3:6, 8). The manifestation of wisdom, and the evidence of knowledge and understanding, is a conversation which is energized by the Holy Spirit, and characterized by discipline and ordered by discretion (Jam. 3:13). Proverbs 10:20 seems to relate the tongue to the heart, for the one is controlled by the other: "The tongue of the just is as choice silver: the heart of the wicked is little worth." This is in full harmony with the words of the Lord Jesus, "... out of the abundance of the heart the mouth speaketh" (Matt. 12:34). If the source is pure, the stream will be clear.

> A *careless* word may kindle strife; a *cruel* word may wreck a life.
> A *bitter* word may hate instill; a *brutal* word may smite and kill.
> A *gracious* word may smooth the way; a *joyous* word may light the day.
> A *timely* word may lessen stress; a *loving* word may heal and bless.

<u>**Thought For Today**</u>

Our thoughts control us, but our tongue exposes us!

September 6

N. T. Bible Reading: I Corinthians 15:1-32   **Our Focus: I Corinthians 15:4**

HE ROSE

Christianity is defined as the Christian religion, founded on the life and teachings of Jesus. New Testament Christianity is more specifically meant to identify those followers who *practice* the teachings of Christ. There is a world of difference between those two categories. It is the basic difference between religion and reality. One may embrace the one and not possess the other: we may talk cream and live skim milk! This fact may be applied to any doctrine or aspect of truth. One may accept the truth without experiencing the dynamic of it. To do so produces harshness, coldness, and an argumentative and arrogant spirit. It is cold, calculating, demanding orthodoxy without the humbling, mellowing, and transforming grace which comes with the experimental appropriation of that truth. That is the reason we are admonished to "... grow in grace, and in the knowledge of our Lord and Saviour Jesus Christ ..." (II Pet. 3:18).

Paul emphatically declares that "... he rose again the third day according to the scriptures" (I Cor. 15:4). That, he states, is the essential truth of *The Gospel*. The primary elements of *The Gospel* as defined in I Corinthians 15:1-4 is the person of the Lord Jesus Christ, and the facts of His death, burial, and resurrection. Later he made the personal application of these fundamental truths when he said, "... I die daily" (I Cor. 15:31). He enlarged upon this vital truth in II Corinthians 4:10, "Always bearing about in the body the dying of the Lord Jesus, that the life also of Jesus might be *made manifest* in our body." It is the application of truth which produces the evidence of the power of that truth.

Paul underscored this elusive truth when he said, "That I may know him, and the power of his resurrection, and the fellowship of his sufferings, *being made* (a continuous and ongoing process) conformable unto his death" (Phil. 3:10). It is this aspect of applied knowledge which gives three aspects to salvation: past, present, and future. Paul lacked nothing in the facts of The Gospel. What he yearns for are the unbounded realities of the liberating applications of those facts in daily personal experience. It is in the appropriation of the fact that He rose, that His resurrection is genuinely experienced and consistently manifested.

Thought For Today

We declare the fact of His resurrection by living the miracle!

September 7

O. T. Bible Reading: Proverbs 11-12   **Our Focus: Proverbs 11:27**

DILIGENTLY

The basic thought of "diligent" is earnestness, and includes the elements of continuity and zeal; the opposite is careless, superficial, and indifferent. The dictionary defines it as that which is marked by persevering, painstaking effort and care. The understanding of this word gives new meaning to the Scripture which states that "... he is a rewarder of them that diligently seek him" (Heb. 11:6). What is done carelessly and haphazardly can claim no such results. Peter used the word "diligence" twice in one chapter, II Peter chapter 1: first in verse 5, "And beside this, giving all *diligence*, add to your faith virtue ..." and secondly in verse 10, "Wherefore the rather, brethren, give *diligence* to make your calling and election sure ...."

Perhaps it may help to think of diligence as disciplined enthusiasm. You will never find faith used with lethargy or laziness; they simply do not mix. Ruth, the Moabitess, is a good example of faith mixed with diligence. We are told first that she said, "... Intreat me not to leave thee ... thy people shall be my people, and thy God my God" (Ruth 1:16). She clearly had faith. We are told that she "... gleaned in the field until even, and beat out that she had gleaned: and it was about an ephah of barley (about a bushel)" (Ruth 2:17). Boaz commended her for her diligence, "The Lord recompense *thy work*, and a full reward be given thee of the Lord God of Israel, under whose wings thou art come to trust" (Ruth 2:12). Indeed He did, and she became the wife of Boaz, the mother of Obed, who was the father of Jesse, and the grandfather of David. She became not only a mother in Israel, but also a part of the Messianic line. Her diligence was more than rewarded.

The admonition of Ecclesiastes 9:10 "Whatsoever thy hand findeth to do, do it with thy might ..." seems to accurately describe diligence; put all you have into it. A five year-old child kneeled to pray with the family as they concluded their family altar. They had read and discussed Exodus chapter 27, a passage considered far beyond his age. His prayer may well illustrate what diligence means in our daily lives: "oh my God, make me burn this day with *pure oil*!"

Thought For Today

Many pray __for__ diligence, but very few seem to pray __with__ it!

September 7

N. T. Bible reading: I Corinthians 15:33-58   **Our Focus: I Corinthians 15:58**

ALWAYS ABOUNDING

The statement "always abounding" represents a direct personal challenge. It is amazing how cunning we can be to ingeniously by-pass a call to action. An inquiry into these words from most commentaries will prove to be disappointing and enlightening. They focus on "steadfast" and "unmovable" and the last phrase of the verse, and completely ignore these precious words in between, "always abounding." Why should this be? There are at least two possible answers:

1. The words "always abounding" do not correspond with their experience, and we tend to ignore and avoid that which is strange to us.
2. The words "always abounding" may also be a bomb-shell to our comfortable doctrinal position, and we will always steer clear of what threatens our security. Whatever the reasons, there is no justifiable excuse for omitting the call of the Lord to higher ground.

If this experience is impossible or unattainable it would not be presented in the Word of God. God never mocks His children; He only presents truth and certainty. It may be, and it is, beyond the level at which most of us live, but it stands securely as a heavenly picture of what is possible on the earthly level through faith in Christ. This is not traditional Christianity, and this certainly is not common to our time. It is God's Word, and it represents just one more level of New Testament experience which is nothing short of miraculous and supernatural.

One key to the call of "always abounding" is found in the verse which precedes it in I Corinthians 15:57: "But thanks be to God, which giveth us the victory through our Lord Jesus Christ." It is the Lord Jesus Himself "... who of God is made unto us wisdom, and righteousness, and sanctification, and redemption" (I Cor. 1:30). Our need is not only new light, but new eyes with which to see Divine truth. Not only do we need a Divine teacher, but we also first need *His mind* to comprehend. It is as we receive the mind of Christ that we perceive His Word intuitively. Spiritual truth quickened by the Holy Spirit distills upon the quickened soul as light falls upon the healthy eye or water into thirsty lips. Only then do we understand "always abounding."

Thought For Today

Since He arose victoriously, we may live triumphantly!

<u>**September 8**</u>

O. T. Bible Reading: Proverbs 13-14   **Our Focus: Proverbs 14:11**

THE TENT

The King James Version uses "the tabernacle" in Proverbs 14:11; however, the Hebrew word used here is "ohel", and many translations will render it "tent." The thought is clear: *the house* of the wicked appears to be much more secure and stable than *the tent* of the upright. It only appears so, for their house has no foundation upon which to rest, and therefore, it is destined to crumble or be overthrown. The pilgrim's tent, by contrast, is his temporary dwelling as he journeys through this foreign land, and it will abide and flourish until tenting days are over, for in truth "… he looked for a city which hath foundations, whose builder and maker is God" (Heb. 11:10).

Two words characterize the life of Abraham; *the tent*, and *the altar*. Both have great spiritual significance. We can accurately make spiritual applications of each. Hebrews tells us that he "*sojourned*" in the land of promise. That is, as the word suggests, he dwelt beside or among, but only as a stranger, but more accurately as a pilgrim. He was a foreigner on his way to a "… better country, that is, an heavenly: wherefore God is not ashamed to be called their God: for he hath prepared for them a city" (Heb. 11:16). *The tent* spoke of the temporary nature of his journey, and of ours. We must be ever alert to the temptation to get our roots too deeply attached to anything in this world. We are pilgrims, and we are only passing through.

The altar speaks of worship, and that is to be a *primary* element in our lives. The spiritual must come first, and it must be the most significant element for each of us. When our priorities are right, God is first, foremost, and final. Jesus set the standard when He said, "But seek ye first the kingdom of God, and his righteousness; and all these things shall be added unto you" (Matt. 6:33). Perhaps Oswald Chambers may have said it best: "Jesus taught that a disciple has to make his relationship to God the dominating concentration of his life, and to be carefully careless about everything else in comparison to that." Let us not drive our tent stakes too deeply; we must *move on* as we move upward.

<u>**Thought For Today**</u>

Things must perish with their using; only the heavenly survives!

September 8

N. T. Bible Reading: I Corinthians 16   **Our Focus: I Corinthians 16:13**

BE STRONG

The words "be strong" occur at least 26 times in the Bible. It is quite obvious that strength is the very opposite of weakness; weakness is *a lack* in whatever way it is used. Physical weakness is a lack of muscle, energy, or vigor. Moral weakness is a lack of will, character, or principle. Spiritual weakness is a lack of resolve, response, resources, or revelation. It seems clear that the Lord knows the human inclination toward weakness, and appeals for a decisive response. When He spoke to Joshua He repeated the words "be strong" four times as recorded in nine verses (Josh. 1:1-9). He spoke in a vision to Daniel the prophet saying, "... O man greatly beloved, fear not: peace be unto thee, *be strong*, yea, *be strong* ..." (Dan. 10:19). The word of the Lord to the returned remnant in their task of rebuilding and restoration was, "... *be strong*, O Zerubbabel, saith the Lord; and *be strong*, O Joshua, son of Josedech, the high priest; and *be strong*, all ye people of the land ..." (Hag. 2:4).

The very fact that God commands us to be strong is proof that we are more likely to be weak, and that there is a human responsibility, as well as an ability, to carry it out. Human willingness attached to the Divine enablement produces miraculous results. His commands are His enablings. What He requires on the human level, He provides for at the Divine level. This leaves no excuse for weakness on our part. The resources are available; failure is ours only when and if we fail to take what He has promised and provided.

The true expression of Christian character is not good deeds, it is God-likeness. It is truly "... Christ in you, the hope of glory" (Col. 1:27). Certainly, this is a mystery, as Paul stated; but it is a revealed mystery, and a blessed reality to be laid hold of and personally appropriated. His life within us will express itself for what it is: *God's life*. It is not human life trying to be godly; it is Divine life manifesting itself, and that is *strength* at the highest level.

Thought For Today

The only thing that limits God is our limited response!

September 9

O. T. Bible Reading: Proverbs 15-16   **Our Focus: Proverbs 15:24**

ABOVE

"Above", what a beautiful word. It seems to vibrate with energizing force, and it inspires the heart and mind like a breath of omnipotence. The adverbs "higher" and "highest" can only adequately define that which is "*above*." When you add the word "all" to the word "above" (above all) you have a clear picture of what is unique in and of itself, and an idea of what is *absolute*. It is perfect in essence and nature; it is complete and unlimited; it is pure and unmixed; it is total and without equal. It can only be God Himself in its highest meaning. "That men may know that thou, whose name alone is Jehovah, art *the most high* (above all) over all the earth" (Ps. 83:18), He is "… King Of Kings, And Lord Of Lords" (Rev. 19:16), "… I am the Almighty God; walk before me, and be thou perfect" (Gen. 17:1).

It is because He is The Most High, above all, that we His children are to be "… the head, and not the tail; and thou shalt be above only, and thou shall not be beneath; *if* …" (Deut. 28:13). The only "if" is connected with "thou." There is no qualifier on His part, only on our part. Paul urged the Colossians to "… *seek* those things which are *above*, where Christ sitteth on the right hand of God. *Set* your affection on things *above*, not on things on the earth" (Col. 3:1-2). The word "seek" means to search for something with a sense of urgency, a keen desire, and with animated ambition.

That which is above is either *higher* than or *more* than; both or either involve stretch and effort. The very word "above" has to include a vision. You may have ideals, and have no vision at all. An ideal is an idea with an "L" added. It has to do with thoughts, and thoughts are human; ideals have to do with *thinking*. Vision has to do with *seeing*. The heroes of faith listed in Hebrews chapter 11 *saw* what was *above*: "… having *seen* them afar off …" (Heb. 11:13). Moses refused, chose, and endured, "… as *seeing* him who is invisible" (Heb. 11:24-27). If we have a vision then the word "above" is a vital part of our daily lives.

Thought For Today

Those who rely on reason have no reason to include "above!"

September 9

N. T. Bible Reading: II Corinthians 1   **Our Focus: II Corinthians 1:21**

STABLISH

The word "stablish" is, of course, an obsolete old English word for the more common word "establish." It becomes abundantly clear to any sincere student of Scripture that there is so much more involved in salvation than just to believe. This word is used approximately 150 times in the Bible. It is used of churches as well as individuals, "And so were the churches established in the faith …" (Acts 16:5), "For I long to see you, that I may impart unto you some spiritual gift, to the end ye may be established" (Rom. 1:11). Most Bible dictionaries will say it means to fix, make fast, to set, or to strengthen and confirm. It certainly includes something which is very important, and which evidently involves a process. "As ye have therefore received Christ Jesus the Lord, so walk ye in him: Rooted and built up in him, and stablished in the faith …" (Col. 2:6-7). The walk is definitely a process, and being rooted and established involves both time and a series of events or experiences. A process implies progress; progress involves change and improvement.

Peter seems to express the thought in I Peter 5:10 "… after that ye have suffered a while, make you perfect (fully mature), stablish, strengthen, settle you." That is quite a package indeed; very difficult to wrap up, and even more difficult to deliver. This is no automatic push button one-timer. The variety of expressions seems clearly to tell us this is an issue of considerable difficulty which will require consistent diligence and concentration on the human side, and supernatural grace, strength, and power on the Divine side.

Continuity is the key to consistency. "But whoso looketh into the perfect law of liberty, and *continueth therein*, he being not a forgetful hearer, but a doer of the work, this man shall be blessed in his deed (activity)" (Jam. 1:25). Consistency is essential to success. A forgetful hearer is not only one who fails to remember the truths he has heard, but who fails to practice them. Phillips translation says, "… makes a habit of doing so …"; the habit is a product of repeated actions, and this leads to being established.

Thought For Today

Those who know the Lord are those who follow on to know Him!

September 10

O. T. Bible Reading: Proverbs 17-18   **Our Focus: Proverbs 17:16**

NO HEART

Everyone knows what it means to have "no heart"; the reason we know is because there are so many examples of it in every phase of life, we see it every day. Those who do things half-heartedly are in the failing majority, and will never be found at the top. Only those who have a _single_ eye and a _whole_ heart will ever receive a _full_ reward (II John 1:8; II Pet. 1:11).

The words "lackadaisical" and "lackluster" are on the same page in the dictionary. They also occur together in every-day life. They both indicate something which is sadly lacking. The lackadaisical, lack spirit and interest; the lackluster is that which lacks luster and vitality. They may best be described as "no heart." They are two elements you will never find in heaven, but you will bump into both, many times on your journey there. It seems to be a spiritual disease which infests churches, and would appear to be very contagious judging from the prevalence of it.

The children of Zebulon were, we are told, "… such as went forth to battle, expert in war … which could keep rank: they were not of _double heart_" (I Chron. 12:33). The margin gives it as "without a heart and a heart." A very practical application can be made from this Scripture. The name Zebulon means _dwelling_ or _habitation_; the unique and special dwelling place of the Lord is with those whose heart is fully set upon Him. "For the eyes of the Lord run to and fro throughout the whole earth, to shew himself strong in the behalf of them whose heart is perfect toward him …" (II Chron. 16:9). Surely this is what the apostle Paul had in mind when he said, "And whatsoever ye do, do it heartily, as to the Lord …" (Col. 3:23). Williams translates it: "whatsoever ye do, do it with all your heart", and Phillips has it as: "… put your whole heart and soul into it." Only the individual can determine the degree or measure of his responses to the Lord. It is our responsibility to put our _whole heart_ into the worship and service of the Lord.

Thought For Today

God dwells where He is given the keys to every room!

September 10

N. T. Bible Reading: II Corinthians 2   **Our Focus: II Corinthians 2:14**

TRIUMPH

To triumph is to be victorious or successful; it is to win. The word "always" leaves little room for anything else. The difference between *constant* victory and frequent or occasional victory is the difference between success and failure. Anything less than constant victory allows for occasional defeat and the word "always" excludes that.

This certainly outlines a most beautiful relationship which is made possible in and through the purchased victory of the Lord Jesus Christ. The picture in Revelation 6:2 is that of One who is triumphant and wears the victors crown and presses forward conquering and to conquer. The conclusion is obvious; there has been a major victory in the past, and there is yet to be another in the future. The rider on the white horse is a winner; He has won already, and He will win again. This seems in perfect agreement with Romans 8:37, "Nay, in *all* these things we are more than conquerors through him that loved us." Philips renders it, "no, in all these things we win an overwhelming victory." Surely this is to overcome. A personal application is that the rider on the white horse has secured such a major triumph at Calvary, and He has now conquered us also, He leads us in the train of His triumph. United with Him (chained to His chariot wheels) we march forward in His victory celebration. There is no room for defeat, for He cannot fail. When we fail it is because somewhere, somehow, we have failed to be led forward *in His* triumphant victory.

The procession continues in I Corinthians 15:57-58, "But thanks be to God, which giveth (now and always) us the victory through our Lord Jesus Christ. *Therefore*, my beloved brethren, be ye steadfast, unmovable, *always abounding* in the work of the Lord …"; it may be necessary and somewhat comforting to notice that Paul did not say, "always bounding", but "always *abounding*." To bound is to skip or jump, but to abound is to be fully supplied. Thank God for His abundant provision!

Thought For Today

The triumph of Christ at Calvary is firm, final, and for me!

September 11

O. T. Bible Reading: Proverbs 19-20   **Our Focus: Proverbs 20:27**

THE SPIRIT OF MAN

The Scriptures reveal what the human sciences ignore or fail to discover. The tripartite nature of man is taught in the Word of God, not in the textbooks of psychology or physiology. The apostle Paul clearly states in I Thessalonians 5:23, "And the very God of peace sanctify you wholly (completely or in every aspect of your being); and I pray God your whole spirit and soul and body be preserved blameless unto the coming of our Lord Jesus Christ." This is the total being as viewed by The One who created it. The prophet Zechariah also recognized the spirit as an essential part of man: "... the Lord ... formeth the spirit of man within him" (Zech. 12:1). "God is a Spirit: and they that worship him must worship him in spirit and in truth" (John 4:24). Jesus, the Creator of all that is in heaven or earth (Col. 1:16), made this statement, since as the acting Creator, He certainly knew all the parts and pieces which He placed within man (John 2:25).

The spirit of man is that unique faculty which is to be found only in the human family, and in no other creature. It is there because he was created "... in the image of God ..." (Gen. 1:27). It is the God-conscious aspect of his complex being; and it is the faculty by which true worship is possible. "For what man knoweth the things of a man, save the spirit of man which is in him ..." (I Cor. 2:11). Perception is a faculty of the spirit and not a function of the mind. "And immediately when Jesus perceived in his spirit that they so reasoned within themselves ..." (Mark 2:8). This is why people can see (read and observe with the natural physical eye), and hear (again with the physical ear), but never really grasp or understand the things of God because they are only spiritually discerned (I Cor. 2:14). This inward capacity when quickened by the Holy Spirit makes possible the spiritual gift of discernment.

Surely we are fearfully and wonderfully made (Ps. 139:14), and that to glorify, worship, and serve the Lord. True fulfillment is possible only when the whole being is quickened to a living relationship with the Lord. It is then and only then, that we begin to discover <u>the ways</u> of the Lord. Oh, that we may <u>know</u> Him in all His fulness!

Thought For Today

He who has begun a good work in us has the tools to complete it!

September 11

N. T. Bible Reading: II Corinthians 3   **Our Focus: II Corinthians 3:18**

CHANGED

To change is to transform or fashion anew. The first meaning of "change" in the dictionary is, "to be or cause to be different"; the second is "to alter." The wise men searched out and found the baby Jesus and "… they departed into their own country another way" (Matt. 2:12). And so it has ever been from that day to this. Those who find the Savior go from that encounter in a different direction, and on a different road because they have had a transforming experience and are now being fashioned anew. Any claim to Christianity which does not involve a change in behavior and life-style is foreign to Scripture. It is counterfeit; it claims the same value, but lacks the genuine ingredients which give it value and make it real. It is the vital element of *life* which spells the difference. Where there is no life, the old habits and life-style continue as they have been; where there is a new life in Christ Jesus there also is a new nature with new desires. This new life cannot help but express itself in a total change inwardly and outwardly. "Therefore if any man be in Christ, he is a new creature: old things are passed away; behold, all things are become new" (II Cor. 5:17).

There are two key words in II Corinthians 3:18; they are "changed' and "beholding." It is what you *see* either with the physical eye or with the inner eye of the soul which causes you to change. We must first behold the glory of God, and in the measure this transforming encounter takes place, the miracle of renewal continues. "Beholding" is in the present tense, and the resulting change will be a continuous ongoing reality. By an encounter with the risen Savior we are transformed, and by beholding Him and His glory we become mirrors to reflect Him. It is the beauty and glory of His very nature and character reproduced in our lives which draws others to Him. The magnitude of such a miraculous change is the greatest proof of the power of the Gospel of Christ (Rom. 1:16).

Thought For Today

To profess is to make a pretense; to possess is to own!

September 12

O. T. Bible Reading: Proverbs 21-22   **Our Focus: Proverbs 21:20**

TREASURE

The word "treasure" as used here refers to the store-house. A store-house is where valuables are stored, and it is a place of abundant supply. Jesus said, "… every scribe which is instructed unto the kingdom of heaven is like unto a man that is an householder, which bringeth forth out of *his treasure* things new and old" (Matt. 13:52). Wisdom and truth are joined with riches, gold, and precious gems in the Word of God. Those who seek out wisdom are to do so diligently and eagerly as those searching for hid treasures (Prov. 2:4). We are to put just such value on the Truth of God and the things of the Lord. Our concept of their worth or value will determine our attitude and actions toward them. A gem of great value may be but a stone to the untrained eye.

There is both treasure and oil in the dwelling of the wise. A helpful application of this fact is to recognize that there are valuable and costly truths, as well as the spirit of inspiration and understanding, where true wisdom is found. The ministers who labor there will not have to hurriedly seek for and buy provisions for his guests, but will tap into his already stocked shelves for every provision needed. In addition, the fresh quickening of the Holy Spirit will also provide new thoughts and new truths with which to feed the hungry souls. These are treasures far beyond the worth of anything which is human or corruptible.

The Lord Jesus taught "For where your treasure is, there will your heart be also" (Matt. 6:21). If we place the greatest value on material things, things of time and sense, then our heart will be there also, thinking upon it, and delighting in it. Concluding this thought He added, "But seek ye first (of primary importance) the kingdom of God, and his righteousness; and all these things shall be added unto you" (Matt. 6:33).

Thought For Today

We may not properly esteem what is beyond earthly value!

September 12

N. T. Bible Reading: II Corinthians 4   **Our Focus: II Corinthians 4:17**

ETERNAL

The word "eternal" means endless; beyond the scope of time and sense. It is not a word which you will hear in common every-day conversation; it is not a word ever used in the entertainment world; it is not a word in the language of the business world; it is not something you will hear in the educational world. It is a foreign word to anything which is of this world. It is a word from and of another world which only the Scriptures describe. It is a word which is unique and precious to those who _know_ the Scriptures, and who _know_ the Christ of the Scriptures.

Perhaps the single most helpful practice of any child of God is to view everything in the light of eternity. That puts it in true perspective. It may weigh heavily in terms of the here and now, but lose its weight entirely when viewed from the illuminating light of eternity. The key is what we are looking at. If we look only at the issues of this life and the elements which affect and control it, we will conduct ourselves accordingly. Paul clearly states that the determining issue is "While we _look_ …" (II Cor. 4:18). It is only then that we see the true value and worth of anything.

Michael Angelo went into the studio of one of his understudies who was completing a statute which was to stand in a public square. The young man was not happy when the great artist pointed out the grave defects. Not a little irritated he complained somewhat sneeringly that in the dimness of his shop, in his opinion, they could not be seen at all. "Well," said Angelo, not the least deterred by his students' objections, "the light of the public square will test it." Many may object to the demands and disciplines of godly living, and to the standards of conduct required by the Word of God; the best response is, "the light of _eternity_ will test it!"

Thought For Today

He lives wisely, he who lives with eternities values in view!

September 13

O. T. Bible Reading: Proverbs 23-24   **Our Focus: Proverbs 23:23**

BUY THE TRUTH

To buy is to acquire in exchange for something. It is obvious that salvation cannot be bought any more than it can be earned. "Forasmuch as ye know that ye were not redeemed with corruptible things, as silver and gold ... But with the precious blood of Christ, as of a lamb without blemish and without spot" (I Pet. 1:18-19). However, truth is another issue, and sometimes the price paid to secure it, is very dear indeed. No amount of money or personal effort will ever buy it. But when you find that you must surrender some false view or doctrine "received by tradition from your fathers" the price tag seems huge.

Jesus always connected truth with "*the way*" as well as "*the life*" (John 14:6). The truth of God will immediately challenge the pathway on which you walk, and the way in which you conduct your life. Both must and will change when you meet The Master. To walk with Him you must keep in step with Him. The things which He loves, you will also love; the things which He hates, you will also hate; the things which He does, you also will do; the things which He avoids, you also will avoid. This is a huge price to pay, and many will not pay that price; however, the conditions of discipleship are not negotiable. That is why the truth is also defined as "... the doctrine which is according to godliness" (I Tim. 6:3).

"*The way of truth*" is a phrase used in the Word of God: "And *many* shall follow their pernicious ways (no restraints); by reason of whom *the way of truth* shall be evil spoken of (or brought into reproach)" (II Pet. 2:2). Jesus said, "And ye shall know the truth, and the truth shall make you free" (John 8:32); that is, freedom from every bondage and from every false way; it is freedom to follow the Lamb and to do His perfect will. "Buy the truth ..." (Prov. 23:23), it is available to all who will pay the price.

Thought For Today

To know the truth is to know Jesus and to know His Word!

September 13

N. T. Bible Reading: II Corinthians 5   **Our Focus: II Corinthians 5:21**

RIGHTEOUSNESS

The two words "righteous" and "righteousness" are used nearly 600 times in the Bible. That fact alone gives them significance through repetition. We should never ignore or lightly esteem what the Word of God emphasizes. It is all too easy, and very human, to put a pound of emphasis on an ounce of truth, while at the same time putting only an ounce of emphasis on a pound of truth.

Perhaps the simplest definition for righteousness is purity of heart and uprightness of conduct; it is *being* right and *doing* right ... and not one or the other, but both. The root word for right occurs about 100 times in the Word of God, and there are nine different words used which stem from the root word. It is a very big subject which requires a very thorough study. However, for our purposes we can make a few practical applications.

The word "made" is used twice in II Corinthians 5:21:

1.   God has "... *made him* to be sin for us ..."
2.   "... that *we might be made* the righteousness of God in him."

To make is to bring about or to create. Jesus was not guilty of a single sin; He "... did no sin, neither was guile found in his mouth" (I Pet. 2:22); yet God, in His infinite wisdom, caused Him to be "... numbered with the transgressors; and he bare the sin of many ..." (Isa. 53:12). That is, by imputation, our sins were reckoned to Him, and He became our substitute. Amazing mystery! Glorious reality!! The sequel is even more amazing and miraculous; "... that we might be made the righteousness of God in Him" (II Cor. 5:21).

God is a righteous God, "Righteous art thou, O Lord ..." (Ps. 119:137; Jer. 12:1); therefore, His children will and must also be righteous, "If ye know that he is righteous, ye know that everyone that doeth righteousness (habitually practices righteousness) is born of him" (I John 2:29). It is as normal for a Christian to live a righteous life as it is for an apple tree to produce apples. This is the New Testament norm; anything less is sub-normal or altogether spurious. The very beauty, nature, and life of Jesus is reproduced in us, and the experience of "... The Lord Our Righteousness" (Jer. 23:6) becomes a blessed reality.

Thought For Today

To be right with God is also to be right among men!

September 14

O. T. Bible Reading: Proverbs 25-27   **Our Focus: Proverbs 26:1**

A FOOL

The word "fool" and its derivatives are used about 100 times in the book of Proverbs; the first 12 verses of Proverbs chapter 26 deal with this subject. The fool, as here described, is an individual who lightly regards evil, and makes a mock of sin; he finds great pleasure from iniquity, and revels in the atmosphere of ridiculing the wise and righteous. He readily rejects the appeal of Scripture, and refuses to heed the voice of wisdom. This speaks of moral more than of intellectual deficiencies. It is not primarily a matter of lacking in mental powers, but is more related to the misuse of them. He is not an individual who lacks reason, but is one whose mind is warped, causing him to reason and think wrongly. The many references reveal the many-sided and complex nature of one who is thus named. It is safe to conclude that one who is so characterized is a willful individual who chooses to reject the fear of God, and who thinks and acts as if he can carelessly and safely disregard the eternal principles of God's righteousness, with no consequences or retribution.

It should be apparent that there are those who are self-proclaimed atheists, and there are those who are practical atheists; that is, they would reject the label while living in such a way as to fit the description. Such is certainly true as regards the fool. Many, indeed most, individuals would vehemently reject any relationship to the classic description of a fool as outlined in the Scripture, yet they conduct themselves in such a way as could only be accurately described as "foolish behavior."

Proverbs chapter 9 gives a beautiful description of wisdom building her house. This can be applied also to the Lord (the personification of wisdom) and to the House (the church) which He promised He would build. The first use of the term "foolish" in Proverbs concludes the portion which speaks of wisdom and her house. It emphatically directs us to "*Forsake* the foolish, and live; and *go in the way* of understanding" (Prov. 9:6). To forsake backbone is to give up, it is to renounce, it is to leave altogether, and it is to abandon completely. This we must do with the way of folly.

Thought For Today

Only the application of wisdom can avoid the pitfalls of folly!

September 14

N. T. Bible Reading: II Corinthians 6   **Our Focus: II Corinthians 6:18**

THE LORD ALMIGHTY

God is so infinite that mere human words and adjectives are frail vehicles to describe what is beyond description. The names and titles ascribed to God occur over 19,000 times in the Scriptures; no one has ever dared to attempt to give their exact number. He has revealed Himself to humanity, and without a revelation none can comprehend God: "... and no *man* knoweth the Son, but the Father; neither knoweth *any man* the Father, save the Son, and he to whomsoever the Son will reveal him" (Matt. 11:27). Any human spiritual encounter with God which produces lasting and effective results will always include some new discovery of God. That which revolves around us is human, natural, and shallow; that which involves God is Divine, supernatural, and always very deep. It is as His infinite power and Divine nature is revealed as a provision for our frailty and weakness, that we grow to know Him, whom to know aright is life eternal (John 17:3). Each progressive revelation of Him includes a corresponding revelation of our great need for just such an Almighty Savior, and we appropriate His power for our weakness and prove His unfailing faithfulness. It is thus that He "... is made unto us wisdom, and righteousness, and sanctification, and redemption (and all we could ever need)" (I Cor. 1:30).

There is a progressive revelation of God in the Scriptures, and there will be a progressive revelation of God in the experience of all who go on to know Him in His fulness. Can a teaspoon hold the fulness of the ocean? It can hold the full measure of which it is capable, but that could scarcely be presumed to represent the fulness of the ocean. God revealed Himself to Abraham for the first time by the title "*Almighty*" in Genesis 17:1. He is the Supreme One who has and is absolute unlimited power. We, too, will need to know this as we claim His promises and appropriate His grace and strength. We are left only to answer a very personal question: "Is anything too hard for the Lord? ..." (Gen. 18:14).

Thought For Today

It is the Almighty who makes the impossible a reality!

September 15

O. T. Bible Reading: Proverbs 28-29   **Our Focus: Proverbs 28:18**

UPRIGHTLY

Proverbs are wise sayings of few words which are used in place of many, with the intent of condensing wisdom in the briefest possible form. The design is to make them easier to remember, but also to act as a stimulant or challenge, to further study, meditation, or research. They are not for the careless and the superficial reader. They are deep wells which evade those who look only for bubbling springs. They are really parables which must be "*searched out*" before they will yield their hidden riches of moral and spiritual values. "It is the glory of God to conceal a thing: but the honour of kings is to search out a matter" (Prov. 25:2). The book of Proverbs will prove to be to our *practical life*, what the book of Psalms will be to our devotional life. They are pithy and witty precepts for daily living, and when incorporated into personal conduct, the individual will be soundly guided and safely guarded.

The words "upright", "uprightly", and "uprightness" will be found 23 times in the book of Proverbs. Upright is the exact opposite of crooked, bent, or warped. It is, in a single word, straight. It is significant that Jesus said, "Enter ye in at the strait gate … Because strait is the gate, and narrow is the way, which leadeth unto life, and few there be that find it" (Matt. 7:13-14). Before Him, John the Baptist had proclaimed, "… Prepare ye the way of the Lord, make his paths straight" (Matt. 3:3). The apostle Paul urged the Philippian believers to "… be blameless and harmless (void of duplicity and devious ways), the sons of God, without rebuke (above reproach), in the midst of a crooked and perverse nation …" (Phil. 2:15). The warped and twisted thinking of the ungodly world leads to lives that are contrary to everything which is pure, moral, and upright. Let us shine as lights amid this darkness.

Thought For Today

The Mighty Gospel truth will straighten what was crooked!

September 15

N. T. Bible Reading: II Corinthians 7   **Our Focus: II Corinthians 7:10**

GODLY SORROW

Sorrow is a human word; it is associated with the element of sin and suffering; it is never experienced by God, nor will it be found in heaven (Rev. 21:4). It was imposed upon the human family because of rebellion and disobedience. "In sorrow" is the epitaph of departure from God (Gen. 3:16). Godly sorrow is sorrow on the human level, and experienced by humans, but of such a nature as God requires. It is a condition which must be produced in the heart by the Holy Spirit and, as such, is the gift of God (John 16:8; Rom. 2:4). It is a product of conviction, and conviction is a work of the Holy Spirit. The reason there are so few convictions (strong inward persuasions), is that there is so little genuine work of the Holy Spirit permitted or experienced in the church or in the individual life.

There could be no better definition of godly sorrow than in the verse which follows (II Cor. 7:10) and which again repeats the very words, "... ye sorrowed after a godly sort ..." (II Cor. 7:11). It is what follows which so thoroughly describes that of which it consists: "... what carefulness (nothing superficial or chaffy) ..." (II Cor. 7:11); that is, thorough, painstaking, and conscientious attention to make our peace with God, and to maintain it by avoiding anything and everything which disturbs that peace or violates His word and will. What clearing of yourselves! (II Cor. 7:11); this is squarely and honestly facing the fact of sin and rebellion, dealing with it on God's terms, and having forsaken the way of life which produced the problem. What indignation (II Cor. 7:11); that is, what holy disgust and displeasure with ourselves, and the inherent element of sin. What fear (II Cor. 7:11); that is, a wholesome caution of mind and conduct lest we offend the holiness of the blessed Savior whom we have come to love, and long to serve. What vehement desire (II Cor. 7:11); it is stamped with intensity, forcefulness, and vigor. It seems there are too many "stillborn" in our time.

Thought For Today

Godly sorrow is the foundation upon which godly living is built!

September 16

O. T. Bible Reading: Proverbs 30-31   **Our Focus: Proverbs 31:1**

LEMUEL

"The words of king Lemuel, the prophecy that his mother taught him" (Prov. 31:1). There is no record of any king Lemuel who sat on the throne of Judah, nor of Israel; neither is there any record of any king by that name among the surrounding nations. The prophet Nathan, apparently at the word of the Lord, gave the name "Jedidah" to the child whom David called "Solomon." Jedidah means, "beloved of the Lord"; Solomon means, "peaceable." Lemuel means, "devoted to the Lord." Most commentators agree that this was very likely a nick name or a pet name which his mother, Bathsheba, gave to Solomon.

We are distinctly told of this child that "… the Lord loved him" (II Sam. 12:24). It seems clear that both David and Bathsheba genuinely repented of their sin, and that both were forgiven and restored (Ps. 51). Solomon was born later, and was destined to become the king of Israel after the death of his father, David.

His mother is heard in Proverbs 31:2 as saying, "What, my son? … and what, the son of my vows?" This seems to speak volumes about her. She is basically saying, "what can I say?" She must speak her heart, but where to begin? Great travail was experienced on his behalf long before the birth pains ever came. She had dedicated this yet unborn child to the Lord and had offered many prayers to God on his behalf, with solemn vows and promises to God. This is a beautiful example for all expectant parents. The value and importance of prayers and promises on behalf of the unborn is a matter of overwhelming statistics and facts. It includes the dedication of the infant, but of equal importance, the dedication of the parents to the awesome task of raising the child in the nurture and admonition of the Lord.

Thought For Today

A dedicated child calls for devoted parents!

September 16

N. T. Bible Reading: II Corinthians 8   **Our Focus: II Corinthians 8:7**

THIS GRACE

Paul uses the word "grace" seven times in II Corinthians 8 and another three times in chapter 9. The subject is the grace of giving. The emphasis in the first seven chapters is *Christian living*, and with the jolting thought he changes the subject to *Christian giving*. He deals with the very important issues of "offerings" and "collections" and clearly shows the difference. It should deeply affect our attitude and our actions in the matter of giving to know that Paul used nine words when speaking of it:

1.   *Collection* (I Cor. 16:1-2).
2.   *Grace* (II Cor. 8:6).
3.   *Fellowship* (II Cor. 8:4, 9:13).
4.   *Service* (II Cor. 9:1, 12-13).
5.   *Abundance* (II Cor. 8:20).
6.   *Blessing* (II Cor. 9:5).
7.   *Ministration* (II Cor. 9:12).
8.   *Alms* (Acts 24:17).
9.   *Offerings* (Acts 24:17).

The occasion was that persecution had scattered the New Testament believers from Jerusalem; that caused the local church there to be weakened. In addition, they were experiencing a severe drought and near famine conditions. Paul was on his third missionary journey as these conditions existed and collected an offering to help relieve a very distressed church in Jerusalem. Obviously, these local conditions and the events that gave it color have passed into history; however, the Biblical principles laid down by Paul remain for all times.

The Macedonian believers set a beautiful example. They were not wealthy by any means; Paul states that they gave out of "… deep poverty …" (II Cor. 8:2). If the standard was "as the Lord has prospered" there would have been no offering of any kind.

The standard for New Testament giving is not the measure of what we possess; it is the Lord Jesus Himself (II Cor. 8:9). The term "grace", as used here (II Cor. 8:7), means a disposition (actually a passion), an overwhelming desire, to share with others all that God has so freely bestowed upon us. It is to be done systematically, regularly, and sacrificially. The real test and proof of love is sacrifice; and the real test and proof of practical applied Christianity is in what we give. There are too many people who, when it comes to giving, *stop at nothing*.

Thought For Today

It was God who first "gave", and the most godly are the most giving!

September 17

O. T. Bible Reading: Ecclesiastes 1-3   **Our Focus: Ecclesiastes 1:1**

THE PREACHER

The book of Ecclesiastes was written by Solomon in his later life. He refers to himself seven times as "koheleth", which in turn is translated preacher. To preach is to proclaim, and perhaps this thought would better be expressed as, "the philosopher." That is precisely what we have here; the philosophy, strictly from a human and natural point of view, of a man who left God out of his life. He uses the word "vanity" 37 times, and it is the key word to the book. It means "empty, purposeless, without direction or goal." The key phrase is "under the sun" which is used 29 times. The key fact is, that all of the conclusions listed, originated in his heart (39 times) or more accurately in his own distressed, depressed, and disillusioned *mind*.

The book of Ecclesiastes *is not* at all a true picture of life, and certainly, it is no picture at all of a life which is lived for God. It is rather a graphic picture of a very wise, very wealthy, and very worldly man who forgot God and lived for this world only. It is the inspired record of a confession of failure, futility, and frustration from a man who "lived it up" but only *under* the sun. Life has no real meaning nor purpose apart from God, and poor Solomon proved to himself and to all who will heed his pathetic findings, that there is nothing but emptiness in a life which pursues satisfaction and meaning in this present evil world.

The sum of any life which is spent on the natural level and for time alone is well expressed by Lord Beaconsfield, "youth is a mistake, manhood a struggle, and old age a regret." How tragic! How sad! How very different the conclusion of a life lived for God, and spent in His happy service: hear the Apostle Paul "I have fought a good fight, I have finished my course, I have kept the faith: Henceforth there is laid up for me a crown of righteousness ..." (II Tim. 4:7-8).

Thought For Today

Philosophy apart from God is really only "fool"osophy!

September 17

N. T. Bible Reading: II Corinthians 9   **Our Focus: II Corinthians 9:15**

HIS UNSPEAKABLE GIFT

It is significant that Paul concludes the two chapters (II Cor. 8 and 9) which deal with the subject of Christian giving with *thanksgiving*. The real basis of all giving, from a human viewpoint, is thanksgiving. It is the foundation upon which every expression of love rests. If there is no real gratitude, anything which is done, and anything which is given, will be done either "… grudgingly, or of necessity …" (II Cor. 9:7). That which is given from a heart of love and in the spirit of gratitude will be cheerful (II Cor. 9:7), wholehearted, and will be done liberally (Rom. 12:8, margin).

The standard for our service and giving is "… his unspeakable gift" (II Cor. 9:15). The original Greek word for "unspeakable" is used only in this verse; it does not occur anywhere else in the Word of God. His supreme gift to us, the blessed Lord Jesus Christ, is beyond the reach of words to describe. Paul reserved a *special* adjective to describe a *very special* gift. This is a gift of such an infinite nature that finite language utterly breaks down before it. The precious Savior, the Father's gift to humanity, is an absolute Divine *wonder*; His very name is *Wonderful* (Isa. 9:6). He is the supreme superlative; He is truly and accurately "unspeakable."

The mystery and wonder of it all is that He is *a gift*. The fact that "*God gave*" is one of the most cardinal and far-reaching truths of the New Testament. It is a genuine expression of His infinite love, and it is the supreme manifestation of His Divine grace. This "unspeakable gift" is just that. It was in no way deserved, and it can in no way be earned. Thankfully, it is to be received with gratitude and enthusiasm. Tragically, it may also be refused and rejected. Only those who have received the gift can really give thanks for it, and they will eagerly join Paul in praise for "… his unspeakable gift" (II Cor. 9:15).

Thought For Today

True praise cannot be extracted … it must freely flow!

September 18

O. T. Bible Reading: Ecclesiastes 4-6   **Our Focus: Ecclesiastes 4:4**

VANITY

There are two conclusions as to human existence; one is *vanity* ... the other is verity. The first sums up life, bulking it into a tragic bundle as being vain, futile, and worthless. The second is the very opposite; life has yielded her hidden meaning, and the baffling mysteries of the purpose of life itself have been discovered. The missing element is "truth", and truth can only be realized when God is included in the formula. He is *the God of truth*; His Word is *the Word of truth*, and the precious Holy Spirit is *the Spirit of truth* (Deut. 32:4; Jam. 1:18; John 14:6). Solomon knew much of the first and very little of the second. That is why he uses the word vanity 30 times in the book of Ecclesiastes; he underlines it with emphasis by adding "... *vanity and vexation of spirit*" (mentioned 7 times). He had experienced a great deal of both.

Solomon was a very gifted man, the wise king and administrator of the nation of Israel, and the acknowledged father of Hebrew wisdom and science. He was a man of immense wealth, as well as fame. He was a naturalist, a botanist, a zoologist, a philosopher, a trader, a builder, a poet, a keen administrator; yet in the end, he sadly defined it all as vanity and vexation of spirit. All of this was because his many wives "... *turned away* his heart after other gods ..." (I Ki. 11:4). His end and his conclusions as to life will also prove to be the experience of all who *turn* from the Lord, from the Word of God, and from the ways of the Lord.

Solomon knew what was right, but like many others *he chose* the wrong way. His knowledge of God, and that part of His Word which was available, enabled him to inject some positive truths, and to give an accurate conclusion, "Let us hear the conclusion of the whole matter: Fear God, and keep his commandments: for this is the whole duty of man" (Eccl. 12:13). The word vanity means foolish pride, but it also means emptiness and worthless effort. The central message rings loud and clear: "Set your affection on things above, not on things on the earth" (Col. 3:2). All else is *vanity* (worthless emptiness).

Thought For Today

Those who forget God can only sigh; those who serve Him will sing!

September 18

N. T. Bible Reading: II Corinthians 10   **Our Focus: II Corinthians 10:5**

EVERY THOUGHT

The human mind is a great battleground; our greatest warfare is the battle for control of the mind. Reason is the governor and master of the soul; "For as he thinketh in his heart, so is he ..." (Prov. 23:7).   When King Uzziah arrogantly presumed to go into the temple of the Lord and perform what only the God-ordained priests were to do, he was smitten with the most feared and dreaded type of leprosy, "... the leprosy even rose up in his *forehead* ..." (II Chron. 26:19). The forehead, in the Scriptures, is symbolic of the mind. Those united with the victorious Lamb on Mount Zion had "... his Father's name written *in* their foreheads" (Rev. 14:1). In contrast to this, the woman who rode the scarlet colored beast had "... upon her forehead was a name written, Mystery, Babylon The Great, The Mother Of Harlots ..." (Rev. 17:5). The mind of man is directly and tragically affected by the fall of man; the human mind, apart from God, is depraved and "... receiveth not the things of the Spirit of God: for they are foolishness unto him ..." (I Cor. 2:14).

The transforming miracle of salvation is both a crisis and a process. The grace of God, through the work of Christ on Calvary, declares us forgiven and Holy in the sense of innocence. God does not make us Holy in the sense of character; this must be done through a series of moral choices. It is thus that we are to "... *grow* in grace, and in the knowledge of our Lord and Saviour Jesus Christ ..." (II Pet. 3:18). We are commanded *to bring* every *thought* into captivity and under discipline, until it is yielded to His control and functions obediently to His will (II Cor. 10:5). Moffat's translation says we are to "take every project prisoner to make it obey Christ."

There are exalted notions and opinions in the castle of the human mind which must be conquered and demolished. Some prejudices may be destroyed by neglect, but there are many more which must be stormed by violence (Matt. 11:12). This can only be accomplished by Divine strength imparted by the Holy Spirit and the dynamic Word of God. There are some areas in which we must simply stand still and see the salvation of the Lord (Ex. 14:13); there are others in which we are to fight the good fight of faith (I Tim. 6:12).

Thought For Today

The discipline of the mind is the last frontier of maturity!

September 19

O. T. Bible Reading: Ecclesiastes 7-9   **Our Focus: Ecclesiastes 9:16**

WISDOM IS BETTER

It is essential to know what wisdom is. There are 28 passages of Scripture in which wisdom is linked to the little word "*is*." In Ecclesiastes 7:12 he has stated that wisdom is a defense, he also says in the same verse that money is a defense; the Hebrew word is *a shadow*. Shadows are fleeting, and are only a faint reflection of an object. However, they provide a temporary shelter or protection while they last. Money can provide many temporary and temporal benefits, but it can never buy the gift of life. A dying king may say in desperation: "my kingdom and my treasure for a moment of time", but no exchange is possible. The beauty of wisdom is that it brings with it the promise of life; only wisdom (which in its fullest expression is the Lord Jesus Christ Himself), can impart life everlasting.

"Wisdom is the principal thing; therefore get wisdom: and with all thy getting get understanding" (Prov. 4:7). Foolish men put great emphasis on fleeting pleasures and entertainment. The highest paid individuals in our society are entertainers. Young athletes sign multi-million dollar contracts, while teachers and educators are among the lowest on our pay scale. This is a symptom of distorted thinking and out of focus priorities. Let us not be caught up in the same snare, but diligently "… seek ye first the kingdom of God, and his righteousness …" (Matt. 6:33).

Wisdom is an attribute of God, and is inevitably and intimately related to the Divine knowledge. Those who possess wisdom, on the human level, have accepted Divine revelation as the ultimate and final word on any subject. It is the practical understanding of issues relating to this life. It expresses itself in the choice of proper ends and the right means for their achievement. The world knows much about knowledge, but very little about wisdom. It is reserved for those who know and serve God.

Thought For Today

Human knowledge and Divine wisdom dwell poles apart!

September 19

N. T. Bible Reading: II Corinthians 11:1-15   **Our Focus: II Corinthians 11:3**

SIMPLICITY

This is yet another passage of Scripture which exposes the danger and problems caused by the carnal mind. In this case, the evil is duplicity, guile, and complicated reasoning. There is a "corrupting" or defiling of the mind and thoughts which robs them of the purity and focus which they found "in Christ." Man complicates, confuses, and contaminates everything of God which he tampers with. Only the renewed mind, otherwise referred to, as "... the mind of Christ" (I Cor. 2:16), can remain guileless, single-minded, and uncomplicated. That is what the Apostle Paul is saying in II Corinthians 11:3. Conybeare translates it as, "... and you should be seduced from single-minded faithfulness to Christ." The Revised Standard Version gives it as, "... your thoughts will be led astray from a sincere and pure devotion to Christ." This may help us to get to the root problem which is the lack of faithfulness and devotion; and both have to do with practice or execution.

The most subtle aspect of any human thoughts, doctrines, or philosophies is that they will always lead to watering down, diluting, or seducing in the areas of *Christian living* and *conduct*. The true Gospel, when preached in sincerity and purity, will always produce true and genuine results. The very first response of a truly repentant soul to the Lord Jesus is "yes Lord!" Yes is an adverb used to express agreement or consent. It is also an expression of submission, which manifests itself in obedience.

Spiritual understanding and insight does not come from study, thinking, and reasoning; it comes from *obedience*. We do not think our way through; we see our way through when we *obey*. Clear vision and spiritual insight come from the inner man and not from the carnal mind. The process of obedience releases the inner man from fog and fuzzy thinking. The entrance of Divine life, gripping the heart and life through submission and obedience, purges the conscience and thereby clears the mind. The more fully we obey, the clearer we see.

Thought For Today

The obedient soul will always be able to say, "and now I see!"

September 20

O. T. Bible Reading: Ecclesiastes 10-12   **Our Focus: Ecclesiastes 12:1**

REMEMBER NOW

Solomon says "vanity of vanities" (Eccl. 1:2, 12:8); John says "blessed is he" and again "blessed are they" (Rev. 22:7, 14). The first words are from the Old Testament, and from a disillusioned man who sought meaning and purpose "*under the sun*." The second is from an aged Apostle who, though banished to Patmos, was in the Spirit, clearly understood the reality of salvation, and who knew God and walked in sweet fellowship with Him. It almost seems one can hear the great Apostle saying triumphantly, "reality of realities!" What a contrast, what a conclusion, what a lesson!

Solomon was another preacher who had to say, "do as I say, but do not do as I do." Everyone knows that does not work. The man is his message; when his life is inconsistent, his words fall flat, and his message is muted. He said at the conclusion of his life, "Remember now thy Creator in the days of thy youth …" (Eccl. 12:1); this was something which he himself had failed to do. He had forgotten, "… his heart *was turned* from the Lord God of Israel, which had appeared unto him twice … but *he kept not* that which the Lord commanded" (I Ki. 11:9-10). Solomon sadly lived *to get* and not *to give*, his self-centered choices only proved that the more one gets the less one possesses. In the spiritual realm, the paradox is that the more one gives the more one truly possesses; we conquer only where we yield. How strange are the ways of God, but they are perfect (Ps. 19:7-10).

What Solomon could not find "*under the sun*" millions have found "*in the Son*!" Revelation is progressive, and we must have the light of New Testament truth to fully grasp the real meaning of life. Solomon said, "… I gave my heart to know …" (Eccl. 1:17), but the end of his futile search for earthly pleasures and human knowledge was only "… vanity and vexation of spirit" (Eccl. 1:14). John declares "… *we may know him* that is true, and *we are in him* that is true, even in *his Son* Jesus Christ. This is the true God, and eternal life" (1 John 5:20). Reality of realities!!

Thought For Today

Those who find the Savior also find meaning, purpose, and reality!

September 20

N. T. Bible Reading: II Corinthians 11:16-33   **Our Focus: II Corinthians 11:30**

MINE INFIRMITIES

The Apostle Paul demonstrated his gift and his call by an amazing and powerful ministry. For 20 years he covered over 12,000 miles by land and sea, and most of his journeys were on foot. He wrote 13 of the 21 epistles of the New Testament. He had a unique conversion, a personal encounter with the risen Savior, a broad ranging "abundant" revelation of truth, and a truly miraculous ministry. Yet, for all that, his many sufferings (here referred to as infirmities) were of such a magnitude, as to shock the conscience and startle the mind. Never could another Apostle chronicle such an awesome list of horrific experiences. If these are the marks of an Apostle, and many feel they are, it should at least thin the ranks of those who desire the title.

One of the great revelations given to Paul, and through Paul to us, is that God allows suffering, permits infirmities, but always provides the grace needed to bear whatever we may experience. The experiences of God's people are widely different. Some may sail calm seas, enjoy robust health, and generally experience mostly blessings and abundant living. On the other hand, others, as did the Apostle Paul, will encounter "… a great fight of afflictions" (Heb. 10:32), "In weariness and painfulness …" (II Cor. 11:27), but to the glory of God they are "… more than conquerors through him that loved us" *in all these things* (Rom. 8:37).

The great Apostle gives us a powerful key by inserting the little word "mine" afflictions. There is a unique cup from which each soul must drink; there is "*a lot*" which bears our very name. There is a personal cross which each disciple must bear. Jesus designated it as "*his cross*" and it is as personal as "*his life*" with which he connects it: "And he that taketh not *his cross*, and followeth after me, is not worthy of me. He that findeth *his life* shall lose it: and he that loseth *his life* for my sake shall find it" (Matt. 10:38-39).

Thought For Today

God provides abundant grace for all which He permits!

September 21

O. T. Bible Reading: Song of Solomon 1-3   **Our Focus: Song of Solomon 1:2**

THY LOVE

The Song of Solomon is a very different and unique part of the Word of God. It is one of the most neglected and misunderstood books in the Bible. It is not our purpose here to get into the literary, historical, or theological viewpoints, but rather to stick to the inspirational studies of which it is a part. Many thoughts have been expressed and written about this book, and they all have at least some merit. We may safely suggest, as have many others, that this exchange makes a beautiful setting for the love relationship which exists between the Great Bridegroom, the Lord Jesus Christ, and His bride who will share the marriage supper (Rev. 19:9) before the millennial reign of Christ.

The word "love" is very prominent in this book; in one form or another it is used 32 times in these eight chapters. This fact illuminates a very vital truth; there is to be, and there must be, a flow of the very highest emotion (love) between the Lord Jesus and His bride. It is well that we know and emphasize the love of God, and the supreme sacrificial love of the Lord Jesus Christ. This is basic to the Gospel, and to the whole message of salvation; it is redeeming love which is the theme of the soul set free. However, there is a reciprocal love *from* the bride about which we seldom hear anything, but which is a vital element to the love relationship which is involved.

Many songs have been written and sung about the love of God. Those who know the real meaning of that love in their personal experience, sing them with genuine and moving expressions of appreciation and delight. Many fewer songs have been written about our love *for* the Lord, and the depth of our devotion *to* Him. Certainly the one is basic to the other, but we shudder to think of a marriage relationship where only the groom has and displays the sacred emotion of love. We should not hesitate to sing enthusiastically, "I love the Lord!"

Thought For Today

Love is the tender chord which gives life meaning!

165

September 21

N. T. Bible Reading: II Corinthians 12   **Our Focus: II Corinthians 12:10**

WEAK

No one wants to be weak, although everyone is. You will never hear anyone boast about being weak, but even a four year-old boy will brag about being "super strong." The weakness here spoken of is, by no means, moral weakness, nor is it a lack of resolve or fortitude. It is rather a sense of human insufficiency and inadequacy. This attitude is seldom realized apart from "infirmities" or sufferings and sorrows. It is in the hours of deepest need that we are made to realize the utter inabilities of our own resources, and very rarely before that.

A true spirit of humility is the ever-present awareness of our own limitations, and the frank and honest confession of our bankrupt condition. It is really a revelation of our depravity and utterly lost condition apart from Christ. Many believe, and I certainly concur, that there can be no genuine salvation without this awareness. However, there must be a two-fold revelation. To grasp and experience real salvation there must also be a great picture of the sufficiency of Christ, and of His unlimited power to redeem and transform. The first aspect brings despair and causes sorrow and remorse for such a condition. This is an element which is sadly lacking in today's shallow and superficial services. The old song says, "Then Jesus Came", and gloriously He does, flooding the soul with hope and raising a chorus of joy.

The Word of the Lord to the burdened, from Paul was, "… My grace is sufficient for thee …" (II Cor. 12:9). This may very well be one of the all-time most comforting Scriptures to God's needy people. It is *His grace*, and it is personal delivery "*for thee*." The supply is in direct proportion to the need; never too much, and never too little, but always "*just what I need*"; never too soon, and never too late, but always "*just on time*." There is no grace given for tomorrow, until the needs of tomorrow are experienced.

Thought For Today

When He shows us our need, He will also reveal His supply!

September 22

O. T. Bible Reading: Song of Solomon 4-5   **Our Focus: Song of Solomon 4:1**

DOVES' EYES

Turtledoves and pigeons were very common birds in Israel, they were considered a clean bird, and were the only birds that could be offered in sacrifice to God. The poor were allowed to offer them, since they were readily available, and dealers in sacrificial creatures were permitted to sit about the precincts of the temple, selling them.

The dove was dispatched by Noah to test the levels of vegetation reappearing from the receding waters of the flood. The dove found "… no rest for the sole of her foot, and she returned …" (Gen. 8:9); seven days later "… he sent forth the dove out of the ark; And the dove came in to him in the evening; and, lo, in her mouth was an olive leaf …" (Gen. 8:10-11). The olive leaf has since become the universal symbol of peace and reconciliation. When sent forth the third time, the dove returned not again and Noah knew then that the flood waters were dried up (Gen. 8:12). This has been applied to the dispensational ministry of the Holy Spirit in our time; the abiding or remaining abroad in the earth, convicting, convincing, confirming, and converting. "And I will pray the Father, and he shall give you another Comforter, that he may abide with you forever" (John 14:16).

The crowning picture of the dove was at the baptism of Jesus in the river Jordan, "… lo, the heavens were opened unto him, and he saw the Spirit of God descending like a dove, and lighting upon him" (Matt. 3:16). From that time on, the dove became the visual emblem of the Holy Spirit.

A "doves eyes" represent the unique operation of the Holy Spirit giving prophetic insight, spiritual perception, and discernment. The bride of Christ, symbolically represented by Solomon's Shulamite, will be a Spirit-led and Spirit-directed body of people. They will have what nothing on the human level can provide, the supernatural and anointed vision which gives "night vision" to the quickened pilgrim. It is both a privilege and responsibility for all of us to become Spirit-led (Rom. 8:14).

Thought For Today

When the heavenly dove descends human eyes are opened!

September 22

N. T. Bible Reading: II Corinthians 13   **Our Focus: II Corinthians 13:4**

HE LIVETH

The resurrection of Jesus was unique; that is why He is called "... the firstfruits ..." (I Cor. 15:20). He was not the first to rise from the dead; there were eight others of which we are told in the Scriptures: three in the Old Testament, three in the Gospels, and two in the book of Acts. However, each of these later died, and returned to the grave. Jesus arose to never die again, and to impart this *new life*, resurrection life, to His children. His resurrection life, we are told, was "... by the power of God ..." (II Cor. 13:4); "that like as Christ was raised up from the dead by the glory of the Father, even so we also should walk in *newness of life*" (Rom. 6:4). This new life, in and through Christ, is not an old life patched up, it is in fact His new and risen life imparted to us by the same Spirit by which He was raised from the dead: "But if the Spirit of him that raised up Jesus from the dead dwell in you, he that raised up Christ from the dead shall also quicken your mortal bodies by his Spirit that dwelleth in you" (Rom. 8:11). That is why Paul longed to know Him in "... the power of his resurrection ..." (Phil. 3:10), in an ever-increasing measure.

There were two offerings of firstfruits which were to be brought and waved before the Lord according to Leviticus 23. The first (Lev. 23:10-11), was the sheaf, on the morrow after the Sabbath (the first day of the week). Surely this must typify the victorious resurrection of Christ who had made Himself an offering for sin "... *without leaven* ..." (Lev. 10:12) "... an he lamb without blemish ..." (Lev. 23:12) "But with the precious (rare) blood of Christ, as of a lamb without blemish and without spot" (I Pet. 1:19). The second, 50 days later, was to be "... two wave loaves ... of fine flour; they shall be baken *with leaven* ..." (Lev. 23:17). The first, we must apply to Christ, "the firstfruits"; the second, to His saints, "... afterward they that are Christ's at his coming" (I Cor. 15:23). This second offering must include "a sin offering" (the first representing Jesus needed none). It also must include leaven (absent from the first) because it represented us and the element of imperfection and sin which is a present reality. The new life imparted to us through the resurrected life of Christ is the guarantee of our resurrection also. All of this is gloriously possible because "He liveth."

Thought For Today

There is a newness of life which flows through and from the quickening Spirit!

September 23

O. T. Bible Reading: Song of Solomon 6-8   **Our Focus: Song of Solomon 6:13**

RETURN

The most simple, and perhaps the most common, use of the word "return" is to come back again. This, of course, assumes that there has first been a departure from. If one has not left a certain place, he could never return to that place because he has remained there. The word is used often in the Scriptures, and emphasizes the human tendency to stray, to be enticed away from, or simply to drift from a given position. The flow of the stream of life is always downward, the pull of the tides of time is always away from the shore, and all you have to do to drift is simply *do nothing*.

There is a parallel between the physical realm and the spiritual realm. The Scriptures often depict the personal relationship with God and the walk with God as *higher* ground. When God communed with Moses he was commanded to "... Come *up* to me into the mount, and be there: and I will give thee ..." (Ex. 24:12). Abraham was instructed to journey to "... one of the mountains which I will tell thee of" (Gen. 22:2), for the offering of Isaac and the revelation of "Jehovah-Jireh." The angel of the Lord called John to "... *Come up* hither, and I will shew thee ..." (Rev. 4:1); "... the mountain of the Lord's house shall be established in the top of the mountains, and shall be exalted above the hills ..." (Isa. 2:2).

The call of the Lord is a "*high calling*" and will require both diligence and skill. The calling to "return unto the Lord" (repeated seven times) anticipates the tendency to drift. How encouraging to know that the gracious and merciful Redeemer stands ready and willing to forgive our waywardness. Those who walk in close fellowship with the Lord will correct these driftings in their very earliest stages and return to the place of His favored blessing.

Thought For Today

Those who heed the call to return shall do so with joy and singing!

September 23

N. T. Bible Reading: Galatians 1   **Our Focus: Galatians 1:4**

JESUS ... GAVE HIMSELF

The Bible declares categorically "For God so loved the world, that *he gave* his only begotten Son ..." (John 3:16). The very next verse, John 3:17, states just as emphatically "For *God sent* not his Son into the world to condemn the world ...." The salvation of the soul is provided for *by* and proceeds *from* the eternal love of God; it is based upon the atonement wrought by Christ at Calvary. The plan was designed in heaven, and accomplished on the earth. Jesus was the effective agent, and because of this we can say "... that God was in Christ, reconciling the world unto himself ..." (II Cor. 5:19).

Jesus chose to fulfil the Father's plan, and plainly stated that, "... My meat is to do the will of him that sent me, and to finish his work" (John 4:34). Therefore, the Scriptures declare that He "... *gave himself* for our sins, that he might deliver us from this present evil world ..." (Gal. 1:4). Paul repeats this fact again in Titus 2:14, "Who *gave himself* for us, that he might redeem us from all iniquity ...." Paul spoke again of the miracle of this new exchanged life in Galatians 2:20, "... Christ liveth in me ... I live by the faith of the Son of God, who loved me, and gave himself for me." The church is His special sanctuary at this time, and we know that, "... Christ also loved the church, and *gave himself* for it ... That he might present it to himself a glorious church, not having spot, or wrinkle ..." (Eph. 5:25, 27). In this relatively short Epistle of Galatians, Paul refers to Christ 47 times under eight separate names or titles. Apart from His unique person and work, there could be no Gospel message. The Gospel *centers* in Christ; the Gospel *is* Christ.

The real passion of Christianity is that we become bond-slaves of Jesus Christ. It is the love of God which is shed abroad in our hearts by the Holy Ghost which is given unto us (Rom. 5:5). It also is the love of Christ which constraineth us (II Cor. 5:14), and we are Divinely enabled to manifest the very spirit of Christ Himself. "And be ye kind one to another, tenderhearted, forgiving one another, even as God for Christ's sake hath forgiven you" (Eph. 4:32). It is because He gave Himself freely that we in turn can say with the Apostle Paul, "For we preach not ourselves, but Christ Jesus the Lord; and ourselves your servants for Jesus' sake" (II Cor. 4:5).

Thought For Today

The supreme sacrifice of Christ is God's standard for us!

170

September 24

O. T. Bible Reading: Isaiah 1-3   **Our Focus: Isaiah 1:1**

ISAIAH

What Beethoven and Handel were to music, and what Longfellow and Shakespeare were to literature, that was what Isaiah was among the prophets of the Bible. The book of Isaiah has been called the Gospel of the Old Testament. There is a sense in which it is a Bible within the Bible. There are 66 books in the Bible, and there are 66 chapters in Isaiah. The Bible is divided into two sections; 39 books of the Old Testament, and 27 books of the New Testament. Isaiah consists of two distinct parts; the first 39 chapters concern themselves primarily with the thought of God's laws and covenants and Israel's judgments for disobedience, and the last 27 chapters give some of the clearest insights into the Divine mercy and grace and the coming salvation for Israel.

Isaiah prophesied and ministered in Israel for over 60 years. Jewish tradition maintains that he continued until the reign of the wicked king Manasseh. They hold that he resisted the evil ways of the king and suffered a horrible death at his hands, being thrust into the hollow trunk of a tree, and then it was "sawn asunder." Many believe that the reference in Hebrews 11:37 was directed to Isaiah's method of death. The prophetic clarity and vividness of his description of the person and ministry of The Messiah have earned him the well-deserved title as "the evangelical prophet."

The name Isaiah means "Jehovah saves." God gave him a far-ranging vision concerning "… Judah and Jerusalem …" (Isa. 1:1). His ministry began 217 years after the division of the United Kingdom. He appears on the scene of history midway between Moses and the birth of the Lord Jesus. The Book of Isaiah is quoted freely in the New Testament; 20 of the 27 books have direct quotations from Isaiah (some have claimed there are actually 66 quotations). His words are woven into the fabric of the New Testament; his message rings out through the centuries: "… though your sins be as scarlet, they shall be as white as snow …" (Isa. 1:18).

Thought For Today

The prophets fore-told what the apostles forth-told!

September 24

N. T. Bible Reading: Galatians 2   **Our Focus: Galatians 2:19**

THE LAW

Each of the Epistles was written with a specific purpose in mind. Paul summarized, in a broad sense, a simple outline of their message in II Timothy 3:16: "All scripture is given by inspiration of God, and is profitable for doctrine, for reproof, for correction ...." The epistles of Romans, Corinthians, and Galatians seem to fit exactly into those descriptions. Romans certainly is primarily a thorough presentation of *doctrine* by which we may become "rooted and *grounded*" in the faith. Corinthians falls mainly into the category of *reproof* for careless living and provides a good set of directions for personal conduct whereby our feet (our walk) may be *guided* into His ways (Luke 1:79). And now Galatians is clearly for *correction* from devious and seducing doctrines so that we may be *guarded* and kept in the purity of the Gospel.

The well known Charles Spurgeon declared: "no man can be a Christian in these days without being a controversialist." It seems to me we could leave out "in these days" and give it a blanket application to all times. In the days of the Apostle Paul, it was abundantly evident. There were at that time many who continued to hold to the keeping of the law of Moses, and to the right of circumcision in particular, as essential to salvation. This created a major controversy with Paul being the primary preacher and teacher of the gospel of "... by grace are ye saved through faith; and that not of yourselves: it is the gift of God: Not of works, lest any man should boast" (Eph. 2:8-9).

In our time we have just the opposite problem. The popular modern version of the Gospel gives license for any and every warped and perverted manner of life. It is very controversial indeed to preach and teach that we "... are his workmanship, created in Christ Jesus unto good works, which God hath before ordained that we should walk in them" (Eph. 2:10). We must hold to the Word of God and stand firm on the sure foundation "... The Lord knoweth them that are his. And, let everyone that nameth the name of Christ depart from iniquity" (II Tim. 2:19).

Thought For Today

Where there is a new life there also will be a new manner of life!

September 25

O. T. Bible reading: Isaiah 4-6   **Our Focus: Isaiah 6:3**

HOLY, HOLY, HOLY

The word "holy" occurs in the Scriptures over 600 times; it is prominent in the book of Leviticus being repeated in one form or another 150 times. No one would question that we are living in a very _unholy_ world. Our culture and society is saturated with secularism and humanism; neither of those two will ever use the word "holy." They are bounded by that which is mortal and mundane, and are blinded by the notion that we are creatures of time only. Ours is a secular society; secular is the very opposite of spiritual. It is most significant that the Scriptures which point to a time of restitution and return specifically say: "... they have put no difference between the holy and profane ... And they shall teach my people the difference between the holy and profane, and cause them to discern between the unclean and the clean" (Ezek. 22:26, 44:23).

The study of contrasts is a primary element in art, politics, and religion. In the first, one element is used to show the beauty of another by contrasts, sometimes subtle and sometimes obvious. In the latter, contrast is one sure test of the false from the true; if there is no contrast then there is no fundamental difference. It is just here that the real issue becomes apparent. Our culture would blend everything into some nebulous realm of a neutral and all-encompassing "grey zone." Everything blends into nothing; there are no absolutes.

The Bible allows for no such nonsense. It states the facts as they are. God is a holy God ... man is not. A solution has been provided. Only God could bridge the gap, and He did, by providing a Savior who offers redemption and the forgiveness of sin. He also imparts a new nature, a new creation, and a new capacity to live "... according to God in the spirit" (I Pet. 4:6), putting on "... the new man, which after God is created in righteousness and true holiness" (Eph. 4:24).

Thought For Today

Those who are born of God will also manifest the nature of God!

September 25

N. T. Bible Reading: Galatians 3   **Our Focus: Galatians 3:8**

GOD PREACHED

The word "preach" is used frequently in the Bible; three times in the Old Testament, and 32 times in the New Testament. It simply means to proclaim. Not everyone is aware of the fact that Paul tells us that God preached to Abraham. What was His message? What did He proclaim? He proclaimed the Gospel, according to Paul. The occasion was recorded in Genesis chapter 22 which gives us the record of the trip to Mount Moriah and the willingness of Abraham to offer Isaac as a sacrifice. The Lord said, "... *because* thou hast done this thing, and hast not withheld thy son, thine only son: That in blessing I will bless thee ... And in thy seed (that seed was Christ) shall all the nations of the earth be blessed ..." (Gen. 22:16-18).

The offering up of Isaac is one of the clearest pictures of the death of Christ, and what that means to us. God did not spare His own Son, although he did spare Abraham's son. The emphasis is on the fact that Abraham obeyed the voice of the Lord. The fact is distinctly mentioned twice, at the beginning and again at the end of the exchange: "... *because* thou hast ... not withheld thy son ... *because* thou hast obeyed my voice" (Gen. 22:16, 18). He obeyed the voice of the Lord; he clearly manifested his faith in God and in His word by his actions. His faith worked; it produced the action which God required. The *root* of faith is absolute and total confidence in what God has said and promised. The *fruit* of faith is the carrying out in action and obedience in the directions of the Lord. This is the very heart of the gospel. We must believe what God has said and place our complete trust in Him and in His word. This will always produce results which demonstrate genuine faith and justify God.

There is no contradiction between the teaching of Paul and the teaching of James. Paul stated of Abraham that "... Abraham believed God, and it was accounted (imputed) to him for righteousness" (Gal. 3:6). James says, "Was not Abraham our father justified by works ..." (Jam. 2:21). They both teach the same thing. Faith is the basis of salvation; faith alone saves. However, faith which saves is never alone; it will always produce acts of obedience to God and to His Word. True and genuine saving faith is a dynamic element which always leads to conduct and life-style which is in harmony with God and with His Word.

Thought For Today

Those justified by faith justify God by their lifestyle and behavior!

174

September 26

O. T. Bible Reading: Isaiah 7-10   **Our Focus: Isaiah 7:14**

IMMANUEL

The birthday of great men of historic proportions are remembered, and in some cases become national holidays. There is only one truly Great Person (so declared by the angel to Mary, Luke 1:32) who was foretold 700 years before His actual birth. His Divinely pre-written name defines His Divinely appointed mission and ministry. We know, of course, that you will not find any place in the Gospel accounts where He is given that name. The Scripture actually says that the virgin mother would so call Him: "… a virgin shall conceive, and bare a son, and (she) shall call his name Immanuel" (Isa. 7:14). Mary knew better than anyone else that the Almighty had performed the unheard of miracle and that it was no less than "… God with us" (Matt. 1:23). We also know that the same prophet, Isaiah, declared that "… his name shall be called Wonderful, Counsellor, The mighty God, The everlasting Father, The Prince of Peace" (Isa. 9:6). Jeremiah joined the chorus announcing prophetically that, "… this is his name whereby he shall be called, The Lord Our Righteousness" (Jer. 23:6).

It is not a proper name which is intended; there are several issues involved:

1. He shall *be* … that is, His nature and qualities will thus be defined.
2. It is a defining and comprehensive picture of His mission and ministry.
3. He will be so named by *His people*, those who have come to know Him and have experienced the miracle of His indwelling.

That is why they called His name "… Jesus: for he shall save *his people* from their sins" (Matt. 1:21). Jesus means Saviour, and Saviour means Rescuer, Redeemer, Deliverer, Restorer, Preserver, and whatever else may be involved in God's great plan of salvation. What a Name!

"… Christ Jesus *came* into the world to save sinners …" (1 Tim. 1:15), "For ye know the grace of our Lord Jesus Christ, that, though he was rich, yet for your sakes he became poor, that ye through his poverty might be rich" (II Cor. 8:9). The Gospel is good news, it is glad tidings, it is a proclamation of the message of salvation through, and only through, the mission and ministry of the Lord Jesus Christ, "… God hath visited his people" (Luke 7:16). His name shall be called Immanuel … God with us (Matt. 1:23). What a Saviour!

Thought For Today

Because He came we can now become the sons of God!

September 26

N. T. Bible Reading: Galatians 4   **Our Focus: Galatians 4:1**

THE HEIR

An heir is an individual who will inherit something or is entitled to inherit the estate, rank, title, or office of another. Some people spend their lives anticipating and planning for an inheritance which they know has been assigned them in the will of a living person. The will only goes into effect after the death of the one who signed it. Through faith in Christ we are now declared to be the sons of God: "Beloved, _now_ are we the sons of God ..." (I John 3:2). The witness of the Spirit gives us the assurance "... that we _are_ the children of God" (Rom. 8:16). This is a function of the Holy Spirit upon the human spirit, and is one of the most precious experiences possible to any human being. It also is "unspeakable" for it is beyond the reach of words to describe. It is another "operation of God" by the Spirit (Col. 2:12); the first taste of heaven in the spirit of a newborn child of God: "... and have tasted of the heavenly gift ..." (Heb. 6:4).

Because of this blessed reality of becoming the sons (children) of God, we are also included in His will as "... heirs of God, and joint-heirs with Christ; if so be that we suffer with him, that we may be also glorified together" (Rom. 8:17). He is not ashamed to identify us as "brethren" or members of His royal family (Heb. 2:11). The inheritance is His by nature, and now through His mercy and saving grace it is extended to us also. The will (testament) is now in effect, for the testator (Jesus) has not only died, but has risen from the dead to personally see that the provisions of the will are fully kept by us.

The inheritance is both for the present and for the future. There are many things which are given as a possession in this present life. The Scriptures declare that we have been "... sealed with that holy Spirit of promise, Which is the earnest (down payment or pledge) of our inheritance ..." (Eph. 1:13-14). There is more, much more, included in the will for this present life, and for that which is yet to come. It also even includes the provision and "... the promise of eternal inheritance" (Heb. 9:15). No wonder the Scriptures speak of "... the unsearchable riches of Christ" (Eph. 3:8). What a will! What an inheritance!

Thought For Today

To comprehend the inheritance, you must carefully study the will!

<u>**September 27**</u>

O. T. Bible Reading: Isaiah 10-12   **Our Focus: Isaiah 12:3**

THE WELLS OF SALVATION

The subject of Isaiah chapters 11 and 12 is the final and yet future restoration of "… the remnant of His people …" (Israel) (Isa. 11:11, 16), "… the dispersed of Judah …" (Isa. 11:12); *the time* is "… in that day …" (Isa. 12:1, 4), when "They shall not hurt nor destroy in all my holy mountain: for the earth shall be full of the knowledge of the Lord, as the waters cover the sea (certainly a *future* prophecy)" (Isa. 11:9). *The prospect* is abundance of refreshing, abounding vigor and prosperity, and the abiding Divine presence. Thank God for the element of hope. Twice the blessed Savior is referred to by Jeremiah as "… *the hope* of Israel …" (Jer. 14:8, 17:13); indeed, He is their hope, and their only hope, as well as ours.

Once the nation of Israel journeyed "… through all that great and terrible wilderness …" (Deut. 1:19), and cried in anguish to Moses to "… Give us water that we may drink …" (Ex. 17:2), and the whole nation "… thirsted there for water …" (Ex. 17:3). The Lord stood before them upon the rock in Horeb; Moses smote the rock, as directed, and there came precious water out of the rock from which they all drank (Ex. 17:6). How well they remembered those days. No such lack will be experienced *in that day* when "… the desert shall rejoice, and blossom as the rose" (Isa. 35:1). The natural prospect is sweet and glorious, but the spiritual is even greater and more amazing. They, with exuberant joy, will draw refreshings from the overflowing and abundant sources of salvation. They will then sing in unison the happy and harmonious chorus, "… O Lord, I will praise thee … Praise the Lord … Sing unto the Lord … Cry out and shout …" (Isa. 12:1, 4-6). Does all of that in any way sound familiar? It should!

Where there is an unlimited *flow* there will also always be an *over-flow*: "And the floors shall be full of wheat, and the vats (the vessels) shall overflow with wine and oil" (Joel 2:24). Salvation is always connected with abundance and fulness; never with want and starvation. Salvation is spiritual, not physical, and God's true people should enjoy spiritual enrichment, growth, and an abundant harvest. "… I am come that they might have life, and that they might have it more abundantly" (John 10:10).

<u>**Thought For Today**</u>

In Christ there is always <u>more</u>; never is there <u>less</u>!

<u>**September 27**</u>

N. T. Bible Reading: Galatians 5   **Our Focus: Galatians 5:1**

LIBERTY

The word "liberty" sometimes translated "free" is used 10 times in the Epistle of Galatians. The key thought which runs through all six chapters is liberation through the Gospel. The climax and conclusion is reached in Galatians 5:1 "Stand fast therefore in the liberty wherewith Christ hath made us free …." Paul first shows in Galatians 5 that this liberty in Christ is a love-service and not, as under the law, a burden and a bondage. It is now not the letter of mere precepts, it is love for a Person. Our joy is not just to believe the Word of God and obey it, but to love and thus believe in and on the Blessed Redeemer whom the Good Book reveals. The Mosaic Law placed great emphasis on doing and keeping the letter of the law; the Gospel puts the emphasis on knowing, loving, and thus serving the Lord Jesus Himself. It is not the dominion of commandments and ordinances; it is rather the dominance and beauty of the Life Imparter.

The second theme of Galatians 5 is to show that this glorious and wonderful freedom issues in righteous and godly conduct, because it is a walk *in the Spirit*, and therefore the *fruits of the Spirit* will be produced. The *Holy* Spirit can only yield *holy* living; because the seed is pure, it can and will also produce the same pure fruit. This is the very core of New Testament truth. Careless conduct and loose-living are both foreign to the true Gospel: "… thou shalt call his name Jesus: for he shall save his people *from* their sins" (Matt. 1:21). Glorious liberty!

The key truth is the difference between a rule and a relationship. The one is cold, calculating, and compelling: the other is inspiring, illuminating, and impelling. All young men know that you cannot demand the love of the fair maiden: you must first win her heart; when that is done, her loyalty and allegiance follow as surely as day follows night. Those who truly love the Lord Jesus long to please Him, and their greatest thrill is to do those things that are pleasing in His sight. Wonderful freedom!

<u>**Thought For Today**</u>

Real and lasting fulfillment flows from loving service!

September 28

O. T. Bible Reading: Isaiah 13-15　　　　　　**Our Focus: Isaiah 14:24**

IT SHALL

The forecasters and meteorologists say "it may"; scientists and inventors cautiously say "it should"; speculators and prognosticators say "it could"; but God alone is able to say "*it shall*." His word is final, and His counsels will stand. He alone can say "I will", because He alone can also say "I can." His authority is absolute, His power is unlimited, His dominion is beyond definition, and His Word and counsel are supreme. What a Mighty God! The thrill and wonder of it all is that "… this God is our God forever and ever: he will be our guide even unto death" (Ps. 48:14). Blessed be His worthy Name!

The admonition of the Psalmist is most fitting for our time: "… let all the inhabitants of the world stand in awe of him. For he spake, and it was done; he commanded, and it stood fast" (Ps. 33:8-9). If we would *reflect* more on Him and His attributes, we would *react* very differently to men and their actions. "For we can do nothing against the truth, but for the truth" (II Cor. 13:8). We are not called upon to *defend* God or the truth; we are simply to *declare* His name and power and *proclaim* the joyful sound. Facts and truth are both absolutes, and our culture and humanistic thinking admits of neither. They are firm and relentless, and after they have been ridiculed and scoffed at by arrogant men, whose breath is in their nostrils, the facts and the truth both stand steadfast and unscathed.

Confidence is unwavering faith and absolute trust. We may and must place our confidence in the Almighty God, and in the Blessed Redeemer who cannot fail and who enables us to say "great is thy faithfulness, Lord unto me." It is when our hearts *condemn us not* that we have just such an unwavering confidence (I John 3:21). This Great and Mighty God is the very One who declared, "… Behold, I make all things new …" (Rev. 21:5), and because He can and does, *He shall* "… wipe away all tears from their eyes; and there *shall* be no more death, neither sorrow, nor crying …" (Rev. 21:4).

Thought For Today

Those who know He will, and He can, fret not at plans of others!

September 28

N. T. Bible Reading: Galatians 6   **Our Focus: Galatians 6:14**

THE CROSS

There has always been a great stigma attached to the cross. The death penalty in Israel was not by hanging, it was by stoning. But in some extreme cases of horrible crimes, after the stoning, the body was strung up on a tree as a final act of rejection and reproach (Deut. 21:22). We are told that Christ was made a curse for us, "… Cursed is everyone that hangeth on a tree" (Gal. 3:13), and it was on the cruel cross of Calvary where this was fulfilled.

It is legitimate to ask the question, "exactly *when* did Christ become a curse *for us*?" Everyone rejoiced, angels sang, wise men sought Him out, and shepherds were given good tidings of great joy, so surely it was not at the time of His birth. There are years of growth and maturity which are termed "silent years", but in those years he *grew in favor* with God and with men (Luke 2:52); there is no clear sign of any curse in all of that. In His public ministry, God sanctioned His ministry and mission, hundreds were healed and blessed, disciples were chosen and taught, and the fame of Him spread far and wide; there is no obvious or even slight hint of a special curse during that time. Even as he hung on the cross in agony and physical suffering for three hours, His offering was without blemish, so the birds continued to sing, the sun continued to shine, and we look in vain for some sure token of a Divine curse. Then suddenly everything changed and the stroke fell heavily; there was darkness; that is all we are told, just darkness; horrible, frightening, rare and strange darkness. One can only ask: "was not this the exact time He was made a curse *for us*?"

Jesus hung and expired on *the tree* (the cross) of Calvary; this was for Him *the Tree of death.* That was His cup from which He drank the last bitter drop. The miracle of the resurrection transforms that cruel Roman gibbet into *a tree of life* for every needy soul. "… To him that overcometh will I give to eat of the tree of life, which is in the midst of the paradise of God" (Rev. 2:7). The cross is the center and core of the Gospel; we must never stray far from it. God forbid that we should glory save in *the cross* of our Lord Jesus Christ.

Thought For Today

Out of His death flows our new life, life everlasting!

September 29

O. T. Bible Reading: Isaiah 16-18　　　　　　**Our Focus: Isaiah 17:1**

THE BURDEN

The word "burden" is closely associated with the prophets of Israel. Isaiah and Jeremiah use the word about 30 times. Their use of the word primarily has to do with the judgments of God. A burden is a load; it is something to be carried or that which you bear. The burden is an oracle or simply a message, of which there are nine mentioned by Isaiah. Most of these specific prophecies regarding these nine surrounding nations have already been fulfilled. They were accurate, exact, and Divine predictions of precisely what was soon to happen to these nations. True prophecy is history written in advance, it is what will happen tomorrow, but it is written today. It is an element of God's omniscience and one of the most convincing proofs of the Divine inspiration of the Scriptures.

The burden of Isaiah, chapters 15 and 16, is a message of judgment to the kingdom of Moab. They were once a proud and powerful nation, but the prophecy dooms them to a small and feeble remnant (Isa. 16:14). The Assyrians struck suddenly and decisively, and Babylon later practically destroyed them. The prophet Zephaniah further prophesied that: "… Surely Moab shall be as Sodom, and the children of Ammon as Gomorrah, even the breeding of nettles, and saltpits, and a perpetual desolation …" (Zeph. 2:9). This area is the modern Hashemite kingdom of Jordan, a very arid and unfertile land of poverty and squalor.

Moab was the illegitimate child of Lot's oldest daughter; his name means "of my father" … the very name was a stigma. They became a mischievous and infamous people. It was the daughters of the Moabites who enticed the men of Israel into their idolatrous practices. They were forbidden and excluded from the congregation of the Lord to the 10th generation because they hired Balaam to curse Israel and were very antagonistic in reviling Israel (Deut. 23:3-4; Zeph. 2:8). They were thus among the nations with whom God had a controversy.

Thought For Today

Those who despise the Lord exclude themselves from His favor!

September 29

N. T. Bible Reading: Ephesians 1   **Our Focus: Ephesians 1:3**

IN CHRIST

The cadence and repetition of certain words in the book of Ephesians flows like the gentle waters of a brook, and glows like diamonds in the clear sunlight. They recur over and over again ... in Christ, in Him, in Whom, in the Lord Jesus, in the Lord. They are too frequent to miss, too important to overlook, and too rich in meaning to ignore. Someone has said that one or the other of these phrases occurs 30 times in the book of Ephesians alone. In Ephesians the emphasis is too obvious to miss, and much may be gleaned from a careful consideration of their significance. It is the central union of two separate entities into a whole new element. The element of copper, when combined with the element of zinc, unites to form a new element called brass. When a sinner is united to Christ, a whole new being is created, sometimes referred to as a saint. There are two key words in Ephesians, they are "in Christ"; the following is not original with me, but was copied out many years ago without the source being indicated:

- In Christ Jesus we have *a title* which can never be disputed (Rev. 5:9).
- In Christ Jesus we have *a pardon* which can never be doubted (Heb. 8:1).
- In Christ Jesus we have *a justification* which can never be forgotten (Rom. 8:33).
- In Christ Jesus we have *a hope* which can never be disappointed (I Pet. 1:3).
- In Christ Jesus we have *a glory* which can never be darkened (Jer. 31:3).
- In Christ Jesus we have *a love* which can never be exhausted (II Cor. 12:8).
- In Christ Jesus we have *a wisdom* which can never be baffled (Rom. 11:33-34).
- In Christ Jesus we have *resources* which can never fail.

Paul stated in Ephesians 1:4 that, "... he hath chosen us in him before the foundation of the world, that we should be holy and without blame before him in love." C. H. Spurgeon is quoted as saying: "God chose me before I came into the world, because if He had waited until I got here, He never would have chosen me at all." G. Campbell Morgan made this interesting comment on the statement which Jesus made, "Ye have not chosen me, but I have chosen you ..." (John 15:16): "that puts the responsibility on Him, if He did the choosing, then He is responsible." We can certainly add, for His part, He cannot fail.

Thought For Today

The account of every human reads: "zero balance", outside of Christ!

September 30

O. T. Bible Reading: Isaiah 19-21   **Our Focus: Isaiah 21:1**

THE DESERT

Isaiah, Jeremiah, and Ezekiel use the Hebrew word "Araba" or "Arabah" which literally means "sterility", and thus stands for an area of land which is non-productive, parched, and barren. It is elsewhere rendered "plain", which indicated a level or hollow section of land; and in the east, wide extended plains are vulnerable to and very likely to become scenes of drought and barrenness, commonly known as desert.

This is a daring adventure; have you ever heard anyone preach on or discuss Isaiah chapter 21? The first verse of Isaiah 21 sounds like a paradox of terms: "The burden of the desert of the sea …"; you can't have both. If you have a desert, the water has deserted the area; it is arid, sandy, and barren. If you have a sea, you have plenty of water, but really nothing but water. "The desert of the Sea", what kind of a monstrosity is this? Some things do seem like a contradiction. The doctor may explain, "we will burn this off", when referring to a troubled piece of flesh, but in reality they freeze it off. We also are familiar with dry ice, which sounds somewhat contradictory, but it works. It will make good sense when we identify what the subject is.

He is speaking here of Babylon. In verse two of Isaiah 21 he calls for the combined kingdoms of Medo-Persia to employ the same treachery and violence which Babylon herself has used for her own destruction. Isaiah 21:9 further identifies this desert of the sea, specifically naming her as Babylon. Jeremiah referred to the same enigma: "O thou that dwellest upon many waters, abundant in treasures, thine end is come …" (Jer. 51:13). There was a literal empire called "Babylon", and there also is a false religious system defined in the Scriptures as "… Mystery, Babylon The Great, The Mother Of Harlots …" (Rev. 17:5). The mystery of the waters (the sea in Isa. 21:1) is solved: "… The waters which thou sawest … are peoples, and multitudes, and nations, and tongues" (Rev. 17:15).

Babylon, a false and deceptive counterfeit religious system, is a *mirage* in the desert. It was the first united rebellion against God at the Tower of Babel; it symbolizes the last stronghold of united false religious rebellion against God and His order in a federated world-church system. It appears to offer water, but it is really a barren desert. The water of life will never be found, except where Jesus is recognized and honored as the Giver of Life and the One True Head of the church, which is *His* body.

Thought For Today

The Bible clearly exposes what appears to men to be otherwise!

September 30

N. T. Bible Reading: Ephesians 2   **Our Focus: Ephesians 2:10**

WALK IN THEM

Here is yet another "*in*": "… good works, which God hath before ordained that we should walk *in them*" (Eph. 2:10). It is God who graciously enables us to "… walk worthy of the Lord …" (Col. 1:10); He has made provision for us to "… Walk *in* the spirit, and ye shall not fulfil the lust of the flesh" (Gal. 5:16); He has also given us understanding and illumination whereby we may "… walk *in* the light …" (I John 1:7), "… walk *in* love …" (Eph. 5:2), "Walk *in* wisdom …" (Col. 4:5), and triumphantly to "… walk ye *in* him" (Col. 2:6). He has so planned and purposed for every child of God; surely this magnifies the Great Provider and illustrates and illuminates what His will is for His obedient children. The plan is clearly drawn, the path is clearly marked, the purpose is plainly taught, and the guide stands ready and prepared to lead us to an abundant entrance into the everlasting kingdom of our Lord and Savior Jesus Christ (II Pet. 1:11). All that remains is for *us* to make *the choices* and to take *the steps* which will get us there.

A step is one of a series of actions or measures taken to achieve a goal. We first must see the goal, we must desire that goal, determine that it is the very thing which we need and want, and then take deliberate and directed individual steps which will bring us to the desired destination. Those steps are taken one at a time. No single step, except the last one, will get us there, but all added together and continued certainly will. We are admonished by Paul to *so walk*; "… as the Lord hath called every one, *so* let him *walk* …" (I Cor. 7:17); and again, "As ye have therefore received Christ Jesus the Lord, *so walk* ye in him" (Col. 2:6); obviously, it is possible to walk otherwise or the admonitions are meaningless.

Only we can take the steps. God has provided, others may help and encourage, friends and relatives will pray and plead, a faithful pastor will teach, preach, and lead; only you can lift that foot and start it moving in the right direction. It does seem to make sense to apply these many Scriptures that speak of the walk as taking steps: "walk in the Spirit" … takes steps so as to be in the Spirit; "walk in the light" … takes steps in the direction the light is pointing etc. To do so is to act promptly, purposefully, and progressively. Those who would walk with God must keep step with Him.

Thought For Today

His is the plan, ours is the will, but mine are the steps!

October 1

O. T. Bible Reading: Isaiah 22-23   **Our Focus: Isaiah 22:22**

THE KEY OF DAVID

Isaiah chapter 22 deals with the ninth "burden" of the prophecies regarding the Gentile nations; there are ten specifically named in chapters 13-23. This one is unique in that it is not directed to any specific nation, but rather to "The burden of the valley of vision …" (Isa. 22:1). The immediate and primary interpretation of these words, appear almost certainly directed at Jerusalem, her people, and the pending sorrows which lay just ahead at that time. However, as is often the case with Scriptural prophecy, there is a duality involved; an immediate and a distant aspect of fulfillment. There can be very little doubt that someone beyond and much greater than Eliakim must be involved in the fulfillment of Isaiah 22:22 and 22:23 in particular.

The phrase "The key to the House of David", in the finality of its meaning can apply only to the Lord Jesus, "… These things saith he that is holy, he that is true, he that hath the key of David, he that openeth, and no man shutteth; and shutteth, and no man openeth" (Rev. 3:7). If there is any doubt in Isaiah chapter 22, all doubt is removed later in Revelation chapter 3. There is only One who is specifically designated as both Holy and True, "… How long, O Lord, holy and true …" (Rev. 6:10); "… These things saith the Amen, the faithful and true witness …" (Rev. 3:14); "… behold a white horse; and he that sat upon him was called Faithful and True …" (Rev. 19:11). It is significant that this "Key Person" bears the key to the House of David on *His shoulder*, and not in His hands. That is an apparent reference to final responsibility as well as authority. The shoulder speaks of strength; and the government of His kingdom, and eventually that of the world, will rest upon the shoulder of Him who is named, "… *The mighty God* …" (Isa. 9:6).

The House of David certainly refers to the nation of Israel. The historic record of that nation and of her people, their dispersion among the nations, the mystery of their sad and unparalleled suffering and sorrow, their re-gathering to their homeland, and now all of their endless conflict with their neighbor nations is a deep dark and hidden mystery apart from their Messiah, our Saviour, the Lord Jesus Christ. He is *The Key*, and when He is injected into the formula it all clears up. It is true that the history of Israel also is more than anything else "His-story."

Thought For Today

It is but a tiny key which unlocks the royal palace!

October 1

N. T. Bible Reading: Ephesians 3   **Our Focus: Ephesians 3:19**

ALL THE FULNESS

Can a mere mortal be "*filled* with all the fulness of God?" The Apostle Paul records this prayer for the Ephesian believers that they might come to *know* (that is, to personally and experimentally realize) this very thing (Eph. 3:19). Is it possible for a tiny shell to be filled with all the fulness of the mighty ocean? Yes, to the extent that it is completely filled, it may be so. Certainly, it did not drain the ocean, but it did truly fill the shell.

Ignatius died a martyr on February 1,107 AD. He once wrote, "few suspect what God would do in their souls, if only they would let Him do it." Trajan, the Roman emperor, is said to have offered him a great reward if only he would sacrifice to and acknowledge the Roman deities. He responded, "should you offer me all the treasures of your empire, I would not cease to adore and serve the only true and living God." He was tormented by scourging, his flesh was seared by burning papers dipped in oil, his flesh was torn by red hot pincers, and finally he was hurled into a den of vicious lions. On his way to the Coliseum he said, "now I *begin* to be a disciple. I thank thee, O Lord, that it has pleased thee to make me worthy to give this testimony of a complete love for thee." This does not sound like the words of some shallow, half-hearted believer. Only *fulness* could produce such a testimony. He triumphantly announced, "now I am ground by the wild beasts that I may be found the pure bread of Christ."

Paul uses the word "*that*" three times in Ephesians 3, verses 17 and 19. Each reference zeroes in on some aspect of personal experience:

1. "That Christ may dwell in your hearts by faith ..." (Eph. 3:17).
2. "... that ye, being rooted and grounded in love, May be able to comprehend ..." (Eph. 3:17-18).
3. "... that ye might be filled with all the fulness of God" (Eph. 3:19).

The knowledge is not an end in itself; it is to lead us into these glorious and blessed realities of experience. The knowledge for which Paul prays is that which enriches the personal relationship, and enhances or adorns the testimony. Those who know God have at least *tasted* of His fulness. It is the satisfying and soul-enriching reality which quickens the heart and generates the heart-cry, "That I may *know him* (that is, in His fulness) ..." (Phil. 3:10). It is evident and challenging to know, "... there remaineth yet very much land to be possessed" (Josh. 13:1).

Thought For Today

His "all" is reserved for those who give Him their "all!"

October 2

O. T. Bible Reading: Isaiah 24-26   **Our Focus: Isaiah 26:3**

PERFECT PEACE

It is very significant that within the Levitical offerings, it included the sacrifice of the peace offering (Lev. 3:1, 3, 6, 9). The word used in "peace offerings" is in the plural number, and seems to speak of peace of *every kind* … "perfect peace." This particular offering, peace offering, was divided into three types:

1. The thank offering, which is otherwise described as, the sacrifice of thanksgiving (Lev. 7:12, 22:29).
2. The sacrifice of a vow, or literally the votive offering (Num. 6:2, 15:3, 8).
3. The freewill offering (Lev. 7:16, 22:18, 21).

A portion of this offering was burned upon the altar with the fat selectively taken and placed upon the sacrifice. This element was hidden and unique to the "inward parts" and seems to typify health and inward vigor, vitality, and stamina. Another portion was divided and became the food for the officiating priests; it consisted of "… the wave breast and the heave shoulder …" (Lev. 7:34). The shoulder in Scripture is symbolic of strength and stability; the breast is the place of the heart, and stands for the seat of affections. These were uniquely the portion for the priests, and it symbolizes the thoroughness and completeness of our inheritance in Christ. To apply it to this special ingredient of peace; it is strong, stable, and sure, and it reaches to the very core (the heart) of our emotions and there it rules and reigns (Col. 3:15). As one translation renders it, "… settles all questions." It is truly *perfect peace*.

The marginal reading of Isaiah 26:3 for perfect peace is "peace, peace", no doubt to signify the certainty and the abundance of that precious and rare attribute which we know as peace. The very specific offer to every troubled soul is, "… Peace, peace to him that is far off, and to him that is near, saith the Lord …" (Isa. 57:19). It is highly significant that the Lord Jesus communicated this special gift to His disciples, "Peace I leave with you, *my peace* (surely that is perfect peace) I give unto you …" (John 14:27). The peace which He possessed and experienced stood every test, every form of stress and strain, and it is ours through His grace and mercy.

Thought For Today

Perfect peace will ride out every storm and prevail!

October 2

N. T. Bible Reading: Ephesians 4   **Our Focus: Ephesians 4:30**

GRIEVE NOT

The admonition of Ephesians 4:30 is, "And grieve not the holy Spirit of God …", that is both a revelation and an appeal. It is illuminating and instructive to understand that there are certain things which we can do which will disappoint, pain, sadden, and offend the Holy Spirit. So also there are certain other things which we can do which will please, delight, and satisfy the Lord Jesus. Jesus was very careful to record the fact that, "… I do *always* those things that *please* him" (John 8:29). Paul reminded the children to obey their parents, "… for this is *well pleasing* unto the Lord" (Col. 3:20). The appeal is to an attitude, which is so in tune with God and His nature that a wholesome fear grips the heart and rules the conduct lest anything we do or say should cause sorrow or grief to Him. This is only possible in a love relationship, and it is the reason why Jesus said, "If ye keep my commandments, ye shall *abide* in my love …" (John 15:10). Nothing will be said or done which would pain or disappoint this tender (Dove-like) Divine love; and therefore, you remain (abide) in that unhindered and uninterrupted flow of love and communion. Fellowship is broken when someone is grieved; the tender chord is most sensitive to anything which offends or pains. This is in no way a negative proposition; it requires the most positive attitudes and actions to "grieve not" the Holy Spirit. It is an urgent appeal to avoid anything which is negative.

Paul very thoroughly traces the offences which will grieve the Holy Spirit earlier in this very chapter. He has said that we are to put off (cast away) the old man with his deeds (Col. 3:9). We are to put away lying (Eph. 4:25), and be truthful in our words and conversation. The Holy Spirit is designated, among other things, as "the Spirit of truth" at least four times in the New Testament. Any falsehood, deception, or deliberate lie will instantly grieve the Holy Spirit, and break fellowship and communion. He also speaks of anger and wrath. An unbridled temper is like an unbridled tongue, it runs wild like a wild horse which refuses bit and bridle. When the two combine, and they will in a fit of anger, the Holy Spirit is deeply grieved into pained silence. Thus the sign-posts are clearly marked enabling us to avoid the by-paths which grieve the Holy Spirit.

Thought For Today

An ungrieved presence produces an unhindered flow!

October 3

O. T. Bible Reading: Isaiah 27-28 **Our Focus: Isaiah 27:6**

FRUIT

The purpose of planting is the joy of reaping, "... Behold, the husbandman waiteth for the precious *fruit* of the earth, and hath long patience for it ..." (Jam. 5:7). Until now, weeds, thorns, and tares have by far outnumbered the precious fruit He intended. It will not always be so, for there is a day coming when the angel will emerge from the temple, and cry out with a loud voice, "... Thrust in thy sickle, and reap: for the time is come for thee to reap; for the harvest of the earth is ripe" (Rev. 14:15). Thus we see that God also has designed a harvest from this earth. There can be no ripened fruit unless there is maturity present and manifest in individual lives. If there were a group of 100 people, and the question were asked, "do they represent and include the quality and kind of fruit God has intended?" That group could never provide the answer as a corporate body, for the group could produce and manifest only what the individuals themselves possessed. An orchard never produced any fruit; it is only the production of each individual tree which constitutes the harvest. It is just as true regarding the great experience of salvation. No family, community, or church can be spoken of as born-again children of God until and unless each individual involved enjoys that personal experience.

What God has promised, He will certainly produce. The vineyard of which the prophet Isaiah speaks is the nation of Israel, "He shall cause them that come of *Jacob* to take root: *Israel* shall blossom and bud, and fill the face of the world with fruit" (Isa. 27:6). The fruit is godly life and conduct; it is judgment, justice, and righteousness, "Judgment also will I lay to the line, and righteousness to the plummet ..." (Isa. 28:17). God has not cast off His ancient people forever; they are promised a great restoration, not only to their own land, but also to the favor and blessing of God. They will be purged and cleansed from their pollutions, restored to His government, and from them shall flow His blessings to all peoples.

Thought For Today

God's promises are His pledges of fulfillment!

October 3

N. T. Bible Reading: Ephesians 5   **Our Focus: Ephesians 5:18**

BE FILLED

God does not provide starvation rations, nor does He intend that His people should settle for tiny portions. It is His plan that they should experience the reality of *His fulness*. Jesus carried with Him no doctor's bag; He never applied a bandage, nor a band-aid. He provided complete and total healing. Paul prayed for the Ephesian believers that, "... ye may *know* (personally experience) what is the hope of his calling ... And what is the exceeding greatness of his power to us-ward who believe ..." (Eph. 1:18-19). Again he earnestly prayed that they might "... *know* the love of Christ ... that ye might be filled with *all the fulness* of God" (Eph. 3:19). The word "*know*" means in the original, to *know fully*, to *experience* to *the utmost*.

There is also the thought of an ongoing process. We are commanded to be in the process of ever being filled and refilled to the point of overflowing. Williams translation seems to capture this blessed reality, "... but ever be filled with the Spirit ...." The tense is in the present progressive, "be ye being filled." This same truth is also emphasized in Acts 5:32, "... the Holy Ghost, whom God hath given to them that obey him." So, in the truest sense of reality, the measure of our fulness of the Holy Spirit is directly proportionate to the measure and completeness of our obedience.

Once again this brings the whole issue down to the level of human responsibility. It is up to us to yield ourselves to His inspection; to carefully heed His directions (mainly by and through the word of God), and to diligently follow His leadings. That is an individual and personal matter; no one else can do that for us, and the Lord Himself watches and waits for our response. Paul identifies two specific evidences or results of such a continuous relationship (Eph. 5:19-21):

    1.   The overflow of praise, which glorifies the Lord.
    2.   The spirit and attitude of mutual submission, which ministers to the needs of others.

Thought For Today

There is a new and greater fulness with every step of obedience!

October 4

O. T. Bible Reading: Isaiah 29-30   **Our Focus: Isaiah 29:23**

ISRAEL

Men carelessly speak of the Divine history of the human race, but the fact is, there is no such history. The Old Testament is the Divinely inspired record and history of the family of Abraham, and of the nation of which he was the father, Israel. The word "Israel" occurs over 750 times in the Bible, and by far the most of those references are in the Old Testament. Other nations are spoken of, but very few of them are named; only those that were near neighbors or who directly impacted the history of Israel. The call of Abraham fits in chronologically to the very center of the time between the creation of Adam and the life and death of the Lord Jesus. The entire record of the history of man from Adam to Abraham is dismissed, almost casually, in 11 brief chapters of the Bible. The Bible is the unfolding record of the drama of redemption. It is not just history, but history as it relates to God's great plan of salvation, and the nation of Israel was at the very heart of that plan.

There are three divisions of humanity as viewed from God's perspective; "… to the Jews, nor to the Gentiles, nor to the church of God" (I Cor. 10:32). The fact is clear and often repeated; "… to the Jew first …" (Rom. 2:10), and that because they were a chosen people for a Divine purpose (Deut. 14:2). The record of the nation of Israel falls clearly into three intervals:

1. The *selection* of Israel primarily relates to *the past*.
2. Their *rejection* relates to *the present*.
3. Their *restoration* relates to *the future*.

Herein lies one of the great mysteries of the New Testament, and one of the keys which unlock the Scriptures (Eph. 3:3-6; Rom. 11:25).

Isaiah issues his "woe" message to the "Ariel" which is the city of Jerusalem (Isa. 29:1). The word Ariel means "lion-like." Jerusalem was "… the city where David dwelt …" (Isa. 29:1), and the Lion is the insignia of that family. It is likely that Jerusalem has been besieged and captured more times than any other city; one writer lists 27 sieges. However, it is very important to remember that the rejection of Israel was neither total nor final; *they will* be restored (Rom.11:26; Isa. 27:9, 13).

Thought For Today

The Covenant of the Lord is certain of fulfillment!

October 4

N. T. Bible Reading: Ephesians 6   **Our Focus: Ephesians 6:14**

STAND THEREFORE

A little child must learn to stand before it can learn to walk. Both are skills which must be learned by experience. No amount of teaching or lectures could ever accomplish either one. It is included in the *process* of growth; and involves strength, balance, and co-ordination. Paul turns to one of the most basic skills as he concludes one of the most profound and advanced teachings of the entire Bible. From the sun-kissed peaks of the heavenlies, he brings us back down to one of the most fundamental of all physical functions, "*Stand* therefore ..." (Eph. 6:14).

This fact brings into focus a most important spiritual principle of truth. No matter how deep, profound, or lofty any teaching may be; it is of little or no real value if it does not contribute to the two most basic of human activities. It must empower and enable us *to stand* uprightly, confidently, and courageously. It must also inform, influence, and infuse us with Divine energy *to walk* in a new manner, on a new level, and with a new strength and vigor unknown before. This is the acid test of any theory or doctrine; what does it produce in the daily life and conduct of the one who believes it? "Wherefore by their *fruits* ye shall know them" (Matt. 7:20). This applies to the professors, but it also applies to their professions.

Paul urges the Ephesian saints to, "... *be strong* in the Lord, and in the power (or by the empowering) of *his might*" (Eph. 6:10). He adds, just a few verses later, "Stand therefore ..." (Eph. 6:14) in full armor, and in complete victory. Through the thunder of the raging battle, and the draining intensity of the conflict, "... having done all, *to stand*" (Eph. 6:13). Let nothing ever jolt us from the uprightness of our spiritual posture. It is *where* we stand, *how* we stand, and *when* we stand which constitutes our real testimony and our true effectiveness.

Thought For Today

Even those who learn to fly must first know how to land!

October 5

O. T. Bible Reading: Isaiah 31-33 **Our Focus: Isaiah 33:14**

THE FIRE

There are three basic cleansing agents in nature; they are water, wind, and fire. The first two are apparent and are recognized by almost everyone. The third is less obvious, but very much a part of the Divine scheme of things. There is a slow but inevitable process of a consuming fire in nature which produces the brilliant colors and tints of the autumn season. It also produces the rust on the nail and the corrosion on other metal objects. The world of science has a technical name for it; it is "eremacausis." It is defined in the dictionary as, "a slow combustion or oxidation of organic matter"; it is from the Greek words "erema", slowly; and "kausis", a burning. This unseen but unrelenting process goes on without intermission in the realm of nature. Just so in the spiritual realm, there is an eternal consuming fire which will eventually consume and destroy everything which is out of harmony with God's eternal purity.

The question of Isaiah 33:14 is, "... Who among us shall dwell with the devouring fire? who among us shall dwell with everlasting burnings?" The answer is given in the very next verse, "He that walketh righteously, and speaketh uprightly ... He shall *dwell* on high ..." (Isa. 33:15-16). The real test is the quality and integrity of the daily walk and conduct of life. This expresses itself in a conversation or life-style which is upright in appearance and righteous in principle.

Every element of truth consists of light and life, and each of these will always expose whatever is of evil and darkness. The universal expression of real genuine faith is prompt action, and a quick response: Abel "offered", Enoch "walked", Noah "built", Abraham "journeyed", Moses "chose", and Daniel "purposed." The universal ear-mark of unbelief is inaction and delay; and delay is disobedience in slow gear. Those who are enlightened are also energized and quickened.

Thought For Today

The essence of wisdom is to prevent problems not to solve them!

October 5

N. T. Bible Reading: Philippians 1   **Our Focus: Philippians 1:18**

I REJOICE

The Christian experience, and the experience of Christians, are not synonymous terms; nor are they always in harmony. To put it in the vernacular, all too many times the saints are "aints"; we believe in and talk cream, but we live skim milk. Paul is writing this Epistle from a prison in Rome, he is chained day and night to an assigned soldier; he has very few friends, and very many enemies. Yet the very heart of this epistle seems to be, "I rejoice, and I pray that you too are rejoicing." Paul transports us from the majestic heights of the "heavenlies" in Ephesians to a Roman prison in the book of Philippians. However, he is certainly not "*under* the circumstances." He, a prisoner of Rome, is triumphant and victorious "in Christ." It is significant that it was at Philippi that Paul and Silas were cast into prison. *Then* God sent a mighty earth-shaking and miraculous deliverance. *Now* he languishes in a Roman prison. In that atmosphere, but by no means imprisoned by it, he is rejoicing in the Lord and implores the saints at Philippi to do the same. Natural circumstances do not determine the experience of God's people, nor should they be allowed to affect it.

Some writers claim the words "joy" and "rejoice", or their equivalent occur 19 times in these brief four chapters, and that the name of "Jesus Christ" is used 40 times. There is a vital connection. Joy is not the real theme; it is the product. The Lord Jesus is both the source and the supplier of our joy; it does not come from cozy circumstances. Christian joy is much more than happiness, because it does not depend on what "happens"; it flows from a risen Savior!

To rejoice is to express joy; joy is a fruit of the Spirit (Gal. 5:22), and it is not a product of anything earthly. It is the overflow of a Divine relationship expressed in harmony and singing. Joy truly is "paradise restored"; it is the realization of that for which we were originally created. Jesus declared that His joy was to do and to accomplish the will of God (John 4:34). His desire for us is, "… that *my joy* might remain in you, and that *your joy* might be *full*" (John 15:11). When "*His joy*" is "*our joy*"; then, and only then, will it be *full*.

Thought For Today

When Jesus fills our lives, our joy will then be full!

October 6

O. T. Bible Reading: Isaiah 34-36   **Our Focus: Isaiah 35:8**

THE WAY OF HOLINESS

God is holy; He is referred to as "*the* Holy One" at least 20 times in the Bible. He is more specifically called "the Holy One of Israel" about 31 times (23 of those in Isaiah alone). The word "holy" is first found in Exodus 3:5. It is not found in the book of Genesis, which is a book of beginnings. Exodus is the book which opens up the theme of redemption, and has been designated as "the book of redemption." Mankind is ignorant of God, and therefore, almost never uses the word holy except as related to some religious ceremony or individuals, falsely so-called. It is only on the ground of redemption that humanity can ever comprehend or grasp the true meaning of holiness. For this reason, one of the eternal unions of Scripture is, "… faith and charity and holiness …" (I Tim. 2:15). It is "… the Spirit of holiness …" alone that makes real the true meaning and message of holiness (Rom. 1:4); and even more so the glorious possibilities of worshiping "… the Lord in the beauty of holiness" (Ps. 29:2, 96:9).

Holiness is the opposite of uncleanness; and much more to be desired. That is why the book of Leviticus, which was the priests guide-book for worship and communion, the word "holy" will be found 150 times, and the two words "clean" or "unclean" 186 times. Every sacrifice was to be carefully examined and they were to offer only that which was "without blemish." Those sacrifices were symbolic; they pictured *The One* who would come and offer Himself without spot (Heb. 9:14); He was truly that *One* and only blessed "… fountain opened to (in) the house of David … for sin and for uncleanness" (Zech. 13:1).

"… The way of holiness …" (Isa. 35:8) is the way *to* God, and it is the way *of* God. Those, and only those, who are redeemed (Isa. 35:9) shall *walk* in that way. The Bible uses the word "walk" and its derivatives over 500 times, and the word "talk" about 50 times. Why is there not 10 times more emphasis on the walk than on the profession (talk)? It is for the "… ransomed of the Lord …" to discover and forever sing "… songs and everlasting joy …" (Isa. 35:10). They have come to know *Him* who is holy, and have found His way to be "… The way of holiness …" (Isa. 35:8).

Thought For Today

Those who find Him have also discovered the way of holiness!

October 6

N. T. Bible Reading: Philippians 2   **Our Focus: Philippians 2:25**

EPAPHRODITUS

It could be said of many politicians, and perhaps of a few preachers, what Winston Churchill once said of one of his political opponents, "he has a genius for compressing a minimum of thought into a maximum of words." The very opposite can be said of the great Apostle Paul, and of the method of the Lord. When God speaks, His words are usually few but their message is almost beyond words to explain, "… This is my beloved Son, in whom I am well pleased; hear ye him" (Matt. 17:5). Few words, but a volume could be written on their meaning and message. Paul also says volumes in one small concentrated sentence, "… Epaphroditus, my brother, and companion in labour, and fellowsoldier, but your messenger (Angel), and he that ministered to my wants" (Phil. 2:25).

"My brother" (Phil. 2:25), surely that has great meaning! He was an individual identified with Paul as to origin of life; he was united by a common birth, by a common parenthood, by common family ties, by common interests and vision, by a common call and commission, by a mutual commitment to walk the same road and follow the same guide. He was also a "brother" in Christ, born into the same heavenly relationship by the miracle of the new birth. This new life is much stronger than any natural kinship, and forever shatters the man-made barriers. It makes all such new creatures in Christ dear members of the same family, the family of God.

Paul called his companion both a "fellow-worker" and a "fellow-soldier." It has often been said that zeal without knowledge is bad; but quite frankly, I have felt many times that knowledge without zeal is much more common, and equally dangerous. Lazy saints are like dry trees in the forest; they are perfect firewood, but much too far from the fire. He was also a "fellow-soldier"; he had been with Paul, not in boot-camp, but in the trenches. Those who are united in battle know a kinship which is foreign to all others.

Thought For Today

Those who are united in Christ, have the closest possible bond!

196

October 7

O. T. Bible Reading: Isaiah 37-38   **Our Focus: Isaiah 38:17**

IN LOVE

"The love of God" is a New Testament phrase and revelation; it occurs 13 times in the New Testament only. The revelation was a manifestation; we could not know nor could we understand "the love of God" except as it was manifest or expressed in the person, work, sufferings, and death of the Lord Jesus; "In this was manifested (revealed and clearly shown) the love of God toward us, because that God sent his only begotten Son into the world, that we might live through him" (I John 4:9).

Isaiah chapter 38 records the recovery of king Hezekiah, and the answer to his tearful prayer; 15 years were added to his life, and the sun-dial reversed itself by 10 degrees as a sign. In his song of gratitude and thanksgiving, he makes a great statement of New Testament truth; literally he declared, "... thou hast in love to my soul delivered it from the pit of corruption ..." (Isa. 38:17). This statement is a beautiful and graphic description of the Divine activity in the plan of salvation. All that God ever initiated and undertook in redemption was "in love", "by love", and "through love." Love was the fountain, love was the channel, love is the stream, and love is the agent. God has truly loved our souls out of the pit of corruption, involving but a measure of suffering for us, but of infinitely greater suffering and cost to Himself as expressed at Calvary. Truly, "love won at Calvary", and just as truly, "love continues to win through Calvary."

This fathomless fountain of love must continue to flow and manifest itself through yielded vessels to an unbelieving world. It is this sacrificial and dynamic "love of God" which is "... shed abroad (pours forth as an overflowing stream) in (all) our hearts by the Holy Ghost which is given unto us" (Rom. 5:5). This can only be experienced where there is an uninterrupted *flow*. The love is in the flow, and it is the flow which loves us out of the pit of corruption.

Thought For Today

The Love of God rescues and transforms all who experience it!

October 7

N. T. Bible Reading: Philippians 3   **Our Focus: Philippians 3:14**

I PRESS

Paul uses the familiar picture of an athlete expending full energy, straining every muscle, and demanding maximum effort to win the race. There was a great amphitheater in Ephesus which seated 100,000 people. The Olympic Games were held there at certain times, and Paul spent over three years in that city. He often used these events to picture the Christian race, and those who will win the ultimate prize, the high calling. Not all athletes of that time were qualified to compete at that level, and only the very best of those selected would win. The long process of preparation required commitment, dedication, discipline, and great personal sacrifice. It is a beautiful illustration of the New Testament standard for the Christian life and experience.

All that was intended and meant in the exercise of this "… press …" we may never fully know (Phil. 3:14). However, there are some aspects of it which are quite clearly indicated. The Apostle Paul reminds the saints at Philippi that he "… counted …" (Phil. 3:7), and then 30 years later he is continuing to "… count …" (Phil. 3:8). The word which is translated "count" means to lead the way, to set the pace, and to march at the front of a troop. It has to do, not with the great physical strains of the athlete, but with the transformed mental attitude and actions of a victorious Christian. It is of utmost importance how we start out; Daniel, we are told, "… *purposed* in his heart …" (Dan. 1:8); Moses "*Choosing* rather to suffer …", and in the process "… refused …" certain other opportunities (Heb. 11:24-25); and now Paul adds his "*counted*" and continues to "count" (Phil. 3:7-8). Each of these mental exercises was basic to the victorious result.

Unprotected strength is utter weakness. We are never at more peril than when we are resting on some past experience. When we are able to express the great realities and experiences of yesterday, in terms of today; then and only then, are they of any real and practical value, "… I counted …" (Phil. 3:7) and even now I continue to "… count …" (Phil 3:8). Blessed indeed, is the experience of those who continue to add to the "I counted" of the original *revelation*, the "I count" of the present attitude and commitment. It is the set of the mind which will determine the depth of the relationship.

Thought For Today

A great beginning is but a contribution to a triumphant ending!

October 8

O. T. Bible Reading: Isaiah 39-40   **Our Focus: Isaiah 40:1**

COMFORT MY PEOPLE

The 66 chapters of Isaiah, like the 66 books of the Bible, are easily divided into two parts. The first 39 chapters of the Bible we know as the Old Testament; the first 39 chapters of Isaiah deal primarily with the thought of judgment on the covenant people of Israel for their disobedience to the law. Just as the New Testament message primarily emphasizes the truths of salvation as seen in the mercy and grace of God; so also the final 27 chapters of Isaiah focus on the yet future restoration and salvation of Israel, which has been called "the Messianic poem." Scholars have also found the last 27 chapters divided into three sections of nine chapters; the first two ending with identical words, "There is no peace, saith the Lord, unto the wicked" (Isa. 48:22 and 57:21). Also of great significance, the central chapter (53) of the middle 9 chapters is the great "Lamb" chapter, with its most graphic picture of the atonement and redemption of Calvary. By design God has made the Lord Jesus (The Lamb) the very center of prophecy, history, and redemption; let us be careful to keep Him at the center of our preaching, teaching, thinking, and daily living.

The section begins with the Divine directive: "Comfort ye, comfort ye my people, saith your God" (Isa. 40:1). The Word of God reveals God as: "... the Father of mercies, and the God of all comfort" (II Cor. 1:3); the Holy Spirit is designated as: "... the Comforter ..." (John 14:26). The "woes" and the "burdens" of the first division of Isaiah are passed; now (prophetically) the time will have come to: "Speak ye comfortably to Jerusalem ..." (Isa. 40:2).

All heathen and false religions attempt to appease the anger and displeasure of their gods by bringing offerings and gifts to present to them. It is just at this point that Christianity is forever separated and made unique among all religions. That difference is defined by two great words, "propitiation" and "reconciliation": "... Christ Jesus: Whom God hath set forth to be a *propitiation* ..." (Rom. 3:24-25); "... we were *reconciled* to God by the death of his Son ..." (Rom. 5:10). That is the only basis upon which "comfort" may be offered; either to Israel, or to any individual.

Thought For Today

Comfort is experienced by all who "come-forth" to Him!

October 8

N. T. Bible Reading: Philippians 4   **Our Focus: Philippians 4:13**

THROUGH CHRIST

The "I can ..." of Philippians 4:13 is qualified by the phrase "... through Christ ..."; that phrase is further qualified by yet another oft-repeated phrase, "in Christ" (mentioned more than 70 times). Even that great phrase will be found to be qualified by two very simple words, "by faith"; those two dynamic words are found 41 times in the Bible, and 15 times in Hebrews chapter 11 alone. It is faith which transforms the promises into prophecies. It is so much more than "*positive thinking*", it is also "*positive living*" made possible by a "*positive relationship*" with the Lord Jesus Himself.

Many have found and claimed the promised "I can ..." (Phil. 4:13), only to be disappointed, and sometimes disillusioned when they found out that they couldn't. There are conditions which apply to any contract or covenant; and sometimes they are found only in the "fine print", but they are there and they are basic to the entire transaction. The "... all things ..." of Philippians 4:13 are those things which relate to and result from a personal relationship of being "in Christ." It limits itself to those things which are related to the will of God, and the eternal principles by which He operates. It is entirely true that we can do all things which He asks or requires us to do. God's commands are also His enablings. We cannot go outside of His will, and claim or expect His provision and the fulfillment of His precious promises; that is neither the plan nor the promise.

The powerful locomotives of the train are mighty in their pulling of long columns of cars loaded with heavy contents. Steep grades are climbed, mountain inclines are surmounted, and mile after mile of almost endless stretches of countryside are easily and quickly passed through. All of this amazing accomplishment is made possible by a very simple fact; the train must remain *on the tracks*. It is useless and powerless when it leaves the tracks. So also are we when we are not "... in the way ..." (Gen. 24:27).

Thought For Today

It is the connection which assures the flow of power!

October 9

O. T. Bible Reading: Isaiah 41-42　　　　　　　　**Our Focus: Isaiah 41:1**

KEEP SILENCE

When once we learn to talk, we have another great lesson to learn; there are times when we are to keep silent. This will take much longer to learn, and very few will ever master the art. You cannot talk and listen at the same time. There are many times when it would be very much in our best interests to listen. The Psalmist seems to grasp this fact when he said: "Be still, and know that I am God …" (Ps. 46:10). A more literal translation of Isaiah 41:1 would be, "in silence listen to Me", and that is the only way we will ever be able to hear Him.

There are a myriad of voices all clamoring for our attention in this world. The loud voices of pleasure and entertainment; the subtle and alluring voices of power and prestige; the clamoring voices of friends and associates; the demanding voices of business and industry; and the *still small voice* of the Lord. The other voices may be heard above the din and chatter, but the voice of the Lord will only be detected in the silence when all is still and we are quiet. This is not primarily a matter of physical posture nor even of the environment. It is more a matter of inward condition and the spiritual attitude of the mind. There is a fine line here, and the balance will not be quickly or easily found.

Abraham we are told, "pitched his tent having Bethel on the west (the direction of the sunset), and Ai on the east (the direction of the sunrise): and there he builded an altar" (Gen. 12:8). Bethel will be found to represent worship and communion with God; Ai on the contrary, speaks of the world around us (the word "Ai" means, a mass or a heap). The altar must be built between the two. There is a balance. Life cannot always be lived in Bethel, nor must we allow it to be lived entirely in Ai. We are *in* the world, but not *of* the world; we must not be so heavenly minded that we are of no earthly use. The most difficult thing in the world is to keep balanced.

Thought For Today

A quiet resignation is the key to keeping silence!

October 9

N. T. Bible Reading: Colossians 1 **Our Focus: Colossians 1:27**

THE HOPE OF GLORY

There is a world of difference between earthly glory and heavenly glory, and it is just that which makes the difference. The earth is the realm of mortal existence. It is marked by man; it is limited *to* humanity, and in that sense, is also limited *by* humanity. As the Scriptures define it, "... that which is natural ... is of the earth, earthly ..." (I Cor. 15:46-47). It is bounded by and limited to that of which it is constituted. That is a hopeless plight. The glory (of a heavenly source) of the Gospel truths is also their strength. They originated from God, are the product of His might; and therefore, emanate and impart that very might to those who experience it.

This is one of the mysteries of the New Testament (Col. 1:27). Among the many Old Testament Messianic prophecies there is nothing said about His *indwelling* presence. Paul clearly states that this New Testament revelation and the secret of it, is now made known. He just as clearly declares that there are vast treasures and riches wrapped up in the package: "To whom God would make known what is *the riches* of *the glory* of this mystery ..." (Col. 1:27).

Earlier in this first chapter of Colossians, verse 11, the Apostle prayed that these Colossian believers might be quickened and enlightened so as to comprehend and thus be mightily fortified and "Strengthened with all might, according to his glorious power ...." Another more literal translation gives it as: "... empowered by the might of His glory." That which comes from the *Almighty God* is infused with *His might*. It is heavenly in origin, and therefore, His strength and might are the very ingredients of which it is constituted. Human or earthly glory is temporary and transient by virtue of its very weakness. When once God's glory is seen, it becomes the passion of the life, and in the very vision there is the ingredient of heavenly strength, and in the effort put forth to experience it, is realized the very energy of which it consists.

Thought For Today

Hope realized makes the vision of it a reality!

October 10

O. T. Bible Reading: Isaiah 43-44   **Our Focus: Isaiah 43:1**

BUT NOW

The word "but" carries with it the basic thought of "on the contrary." Something has totally changed, and therefore, to add the word "now" defines the emphasis of the difference as relating primarily to time; "then" some condition or interval having to do with *the past*; "now" a completely changed time and circumstance of *the present*. Thus it is in Isaiah chapter 43.

The great prophet Isaiah has, by prophetic foresight, given us a panoramic view of the Divine plan involved in the proclamation "Behold my servant ..." (Isa. 42:1). The words "But now ..." (Isa. 43:1) form the link between the "manifesto of Jehovah" and the series of messages which are to follow. Each message will be directly marked off by the introductory words, "... thus saith the Lord ..." (Isa. 43:1-10, 14, 16). There are 4 such messages in Isaiah chapter 43. Each of these proclamations are directly tied to, and only made possible by, the fact that Jehovah has commissioned "His Servant."

The first of the significant insights is contained in Isaiah 43, verses 1-9. The Divine relationship to Israel as their Creator and Redeemer (Isa. 43:1) is declared to be the very guarantee of their hope and His pledge that in a yet future day He will "... bring thy seed from the east, and *gather* thee from the west" (Isa. 43:5). Verses 10-13 (of Isa. 43) contain the second message; it is that they (Israel) will yet fulfill His original purpose as they become His witnesses (Isa. 43:10, 12). It is emphasized that all of this will be realized by them only because of who He is and what He will yet accomplish. The third (Isa. 43:14-15) outlines the sure overthrow and destruction of Babylon, both the natural Babylon, and finally the religious Babylon also. He is Redeemer, Creator, and King, and every false pretender will one day be destroyed. The fourth promise is in verses 16-28 which envisions "... a new thing ..." (Isa. 43:19). All of this is predicated by "but now." There will come a day when these visionary prophecies will become reality; when the nation has been purged and purified. The New Testament outlines so many spiritual benefits for God's people by declaring, "but now" and it is gloriously true for us "... *now* is the accepted time ..." (II Cor. 6:2).

Thought For Today

God's revealed season for salvation is "now!"

October 10

N. T. Bible Reading: Colossians 2   **Our Focus: Colossians 2:2**

ALL RICHES

Paul wrote to the church in Colosse to correct two errors which were prevalent in that area, and which had begun to filter into the church. They had a peculiar Greek philosophy known as Gnosticism, and a zealous Jewish traditionalism. The Gnostics essentially said that all matter is evil; therefore, man's problems had nothing to do with the will, but were problems of the mind, and they claimed a superior wisdom ... "they had cornered wisdom in a jug and held the cork in their hand." Water is an essential element of life; it may be frozen, then it is ice; it may also be boiled, then it is steam. That has been, and still is, the problem which every church faces. Too much tradition, forms, rituals, or just plain ruts of repetitious exercises will freeze any church into icy regularity in a frozen and dead atmosphere. The other extreme is to over-emphasize the mind and what feeds the mind; doctrines, theories, ideas, and the intellectualism of mere head-knowledge which will create steam and vapor (hot air). No one can drink ice, nor can they swallow steam. What is needed is "the *Water* of Life" (Rev. 21:6, 22:17).

The book of Colossians, therefore, rivets our attention to Christ, who is *The Head* of the body. He is the fulness of God expressed to humanity. Only "in Him" dwells the very fullness and completeness of wisdom. Apart from Him all else is poverty, waste, and emptiness. In Him are riches (real wealth) beyond comprehension (unsearchable ... Eph. 3:8) which are so vast they can never be fully explored; you cannot count or measure them; you cannot by any mortal means of thought or projection estimate them; and your investigation of them will be endless. Christ is all, and in Him are all the riches of Divine provision hidden and stored.

Material accumulations generally referred to as riches, are subject to moth, rust, decay, and suddenly being vaporized. "True riches" (those that survive every earthly calamity) are to be found only in Christ (Luke 16:11). The alabaster box of very precious and costly ointment needs but to be opened for all to enjoy the fragrance. The attractive attributes and loveliness of the Lord Jesus must be opened up for all to enjoy. It is both our great privilege and solemn responsibility to do just that for a world sickened by the nauseous odors of time and sense.

Thought For Today

The true riches are hidden to those who are without eye-salve!

October 11

O. T. Bible Reading: Isaiah 45-47   **Our Focus: Isaiah 46:4**

I CARRY

When men make an idol, that idol must be carried by the very people who fabricated it. The true God created us, we are His creatures, and therefore, He is also able to carry us.

The two primary gods of Babylon were Bel and Nebo. Bel was the chief idol, and seems to be an abbreviation of Baal, also called by historians "Jupiter Belus"; the word Nebo means "speaker or prophet." At Lystra, Paul and Barnabas were surmised by the people to be the combination of these two gods. Barnabas, they thought of as Bel or Jupiter; Paul was characterized as Mercury or Nebo because he was the spokesman. The Medo-Persian armies reduced these images of gold, silver, and brass to piles of valuable metallic rubble which they crated and carried on their beasts of burden to their homeland. The idols were dumb and defenseless. These false symbols of idolatry could neither help nor deliver their makers, but themselves became a burden to their captors. Every false god and every form of spiritual idolatry is but a burden to those who embrace it. That is why the invitation of the Mighty Creator, The Living God, is to all who are heavy laden "Come … Take my yoke upon you … and ye shall find rest unto your souls" (Matt. 11:28-29).

The contrasts could not be more graphic nor could it be any greater. It is God Himself who declares emphatically: I created … I called you by name "… even to your old age I am he; and even to hoar hairs will *I carry you*: I have made, and I will bear; even I will carry, and will deliver you" (Isa. 46:4). He is supreme, absolute in power and in strength, and has pledged Himself and His unlimited resources to us for personal victory.

An Idol is a fabrication of man, either literally or spiritually, and must be carried by the one who made it. Man is the creation of God, and God alone is able to carry that man. Men create false gods and false concepts of God when they turn from God and from His Word. This always becomes a heavy burden and an encumbrance from which there is neither relief nor respite. He who embraces his *Savior* also finds his Creator, he dumps his burden on Him, and is carried by Him rejoicing in his new-found rest for his weary soul (Matt. 11:28-30).

Thought For Today

Rest is the difference between carrying and being carried!

October 11

N. T. Bible Reading: Colossians 3   **Our Focus: Colossians 3:1-2, 5**

SEEK – SET – MORTIFY

When we read and study the third chapter of Colossians we cannot help but think of the familiar race-track words of instruction: "gentlemen, start your engines." Anyone who imagines the Christian life to be a rocking chair, flower-strewn, bed-of-ease dreamland need only read this chapter to return from fantasy to the real world. These 25 verses are laced with verbs, spiced with action words, and like the barking signals of the Drill- Sergeant, demand an immediate, intense, and whole-hearted response. It is a summons to a battle-field, not a lullaby for a nursery, nor is it a lilting ditty for the recreation room. This is bare-knuckles, down-home, real-world reality where the rubber hits the road and the dream world of theories and philosophies comes to a sudden and wrenching halt. The Australian poet, Adam Lindsay Gordon, wrote:

> Life is mostly froth and bubble
> Two things stand like stone
> KINDNESS in another's trouble
> COURAGE in your own

The bubbles burst in Colossians chapter three!

The whole admonition is prefaced with the tiny preposition "If ..." (Col. 3:1); however, it is not an "if" of relationship; it is a strong and persuasive preposition "since." This is the basis for a very powerful argument demanding an exciting, enthusiastic, urgent, and whole-hearted response. Such is the meaning of the word used in Colossians 3:1 for "seek."

The word "Mortify ..." in Colossians 3:5 means: "to put to death or to make dead", and has been translated by Williams as "so once for all put to death." We must get serious about the project; it is not child's play ... it is grim reality, and it requires a decisive course of action based upon an all-out commitment. It is not surprising that sexual immorality tops the list of sordid evils that must get the axe. This is the devil's strongest chain, and it must be dealt with immediately and with unreserved determination. Purity is the goal, and holiness is the beautiful fruit.

Thought For Today

The call of God shatters ease and smothers complacency!

October 12

O. T. Bible Reading: Isaiah 48-49   **Our Focus: Isaiah 48:22**

NO PEACE

Truths of great importance are underlined by emphasis and repetition in the Scriptures. The very same words are repeated in Isaiah 57:21; "There is no peace, saith my God, to the wicked." Like a concentrated formula in a capsule, God gives us a clear and positive explanation for the absence of peace in the troubled and turbulent world; and with it the equation for peace in this world and the promised world of tomorrow. The basic law of cause and effect was never in clearer focus. There is a primary cause for the violence, warfare, grief, sorrow, and suffering in this present evil world. The culprit is wickedness and evil.

"Righteousness exalteth a nation: but sin is a reproach to any people" (Prov. 14:34). "But the wicked are like the troubled sea, when it cannot rest, whose waters cast up mire and dirt" (Isa. 57:20). "Take away the wicked from before the king, and his throne shall be established in righteousness" (Prov. 25:5). "For there is no faithfulness in their mouth; their inward part is very wickedness ... they have rebelled against thee" (Ps. 5:9-10). "For out of the heart proceed evil thoughts, murders, adulteries, fornications, thefts, false witness, blasphemies" (Matt. 15:19). "From whence come wars and fightings among you? come they not hence, even of your lusts that war in your members?" (Jam. 4:1). It is both an indictment and revelation, "There is no peace, saith my God, to the wicked" (Isa. 57:21).

Thank God there is another reverse side, and we can wash our ears and our mind out with God's proven antiseptic: "And the work of righteousness shall be peace; and *the effect* of righteousness quietness and assurance forever" (Isa. 32:17). "They shall not hurt nor destroy in all my *holy* mountain: for the earth shall be full of the knowledge of the Lord, as the waters cover the sea" (Isa. 11:9). "And God shall wipe away all tears from their eyes; and there shall be no more death, neither sorrow, nor crying, neither shall there be any more pain: for the former things are passed away" (Rev. 21:4). Only the personal return of the Prince of Peace will ever bring universal peace to *the world*. His coming to reign and rule in the hearts and lives of His people, brings peace *individually* to those who know Him, whom to know aright is life eternal (John 17:3).

Thought For Today

The peace of God __rules__, where the Prince of Peace __reigns__!

October 12

N. T. Bible Reading: Colossians 4   **Our Focus: Colossians 4:17**

FULFILL IT

A good beginning is great, but it is just the beginning; a good ending is of even greater importance, because it is the conclusion or summation ... the final result; the bottom line. Many start a race, some with great promise and potential, but not all finish a race, much less win it. To fulfill, as used in the Scriptures, is to fill up or complete; it is to fill up, and to keep filled up to the very completion. Paul urges Archipus, mentioned only here and in Philemon 2 as a "fellow-soldier", to take care that he fulfill the ministry which the Lord had given him. We do not know specifically what his calling or gift may have been, but apparently he heeded the admonition. Tradition maintains that he was one of the 70 disciples whom Jesus dispatched, and was martyred at Chonae, near Laodicea.

Many are surprised to learn that the word "stick-to-it-ive-ness" is actually in the dictionary. The meaning is "unwavering tenacity", and tenacity is holding firmly and faithfully until completion. Tenacity is more than endurance; it includes the element of inspired zeal fired by vision. It is the contagious quality of enthusiasm, perpetuated and maintained by confidence, and certainty of ultimate and victorious completion. It is the fire which burned in the hearts of the early church; it is the glowing inspiration which fuelled and inflamed the great reformers; it is the Divinely imparted passion which drove the overcoming saints to the very peak of Mount Zion from which they shout and sing: "... *thou* hast redeemed us ... *thou* hast made us unto our God kings and priests: and *we shall reign* ..." (Rev. 5:9-10).

To fulfill is much more than "hanging on", that could be little more than the weakness of fearing to fall off. It is "keeping on", and the extra fortitude to "keep on keeping on." It is what sets the over-achiever apart from all others; he is a man with a mission. He is infused with just enough of the Divine to "see the end from the beginning"; at least enough of it to keep him pressing on the upward way, and to fulfill his calling.

Thought For Today

A true vision also includes and magnifies the goal!

October 13

O. T. Bible Reading: Isaiah 50-52   **Our Focus: Isaiah 50:7**

LIKE A FLINT

The greatest example of commitment in the entire Bible is the Lord Jesus Himself. There are others which stood out as exemplary, but His was absolute and complete. Prophesy had pin-pointed this outstanding attribute: "Then said I, Lo, I come: in the volume of the book it is written of me, I delight to do thy will, O my God: yea, thy law is within my heart" (Ps. 40:7-8). Luke carefully and accurately gives us the singular picture of the Lord as He drove steadily forward to complete His mission: "... he steadfastly _set his face_ to go to Jerusalem" (Luke 9:51). We wonder did Luke have the clear and defining prophecy of Isaiah in mind when he recorded: "... therefore have I set my face like a flint ..." (Isa. 50:7). It is very easy for me to believe that he did.

Jesus told the bewildered disciples: "... My meat is to do the will of him that sent me, and to finish his work" (John 4:34). It was not only what He feasted upon; it was also the one thing which consumed Him. A wise person will never _fully_ trust anything but the grace of God in himself or in any one else. When anything or any person, on the human level, is the object of absolute trust we will be disappointed. No one is _absolutely_ right; therefore, sooner or later they will let you down. We become bitter, disillusioned, and if we are not careful and prayerful we will become cynical and despair of everyone. Jesus trusted God implicitly and without reservation, and He was never disappointed. The posted sign near the cash register of the old Country Store sums it up very well: "in God we trust ... all others pay cash."

Hesitation and delay are symptoms of doubt; doubt is unbelief in disguise. Confidence is a product of certainty; and manifests itself in calm assurance, unqualified trust, and consistent steadfastness of purpose and life. We should never begin until we are sure; once we are sure, we should never stop. Jesus was certain of the outcome before His mission ever began. He had God's Word on it, and the triumphant completion was never in doubt. Therefore, He set His face as a flint (Isa. 50:7), and by His grace and with His help, we may do the same.

Thought For Today

The direction is in doubt until the sail has been set!

October 13

N. T. Bible Reading: I Thessalonians 1 **Our Focus: I Thessalonians 1:3**

LABOR OF LOVE

Paul seems to specialize in trios. He concludes this first epistle to the Thessalonians with a comprehensive view of the creation and constitution of man: "… I pray God your whole *spirit* and *soul* and *body* be preserved blameless unto the coming of our Lord Jesus Christ" (I Thess. 5:23). In I Thessalonians 1:3 he lumps the three primary Christian graces of which he spoke in I Corinthians 13:13: "And now abideth (remaineth) faith, hope, charity, these three; but the greatest of these is charity." He combines them with the three divisions of time; past, present, and future. The anatomy of the Christian life in a capsule is:

1. The work of faith is past tense.
2. The labor of love is present tense.
3. The patience of hope is future tense.

The labor of love is the meat of the sandwich. The bottom slice of bread is faith; the top slice is hope; and this makes for a very spiritually nutritious lunch. As is his custom, Paul skillfully transposes this from the abstract to the concrete.

Perhaps you have read of the kind father who often said he loved children when large numbers flocked into his yard to play with his own. He poured a much-needed sidewalk one afternoon, and finished it before darkness fell. He was very irritated early the next morning to find an array of tiny footprints deeply etched in his work of art. His good wife reminded him of his repeated claim to love the little people. He quickly responded, "yes, and I do love them in the abstract, but not in the concrete." Paul now gets both feet into the concrete.

He summarizes the thought in I Thessalonians chapter 1 verses 9 and 10: "… ye turned … from idols …", which is the work of faith; "… to serve the living and true God", which is the labor of love; "… to wait for his Son from heaven …", which is the patience of hope. The labor is where the rubber hits the road. D. L. Moody returned home exhausted from an extended series of meetings, and was urged by his family to cut back on his schedule. His response is a perpetual challenge for all of us, "I *am* weary *in* this great work, but I am not in the least weary *of* the work."

Thought For Today

It is in the labor where the faith is measured!

October 14

O. T. Bible Reading: Isaiah 53-55   **Our Focus: Isaiah 53:11**

SATISFIED

"He … shall be satisfied …" (Isa. 53:11); these may be the most rewarding and calming words in the Scriptures. They bring a sense of relief and rejoicing beyond definition. To satisfy is to gratify or to fulfill; satisfaction is compensation for injury or loss. How thrilling to know that one day He who suffered the most, will be fully rewarded with total and complete gratifying joy.

Isaiah chapter 53 outlines and unveils the sufferings and the agony of Christ in a more graphic way than any of the four Gospel accounts. They seem to treat it with such awe and reverence, that they feared the sacredness of the event might be compromised or diluted by exposure. But here the veil is rent and momentarily, in a single minute (the entire chapter can be read in just one minute) of stunned silence, we see the cost of redemption in the suffering Savior. The awful reality that the spotless Lamb of God was "… made … sin for us, *who knew no sin*; that we might be made the righteousness of God in him" (II Cor. 5:21). We cannot escape the piercing truth; it was "*our*" sin and guilt for which He suffered, bled, and died. The personal pronouns "He, Him, and His" recur, like trip-hammer blows, at least 47 times in 12 brief verses. The finger of guilt points directly to each one of us; "our" is used 5 times in just two verses (Isa. 53:5-6), and "we" is inserted 5 times in Isaiah 53:3-6. The middle verse (Isa. 53:6) begins and ends with the words "all" and "we all." There is no escape, the entire human family is involved in the crime; yet, amazing mystery, it is through His ignominious death that "… we are healed" (Isa. 53:5).

It is the ultimate outcome, not the present distress, which will bring supreme joy to our blessed Savior: "… who for the joy that was set before him endured the cross …" (Heb. 12:2). He passes through pain to fulfillment, through travail to triumph, through rejection to rejoicing, and through grief to gratification. The ultimate completeness of His satisfaction is yet in the future; however, there is "… joy shall be in heaven (which certainly must include Him) over one sinner that repenteth …" (Luke 15:7). How satisfying and rewarding to know that there is deep satisfaction, even now, in every life which is yielded to His control, and manifests the miracle of redemption in their daily conduct. Surely this is one of the greatest possible incentives to live our lives on the highest possible level.

Thought For Today

He is gratified and satisfied as we are transformed into His image!

October 14

N. T. Bible Reading: I Thessalonians 2   **Our Focus: I Thessalonians 2:12**

WALK WORTHY

There are three New Testament passages which urge us to walk worthy; Ephesians 4:1; Colossians 1:10; I Thessalonians 2:12. They specifically admonish us to, "… walk worthy of the vocation wherewith ye are called" (Eph. 4:1); "… walk worthy of the Lord unto all pleasing, being fruitful in every good work, and increasing in the knowledge of God" (Col. 1:10); "… walk worthy of God, who hath called you unto his kingdom and glory" (I Thess. 2:12). Surely, we can say that we have been called with a high and a holy calling (Phil. 3:14; II Tim. 1:9). The call is clear, the will of God is revealed and recorded; it now remains only for us to fulfill the Divinely intended manner of life. This is where the daily walk and conduct become the determining factor. God has designed the plan, He has prepared the blue-print for the building, He also has provided the equipment necessary for the project; only we can complete the beautiful formula for victory and success … we must take the steps of obedience and walk the walk.

Much is involved in *how* we walk, *when* we walk, and *where* we walk. It is a fact that everything that has to do with life and godliness is involved. It means we are to, "… walk in *his paths* … and … in *his ways* …" (Isa. 2:3, 42:24). We are to walk *in the light*, and as children of light (Isa. 2:5; Eph. 5:14). We are also to walk honestly, and in newness of life, and thus to walk circumspectly (Rom. 13:13; Eph. 5:15; Rom. 6:4). We are to walk in the Spirit, to walk in love, and to walk in wisdom (Gal. 5:16; Eph. 5:2; Col. 4:5). There is much more, but this should be sufficient to keep us well occupied for today.

It is at the level of the walk where either success or failure will be recorded. If there is defeat or failure, the problem is not far removed, nor difficult to detect. It is clearly to be found in the steps we took, forward or backward, in response to the truth. To back away from any revelation of precept or principle, is to step away from light and into darkness and confusion. To step forward in that new light, is to emerge from the shadows into His marvelous light and into a glorious personal walk with God.

Thought For Today

The clearly marked way of life is <u>straight</u> ahead!

October 15

O. T. Bible Reading: Isaiah 56-58   **Our Focus: Isaiah 56:1**

MY SALVATION

Salvation is an Old Testament word as well as a New Testament revelation. The word is used nearly 200 times in the Scriptures. "My salvation" is repeated approximately 30 times, and "thy salvation" another 27 times. It has at least eight applications and shades of meaning, and is worthy of careful study. The defining word, "my" restricts the scope and pretty clearly identifies what is being considered. It is first used in Exodus 15:2, "The Lord is *my* strength and song, and he is become *my* salvation …", the context is clear and obvious; the miracle of the Red Sea passage had just taken place. It was Divine deliverance in the truest sense of the word, and that is the heart of salvation. If there is no deliverance, there is no real salvation. If there is genuine salvation, there will always be deliverance. If there is no change, then nothing has changed: "Therefore if any man be in Christ, he is a new creature: old things are passed away; behold, all things are become new" (II Cor. 5:17).

This Old Testament scripture from Isaiah chapter 56 identifies "my salvation" with "my righteousness", and so it always is. The God of salvation initiates the salvation of God. The salvation of God always brings righteousness; and His righteousness is utterly unknown apart from His salvation. It is the coming of "… The Lord Our Righteousness" (Jehovah-Tsidkenu, Jer. 23:6), which makes possible the righteousness of Christ, which is the righteousness, which is by faith (Rom. 9:30), in the experience of the regenerated child of God; "… what doth the Lord require of thee, but to do justly, and to love mercy, and to walk humbly with thy God" (Mic. 6:8).

The issue is salvation, the implication is righteousness, and the inspiration is the coming of the Lord. For *the nation* of Israel, the realization of the promise is yet future, but for both them and us on a personal basis, "… *now* is the accepted time; behold, *now* is the day of salvation" (II Cor. 6:2). The aged Simeon took the infant Jesus in his arms, he knew by the Holy Ghost that his vision had been realized and rejoicingly exclaimed, "For mine eyes have seen *thy* salvation" (Luke 2:30). When we receive Him, "thy salvation" becomes "my salvation", and we too rejoice.

Thought For Today

When the provision becomes our property, our problem is solved!

213

October 15

N. T. Bible Reading: I Thessalonians 3   **Our Focus: I Thessalonians 3:10**

FAITH LACKING

Paul admonished the Corinthian believers to, "Examine yourselves, whether ye be in the faith; prove your own selves ..." (II Cor. 13:5). Now he indicates to the Thessalonians believers that their faith is lacking in certain essential elements. He also states that it is his earnest prayer to be allowed by God to visit them once more in order to correct the problem and perfect their faith. The truth is that we may have a genuine faith, but not have the measure or quality of faith which we need. This is yet another reminder that there is a progressive aspect to salvation. It is a life, and must be nurtured, fed, exercised, and strengthened.

We are told in Romans 12:3 that we are not to be exalted in our thinking and attitude. It is both sobering and humbling to know that, "... God hath dealt to every man *the measure* of faith." That is, God has meted out to each *only* a measure of faith. For this reason, we are informed that some are, "... weak in faith ..." (Rom. 4:19), and that others are, "... strong in faith ..." (Rom. 4:20). James tells us that some are "... rich in faith ..." (Jam. 2:5); it would seem fair to assume that some others may be poor in faith. There are, it is clear, certain positive steps which can be taken which will "nourish our faith" and "build us up" in faith; it can be developed to the point of completeness.

Doubt is dumb; faith is festive. To be silent, as to our faith, is to choke it; to declare our faith, is to fuel and fire it. It is essential to full assurance in the initial phase of salvation, "For ... with the mouth confession is made unto salvation" (Rom. 10:10). The Apostle Paul declared, "... we also believe, and therefore speak" (II Cor. 4:13). Real faith is restful; we struggle when we doubt. "For we which have believed do enter into rest ..." (Heb. 4:3). There is a *rest of faith*. Saving faith is also joyful, "... believing, ye rejoice with joy unspeakable ..." (I Pet. 1:8). To rejoice is to express joy, and if we do not express it, we certainly will stymie it, or lose it altogether. Faith is positive as well as hopeful, "Now faith is the substance of things hoped for ..." (Heb. 11:1). "For we ... wait for the hope of righteousness by faith" (Gal. 5:5). Hope is not faith, and faith is not hope. They are not identical, but they are inseparable. Real faith delivers a knock-out blow to morbid pessimism.

Thought For Today

Faith which is tested and tried will always emerge triumphant!

214

October 16

O. T. Bible Reading: Isaiah 59-61   **Our Focus: Isaiah 61:3**

BEAUTY FOR ASHES

There are times when a contrast is the best vehicle to vividly illuminate some great fact. A contrast is meant to magnify a striking difference. Ashes, especially in Scripture, are a symbol of sorrow, sadness, grief, bereavement, and emptiness. It is associated in the Bible with sackcloth, which is a synonym for deep grief or remorse. The contrast for this morbid scene is the festive *garland*, the symbol of great joy and victory. The Hawaiian "Lei", a wreath of plaited flowers, is familiar to all who visit the beautiful islands. It is placed on the necks of arriving guests to invite them to forget their trials, labor, and drudgery, and to enjoy the sunshine, beauty, singing, and festivities among the happy Islanders. The great prophecy of Isaiah chapter 61 has fulfillment in the Lord Jesus only. It has a spiritual fulfillment now, for all who come to know Him as their Lord and Saviour. It will have final and complete fulfillment in the future restoration and salvation of Israel.

There is a tendency among the ignorant and uninformed to think of Christianity as somber, melancholic, in atmosphere and expression. How tragic and sad is that deception. Jesus came to copiously anoint our heads with the oil of *joy*. Those who do not enjoy their salvation have not allowed the liberating power of the Gospel to release them from their shackles. It is not necessary to have a special instruction class on "how to enjoy life" for a prisoner just pardoned and released from confinement. It is much more likely that his conduct and actions would be a lesson for those who look on.

The joy of the Lord is our strength (Neh. 8:10). It is not some superficial and momentary thrill. It is the abiding and enduring exhilaration of experiencing the fulfillment of that for which we were first created. Jesus, we are told, "... for the joy that was set before him endured the cross, despising the shame ..." (Heb. 12:2). There is great joy when the ultimate purpose is kept clearly in focus. We rejoice *in the Lord*, not in events and circumstances, nor even in apparent successes.

Thought For Today

The heights of joy come from the depths of fulfillment!

October 16

N. T. Bible Reading: I Thessalonians 4   **Our Focus: I Thessalonians 4:11**

MIND YOUR OWN BUSINESS

One of the most down-to-earth practical Scriptures in the entire Bible is I Thessalonians chapter 4. No theory here; this is applied Christian reality, not profound theology. It is salvation in shoe leather, and it is what we all need.

1.   "… study to be quiet …" (I Thess. 4:11); a very interesting topic for the success seminar. Most ads that we see have to do with *speaking* effectively so as to win friends and influence people. Paul really is saying, "… be ambitious to be quiet …"; this is to be one of our goals as followers of Christ. It means that we are to avoid notoriety; don't be headline seekers. The carnal ambition to be seen and known, to be recognized, to excel, to achieve prominence and position must be replaced by a master-passion to be Christ-like in character. Every self-centered ambition, and every ulterior motive, however subtle or cleverly concealed, must give way to the centrality of Christ. This will take some doing, and it will require great ambition and motivation to accomplish it.

2.   "… do your own business …" (I Thess. 4:11), or as a heading for today reads, "mind your own business." Those who meddle are sure to find themselves in the middle of a muddle. One common earmark of the undisciplined is to be lured by curiosity and to be fascinated by the exposure of another's personal affairs. The genuine disciple of Christ will ruthlessly curb this carnal tendency, by a sincere desire to help and to identify. Love, which yearns to minister healing and to be a true friend to those in need, will wisely avoid becoming involved in what is not their responsibility, nor their prerogative to resolve.

3.   "… work with your own hands …" (I Thess. 4:11); learn to love labor, and to enjoy meaningful enterprise. Laziness and idleness are the twin offspring of the loser, and will always lead to failure. It is the hand of the diligent which is promised prosperity, and which leads to effective leadership and success (Prov. 10:4, 12:24). Those who only kill time should learn that the most effective way to do so is to work it to death. One of the early presidents wisely advised, "every good citizen should be a jack-of-all trades, but the *master* of *one*."

Thought For Today

Christianity is not a theory to learn … it is a life to live!

October 17

O. T. Bible Reading: Isaiah 62-64   **Our Focus: Isaiah 63:1**

WHO IS THIS?

Many questions are asked and recorded in the Scriptures; however, there are more answers provided than there are questions asked. When there are more questions than there are answers, there is a real problem. Isaiah asks the question concerning the vision which the Lord had given him. Has anyone ever had a true vision who did not have questions? Daniel, the prophet, was given a vision of the four beasts (Dan. 7), and immediately we are told *he asked* of his heavenly guest the meaning of it all (Dan. 7:16), and was given the meaning and interpretation. Those who interpret their own dreams will awaken disappointed.

The vision was of *One* returning from Edom, with garments dyed from Bozrah, marching in majestic strength, and clothed in garments of beauty and glory (Isa. 63:1). It was the custom, in those days of grape harvest, for foreign individuals to enter the great vat with bare feet, and to tread out the grapes. The red juice thus extracted spurted out in all directions staining the garments of the harvester. So it is in the vision. Edom was the land of Esau, and Esau typifies the flesh. The Majestic One comes from the east, and represents the Lord Jesus in His coming glory to judge the nations, and to bring in everlasting righteousness. In Isaiah chapter 53, He is seen as marred with "... no beauty that we should desire him" (Isa. 53:2). In Isaiah 63, it is different, now He comes clothed with majestic beauty and glory. First He comes as "the Lamb of God" to suffer and die for our salvation, but Isaiah sees Him coming the second time as the "Lion of the tribe of Judah" to rule and to reign on *the earth*.

Jesus came the first time "to proclaim the year of Jubilee" in fulfillment, to announce "... the acceptable year of the Lord ..." (Isa. 61:2). When the Lord read this Scripture in the synagogue of Nazareth He stopped at the comma, and closed the scroll. It was that part of the prophecy which pictured His first coming. Now, however, the time has come to complete the sentence, "... the day of vengeance of our God ..." (Isa. 61:2). It is not a pleasant picture, but it is an accurate one. In the final scene, His judgment precedes His coming, and then "... he shall reign forever and ever" (Rev. 11:15). Hallelujah!

Thought For Today

To know who *He is, is also to know* what *He does!*

October 17

N. T. Bible Reading: I Thessalonians 5   **Our Focus: I Thessalonians 5:16**

REJOICE EVERMORE

Paul launches into a fast-paced staccato-like summary of Christian principles for life and conduct, and gives in the briefest context of 11 verses, 22 Commandments for believers. This is a good shopping list for those who desire maturity in Christ.

The list continues in I Thessalonians 5:16. These are marching orders for the troops; it is an action plan for spiritual success. We are told to "Rejoice evermore" (I Thess. 5:16). That is not an injunction to be happy and jolly. It is much deeper than the emotion which flows from the positive happenings of life. To rejoice is to express joy. Joy is a fruit of the Spirit, and a vital element in Christian stability and maturity. To "rejoice in the Lord" (repeated 9 times in the Bible, twice in Philippians) is to have joy in Him and in His purposes. It is the deep satisfaction of knowing Him, of understanding His will and purposes, and the unspeakable thrill of serving Him. It is communion on the highest level.

"Pray without ceasing" (I Thess. 5:17); this is a revelation of what true prayer really is. He did not say, "stay on your knees", that would be impossible. He did say to continue the exercise of prayer, and never to discontinue doing so. Prayer is not so much an exercise, as it is the very life of the believer. It has been defined as the air in our lungs; as the blood which flows through our bodies. We breathe naturally and normally without conscious effort, and we do so without ceasing. The purifying life-producing flow of blood is mostly undetected, but, thank God, it does not cease. Thus also the deep inner spring of communion will express itself by the habitual flow of earnest desires, petitions, intercessions, and at times real travail.

The third admonition in this series is, "In every thing give thanks ..." (I Thess. 5:18). This is gratitude in motion. It is not so much a once-a-year celebration as it is a continuous flow of appreciation. It is a frame of mind more than a flow of words, although it will certainly include that as well. These three things are identified here as the will of God. When they are genuinely experienced, the other aspects of the will of God will fall into place beautifully.

Thought For Today

Real communion flows unconsciously and vibrantly!

October 18

O. T. Bible Reading: Isaiah 65-66 **Our Focus: Isaiah 66:2**

THIS MAN

The great prophecy of Isaiah closes with a summary of the majesty and greatness of God, and an emphasis on His omnipotence. His earthly people, Israel, may forget their calling and neglect their God, but they cannot escape His government. He is on His throne, and one day His will shall be done, and justice will prevail. All nations will at that time be gathered and will behold His glory (Isa. 66:18). This shall surely be, for thus it has been spoken; so much for the big picture ... the nations, this world order, and the final and sure restoration and salvation. What of this present distress, and then what of the individual relationship involved?

To "... *this man* ..." (Isa. 66:2); now we are dealing with the personal aspect. God will turn His attention to individuals who meet certain conditions. Those who respect and honor His Word, in humility acknowledge their personal needs, and earnestly seek His mercy and forgiveness, will find His favor. It all boils down to a personal relationship with God. We either know God on an individual basis, or we do not know Him at all. That individual whose heart is subdued before God, and who is moved to repentance, will experience God's favor and forgiveness. Those who deeply respect God's Word, and in humility choose the Divine will, shall personally know God's smile, will begin to see and understand God's ways, and will learn how to walk with God. God only walks with individuals, never with crowds or groups. Enoch walked with God as an individual; Noah walked with God as an individual; the imagination and the thoughts of the crowds were only evil continually (Gen. 5:22, 6:9, 6:5).

Every encounter with God is designed to work something of God into our lives, by removing something of the carnal flesh which rebels against God. The mountaintop experiences with God are not meant to *teach* us great mysteries; they are designed to *make* us more Christ-like in our daily conduct. God is not far removed from us when our heart is humbled, and we seek His mercy. The fact is that, "... the eyes of the Lord run to and fro throughout the whole earth, to shew himself strong in the behalf of them whose *heart is perfect* toward him ..." (II Chron. 16:9).

Thought For Today

The eyes of the Lord detect sincerity at a single glance!

October 18

N. T. Bible Reading: II Thessalonians 1   **Our Focus: II Thessalonians 1:10**

HE SHALL COME

It is that coming, the second coming of the Lord Jesus, which is the prominent theme of the Thessalonian Epistles. There are 20 specific references to the second coming of Christ. It is a fact of the future, a certain coming event, and a positive and sure hope for God's people. Paul is emphatic, "*When* he shall come ..." (II Thess. 1:10); it is not "if" or "perhaps", it is dogmatic; an event anticipated by all saints of *all time*, and a positively certain event at *some time*.

Paul writes this second Epistle to correct a false teaching which had affected the church. It was being said that they were already in the great tribulation. They were troubled and persecuted, and were being told by false teachers that this was the tribulation period spoken of in the Scriptures. To correct this erroneous notion, Paul carefully outlines the sequence of events which will precede "... the day of the Lord ..." (I Thess. 5:2). In I Thessalonians the emphasis was on that aspect of His coming when, "... we ... shall be *caught up* ... to meet the Lord in the air ..." (I Thess. 4:17). The Greek word used here is "harpazo", which means "to snatch away." The word which we most commonly use is "rapture", although not found in the Bible, it refers to the catching away of the Bride of Christ. She will be both "waiting" and "watching" for that great event, having faithfully made due preparations to make herself ready (Rev. 19:7-8).

The Lord is to be *revealed* from heaven "*with*" His saints at a later period of time, and after "... the indignation be overpast" (Isa. 26:20). The time of God's wrath being poured out upon the Christ-rejecting nations is called "the great tribulation" and also "the time of Jacob's trouble." We are plainly taught "For God hath not appointed *us to wrath*, but to obtain salvation by our Lord Jesus Christ" (I Thess. 5:9). This, the final phase of His return, is designated "the revelation." It should be very clear that He could not come "*with*" His saints until He had first come "*for*" them. The interval between those two events is marked by "the marriage supper of the Lamb" for the Bride *in heaven*, and by the great tribulation *on the earth*. This great truth is intended to be a comfort to those in suffering, a challenge to patience, a great inspiration to hope, and a motivation to purity of life and to preparedness.

Thought For Today

Unbelief asks "where?"; faith confidently responds, "when?"

October 19

O. T. Bible Reading: Jeremiah 1-2   **Our Focus: Jeremiah 2:13**

LIVING WATER

The diagnosis of a disease is essential to its treatment. Many people will get a second opinion before taking any course of medical treatment. This is wise, because at best, it is only an opinion. In the verse of focus for today, God Himself gives the Divine diagnosis of the malady which had overtaken the nation of Israel. No second opinion is needed; this is 100% accurate; it contains both an analysis of the problem, and a Divine indictment. It is also an insight into the process of spiritual decay.

Living water is that which rises from springs, it is ever-flowing, and always fresh. God is the fountain-head from which source flows the refreshing stream. It is called living water because it is perpetually flowing, moving, and life-giving. Jesus informed the woman of Samaria that He could impart living water, and with no human limitations such as the tiny pitcher which she held (John 4:10). He is referring to the very same Divine provision. At a later occasion in John, He enlarged upon the truth by showing that the believers who are in the channel, will experience that living water (the *flow* of life) gushing forth from their inner being (John 7:38-39). The nation of Israel had forsaken God, they had taken their own way; they had disregarded God's Word, and forsaken His precepts. They had by choice removed themselves from God, and when they did, they walked away from the flowing stream.

Thirst is a primary appetite; men must have water to survive. Once you leave the flowing stream, you must find a substitute, or perish. A cistern is nothing but a tank; it is a storage tank. As soon as water, from whatever source, is placed into a cistern it ceases to be living; it is now stagnant, and the inevitable process of deterioration has already begun. The cisterns which they had chosen were already cracked and could retain no water. So also is every man-made device or concoction which they construct as a substitute for the precious flowing stream of living water. Men have fabricated substitutes and clever counterfeits for almost everything, but *life* itself. There simply are no substitutes for life; only empty and futile tanks of decay and disease. A new substitute is no better than an old one; both will fail utterly, and in cruel emptiness will mock the parched seeker.

Thought For Today

No pump is needed for those who stand in a flowing stream!

October 19

N. T. Bible Reading: II Thessalonians 2   **Our Focus: II Thessalonians 2:15**

STAND FAST

The words "stand fast" are repeated nine times in the Bible. We are told that it is a military expression, and indicates an attitude, a posture, and a commitment. A military person has been trained and disciplined to respect, honor, and obey authority. The skills of argument and debate are not a part of boot camp. The military uniform itself is meant to give them a sense of honor and dignity even in their posture and movement. They are also drilled and repeatedly reminded of a cause which they represent, and are prepared to defend it if necessary with their own lives.

In Galatians 5:1 Paul admonished the Galatians to, "Stand fast therefore in the liberty wherewith Christ hath made us free …." This is not a license to citizens to disregard and ignore the laws of the land; it is not an unbridled freedom for children to challenge and to disobey the laws and principles of their parents; it is not a Magna Carta to the servants to flaunt and ridicule the demands and requirements of their masters; neither is it an excuse for believers to ignore and disobey the righteous standards taught by every book of the New Testament. Any one of these would be rejected by any clear thinking level of sanity as being ridiculous if not outrageous. The liberty wherewith Christ has made us free is the deliverance from every bondage of habit or thought which would prevent us from doing the will of God in all that it involves. It is the cutting of every chain and the snapping of every fetter which would hinder us from obeying and doing all that Jesus, the Apostles, and the Word of God outlines as being righteous.

The root word for "standard" is stand; there can be no standard where there is no firm _stand_, and it should be clear and apparent to all that there simply is _none_. We must be patient with ourselves and with others as we strive toward that goal of maturity outlined in Scripture. There is a huge difference between patience and tolerance. Any attitude or action which dilutes and waters down the Divine standard is <u>compromise</u>. We have been called upon to measure our lives with the standards of Jesus, and not the ways of this world.

Thought For Today

Those who <u>stand</u> with Christ will also <u>reign</u> with Him!

October 20

O. T. Bible Reading: Jeremiah 3-4   **Our Focus: Jeremiah 3:11**

TREACHEROUS

The very word "treacherous" arouses within us a sense of disgust and repulsion, and well it should; it involves betrayal, and the conduct of a traitor. Even the most hardened of criminals have no time for a Judas. Jeremiah repeats the word four times in chapter 3 (Jer. 3:7, 8, 10 and 11); it is found only four times in all the rest of the Old Testament. Zephaniah used it once to describe *the false* prophets of Israel, "Her prophets are light and treacherous persons: her priests have polluted the sanctuary, they have done violence to the law" (Zeph. 3:4). The false teachers and prophets who are chaffy, frivolous, and shifty on the issues are easily identified either then or now. They always pollute true worship, and introduce corrupting elements of compromise and conformity into their practice of religion. They will always act violently to any restraints or standards of righteousness, but will militantly promote whatever the public opinion polls indicate the majority demand. This is treachery on a grand scale, and is a betrayal, parallel to that of Judas.

Jeremiah uses the negative adjective to describe the actions of Judah. The Divine indictment is made vivid by the use of the marriage covenant. Israel, joined to Jehovah by both love and covenant, had violated the sacred vows by embracing strange gods, and was guilty of spiritual adultery and promiscuous whoredom. This would seem to be the ultimate evil; but the sin of Judah was even worse. Judah had experienced the reforms under the influence of Josiah. She was pretending to be identified with those religious movements, but was actually pursuing a path of infidelity and rebellion. God shows His estimate of pretense and hypocrisy. The nation which abandons all pretenses to the ways and to the Word of God is more righteous than another nation which disguises its rebellion under the cloak of pretended conformity. This God hates, and lists it as an outright abhorrence in His sight; it is an ultimate expression of sin, and God rejects it as treachery. This principle is the basis for Jesus fiery denunciations of religious pretense and hypocrisy in His time.

Thought For Today

The worst form of evil is disguised hypocrisy!

October 20

N. T. Bible Reading: II Thessalonians 3   **Our Focus: II Thessalonians 3:13**

BE NOT WEARY

The only person who has never been weary is the one who has never done anything. To be weary is to be tired, worn out, exhausted, and fatigued. We have all been there many times, and we seem to arrive there much sooner than in previous days. This is perfectly normal, and has nothing to do with what Paul is driving at. He clearly identifies the activity in which we must never become faint or fatigued; it is in the healthy spiritual exercise of "... *well doing*" (II Thess. 3:13) that we are not to slack off or cease the effort. You may be physically drained, and still maintain full vigor in pursuing what is right.

The danger in question is clearly pin-pointed in Hebrews 12:3, "For consider him ... lest ye be wearied and faint in your minds." The real battle is for *the mind*, it is there that the warfare is raging; and it is in *the mind* first where the battle is either won or lost. We must be constantly *renewed* in the spirit of our minds or we will wilt and quit fighting (Eph. 4:23). There is a life-giving, regenerating, quickening faculty of our minds which gives vigor, strength, and enthusiasm to our thinking. We must be renewed, restored, and revived in this area lest we give way to mental fatigue and fog. Rest, or sleep, has been called nature's sweet restorer; and so it is on the physical level. It is the renewing of the mind by the Holy Spirit, through the Word of God, which has the same effect on the mind. It is my prayer that these daily inspirational studies may help in this vital area of spiritual activity. If we win the battle here, the rest is both assured and half-won already.

It is a practiced habit of "Looking unto Jesus ..." (Heb. 12:2), which avoids this wilting of our minds and then our spirits. The original word is, "looking *off* unto Jesus"; by an act of intelligent and determined concentration, we must keep our focus on Him. This brings life, vitality, and fortitude to our minds and hearts. If we look only at ourselves, at our circumstances, and at the swirling evils around us we will faint and be overwhelmed. Jesus is the author, the *file-leader*, of our faith; and He alone can supply and impart that very ingredient which initiated our faith at the outset of our spiritual life and experience.

Thought For Today

Those who keep on looking to Him, also keep on being renewed!

October 21

O. T. Bible Reading: Jeremiah 5-6   **Our Focus: Jeremiah 6:16**

THE OLD PATHS

A path is not a road; it is a trail. A trail is a walk-way in the country used only by individuals, and never by any kind of vehicle. The highways, roads, and interstates are for carriers of people and produce, and are intended for speed, convenience, and mass movement. The lowly foot-path is but for the individuals, who must either tread it alone or at least in single-file. Someone else has gone before to break-trail, and has found a route which will lead to the intended destination. Many a hiker has missed the trail, deliberately attempting to take a short-cut, or has mistakenly followed a by-path or a dead-end trail and has become disoriented and hopelessly lost in a strange wilderness. The old path is a proven way, successfully trodden by others in the past, and still accessible and available to those who choose to go this way.

The good way is the right way, in contrast to the wrong way. There are many by-paths each of which will take you elsewhere or, in some cases, nowhere. The importance and significance of the path is not in a scenic route, but that which lies in the end of the trail. The single most important consideration is quite simply, "where will it take me?" We are not just out for a walk, our primary intention is to get to a certain destination; the good way is the correct path which others have used to get there.

Rest is relief from anxiety and uncertainty. The traveler, who carefully follows the old proven path, need not fret about the outcome. The certainty of those who have arrived at the desired goal, gives credibility and legitimacy to the path, and confidence to those who walk in it. The first who pioneered the way were trail-blazers. They left enough cuttings or other identifying markers so that none need miss the sure path. The precious Word of God is our map, and the Holy Spirit is our sure guide. It is for us to be certain that we remain on "the old path."

Thought For Today

The one who marked the trail is always the safest guide!

October 21

N. T. Bible Reading: I Timothy 1   **Our Focus: I Timothy 1:16**

LONGSUFFERING

Longsuffering is a fruit of the Spirit. Most people are short on their longsuffering; it is a comparatively large word consisting of 13 letters in English. It is much larger (it is by any standard … huge) when it comes to practical living. Generally speaking, the value of anything is pretty much determined by its availability. Any item which is seldom found is usually quite expensive; anything which is one-of-a-kind will have astronomical value. If rarity determines worth, then longsuffering is a gem of priceless value beyond rubies and diamonds.

We are told that longsuffering is a discipline; it is restraint in the face of provocation; it does not rush to retaliate, nor does it hasten to punish. In Galatians 5:19 Paul graphically exposes the grisly works of the flesh. One of the clear manifestations of this abhorrent carnality is wrath, which is anger, better known as temper. Longsuffering is one of the beautiful clusters of the nine-fold fruit of the Spirit which is the very opposite of anger. It is one of the Divine attributes of God which is associated with His mercy and His grace (Ex. 34:6; II Pet. 3:9). It is patience in action. Patience is a character quality which must be cultivated and fertilized to survive. It is the sterling attribute of maturity, which is the exact opposite of despondency; it does not succumb to any deep trouble and triumphs over negative conditions. It is truly a genuine and deep work of the Holy Spirit, and is an undeniable manifestation of a truly Spirit-filled disciple of Christ. It is very rare, but not extinct; may God multiply those who possess it.

One evidence of a true vision is the quickened capacity to reach out for more than we have yet grasped. If our reach does not exceed our grasp, then we are complacent, smug, and spiritually inert. Only God can incorporate these great attributes of spiritual maturity into our daily conduct. But God does not, and will not, force them upon us. They are available, but not inevitable. Only those who genuinely "… hunger and thirst after righteousness …" (Matt. 5:6) will be "*blessed*", and also will be faithfully "*filled*."

Thought For Today

To be like Jesus is to conduct ourselves as He did!

October 22

O. T. Bible Reading: Jeremiah 7-8   **Our Focus: Jeremiah 7:4**

THE TEMPLE

Externals are never an end in themselves; at best, they are only a means to an end. The human tendency is to magnify these tangibles, and the more involved they are in our worship, the greater is the temptation to make an idol of it. The very things which God has ordained as an instrument, or vehicles involved in salvation, may very well become a snare to our souls. A church house or building is a convenient place for us to gather for worship, praise, and instruction; however, it is only a building, and it will become sacred and special only in the measure in which we meet with God and God meets with us. Any fellowship of believers, either local or general, is vital to our growth and maturity. We must never place our confidence or hope in that alone. It is important, and it is to be appreciated; however, it is not a substitute for our personal relationship with God. Nothing can be allowed to be a sanctuary, nor substitute for the reality which is in Christ alone. When the life is not right, and the heart is in rebellion, the daily conduct is always contrary to *the way of life* as defined in Scripture; all else is an empty frame-work only. If the heart is unclean, the spotless shining temple does nothing to change it.

Jeremiah warned the nation of Israel that they were trusting in external reforms, and missing God completely. A magnificent temple had been cleaned out, the rubbish had been removed, and the furnishings washed and polished. That was all well and good as far as it goes, but it stops far short of personal cleansing and restoration. The deceived throngs were trusting in the fact that the great Temple was in place, and the services and functions had been restored, to demonstrate their relationship with God. It is ever so; this essential and basic truth is as appropriate today as it was in ancient Israel. There is no substitute for a personal relationship with God.

Thought For Today

The carnal clings to things; the spiritual clings only to Him!

October 22

N. T. Bible Reading: I Timothy 2   **Our Focus: I Timothy 2:1**

PRAYERS

Prayer is as much a part of a Christian life as breathing is to the natural life. Everyone who has any experience with God prays, but very few pray as they should. The subject of prayer occupies a large part of the Bible; the word "pray" and its derivatives occur over 300 times. There are many kinds of prayer; there are many aspects to it. It is a ministry in itself, and many have felt a definite call to this vital spiritual exercise. These are "prayer warriors", and they are at the fore-front of the armies of the Lord. May the Lord increase their number and effectiveness.

Paul enumerates four distinct aspects of prayer in I Timothy 2:1:

1. Supplication is, as the basic word suggests, an earnest beseeching petition. It is a humble request which expresses a need in which all of those offering them share. It certainly seems to refer to those very deepest needs of the human heart; for purifying and cleansing from activities and motives strange to the ways of God; for spiritual enablement and special quickening for daily life and service. These requests are first of all for ourselves, but should also include others for whom we are praying, "My little children, of whom I travail in birth again *until* Christ be formed in you" (Gal. 4:19).

2. Prayers, as used here, seem to indicate those distinct acts of worship in which the saints offer up the pure incense of praise to the Lord. Personal needs, nor even the needs of others, are not the primary focus at this time; it is the transforming basking in His Majesty, Might, and Mercy.

3. The term intercession primarily involves petitions; a petition is a solemn request made to an authority; it is an entreaty on behalf of me or someone else. It seems to refer to that depth of request which disregards all that is personal in order to focus on the needs of another.

4. Thanksgiving is a vital aspect of prayer. It is the outpouring of gratitude overflowing in deep expressions of true worship. But it must be mingled with, and become an essential part of, any and every form of prayer. "Lord, teach us to pray!"

Thought For Today

Prayer is the deepest channel of the inner river!

October 23

O. T. Bible Reading: Jeremiah 9-10   **Our Focus: Jeremiah 9:7**

I WILL MELT

These are the very words which God Himself spoke, and when God speaks let every other voice be silent, "Be silent, O all flesh, before the Lord: for he is raised up out of his holy habitation" (Zech. 2:13). Jeremiah has entered into prevailing prayer on behalf of the nation of Israel. He wept bitterly and regularly over the sufferings and the sins of the nation; he is called "the weeping prophet" as the mention of his tears is recorded 14 times in the book. The anguish of the prophet of the Lord is Divinely attended to, and God speaks from heaven, "Therefore thus saith the Lord of hosts, Behold, I will melt them, and try them …" (Jer. 9:7). The two words "*melt*" and "*try*" are borrowed from the scene of the refinery (Jer. 9:7).

The language was familiar to those who lived at that time. They all understood that precious metals, and especially gold and silver, were thus processed in order to purify the product by literally boiling out the impurities and the dross. It was thus with Israel, and it is the intent and purpose of God in all afflictions and sufferings. God takes no pleasure in adversities, and judgment is His "… strange work …" (Isa. 28:21). It is *the end* for which the process is intended, "For I know the thoughts that I think toward you, saith the Lord, thoughts of peace, and not of evil, to give you an expected (desired) end" (Jer. 29:11). It is the method by which God deals with humanity to accomplish His purifying purpose.

This account brings into clear focus a twofold revelation of God in His person and in His methods with men. As for man, it is God's design that he be restored, cleansed, and in the end purified, enjoying the Divinely intended communion with the Great Refiner. Jesus wept over Jerusalem, and in reality, Jeremiah enters into the very feelings of heaven as he grieved over the fires and purgings in store for his people. This is a true picture of Divine intention, and of Divine compassion in action. Those who walk with God in maturity will share His emotions and manifest His spirit.

Thought For Today

God sees the end from the beginning; we see only the process!

October 23

N. T. Bible Reading: I Timothy 3   **Our Focus: I Timothy 3:9**

A PURE CONSCIENCE

Everyone has a conscience; very few have a pure conscience. The Scriptures speak of a *good* conscience (I Tim. 1:5); we may assume that there would also be a *bad* conscience. It also refers to a *weak* conscience (I Cor. 8:7, 10, 12); it is logical to assume that there would also be a *strong* conscience. The verse of focus for today speaks of a "... *pure* conscience" (I Tim. 3:9); it follows that there is also an *impure* conscience. We are told some have a conscience *seared* (callous, covered by scar tissue) as by a hot iron (I Tim. 4:2); therefore, the opposite quality of *tenderness* and *sensitivity* must also exist. Hebrews 10:2 identifies yet another type of conscience, and it is an *evil* conscience; by deduction we may conclude there must also be a *righteous* or *godly* conscience.

The conscience is a faculty of the mind. The word is derived from two words, "co" and "knowledge"; it is the built-in monitor which, in its intended positive condition, agrees with the law and what is right (Rom. 2:15). It is that process of thought which distinguishes and identifies what it considers morally good or bad, commending what is good, and rejecting what is bad by an impulse or prod, prompting actions in favor of the good, and avoiding the bad. We are told the primary elements which combine to form character are heredity, environment, and training. Nowhere is this more evident than in the study of the conscience. These three factors weigh so heavily upon the condition of the conscience, that to relate them accurately to any one individual is to predict the status, bias, and condition of the conscience involved.

It is clear that the conscience is the eye of the soul, which aligns itself with the very highest and best. It may be trained, directed, influenced, and silenced; therefore, it is our personal responsibility to see to it that our conscience is so accurately taught in the principles of Scripture that it inclines us to walk on the highest possible level. The tender still small voice of the Spirit will be heard only by those who are on the same frequency as God. His voice is so tender, we may easily miss it, or even more tragically, we may ignore it.

Thought For Today

A pure conscience is the pulse of the pure in heart!

October 24

O. T. Bible Reading: Jeremiah 11-13   **Our Focus: Jeremiah 11:5**

AMEN, O LORD

Very few people would ever say that they disagree with God, but the fact is that many do. To agree is to be of one opinion, to concur, and to be in accord with. It is also to *act* in accordance with. The measure of agreement will be directly proportionate to the actions taken. A tacit approval is not by any means a covenant, nor is it a contract. Full accord and agreement involves a voluntary response; which will issue in, "where do I sign, and what is expected of me?"

Jeremiah becomes an object lesson in the vital issue of standing with God. The early part of Jeremiah outlines the way in which Judah had violated their covenant relationship with God (Jer. 11:1-17). He was commissioned to inform them of their failure, and also to enlighten them as to the consequent judgments on their stubbornness and rebellion. His immediate and whole-hearted response was, "... So be it, (margin is amen) O Lord" (Jer. 11:5). He stood with God and with His Word without reservations. The tenacity and loyalty of this great prophet was the product of his own deep and unqualified agreement with God in his own personal life. There is a vast world of difference between the formal or religious "amen" which is conventional and proper, means little or nothing, and costs the same; and the deep meaningful "so be it, amen" of the heart to the will, purpose, and methods of God. The first has no roots in principle or in practice, and quickly fades at the first signs of stress or conflict. The genuine "amen" of commitment grips, like an anchor, the solid bed-rocks of principle, righteousness, and godliness. The shifting sands of human convenience and comfort offer nothing for any anchor to grip.

The promises of God are the sure foundation upon which our faith securely rests; and to those "in Christ" they are yea and amen (II Cor. 1:21, 20). Those who experience the purpose of the promise also enjoy the power of the purpose. The degree in which we have known Him as *Lord* and *Master* of our lives, determines the measure of our ability to say "amen" to His working in our own lives or the lives of others. The quick and decisive, "... thy *will* be done" (Matt. 26:42) is the "echo" of a deeper inner relationship.

Thought For Today

A quiet resignation anchors the soul to the reigning Savior!

October 24

N. T. Bible Reading: I Timothy 4   **Our Focus: I Timothy 4:12**

BE AN EXAMPLE

Every builder must know how to read and interpret a blueprint. That document is a photographic reproduction of an architectural or technical drawing. It is an accurate professional illustration or plan of action which must be followed precisely. God placed an awesome load of responsibility upon the shoulders of His servant Moses. He was commissioned to oversee the building of a sanctuary, which was later identified as a tabernacle, "... that I may dwell among them" (Ex. 25:8). It was to serve also as a type or pattern of the "... true tabernacle ..." of heaven (Heb. 8:2), and would be a pattern for many great spiritual truths and insights; therefore, it must be framed in a very exact way, "According to all that I shew thee, after the pattern ..." (Ex. 25:9). The last two chapters of Exodus use the repeated words, "... as the Lord commanded Moses ..." 17 times. God gave the pattern or blueprint, and it must be followed precisely.

Hebrews chapter 11 gives us a list of role-models of faith; it is the Westminster Abbey of the Bible; these who are specifically named excelled, and generally illustrated at least one unique quality of faith. It is as though a family wished to present a photo of the traits and features which marked them in a special way. The series of photos of several generations would be carefully selected; each one showed at least one pronounced family feature ... the eyes, the nose, the mouth, the fore-head etc; one enlarged picture placed at the end of the exhibit would be presented as the ideal, which would combine all of the family features into one person. That person, in Hebrews chapter 11, is the Lord Jesus (Heb. 2:9).

Paul appeals to young Timothy to be a role-model for all believers. A leader must be respected, and that respect must be earned; it can never be demanded. When any believer, whether young or old, "lives the life" in consistency and humility, they will be respected. Even more importantly, their profession will be believable because it has been demonstrated to be genuine. This involves the total person and every facet of their life, "... in word, in conversation, in charity, in spirit, in faith, in purity" (I Tim. 4:12); "... give none occasion to the adversary to speak reproachfully" (I Tim. 5:14).

Thought For Today

Every life is a green light or a red light to other travelers!

October 25

O. T. Bible Reading: Jeremiah 14-16   **Our Focus: Jeremiah 15:19**

THE PRECIOUS

That which is precious is very costly and of great value. It is clear that there is a vast difference between what is seen as precious on the human level, but is of little or no consequence to God. Conversely, that which is precious in the eyes of the Lord, is given no value whatever by human standards. That which is of the earth, is combustible when exposed to the testing fires of eternity. They are but wood, hay, and stubble and will perish with the using (I Cor. 3:12). They may seem to sparkle like diamonds, glowing in the rays of the beaming sun, which measures the seasons of men's short day. Whether it be riches and wealth, prestige and prominence, position and power, or any other coveted thing of earthly value, it will not register on heaven's scales, nor would it survive when injected with the pure atmosphere of eternity.

There are a number of things which are said to be precious to the Lord, wisdom is "… more precious than rubies …" (Prov. 3:15). "That the *trial of your faith*, being much more precious than of gold that perisheth …" (I Pet. 1:7); "… to them that have obtained like precious *faith* with us through the righteousness of God and our Saviour Jesus Christ" (II Pet. 1:1); "Whereby are given unto us exceeding great and precious *promises*: that by these ye might be partakers of the divine nature …" (II Pet. 1:4).

Jeremiah is given the word of the Lord concerning both the nation of Israel and his own ministry and message. He is understandably perplexed by some of the implications and somewhat doubtful as to his own sufferings involved. God directly answers his words, and in doing so, gives a great insight into Divine values. In the thoughts and expressions of Jeremiah were concepts of God which were in error. It is these erroneous thoughts which God requires Jeremiah to purge from his mind. He is to purify himself from those unworthy ideas which God calls vile or impure. The mind of the prophet must be in perfect harmony with God so that he thinks and feels with God. This is maturity for a prophet and for any saint of God; and it is *precious* in His sight.

Thought For Today

To have the mind of Christ is an evidence of maturity!

October 25

N. T. Bible Reading: I Timothy 5   **Our Focus: I Timothy 5:8**

HIS OWN HOUSE

There are two great institutions which are Divinely chosen and ordained among men:

1.   The true church of which Christ is the head.
2.   The godly or Christian home.

Both are in contempt by the secular world, and both are primary goals for elimination by humanism. Since neither can be destroyed they must both be restructured in such a manner as to render them impotent and powerless in the interests of religion. By infusing them with the watered-down and diluted ideas and the natural theories of popular life-styles, they can both become agents to promote decay and corruption.

The family circle is God's ordained institution, and is the very foundation upon which our society was built; it is man's primary responsibility. Paul clearly outlines the Divinely intended pattern for provision and protection. Each man is shown to be primarily responsible *to provide* for *his own house*, or more accurately, for *his own kindred*. There is a vastness involved which is almost overwhelming. He is to furnish, to make available, to make all necessary preparation, and by fore-thought and planning, to make provision for his household. This obviously involves so much more than simply a roof over-head, and food on the table. It also includes anticipating and providing for the moral, ethical, mental, emotional, and primarily the *spiritual needs* of his own house, and insofar as it is possible, for his kindred.

First things must be given prominence and priority. No other obligation, responsibility, interest, or enjoyment is to come before or take precedence over the domestic duties and household responsibilities. This truth is not taught, nor is it practiced in many places. It is central to all balanced and Biblical behavior. To neglect or to fail at this point is to deny the faith, and to be more damaging than the blatant infidel. To carry out commonplace duties is to transform them into glowing pictures of genuine salvation, and it is carrying out human obligations on the highest possible level of godly conduct.

Thought For Today

The most effective witness is in the first circle of responsibility!

October 26

O. T. Bible Reading: Jeremiah 17-19   **Our Focus: Jeremiah 18:6**

THE POTTER'S HAND

The art of pottery making is one of the earliest crafts learned and practiced by mankind. Science dates some recovered artifacts of pottery as early as 4,000 BC. The invention of the potter's wheel was a revolutionary introduction to the industry in about 3,000 BC. Pottery has been found in most archaeological historic excavations in the land of Israel. It was a major industry in the ancient world, and remains a multi-billion dollar industry in the world markets of our generation. But it is used extensively in the Scriptures of both the Old Testament and the New Testament. The picture is simple and clear, the lessons are practical and profitable, and the applications are universal and personal.

It was Jehovah Himself who used the common scene in a picture of His relationship to the nation of Israel (Jer. 18:8). There is a prophetic aspect to this application which offers both hope and promise to His chosen people. The intended vessel has been marred and disfigured not once but many times. The patient Potter has a finished product in mind, and he will not abandon the project until he has completed the vessels of honor, "For he will finish the work ..." (Rom. 9:28), "Behold, I have created the smith that bloweth the coals in the fire, and that bringeth forth an instrument for his work ..." (Isa. 54:16).

There are many beautiful applications for this familiar scene of the Potter and the clay. Whatever experience we may encounter; whatever heart-breaking sorrows we may go through; whatever bitter disappointments and human failures we may encounter; it is both refreshing and encouraging to know that we are in the Great Potter's hands. There is a picture of a beautiful polished vessel in the mind of *The One* who sits at the wheel. He is patient and long-suffering, and does not grow weary in the long process. He will not abandon the project until the vessel of anticipation is fully realized. The all important element for us is that we keep in mind that we are still in the process of being molded; He still has His fingers in our clay.

Thought For Today

The thing being formed is the vision realized!

October 26

N. T. Bible Reading: I Timothy 6   **Our Focus: I Timothy 6:10**

A ROOT

The tree is but one; the roots are many. Most commentaries agree the article is not "the root", but "a root"; the love of money it is *a root* of all evil (I Tim. 6:10). There are many evils which have nothing whatever to do with money, nor even with the love of it. However, there is a significant cluster of evils which do indeed stem from the love of money. The love of money, and what it will buy, is a driving desire to have and to hold. It is a passion for possessions, which can grip and master the lives of those who have riches, as well as those who are utterly devoid of them. It is one more lust which must be conquered and overcome. Those who have mastered it have fixed their focus on things eternal and have proven on a daily basis that, "… godliness with contentment is great gain" (I Tim. 6:6). Those who were mastered by it find themselves in the ever-tightening grip of a giant web of selfishness and greed.

There are many other roots; Hebrews 12:15 "… lest any root of bitterness springing up trouble you, and thereby many be defiled." Many struggle a life-time with feelings of hatred, unforgiveness, rejection, bitterness, distrust, and even a fiendish desire for revenge, and never discover that it all stems from a root of bitterness. Meanwhile their inner strength is utterly wasted, their minds are tormented and confused, their nerves are strained to the breaking point, and in many cases, their health is gone; an unforgiving spirit has taken its awful toll.

The vital principle involved is that we must learn to deal with the *root* problems instead of forever trying to find a cure for symptoms. Preventive medicine is the best solution and the surest formula for good health. When the heart is strong and healthy the pulse will be regular and distinct. We must flee from the disease laden swamp of evil, and this we do diligently, following after (pursuing aggressively) all that is good and godly (I Tim. 6:11).

Thought For Today

The root of righteousness yields the fruit of the Spirit!

October 27

O. T. Bible Reading: Jeremiah 20-22   **Our Focus: Jeremiah 20:3**

MAGORMISSABIB

A very brief paragraph of history (three verses) is recorded in Jeremiah 20. A major change takes place in the life and ministry of the prophet Jeremiah. His good friend, the godly king Josiah, was now dead. Josiah succeeded his father Amon at the tender age of eight, and at sixteen, eight years later, "... he began to seek after the God of David his father ..." (II Chron. 34:3). Jeremiah wept over the loss of this good friend and worthy king (II Chron. 35:25-26). Those who next came to the throne were both weak and evil, and the environment changed completely for God's messenger. The Lord directed him to take an earthen potter's vessel and smash it to pieces in the sight of the ancients of the people and of the priests (Jer. 19:10). This was a sign-message of their impending siege and destruction (Jer. 19:10-11).

The false, official, organized religious leaders reacted. Pashur, the chief temple officer, smote the prophet of God, and put him in stocks. The word "*smote*" is a legal term which many believe involved the official scourging of "... forty stripes save one" (II Cor. 11:24). Jeremiah is then detained in the pillory and exposed to public scorn and ridicule. The next day he is "... brought forth ..." (Jer. 20:3), at which time he pronounced God's judgment upon his persecutors. Pashur is now to have a name change; he would be identified by the Lord as "... Magormissabib" (Jer. 20:3). This strange sounding name means "terror on every side", and accurately describes the impending disaster.

The lonely and dejected Seer now suffers the prophet's disease known as "the Elijah syndrome"; "... and I, even I only, am left; and they seek my life, to take it away" (I Ki. 19:14). Jeremiah was swept into a swirling tornado of conflicting emotions and thoughts. He mourned the day of his birth, was puzzled and peeved at his treatment, and sang the blues. He began to compose his resignation; what true prophet of God has not done the very same thing? Then the true experience of a Divinely ordained messenger is revealed, "... *But* his word was in mine heart as a burning fire shut up in my bones ..." (Jer. 20:9). Only those who have experienced it can understand or explain it.

Thought For Today

The rejection of the prophet only underlines his message!

October 27

N. T. Bible Reading: II Timothy 1   **Our Focus: II Timothy 1:5**

UNFEIGNED FAITH

There is no pretense here; there is nothing "phony" or "fake" about it. This is bare-bones, brass tacks, and Bible-based reality. *Unfeigned faith* is the expression, of a caliber of trust, which brings peace and joy, and which manifests itself in the transformation of both life and conduct. It is a marvel to those who possess it, a manifesto to those who witness it, and a mantle to be transmitted to another generation.

This true and trustworthy faith is the work of the Holy Spirit in the heart and life, and is contained in the vehicles of a good conscience and a pure heart, "Now the end of the commandment (the thing aimed at) is charity out of a pure heart, and of a good conscience, and of faith unfeigned" (I Tim. 1:5). A good conscience is   one in good working order; it functions in its originally intended way. It is tender and sensitive, and registers strongly against what is wrong or evil. A pure heart is one that is clean and thoroughly washed. It has been to the cleansing fountain which has been opened in the House of David for sin and uncleanness (Zech. 13:1); and it has been scoured by the purging and purifying Word of God (Eph. 5:26; Tit. 3:5). From this good ground, the good seed produces a truly abundant harvest, even unto one hundred-fold (Matt. 13:8, 23).

Timothy had a very precious and rare heritage; his Mother and his Grandmother were both possessors of this very same unfeigned faith. This brings up a very important and basic spiritual insight. It is certainly true that we cannot impart neither our faith, nor our spiritual experience to our children. It is not something in our genes, nor is it an element of any will or inheritance. However, if it is certainly true that we can live such a life of consistency and vibrant faith, it is very difficult for those who know us best, not to desire and experience the same glad and glowing faith. The odds are greatly increased and the pathway much clearer for those who witness reality in the home environment.

Thought For Today

Unfeigned faith cannot be imparted, but it is very contagious!

October 28

O. T. Bible Reading: Jeremiah 23-24   **Our Focus: Jeremiah 23:16**

HEARKEN NOT

Life is filled with complexities, competitions, complications, and compromises. There are good friends, and there are bad friends; there are good thoughts, and there are bad thoughts; there are good habits, and there are bad habits; there are good people, and there are bad people. How are we ever to survive and succeed? We need help, we must have advice and instruction, and we must find a trusted, experienced, and faithful guide who can direct us through the maze of paths to our desired destination. We have not been left hopelessly abandoned. God has graciously given us a true and faithful Friend, a clearly marked pathway, and a chart and compass to assure our safe passage. The guide is the Lord Jesus Himself; the way is outlined in the Word of God and is explained by the Holy Spirit. It is left to us to hearken, to harmonize, and to heed.

We must settle in our minds the absolute fact that God Himself *has* indeed spoken. In just three books of the Old Testament, Exodus, Leviticus, and Deuteronomy the words "God said", "the Lord spake", "thus saith the Lord" are repeated 1,770 times. Indeed, God *has* spoken many times and *the voice of the Lord* has sounded forth in various ways (Ps. 29, repeated 7 times). It is plainly stated that, "… God hath spoken by the mouth of all his holy prophets since the world began" (Acts 3:21). Certainly, God has spoken unto us; "… in these last days (God has) spoken unto us by his Son …" (Heb. 1:2).

There is a world of difference between a false prophet and a true messenger of God. The false teacher dwells on vanities, and speaks from his own mind. The true teacher is a messenger of wisdom, is in direct and personal communion with God, and makes clear the way and the will of God. There is an accurate two-fold test:

1.   Do they faithfully and accurately adhere to the basic truths and principles of the Word of God?
2.   Does their ministry produce righteousness and true holiness in their own lives and in the lives of their hearers (Luke 1:75; Rom. 6:19)?

If they cannot pass the "fruit test", then "… Hearken not …" (Jer. 23:16); just do not listen to them.

Thought For Today

It is not what is claimed, but what is produced that counts!

October 28

N. T. Bible Reading: II Timothy 2   **Our Focus: II Timothy 2:4**

A SOLDIER

The Christian life and experience is a multi-faceted relationship. In just one chapter with but 26 verses, the apostle Paul lists seven figures of speech to describe the duties and activities involved. They are by no means intended to be a complete list, but they are a good beginning into the understanding of the anatomy of the "faithful men (man)" of II Timothy 2:2. Any one of the seven makes for a challenging study of the essential elements of salvation as defined in the New Testament:

1. *A son* (II Tim. 2:1).
2. *A soldier* (II Tim. 2:4).
3. *An athlete* (II Tim. 2:5).
4. *A farmer* (II Tim. 2:6).
5. *A student* (II Tim. 2:15).
6. *An instrument* (II Tim. 2:20).
7. *A servant* (II Tim. 2:24).

The word "*soldier*" is derived from the Latin root word "solidus" which means *firm* or *solid*. The very word itself exudes an atmosphere of dignity and devotion, and involves the basic ingredients of duty and discipline. The sole reason we are to be soldiers, is because we are by virtue of our new relationship with Christ, involved in a warfare. We are told in Ephesians chapter 6 to get into full battle gear, the full armor of God. Every single piece of that armor is of supreme importance, and will be found essential for victory. It will be quickly recognized that it is all external equipment; and therefore, will involve a heated battle from without. None of the equipment is for the protection of the back; no provision is made for any retreat. If we fail to *stand*, and turn away from the conflict, we are on our own, and unprotected.

> From craven inner selfishness
> Whatever be its outward dress
> From fainting when the goal is near
> From faltering in my song of cheer
> From all that is unsoldierly
> Captain of souls, deliver me.
>
> – Amy Carmichael –

Thought For Today

The word "retreat" is not in our book of battle strategy!

October 29

O. T. Bible Reading: Jeremiah 25-26   **Our Focus: Jeremiah 26:3**

I MAY REPENT

The Word of God, when correctly understood, will never contradict itself. It may, at times, from a superficial point of view, appear to do so. In reality it never does, and the problem will be found to be our inability to grasp the truth.

There are at least 10 Old Testament Scriptures which specifically state that "God is not a man that he should lie; neither the son of man, that he should repent", and many others which affirmed that "He is God, He changeth not." There is no contradiction in these Scriptures. Both are absolutely correct, and in no way do they disagree when we correctly understand them.

God never changes in His essential attributes and character: "For I am the Lord, I change not ..." (Mal. 3:6; Jam. 1:17). It is because He never changes in His perfect love, and in His purpose to bless, that He does in fact and of necessity, change His methods in dealing with a volatile and ever-changing humanity. When man, who is the creature, vacillates, changing his loyalties and his priorities; the God, the Creator, changes His method, either to bless and reward, or to punish and correct. God's nature and His love are immutable; therefore, His dealings with fickle humanity must change from blessing to punishing and correcting. What has really changed is on the human level. The unchanging God must continue on in His eternal purposes; He will always pardon and forgive the repentant sinner; and He will just as certainly punish the rebellious and wayward child.

Repentance, on the human level, is an entirely different issue. It is a thorough and fundamental change of mind, attitude, and behavior which involves:

1. A deep and genuine sorrow for sin which is produced by the conviction of the Holy Spirit (John 16:8; II Cor. 7:9-10).
2. An inward repulsion toward sin, and the forsaking of sinful behavior and conduct (Matt. 3:8; Acts 26:20).
3. A sincere and unconditional surrender of the human will, and a love for and acceptance of the good and acceptable and perfect will of God (Rom. 12:1-2).

Thought For Today

Faith alone sees the realm of unchanging certainty!

241

October 29

N. T. Bible Reading: II Timothy 3   **Our Focus: II Timothy 3:1**

THE LAST DAYS

It is generally agreed that II Timothy is the very last communication we have from the apostle Paul. He knew that his time was short, and wrote his own epitaph: "… the time of my departure is at hand. I have fought a good fight, I have finished my course, I have kept the faith" (II Tim. 4:6-7). This gives the book a very special significance; what would the great Apostle leave as his last words to the youthful Timothy, and to us?

He concerns himself with "… the last days …" (II Tim. 3:1); not the last days of his own life, but rather the end-time conditions and events of this church age. The expression "the last days" is used seven times in the Gospel of John. It is interesting that it is first used in Genesis 49:1; Jacob insightfully projects the events which lay ahead for his son's posterity when they would enter the land of promise. It occurs 15 times in the Bible, and is closely associated with the "last time or times" which is used 5 times. In II Timothy 3, Paul is referring to the closing days of this dispensation; the interval of time just before the promised second coming of Christ. In that context he speaks of the *two departures*.

The first departure has to do with the true church. For them the word "harpazo" is used. It means "caught up", and that has been commonly called *the rapture*: "Then we which are alive and remain shall be caught up (raptured) together with them in the clouds, to meet the Lord in the air …" (I Thess. 4:17). This is our blessed and glorious hope.

The second departure is sad and tragic; it is the apostasy of the professing church. The word apostasy is defined as "the total desertion of the principles of faith." The Gospel which is transforming is abandoned and a watered down and anemic social substitute is deliberately chosen. Someone has described it as "the preaching of sermonettes which are proclaimed by preacherettes to an audience of Christianettes." Paul called these conditions "… perilous times …" (II Tim. 3:1); they are grievous, desperate, precipitous, dangerous, violent, and deceptive. We have been duly warned, but are we diligently watching?

Thought For Today

We are both _pilgrims_ and _strangers_ in this present evil world!

<u>October 30</u>

O. T. Bible Reading: Jeremiah 27-28   **Our Focus: Jeremiah 27:10**

THEY PROPHESY A LIE

There are false prophets as surely as there are true prophets. There are counterfeits and fraudulent imitations for almost everything that is real and genuine. In our time it is more in the area of false teachers than that of false prophets. However, the effect of their devious ways is much the same, and the profile of one is a very accurate picture of the other.

The words "they prophesy lies in my name" are the words of the Lord concerning these imposters of Jeremiah's time; those very words are repeated seven times in a short frame within the book of Jeremiah. A lie is a falsehood, and it is that whether done deliberately or simply repeated innocently. In the first case it is a conscious strategy to promote something which is known to be false under the pretense of being true; this person is a liar, and falls under the wrath of God. Those who perpetrate a falsehood without knowing the source or the motive are deceived, but still called liars for they are advancing that which is false. Yet they loudly maintain Divine ordination and approval saying, "Thus speaketh the Lord of hosts, the God of Israel ..." (Jer. 28:2). A claim is not a fact; it is only an assertion, and must be carefully examined. The acid test for all time remains "... by *their fruits* ye shall know them" (Matt. 7:20, 16). What fruits of righteousness and true holiness (Eph. 4:24), and what similar fruits do their teachers produce in the lives of those who hear them?

The true prophet, God's messenger, Jeremiah, accurately prophesied 70 years of captivity in Babylon (Jer. 25:11-12). Hananiah, the chief spokesman for the false prophets, did what was politically motivated, telling the people what they wanted to hear, contradicted the true message and declared instead that the yoke of Babylon would be broken in 2 years, and the land would be liberated (Jer. 28:11). The true prophet was vindicated by the removal of the false prophet within that very year as prophesied (Jer. 28:16-17), and by the fulfillment of his true prophecy of 70 years captivity. It is a very dangerous thing to presumptuously stand against God's messengers.

<u>Thought For Today</u>

The Word of the Lord is never popular with those in rebellion!

October 30

N. T. Bible Reading: II Timothy 4   **Our Focus: II Timothy 4:5**

MINISTRY

The aged Apostle challenges the youthful Timothy to fulfill the ministry to which he had been called, "… thy ministry" (II Tim. 4:5). He prefaced that with a resume of his own ministry; it was *a battle*, *a race*, and *a sacred trust*.

"I have fought a good fight …" (II Tim. 4:7); these are resting words from a much decorated veteran of many battles: "… Let not him that girdeth on his harness boast himself as he that putteth it off" (I Ki. 20:11). In one brief terse statement, Paul uses three metaphors to describe his or any other true ministry which demands bravery and commitment, perseverance and discipline, faithfulness and loyalty. It is no child's play, it is not theatrical entertainment, nor is it a recreation room. It is a call to arms; it is a summons which forever separates the casual followers from the dedicated disciples. There is no room here for cozy rest, casual slumberings, or pious platitudes. This is warfare of the most fierce and intense kind. It demands sacrifice, blood, sweat, and tears; every triumphant and victorious warrior will be faithfully and finally decorated and rewarded with an eternal "… crown of glory …" (I Pet. 5:4).

The ministry is also a strenuous and demanding race; "… I have finished my course …" (II Tim. 4:7). In a relay race each runner has a particular phase of the race for which he individually is responsible. At the finish line of his course, he must pass the banner to the next runner. In any natural race there is a race track, a starting and a finishing line, and a prize or trophy for the winner; so also in the spiritual. To see this clearly, transforms any ministry.

"… I have kept the faith" (II Tim. 4:7); this is a sacred trust. It is a solemn responsibility to maintain and enunciate the truth accurately, "… as the truth is in Jesus" (Eph. 4:21); but of equal importance, to so live that every phase of conduct would "… adorn (or decorate) the doctrine …" preached (Tit. 2:10). Timothy is urged to "… keep that which is committed to thy trust …" (I Tim. 6:20; II Tim. 1:14), or simply "guard the deposit." This is indeed a solemn responsibility which is incumbent upon the ministry.

Thought For Today

The first duty of a teacher is to demonstrate the subject!

October 31

O. T. Bible Reading: Jeremiah 29-30   **Our Focus: Jeremiah 29:11**

AN EXPECTED END

The focus of God is on *the end* of the process of life and its experiences, because He is omniscient and eternal.   The focus of man is the present distress, the present time and the immediate circumstances, and how they relate to our comfort and well-being, because he is mortal and lives for today only.   It takes a supernatural adjustment of our mind and of our motives for us to measure things in the light of eternity.   "Now no chastening for the present seemeth to be joyous, but grievous: nevertheless afterward it yieldeth the peaceable fruit of righteousness unto them which are exercised thereby" (Heb. 12:11).   The young boy who was about to be disciplined by his father was told, "my boy, this is going to hurt me even more than it hurts you."   The boy responded, "but not in the same place."   It is a momentary discomfort which is foremost in our minds.   The key words are "afterward" and "exercise"; those who "get the message" and are instructed by the unpleasant lesson will eat the pleasant fruits.

The Word of the Lord to Israel by His messenger, Jeremiah, was that God had an intended purpose for their captivity in the 70 years of servitude.   There was a tomorrow, the bondage would cease, and in the end they would flourish in their own land once again.   The purpose of God's love, the intent of His heart, was ever their best good as well as their blessing.   The temporary discipline, made inevitable by human rebellion, must be seen as a means to an end.   So also is it ever the very same in our own lives, and daily experience.   God is good ... *all the time*; when we cannot *trace* the process, we must patiently *trust* the designer.

It is our *reaction* to the process which determines the results:

1.   We may, and often do, *despise* the chastening (Heb. 12:5); we either get upset by it, flippantly dismiss it, or take no serious note of it.
2.   We may *faint* (Heb. 12:5); the greatest temptation will be found to engage in self-pity.
3.   We may *endure* the experiences (Heb. 12:7); that is, grit our teeth, and tenaciously hold our breath until the storm passes over.
4.   We may in a positive way respond to the "strange things" which God's providence has permitted to come our way (Heb. 12:11).

We accept it as allowed of God, only for our best good, and in the end for His greater glory.

Thought For Today

There is no defeating those who see time from eternity's perspective!

October 31

N. T. Bible Reading: Titus 1　　　　　　　　　**Our Focus: Titus 1:1**

GODLINESS

The two words "godliness" and "godly" occur 28 times in the Bible; Paul uses the word godliness 11 times in the pastoral epistles of Timothy and Titus ... it is used only 14 times in the entire New Testament. It is a good word, and an outstanding attribute of Christian behavior, also a rare quality which characterizes the most spiritual people of God. It is God-likeness in shoe leather. It has to do with behavior and conduct; the Greek word literally means "well-pleasing" to God. It is the attitude of heart, the manner of thinking, and the pattern of behavior which Paul defines as "good works." Nine times Paul associates this pattern of godly conduct, good works, and Christian behavior in the books of Timothy and Titus.

He is not talking about the human and futile effort to be justified by our own works or merits. The basis of our salvation is well established; we are justified by faith, in the finished work of Christ on Calvary: "For by grace are ye saved through faith; and that not of yourselves: it is the gift of God: Not of works, lest any man should boast" (Eph. 2:8-9). We are saved by grace, we live by faith, and we conduct our daily lives in a manner which is well-pleasing to the Lord. Any pretended faith which does not produce righteousness and the vital change in life-style and conduct, is foreign to the Scriptures, and is by them called vain.

The basis of our relationship to God by the transformation of regeneration is one of love: "We love him, because he first loved us" (I John 4:19) and to His eternal praise, the love *of* God as well as a great love *for* God "... is shed abroad in our hearts ..." (Rom. 5:5). Where there is genuine love there is also an automatic desire to please, and to manifest that love in sacrificial service. When we come, through the new birth to love God, we inherit also a compelling desire to "... do always those things that please him" (John 8:29; I John 3:22). The central element of "... godliness" (Tit. 1:1) is not just to do that which is right, but that which is *well pleasing* (Col. 3:20).

Thought For Today

The seed of Divine planting will produce "after its kind!"

November 1

O. T. Bible Reading: Jeremiah 31-32   **Our Focus: Jeremiah 31:4**

I WILL

Jeremiah chapter 31 may very well be given the title of the "I will" chapter, because the words "I will" are repeated 15 times. The most arresting fact of all is that these are the words of God Himself. These few segments of Jeremiah, chapters 30-33, are indeed a "... song in the night ..." (Ps. 77:6). They have been defined as "the triumphal hymn of Israel's salvation." To rule out any future restoration and Divine purpose for the nation of Israel, is to deny categorically the very words which God Himself has spoken concerning them. However, this is the word of prophecy. The most difficult aspect of prophecy is the element of *time*. The Word of the Lord for this and for many prophetic pronouncements is: "For the vision is yet for an appointed time, but at the end it shall speak, and not lie: though it tarry, wait for it; because it will surely come, it will not tarry" (Hab. 2:3).

The great promises of the prophetic Word are sure of fulfillment. Certainly the promises will have to wait or tarry until the appointed time for the fulfillment of them. One thing is clear; it will not tarry one moment beyond that time. Every such inspired word is dated with an invisible ink which can be read only by the Holy Spirit quickened eye of faith. Genuine faith not only sees, but also confidently rests in God's purposes.

God spoke to Israel, through the prophet Jeremiah, by declaring emphatically and categorically "... I will ..." (Jer. 31:4); certainly and absolutely *He will*. What He promises, He also performs. In a much less dramatic and much more solitary way, the Lord may whisper to His troubled children today, and it too will include the words, "I will." We must cling to those assuring words. As surely as God has spoken them, just as surely they will come to pass.

Thought For Today

When God says, "I will" true faith says, "thank you Lord!"

November 1

N. T. Bible Reading: Titus 2   **Our Focus: Titus 2:1**

SOUND DOCTRINE

There are doctrines which are "… according to godliness" (I Tim. 6:3), and then again there are man-made concoctions which gender rather to ungodliness and careless living. Paul warned Timothy that, "… the Spirit speaketh expressly (explicitly and distinctly), that in the latter times some shall depart from the faith, giving heed to seducing spirits, and doctrines of devils" (I Tim. 4:1). There is nothing new in this intrusion into the ranks of God's people. The church at Corinth came together and every one of them "… hath a psalm, hath a doctrine … hath a revelation …" (I Cor. 14:26). Not all, by any means, were the Apostles' doctrines (Acts 2:42) nor were they a doctrine of the Lord (Acts 13:12). Just a few verses later in I Corinthians 14:33 Paul added "For God is not the author of confusion …", and the strange doctrines (that is, strange to the truth, Heb. 13:9) were not edifying the church. Any false teaching always brings with it some dubious and damaging way of life.

Instruction and teaching are important, but so also is conduct and character, both as to the people who hear and of those who teach. The truth must be proclaimed, and the most effective way to declare it is to illustrate it by a godly and holy life. Principle and practice are essentials to preaching.

The words, "sound doctrine" are repeated four times by the Apostle Paul: twice in Timothy and twice in Titus. It means "healthy or health producing." Could there be some relationship between the sickly and anemic condition of the modern church and the doctrine, or type and tone of the message being preached? We do know that the good old-fashioned Bible preacher is rejected, while the shallow religious entertainer becomes a celebrity. Tragically, these itching ears, which clamor for theatrical Christian performers, soon, will become deaf ears, having turned from the truth and having believed substitute and man-made fables (II Tim. 4:4).

Thought For Today

Blessed are those who refuse to eat at tables with only substitute victuals!

November 2

O. T. Bible Reading: Jeremiah 33-35   **Our Focus: Jeremiah 34:4**

ZEDEKIAH

The history of nations, as well as individuals, is very fascinating and instructive when studied in the light of Bible prophecy and truth. History is truly "His-story" when it is studied with anointed eyes. In the case at hand, Jeremiah is the God-appointed messenger or prophet to the nation of Judah (the two tribes of Judah and Benjamin). The last and final king of the 19 kings of the southern division was Zedekiah. The northern kingdom had been crushed by Shalmanezer the Assyrian 136 years earlier. The false prophet, Hananiah, had prophesied seven years earlier that the Babylonian empire of Nebuchadnezzar would be broken in two years. The true prophecies of Jeremiah prevailed and now, alas, Jerusalem is under siege and will soon fall into the hands of Babylon. Jehoichin the king is taken prisoner of war and deported to Babylon. His uncle Mattaniah was made king by Nebuchadnezzar and he, the Babylonian conqueror, changed his name to Zedekiah (II Ki. 24:15-17).

The original name Mattaniah meant the gift of Jehovah. Zedekiah, in turn, means the righteousness of Jehovah. This seems to be a scathing rebuke by Nebuchadnezzar of Judah's dereliction and of their defection from their God and from His word. It may also have been an attempt to vindicate the justice and righteousness of the Great Jehovah in the tragic events at hand, and the judgment about to fall upon the nation.

The yet future prophecies of Jeremiah (chapters 30-33) for Judah and for Israel beam forth with almost blinding sun-bursts through the dark, dismal, and cloud-draped skies. The amazing and glorious fact that God "... loved thee with an everlasting love ..." (Jer. 31:3) brings hope to the hopeless. This wonderful truth is crowned with a glowing gem of promise, "In those days shall Judah be saved, and Jerusalem shall dwell safely: and this is the name wherewith she shall be called, The Lord our righteousness" (Jehovah-Tsidkenu, Jer. 33:16). What a hope for Israel: what a great revelation for us ... Jesus is now our righteousness! Blessed be His worthy name forever!

Thought For Today

The darkest clouds cannot hide the brightest promises!

November 2

N. T. Bible Reading: Titus 3   **Our Focus: Titus 3:8**

MAINTAIN GOOD WORKS

Some things need to be said only once; others must be repeated often and with much emphasis. The tide flows in the opposite direction, and without deliberate and determined effort we will drift with it. "… these things I will that thou affirm constantly …" (Tit. 3:8). Circumstances and conditions require urgency and great diligence in this particular issue.

This little epistle of Titus was written by Paul at about the same time as I Timothy. The letters to Timothy, Titus, and Philemon are known as "the pastoral epistles"; they are written by an Apostle to young men in the ministry. They deal with vital issues of great importance from the pastor's point of view. First Timothy is a charge to protect and preserve the purity of the Gospel; second Timothy is a challenge to proclaim the full Gospel; Titus is a caution to practice what you preach. Twice in Titus chapter 3 Paul urges that great care must be taken to maintain good works (Tit. 3:8, 14). The very highest expressions of Christian doctrine are to be linked and tied to the very highest ideals of life and conduct. Deep doctrine and shallow living cannot and do not sail in the same waters. The polite modern evasions and compromising indulgences are blown out of the water by this forthright expression of true New Testament Christianity.

The word "maintain" is worthy of careful study. The dictionary will help; the first entry says, "to carry on, to continue." Applied spiritually, it suggests we are not to initiate something new or on our own. We are, rather, to cooperate fully and enthusiastically to further and continue what the Great Redeemer has already miraculously begun. Webster also adds, it means to keep in good repair. You do not have to build it, but like any other tool or machine, it must be maintained and kept in good repair and at top performance level. The manufacturer provides the equipment, but the responsibility of maintenance rests with the user. Another interesting slant to the meaning is to protect against criticism. The conduct and life-style of the individual has much to do with the demonstration and presentation of the product. We are to be careful to maintain consistently the pattern of conduct which is above reproach lest the Gospel be blamed (II Cor. 6:3).

Thought For Today

Those who maintain good works adorn the doctrine!

November 3

O. T. Bible Reading: Jeremiah 36-37   **Our Focus: Jeremiah 36:4**

BARUCH

Baruch was Jeremiah's scribe or writer. His name means "blessed" and surely he was a blessed man to be secretary to the prophet Jeremiah. He recorded what was dictated or directed by the prophet, and he shared the message and ministry of Jeremiah so fully that he also shared in the prison sentence handed down by the rebellious king. It is interesting and enlightening to notice that God provided "helps" even in another dispensation. It may be that in his ministry, as well as in his personal life, it could be said, "… It is not good that the man should be alone …" (Gen. 2:18). Even the great Apostle Paul had Barnabas assigned by the direction of the Holy Spirit to accompany him (Acts 13:2).

The tiny 45th chapter of Jeremiah is specifically addressed to Baruch (Jer. 45:1). It is dated in the fourth year of Jehoiakim, which would be 20 years after the captivity and exile. The book, which is referred to in chapter 25, verse 13, is no doubt, the Chronicle of the prophecy regarding the Gentile nations as recorded by this very man, Baruch. He spent his final years in exile in the land of Egypt with his friend Jeremiah (Jer. 43:6-7). The record as given in chapter 45 was given much earlier, when Baruch was yet a young man.

The specific promise was precisely fulfilled. God did spare his life, and he came through the ordeal alive. It has been observed that God can pull us through anything, if we can stand the pull. Early on, God warned this able and talented young man not to seek great things for himself. It was timely advice for the youthful Baruch, and it is timely advice for all of God's children. One of the greatest hindrances to God's purposes in any individual life is personal ambition. For the vessel to be fit, it must be purged of this impediment. God will have a people who have, through the furnace of testing and trial, died out to all personal self-seeking in order "That no flesh should glory in his presence" (I Cor. 1:29).

Thought For Today

Blessed is the man who can serve the Lord unselfishly!

November 3

N. T. Bible Reading: Philemon   **Our Focus: Philemon 1:10**

ONESIMUS

The tiny 25 verse book of Philemon is a profound portrait of the Apostle Paul. It is also a miniature but mighty anatomy of the practical aspects of Christian principles applied to social relationships. It also very graphically illustrates and gives a strong emphasis to the basic out-workings of the Mighty Gospel of Jesus Christ in 3 culturally diverse men: Paul, the Apostle; Philemon, an affluent businessman; and Onesimus, a runaway slave. Never has so little said so much to so many!

The background story in this case is essential. Philemon, it would seem, was himself converted to Christ through the ministry of the Apostle Paul (Phil. 1:19, 21). He was a man of means, a slave-owner, a recognized Christian leader and very likely a local pastor (Phil. 1:2). The "... beloved Apphia ..." (Phil. 1:2) is generally believed to be his wife, and Archippus his son, and possibly the pastor either at Colossae or Laodicea (Col. 4:17). Onesimus had probably been a domestic slave, who may have stolen money with which he made his way across the Aegean and the Adriatic seas to Rome. By Divine appointment, he there met the Apostle Paul, who was at the time in prison at Rome. Onesimus was genuinely converted, and this great manifesto of Gospel principles and practice unfolds.

There is a beautiful unveiling of the very core elements of New Testament Christianity in this story. The run-away slave returns to his master not to be "scourged, mutilated, crucified, thrown to wild beasts" (Bishop Lightfoot), but to be embraced as a true brother and companion in the Gospel. The name "Onesimus" means "profitable" and Paul plays on this fact.

The one who once was unprofitable to you, is now, by the transforming power of the Gospel, profitable both to you and to me (Phil. 1:11). The debt (likely stolen money) is not intended to be ignored; restitution is a vital part of regeneration. Paul himself would repay it if Philemon did not specifically and personally forgive the debt and the debtor. No wonder Paul (and thousands of others) was not ashamed of the Gospel of Christ (Rom. 1:16). Personal problems, as well as huge social evils, are effectively and permanently changed by the reality of transformed lives. Glory to God!

Thought For Today

What was "then", is not "now", when Jesus is truly "Lord!"

November 4

O. T. Bible Reading: Jeremiah 38-39   **Our Focus: Jeremiah 38:28**

JERUSALEM WAS TAKEN

There is nothing as powerful as an idea whose time has come. And there is nothing more certain of fulfillment than the prophetic Word of the Lord. What is of vital importance is usually repeated at least once whether by a dream or by admonition. Jeremiah had repeatedly prophesied and warned that the city of Jerusalem would be captured, sacked, and burned by the armies of Babylon (Jer. 21:10, 34:2 et al). It is a matter of history that indeed it was.

Jeremiah was a prophet (Jer. 1:5). God ordained him to that great office, and there is no other appointment or designation which can qualify any person for that or any other office in the ministry. Isaiah had been dead for about 100 years when Jeremiah began his prophetic work. He remained at his post for over 40 years, which covered the reigns of Judah's last five kings: Josiah, Jehoahaz, Jehoiakim, Jehoiachin, and Zedekiah. The very mention of these names spells the darkness and despair of those desperate days. Jeremiah was the prophet of God at the time of Judah's midnight hour. During 40 years of faithful ministry, Jeremiah never once saw any grateful or meaningful response to his message. "Moreover it is required in stewards, that a man be found faithful" (I Cor. 4:2). Men and boards will require success especially in numbers and finance, but the Divine principle prevails, God honors and rewards *faithfulness*.

Jeremiah has been called "the weeping prophet." Every prediction of coming judgment is soaked in tears; and every pleading appeal is punctuated with sobs of sorrow. The ministry of a broken heart (that of Jesus), requires a ministry of broken and bleeding hearts. These are the unmistakable features of a true prophet of God. His humble attitude and spirit when he began his ministry was, "... Ah, Lord God! behold, I cannot speak: for I am a child" (Jer. 1:6). These are great credentials for anyone who is called into the ministry!

Thought For Today

"It came to pass, as the Lord had said" ... it always will!

November 4

N. T. Bible Reading: Hebrews 1   **Our Focus: Hebrews 1:4**

BETTER

That which is "better" has no equal. The book of Hebrews includes the word "better" 13 times; more than in all the rest of the New Testament combined. The writer erases any cause or reason to question who this exalted One is. The very brief but unqualified Divine titles of "Jesus", "Christ", and "Lord" are repeated 68 times. He is described as "... better than the angels ..." (Heb. 1:4); having by His unique and superior sacrifice provided better things (Heb. 6:9, 12:24), a better hope (Heb. 7:19), a better testament (Heb. 7:22), a better covenant (Heb. 8:6), better promises (Heb. 8:6), better sacrifices (Heb. 9:23), a better and an enduring substance (better position) (Heb. 10:34), a better country (Heb. 11:16), a better resurrection (Heb. 11:35), some better thing (or time) (Heb. 11:40), and victoriously "... the blood of sprinkling, that speaketh better things than that of Abel" (Heb. 12:24).

It becomes quite clear that the purpose of the book is threefold:

1.   To establish the typical significance of the Mosaic institutions, and of the tabernacle. There are 86 direct references to the Old Testament in the book of Hebrews, and these can be traced to at least 100 passages from the Old Testament. The Old Testament economy and that of Moses was merely the type and shadow of which Christ and Christianity are the anti-type.
2.   To warn against diluting the pure Gospel with Judaism, and of consequent apostasy. There is a seven-fold emphasis and warning against any "falling away" in doctrine or in practice.
3.   To clearly affirm and establish the superiority and finality of Christ and of Christianity.

New Testament Christianity is not established by the doing away with or by the abandonment of the Mosaic institutions, but rather by the fulfillment of them. It is because He is the fulfillment of _all_ that He is "_better_." Jesus is as much better than the individuals involved and the typical ceremonies, as the substance is better than the shadow. The earthly rituals are fulfilled in the heavenly Redeemer, and "heaven" or "heavenly" are repeated 17 times. Therefore, "let us" (used 14 times) go on to full maturity.

Thought For Today

Because He is "better" we can claim His very "highest!"

November 5

O. T. Bible Reading: Jeremiah 40-42   **Our Focus: Jeremiah 42:7**

AFTER 10 DAYS

Divine delays are not denials. Rush is always wrong. It is not in our nature to wait. Waiting is a discipline, and like any other discipline, it must be learned through a process of teaching, heart and life preparation, and experimental training. Patience must be learned, not from a text-book, but from and in the furnace of trials, tests, and tribulation. If you pray for patience, prepare for trouble. There are phases and aspects of our salvation which are progressive in nature, and are incorporated into our lives only through the process of experience. This takes time, involves change (which requires time), and demands maturity in attitude and action (which involves on-the-job tutoring).

The classic example of Divine delay is Daniel the prophet. He set himself to pray and to seek God through fasting for an answer. The answer came, but there was a strenuous and demanding waiting on the Lord for three weeks. There may be one or more of a large number of reasons for the delay in the answer. In his case, the reason is clearly stated, "But the prince of the kingdom of Persia withstood me one and twenty days …" (Dan. 10:13). This is spiritual warfare, and one reason prayer is hard work, and very demanding.

The Scriptures instruct us to wait on the Lord. There are some very distinct promises to those who do. This is one of the several steps which lead us to spiritual maturity. To wait on the Lord is an *attitude* of dependence and expectancy; it is a cultivated life-long attribute of the spiritually minded. The promise of Isaiah 40:31 is, "But they that wait upon the Lord … shall walk, and not faint." They wait as they walk, and they walk as they wait. One of the reasons for delay is to wean us from all that is earthly and natural. We fret when we fail to get what intrigues us. We fume and worry when some desired potion evades us. The Lord of harvest has long patience with our frailties. In His deliberate delays He wants to teach us that He Himself is the real answer we seek. When He fills our lives with His glorious presence and transforming power, waiting and duty become a delight.

Thought For Today

Real fulfillment is not "some-thing" it is rather "some-One!"

November 5

N. T. Bible Reading: Hebrews 2   **Our Focus: Hebrews 2:17**

RECONCILIATION

Reconciliation involves animosity and enmity. Sin is a fact, and it is a fundamental problem. It is not just commission; it is *condition*. It is not just *doing* wrong, it is much more importantly *being* wrong. The acid test of religion is how it deals with this issue. False religion and false cults deal with *sins* and with *culture*. Only the Bible, and only the Lord Jesus Christ, deal with *sin* and the nature of sin. We are told that the three primary elements which mold every life are heredity, environment, and training. If we have no answer for the first, then we fail utterly in the other two. Jesus laid the axe to the root of the tree. We are not sinners because of the catalogue of evils we commit; we are guilty of these offenses because *we are* sinners. God made His Son "... to be sin for us (note well, not a sinner; He experienced no sin) ... that we might be made the righteousness of God in him" (II Cor. 5:21). He was our substitute; "Who his own self bare our sins in his own body on the tree ..." (I Pet. 2:24).

Man can suffer, but he cannot satisfy. God can satisfy, but He cannot suffer. The Lord Jesus Christ did both. He fully met all of the requirements of a Holy God; He also fully meets all of the needs of fallen humanity. Hallelujah, what a Saviour!! God is now satisfied; man has been reconciled, and there is peace for the pardoned sinner. The basic truth is that, "... God was in Christ, reconciling the world unto himself ..." (II Cor. 5:19). This is impossible, apart from the completed work of Christ at Calvary. Now, correctly and with rejoicing, we can say, "... he is our peace ..." (Eph. 2:14).

Reconciliation represents a fundamental change. It has to do with a vital change in our relationship to God. Now, through Christ, God has His arms outstretched to a lost world. This great reality also involves a vital change in the believing soul. We come to experience His love and mercy, and as forgiven sinners we have a new birth into a new family, with a new nature and a whole new way of living. If there is no vital change, then there has been no reconciliation. The only justifying defense of the mercy of God in forgiveness is the total change in behavior of the one forgiven.

Thought For Today

Those who are reconciled to God have also been recreated!

November 6

O. T. Bible Reading: Jeremiah 43-45   **Our Focus: Jeremiah 45:5**

SEEK THEM NOT

There is a subtlety in the human heart which is so coated with good and great goals that it is almost impossible to detect. It is woven into the vital impulses of the appetites for God and for His very best. It lurks in the shadows of diligent labor and sacrificial service. It is as relentless as it is relevant. It is carnal ambition, and fleshly self-seeking.

Those who live on a carnal level will never have even a hint of concern about ulterior motives. Those who serve only from a sense of duty will warm themselves at the deceptive fires of apparent success. The flattering applause of statistics, size, and numbers spur the human genius to unbelievable levels of dedication and drive. Only the rare souls who walk in closest communion with the risen Savior, sense the call of the Spirit to new levels of abandonment and self-effacing love. This is indeed a high-way; it is found only at the highest peaks of spiritual reality, and enjoyed only by those who abide in the secret place of the Most High. The great George Muller of Bristol was asked by a naive young minister, what was the secret of his success. The young man was stunned and nonplussed by the immediate response: "there came a day when I died." The average Christian would certainly say, "and what does that mean?" It is foreign language to shallow followers. The rare few, those initiated into the post-graduate school of "hidden ones", will smile, bow their heads, and quietly whisper "thank God!" They know the secret, and they deeply rejoice from their strong tower hidden with Christ in God.

It is not God's purpose to make us display pieces of His wise crafting, but to lure us into His banqueting house where we are truly and experimentally made *one* with Him. This vital union transforms the life and mind by the overpowering awareness of His purpose, His will, and His presence. There is a blessed God-consciousness which saturates the life. This glorious relationship fills the life and spirit with the aroma of heaven's atmosphere, which creates a longing after God in other lives, not admiration for me as a person. Self-realization is spiritual dry-rot; self-expenditure is spiritual maturity.

Thought For Today

Those who seek Him first will always know His fulness!

November 6

N. T. Bible Reading: Hebrews 3   **Our Focus: Hebrews 3:1**

CONSIDER HIM

The writer to the Hebrews urges them to "consider" 4 times:

1.   "… consider the Apostle and High Priest …" (Heb. 3:1).
2.   "… consider how great this man (Melchizedek) was …" (Heb. 7:4).
3.   "… consider one another to provoke unto love and to good works" (Heb. 10:24).
4.   "… consider him that endured such contradiction of sinners against himself, lest ye be wearied and faint in your minds" (Heb. 12:3).

We combine the first and the last; as we think seriously and carefully about the Apostle and High Priest of our faith, we are certainly fulfilling the admonition to consider Him.

John Wycliffe (1324-1384), the English reformer, translator, and author of "The English Bible" gave us what he termed "*the golden rule of interpretation*": "it shall greatly help thee to understand Scripture if thou mark not only what is spoken or written, but of whom and to whom, with what words, at what time, where, and to what intent, under what circumstances, considering what goeth before and what followeth." It would be very difficult to improve on that.

The obvious theme of the book of Hebrews is the superiority of Christ. But He is not to be compared, but is clearly contrasted with all that was basic to the Jewish people. He surpasses the outstanding personalities; the Angels, Moses, Joshua, and Aaron; He rises above and fulfills all of the ancient institutions; the Sanctuary, the Covenant, the Tabernacle, the sacred Day of Atonement, and the Levitical offerings. The sun (in Hebrews S-O-N) has risen; the stars must retire. The appeal is not to *go back* to any or all of these, but to *go on* to a full inheritance and to full spiritual maturity in Christ.

Jesus is *the Apostle*, the *One sent* from God, and the great *Messenger* of the new covenant. As God's Apostle, He came from God to man with a Divine message; He spoke for God to man. He is also *the High Priest* for us; He stood before God, and represented man as their only possible mediator. This Jesus is the founder of this new house (used 7 times) which is God's house, and He was faithful as a Son *over* this House (Heb. 3:5-6). Moses, by contrast, was merely the human agent of the old economy and was faithful *in it*. Jesus' unique priesthood is the very theme of the latter part of Hebrews. Let us also duly "*consider Him*."

Thought For Today

Those who reflect prayerfully on Him, will also reflect Him!

November 7

O. T. Bible Reading: Jeremiah 46-48   **Our Focus: Jeremiah 48:10**

DECEITFULLY

To deceive is to misrepresent. The margin helps here again, on our focus Scripture, "negligently." Something is being neglected or simply left undone. When only a portion is manifest, this is a gross misrepresentation. Only a complete and accurate listing of the contents can be described as "truth in packaging." There is a high honor bestowed upon God's people to give our very best to the service of the Lord. What is half-hearted is also haphazard, and must inevitably be a handicap.

The Christian life is not at all an issue of "dos" and "don'ts." It is so much more, so much deeper, and so much more glorious, exciting, and enjoyable. The Lord does not just lay out a set of rules; He, rather, makes the standard clear, imparts His very nature within us, and in so doing, as the song says, "Since I've got my want-to fixed, I'm happy and blessed." It is a relationship which determines the motive. When my relationship to Him is one of genuine love, I delight and enjoy doing whatever pleases Him. Those who harp on legalism and bondage, when referring to Christian behavior and conduct, expose their own utter bankruptcy. Those who have a love-relationship revel in and delight to do that which pleases and ministers to the loved one. There is no sacrifice which is too great and no self-denial is a burden. It is sheer joy to serve and minister to the one you love. This beautiful expression of domestic harmony and sweet fellowship is sadly lacking in most families. It is God's design, and where and when it is found, the home is a little bit of heaven on earth.

When the reality of redemption reaches the point of commitment and glad obedience, it enters into the Divine attribute of creation. Every happy response to the appeals of the Blessed Savior to higher ground opens the floodgates of spiritual abundance. It unites us to the reality of the Almighty God. It is then and only then, that His creative power works mightily *within* us, and miraculously through us, to hungry hearts and lonely lives. Genuine faith in Christ not only claims forgiveness, it also victoriously claims fruitfulness. The half-hearted can never appreciate the exploits of the whole-hearted.

Thought For Today

To be delivered from mediocrity is to enjoy the miraculous!

November 7

N. T. Bible Reading: Hebrews 4   **Our Focus: Hebrews 4:2**

MIXED WITH FAITH

The example of Israel, when they failed to enter the land of Canaan, teaches us that we must grasp the opportunities and claim the Gospel truth presented. Caleb and Joshua had another spirit, saw the Divine plan and provision, and viewed the giants as specks of human effort attempting to stand before the armies of the Almighty God. There is a great secret in quick and decisive action when the Word of God is preached. Delay is a sure component of failure, and procrastination is the sure companion of disappointment. Isaiah gives us a vital key to spiritual success and victory, "If ye be willing and obedient, ye shall eat the good of the land" (Isa. 1:19). One translation renders it, "Obey with a will." This seems to mean that we are to take positive action heartily, decisively, deliberately, and immediately. This has always seemed to me to be the key which enables the Word of God to become "... engrafted ..." (Jam. 1:21).

Real salvation is experienced when the Word of God is engrafted ... the root of that word is "implanted." If the seed of the Word only "falls" upon our ears and hearts, it will be non-productive. The element which opens the heart and mind to allow the Word to enter and to imbed itself in the fertile soil of the obedient heart is a ready response from a surrendered will. Only when the will is surrendered can it act quickly and positively to the appeals of the Gospel message.

There is rich meaning in the word used here and translated "mixed." It is a metaphor borrowed from the science of physical health. Food which is ingested must also be digested to be productive. In the process of assimilation the food must be mixed with saliva and gastric juices. It is then capable of being absorbed by the digestive vessels, discharged into the bloodstream, and becomes the elixir of life. So also is the Word of God. It must be assimilated to be productive. The faithful heart enthusiastically responds to the Word of God, mixing every element of the quickened heart in absolute and unqualified trust and faith to seal that creative Word in the good soil of a surrendered will.

Thought For Today

A hearty response always produces a healthy example!

November 8

O. T. Bible Reading: Jeremiah 49-50   **Our Focus: Jeremiah 50:5**

THEIR FACES

The prophet Isaiah said by inspiration of the Lord, "… therefore have I set my face like a flint …" (Isa. 50:7). Luke records an event which characterized the entire life of the Lord Jesus, "… he steadfastly set his face to go to Jerusalem" (Luke 9:51). There was a singleness of purpose, thus expressed, which is an essential element in every Christian life. Paul stated it in slightly different language, "… this one thing I do …" (Phil. 3:13). Jesus spoke of the very same principle in the Sermon on the Mount, "But seek ye *first* the kingdom of God, and his righteousness …" (Matt. 6:33). Three times in Joshua chapter 14 the Word of God emphasizes the singular element which set Joshua apart from all Israel, he "… *wholly* followed the Lord …" (Josh. 14:8, 9, 14). The victorious band of overcomers pictured in Revelation chapter 14 is represented as those who "… follow the Lamb whithersoever he goeth …" (Rev. 14:4), and there is a single word which I have printed in the margin of my Bible which is "*wholly.*"

The children of Israel failed to enter the land of Canaan when they first came to Kadesh-Barnea because their hearts were divided; they had a heart and a heart. One part of them desired to enter the land, and another part of them wanted something else. In Jeremiah chapter 50 it is said of Zion, and of those who seek the way to Zion, that their faces were pointed only in that direction. This surely means that the single purpose of their entire being is set in that direction. A major problem, and a very common one, occurs when the feet point in one direction and the face is turned in another.

This makes for instability and leads to failure. James tells us that the double-minded man is unstable in all his ways (Jam. 1:8). He later admonished his readers to, "… purify your hearts, ye double minded" (Jam. 4:8). We are told that the sons of Zebulon, which means "dwelling", were "… expert in war … could keep rank: they were not of double heart" (I Chron. 12:33). The margin helps by explaining, "without a heart and a heart." Blessed condition, and blessed reality, for all who set their faces toward Zion.

Thought For Today

When the heart is fixed, the face is steadfastly set!

November 8

N. T. Bible Reading: Hebrews 5   **Our Focus: Hebrews 5:14**

SPIRITUAL GROWN-UPS

There are, it seems, as many definitions of spiritual maturity as there are immature people, who will attempt to justify their own childishness, if it is humanly possible. The Word of God is a clean, clear, and classic mirror which gives a true picture of what really is. No amount of posturing or pretense can mask the facts; all can see them except the one who attempts to disguise them. This inclination is the very essence of immaturity.

Maturity is much more than size, shape, or sight; it is primarily an issue of grown-up faculties and fabric. The fifth chapter of Hebrews gets to the root of the definition. It is not so much demonstration as it is development and consequent demeanor.

The first-mentioned attribute in focus (Heb. 5:12) is that of being an effective teacher. The teacher must be one who has mastered the subject, and has the ability to impart the subject material to the student. This is indeed a fine art and a much-to-be-coveted faculty even in the natural world. The mature saint is one who has listened carefully, studied diligently, and absorbed thoroughly so as to become an expert or specialist in the area of Christian life and conduct. It is not so difficult to teach someone to ride a bicycle if you know how yourself. It is not just an explanation of basic laws; it is imparting a technique. The single most essential attribute of teaching is example or illustration. Those who cannot show what Christian maturity is by their own example of life and conduct are themselves still very immature.

The spiritually mature are no longer dependent on others for their nourishment and daily supply of health producing food. They now enjoy the "… strong meat …" of the Word of God (Heb. 5:14). Tiny children must be nourished with juices and baby food. Their system is not capable of digesting solid foods and meat. Those who have grown and learn how to distinguish between right and wrong, between decent and indecent, between proper and improper, between virtuous and vulgar, and between what God loves and what God hates, have matured. They will also be able to communicate and impart these great skills to others.

Thought For Today

The truly mature inspire hope in those who are youthful!

November 9

O. T. Bible Reading: Jeremiah 51-52   **Our Focus: Jeremiah 52:34**

EVERY DAY A PORTION

On December 25th the King of Babylon lifted up the head of Jehoiachin, King of Judah. That simply means that as sorrow and sadness cause the head to be held down, even so comfort, relief, and gladness cause the head to be lifted up. This kindness and expression of mercy from the heathen King resulted in a changed prison garment into a *caftan* or robe of honor (Jer. 52:33). He was also given a daily portion of food for his nourishment. All of this was quite a surprise and an unexpected turn of events for any prisoner.

The King of Kings has likewise provided daily portions for His children. Jesus taught His disciples to pray, "Give us this day our daily bread" (Matt. 6:11). The manna, or "… the bread of heaven" (Ps. 105:40) (angels' food, Ps. 78:24-25) descended on a daily basis every single day of the work-week. The day of rest was the exception. Even the law taught that (and Jesus added it to the New Testament standard) "… Man shall not live by bread alone, but by every word that proceedeth out of the mouth of God" (Matt. 4:4; Deut. 8:3). The blessed man of Psalm chapter 1 (Ps. 1:2) is said to meditate in His law day and night, and to delight in doing so. The inner man must be nourished and fed daily with the Spirit-quickened Word of God to maintain a strong and healthy spiritual life.

Medical authorities are agreed that the most effective health insurance is preventive medicine. It is a far more difficult task to deal with disease and illness than it is to strengthen the immune system and prevent the onset of the malady. Those who fortify their inner man with regular and strengthening nutrition, fend off many a foul and debilitating virus.

There is an opportunity in every difficulty, and a difficulty in every opportunity. We are instructed to redeem the time (Eph. 5:16); the Revised Standard Version reads: "buying up for yourselves the opportunity." Each moment carries with it some special and unique opportunity. It is our responsibility to seize each one, for they speed away quickly and forever. Like a lonely trek through a barren desert, rarely but occasionally, you come upon a flower; pick it quickly and admire its rare beauty; you may not find another just like it. So are the opportunities of every single new day.

Thought For Today

The daily portion is essential to daily strength and victory!

November 9

N. T. Bible Reading: Hebrews 6   **Our Focus: Hebrews 6:9**

BETTER THINGS

The Lord Jesus Christ is portrayed in the book of Hebrews as superior, sufficient, superb, and sublime. His redemptive plan is complete, comprehensive, conclusive, and consistent. Every provision has been made for every possible need. The supplier is exalted to the highest; the supply is from an eternal source, and the delivery is immediate and personal. Little wonder then, that "… better things …" (Heb. 6:9) are required of all who are privileged to partake of "… so great (a) salvation …" (Heb. 2:3).

There should be neither thorns nor thistles in the garden which is planted and carefully maintained by the Master-Gardener. The nutritious "… good soil …" (Ezek. 17:8) will produce an abundant harvest, but it must be weeded, cultivated, and carefully worked on a daily basis. The richer the soil the more certainly it will produce thorns, thistles, and weeds if neglected. Each person is responsible to maintain and care for their own garden plot. The Landlord has provided the good soil, the good seed, and a good season. We have only to add the good work (Jam. 2:17, 20, 26) of pulling weeds and the "better things" of personal responsibility to enjoy a good harvest and a final "… Well done, thou good and faithful servant" (Matt. 25:21, 23). These facts were brought home to me with great force recently. Due to the pressures of a busy schedule and the constraints of time, I chose not to plant a garden this year. The soil had been carefully built up and enriched over several years. To my amazement, that very same "super soil" which was so productive just last year, produced more varieties, abundant growth and different sizes of thistles than I imagined ever existed in this area. All of this came about for just one simple reason, "neglect."

To "neglect" is to fail to care for or attend to properly; it is to fail to perform through carelessness or oversight. It is for this reason that the Scriptures urge us "… giving all diligence …" (II Pet. 1:5). Provision was made under the law for sins of omission, as well as sins of commission. The failure was personal and specific and there is accountability and responsibility for failure to perform. When "… these things be in you, and abound, they make you that ye shall neither be barren nor unfruitful in the knowledge of our Lord Jesus Christ" (II Pet. 1:8).

Thought For Today

The law of sowing and reaping is modified by the law of effort!

November 10

O. T. Bible Reading: Lamentations 1-2   **Our Focus: Lamentations 2:2**

THE LORD HATH

The *high calling*, when ignored and replaced by *low living*, always results in *deep suffering*. High privilege and great advantage carry with them solemn responsibility and certain accountability. Jeremiah is called the weeping prophet; here in Lamentations he says, "For these things I weep; mine eye, mine eye runneth down with water ..." (Lam. 1:16); in Jeremiah 9:1 he said, "Oh that my head were waters, and mine eyes a fountain of tears, that I might weep day and night for the slain of the daughter of my people!" A true prophet must *speak for God*, and *feel with God*; he must also *speak to* the people with compassion and allow tenderness to blend with the sternness of truth. Jeremiah was a true prophet of God to the wayward nation of Israel.

Where there is law and order there will always be the heavy but sure burden of consequences. When there is no accountability and punishment for the lawless, the inevitable result is anarchy and chaotic confusion. God is not the author of confusion (I Cor. 14:33), and His disobedient and rebellious people, Israel, must experience the inevitable Divine displeasure. The second chapter of Lamentations uses the words "the Lord hath" or simply "He hath" or their equivalent 31 times. The essence of wisdom is in repetition; surely the message here is loud and clear. The nation of Israel has rebelled against God and His Word; therefore, the Lord has brought upon them the inevitable fruits of their own doings. There are great rewards for obedience and heeding the Word of the Lord. There are also dire consequences for deliberate disobedience and rebellion.

The book of Lamentations is not pleasant reading. It is, in fact, depressing and unpleasant. It has been termed: "a cloudburst of grief, a river of tears, and a sea of sobs", and so it is; hardly the making for a "best seller." If anyone could learn the lesson, it would be abundantly justified. What a man sows, he will reap; this is an eternal and an irreversible principle. You have the power of choice, you can do what is right or what is wrong, it is *your choice*. Let the sad dirge of Lamentations remind everyone, there are consequences for those choices. Only you can make them a happy experience.

Thought For Today

The wheels of the inevitable grind slowly and exceeding fine!

November 10

N. T. Bible Reading: Hebrews 7   **Our Focus: Hebrews 7:25**

HE IS ABLE

Never has more been said and by fewer words; "He is able!" They are inspired words of assurance, hope, confidence, and anticipation. We will come to circumstances and conditions in this life where every resource has failed, and these words with resurrection authority shine forth from the Sacred Page; "... *he* is able ..." (Heb. 7:25). Others could not, we cannot, but glorious reality, *He can*! These words and the truth of them echo throughout time like the peeling of the bells of heaven sounding the melody of an eternal chorus, "*He is able*."

There were three Hebrew children who stood before the wrath of the ruthless King and faced the flaming fiery furnace. Their doom was settled, their execution was imminent, and their death was certain; but with calm and confident heaven-born faith they declared, "... our God whom we serve is able ..." (Dan. 3:17). Then one of the finest expressions of commitment ever uttered by a human voice was spoken, "But *if not*, be it known unto thee, O king, that we will not serve thy gods ..." (Dan. 3:18). This great experience has inspired the hearts of severely tested saints of God from that time to this. The refrain of these words vibrates with the very inspiration of heaven, and thrills the troubled heart with hope eternal.

Two blind men followed Jesus crying out, "... Thou son of David, have mercy on us" (Matt. 9:27). They went into the house after Him, and He pointedly asked them, "... Believe ye that *I am able* to do this ..." (Matt. 9:28). They answered (it reads as if both, at the same time) without hesitation, "... Yea, Lord" (Matt. 9:28). They sensed the almighty power of the Great Physician and their hearts were filled with a heaven-born faith as they proclaimed Him Lord, Master, the Almighty One! Immediately their eyes were opened ... "He *is* able!"

Wherefore is the specific reason why; it is the *therefore* of what has been said (the promise), and the *certainty* of what is ahead (the fulfillment). *He is able* to save to the uttermost (Heb. 7:25): that pledge involves all conditions; from the guttermost to the uppermost. It also involves thoroughness and completion. He is able to save, and to keep on saving you. This is a process and He did not begin the work to abandon it in mid-production. He is a faithful Creator, and will stay on the job until it is completed. He is able ... are we willing?

Thought For Today

The absolute promise is the sure pledge of absolute results!

November 11

O. T. Bible Reading: Lamentations 3-5　　　　**Our Focus: Lamentations 3:24**

MY PORTION

People often say they are doing quite well *under* the circumstances. That is not a fit place for God's people to be. We are to be, as God's people of old, "… thou shall be above only, and thou shalt not be beneath; if that thou hearken unto … the Lord thy God …" (Deut. 28:13). Jeremiah was in the midst of circumstances which were as bad as they can get. He prophesied and ministered in Israel without ever one time seeing a positive or grateful response from the rebellious nation of Israel. His suffering may rank second only to the Man of Sorrows. He stood alone, a solitary sentry, crying out from his lonely tower; he was God's messenger and spokesman, disregarded, disrespected, and disgraced, yet faithfully consistent and persistent. Every warning of prophecy of coming judgment is saturated with scalding tears; every plea is punctuated with the sobbing of a suffering sympathy. This must be kept carefully in mind, for it is from such a pit of anguish and suffering we hear the reassuring words, "… great is thy faithfulness. The Lord is my portion, saith my soul; therefore will I hope in him" (Lam. 3:23-24).

David made a similar statement of trust and confidence in God in spite of deep sorrow, anguish, and remorse. He said in Psalm 16:5-6, "The Lord is the portion of mine inheritance and of my cup: thou maintainest my lot. The lines are fallen unto me in pleasant places; yea, I have a goodly heritage." This seems to say exactly what Jeremiah is saying; when I pause to consider the big picture, only then do I get a true perspective. All of the human sufferings and trials are things of time, and when weighed on the scales of eternal values, they are both "…*light* affliction (s) …" and they will endure "… but for a *moment* …" (II Cor. 4:17).

Out of the deepest sorrows and from the most severe tests have come the greatest revelations of God, His mercy, and His faithfulness. Joy is the sweet nectar which the bitter trials of life have squeezed out of the trusting hearts of God's children. The test is not the end; it is but a part of the process. It is the expected (Divinely anticipated) *end* which He has in mind (Jer. 29:11). It is the "… afterward …" which yields the peaceable fruit of righteousness to those who are exercised thereby (Heb. 12:11).

Thought For Today

From the deepest wells of suffering, come the sweetest waters of joy!

November 11

N. T. Bible Reading: Hebrews 8   **Our Focus: Hebrews 8:6**

A BETTER COVENANT

The book of Hebrews is the book of values and perspectives; the word "perfect " in all grammatical forms is used 14 times, the two words "eternal" and "forever" occur 15 times, "heaven" or "heavenly" will be found 17 times, and the very hopeful word "better" is repeated 13 times, more than in all the rest of the New Testament.

Those things which are specifically singled out as being better are as follows: better things (Heb. 6:9, 12:24), better hope (Heb. 7:19), better testament (Heb. 7:22), better covenant (Heb. 8:6), better promises (Heb. 8:6), better sacrifices (Heb. 9:23), better and an enduring substance (Heb. 10:34), better country (Heb. 11:16), better resurrection (Heb. 11:35). The thought of the superiority (better) of the new agreement (covenant) runs all the way through the book. The exalted Lord Jesus is better than even the revered Angels (Heb. 1:4); better than Moses, the great emancipator of Israel; better also than the great national heroes, Joshua and Aaron. Jesus is *the one* (used seven times) who needed only to offer Himself *once* (used eight times), after which He *sat down* at the right hand of God (Heb. 10:12), because He alone could shout victoriously, "... *It is finished* ..." (John 19:30). All Old Testament priests must *stand* to minister, for their sacrifices were continuous and their work was never finished.

The New Covenant or Testament (will) stands above the old, and is "better" because it is officiated by a much superior Priest, and it is based upon a "better" sacrifice (His was *perfect* and needed never to be repeated). The problem with the first (old) covenant was the human element which was involved throughout. Hebrews 8:8 clarifies this by saying, "For finding *fault with them*, he saith, Behold, the days come, saith the Lord, when I will make a new covenant ...." He did not find fault with *it*, but rather *with them*. The solution is the Divine miracle of the new relationship. We now have not only forgiveness and pardon; we have a *new life* imparted by the *new birth*. We are given power through the Word of God and the quickening of the Holy Spirit to overcome. Thank God for a new and better hope.

Thought For Today

The crowning jewel of redemption is a transformed life!

November 12

O. T. Bible Reading: Ezekiel 1-3   **Our Focus: Ezekiel 1:1**

I SAW VISIONS

Ezekiel was among the 10,000 Jews deported to Babylon in the first of two deportations before the fall of Jerusalem. He began his ministry, when he was 30 years of age, as a prisoner of war in a captive colony by the river Chebar, five years before the city of Jerusalem was plundered. He gives the exact time and dates of his visions 13 times, and they are all dated from the traumatic and tragic year in which he was carried captive into Babylon as a young man of 25. God always prepares His servants, and especially His prophets, and the process begins long before their ministry ever starts. It is significant that Ezekiel states in retrospect (many times), "I saw", "I fell", "I heard"; perhaps this may be an autobiography of the making of a prophet. It was when he was *on his face* that the Spirit quickens him and sets him *on his feet*, and not until then.

Ezekiel has been called "the Patmos prophet of the Old Testament." The Apostle John was exiled to the island prison of Patmos, and Ezekiel was exiled to Babylon; both wrote books of prophetic significance, and both are full of symbolic terms and language. The word "likeness" is used 15 times, as he carefully attempts to relate what he saw as nearly as possible to what we could grasp or understand. His commission and his mission are plainly stated, "... I send thee to the children of Israel ..." (Ezek. 2:3). The purpose is also made very clear, "they shall know that I am Jehovah" which he repeats no less than 70 times. This is the key thought and the core message of the book of Ezekiel.

Ezekiel chapters 1-3 are very complex in symbolic language. The bottom line seems to be that God is showing that behind all the confusing events of earth there is heavenly supervision and Divine control. Above all the chaos and confusion among men there still shines a beautiful rainbow and a Divine purpose (Ezek. 1:28); the covenant and the promise prevail as revealed by the storm clouds themselves. How good it is to know, even in our own time, that there is a mighty God in heaven, and that He is in control!

Thought For Today

With every God-given vision, fulfillment is certain!

November 12

N. T. Bible Reading: Hebrews 9   **Our Focus: Hebrews 9:26**

HE APPEARED

There are three *appearings* of the Lord Jesus Christ referred to in the last five verses of Hebrews 9. Hebrews 9:24 declares, "… *now* to appear in the presence of God for us." The ministry of Jesus as our mediator and faithful high priest is an on-going reality, and did not officially begin until after His ascension. The Old Testament type of Aaron as the high priest shows the picture of our Great High Priest. On the Day of Atonement He was to wear his priestly garments of linen, while officiating at the altar on behalf of the congregation. It was only *after* this offering for sin that he was to change his garments and put on "… garments … for glory and for beauty" (Ex. 28:2). We now see the Lord Jesus "… crowned with glory and honour … is not entered into the holy places made with hands … but into heaven itself, *now* to *appear* in the presence of God *for us*" (Heb. 2:9, 9:24). He *now appears* as the mediator of a better covenant.

Hebrews 9:26 states that, "… once in the end of the world (age) had *he appeared* to put away sin by the sacrifice of himself." This is another appearing; it was accomplished when, as John describes it, "And the Word was made flesh, and dwelt (tabernacled) among us …" (John 1:14). Jesus appeared (was born of the virgin Mary) at the end of the law age, and instituted a new dispensation, that of the Gospel, also known as the church age. His mission was distinctly to save His people from their sins (Matt. 1:21). This was no temporary "covering", nor was it partial. He dealt with it in all finality; in His offering of Himself *for us*, His substitutionary death was redemptive. His atoning sacrifice dealt with the guilt, the stain, the power, the condemnation, and the penalty of sin. His work was complete and acceptable to God as proven by His glorious resurrection.

There is yet a third appearing; "… and unto them that look for him shall *he appear* the second time (hence the phrase, the second coming) without sin unto salvation" (Heb. 9:28). This will be the culmination of the process of salvation begun at Calvary. It is not His coming as the Lamb of God (this He did, and finished that mission), but now as King of Kings and Lord of Lords (Rev. 17:14). The established fact of His promised return is spoken of in 318 Scriptures of the New Testament; it is called the "… blessed hope …" (Tit. 2:13), and is also a purifying hope for God's people. He will appear as the Angels promised; "… this same Jesus … shall so come …" (Acts 1:11).

Thought For Today

Only those who know Him in redemption will see Him in glory!

November 13

O. T. Bible Reading: Ezekiel 4-6   **Our Focus: Ezekiel 4:3**

A SIGN

Ezekiel chapters 4-24 mark the first of three divisions of the book. They deal with the impending judgments of God upon the nation of Israel and the city of Jerusalem. The dates which the prophet gives, all fall *before* the overthrow and ruin of Jerusalem. The dark clouds of over-hanging doom and destruction float heavy and low over the city, and God is attempting to get the attention of the nation. False prophets are refuting what Jeremiah and Ezekiel are accurately telling the people. They are falsely saying that the city would be spared, the Babylonians defeated, and those taken captive would be returned. The nation and its people have become so hardened in their rebellion that they are deaf, and cannot or will not hear God's warnings. In this first section of the book (chapters 4-24) there are 10 sign-sermons, and only one such in the rest of the book.

God required Ezekiel, in a unique way, to engage in symbolic and typical actions, since the people were too dumb to spiritual things to hear what God was saying. One of these unusual phenomena was that he himself would be dumb and unable to speak until his prophecies were fulfilled at the overthrow of Jerusalem. At the very beginning of his ministry God told him "And I will make thy tongue cleave to the roof of thy mouth, that thou shalt be dumb ..." (Ezek. 3:26). It was four and one-half years later that God further said, "In that day (at the exact time Jerusalem fell) shall thy mouth be opened ... thou shalt speak, and be no more dumb ..." (Ezek. 24:27). It appears that this interval of dumbness was interrupted only briefly when God directly spoken to him "... I will open thy mouth, and thou shalt say ..." (Ezek. 3:27). For the last one and a half years the dumbness was complete and without intermission.

There is a tragic background scene also, which may be easily overlooked, but is vital to get the full picture. The book begins with a unique expression of the *heavenly glory*, in the first vision; it ends with a spiritual symbolism of final *earthly glory* for a restored nation in millennial blessing. The sad and tragic events between those two occasions are represented by the sure but reluctant *departing glory*. This pictures the present plight of the covenant people ... however, the end is not yet.

Thought For Today

How dull the human ear when once it is closed to God's voice!

November 13

N. T. Bible Reading: Hebrews 10:1-23   **Our Focus: Hebrews 10:20**

A LIVING WAY

Jesus is the expression of spiritual *life* (John 1:4); He also is the provider of spiritual *life* (John 10:10); and He alone is the imparter of that *life* (John 6:51-54). The Gospel of John alone speaks of that *life* over 20 times. To convey this thought to our minds more graphically the Scriptures use the word "living" repeatedly; Jesus describes Himself as the "… living water" (John 4:10), and "… living bread …" (John 6:51); because of this we are referred to as "… lively stones …" (I Pet. 2:5) who now have a "… lively hope …" (I Pet. 1:3). How refreshing it is to be able to fellowship with these lively creatures in an atmosphere expressive of life and liberty.

We are given a beautiful insight into this reality back in the book of Proverbs, "There is *a way* (surely a religious way) which seemeth right unto a man, but the end thereof are the ways of death" (Prov. 14:12). In case we should miss this key message, the very same words are repeated again in Proverbs 16:25. That which originates in the element or principle of death (that which bears the curse of sin … all that is of human origin) can only produce death. There will be dead rituals, a dead environment, dead and dry sermons, boring services, and dead people. We know that He is not the God of the dead, but of the living (Matt. 22:32); "There is a river, the streams whereof shall make glad the city of God …" (Ps. 46:4). We are to serve the Lord and to walk (steps of the living) in newness of life (Rom. 6:4). This is nothing less than His resurrection life which enables us to serve the Lord in "… newness of spirit …" (Rom. 7:6).

The *new* and *living way* is now opened up for us through the veil. In the old economy, the veil of the temple excluded all from the symbolic presence of God in the Holy of Holies. Even Jesus could not open a way for us until the veil (His flesh) was rent. When He was crucified, the veil of His flesh was rent; and at the very instant of His death, the veil of the temple was rent from the top to bottom by an invisible Divine hand (Matt. 27:51). That marked the end and fulfillment of all types and shadows; we are now in a season of fulfillment and reality.

Thought For Today

The Living way opens to ever-new expressions of life!

November 14

O. T. Bible Reading: Ezekiel 7-9　　　　　　　**Our Focus: Ezekiel 7:14**

MY WRATH

The most difficult thing in the world is to keep balanced. We are creatures of extremes; we swing the pendulum from one extreme to the other. The love of God is one of the most used themes in the Christian community of our time, and surely we can all rejoice and be thankful for redeeming love. Few realize that the exact words "the love of God" occur 13 times in the Bible, and all in the New Testament. "The wrath of God", the very opposite emotion, is also found 13 times in the Scriptures; three times in the Old Testament, and 10 times in the New Testament. However, if you include the additional expressions, "His wrath", "my wrath", and "thy wrath" the total swells to 87. Add to that, the use of the word "anger" as related to God, you would at least double that figure; the actual words, "the anger of the Lord" are used 18 times. These are impressive statistics, and you cannot help but wonder why we are not informed of them from the pulpits.

The reason seems obvious; people simply do not want to hear about God's wrath. It certainly is not a popular subject, and the temptation is very strong to give the people what they want to hear, and to avoid those things they resent hearing. It is certainly not to be used as a big stick or a hammer with which to rail on an indifferent person or persons. It must be handled with tenderness and compassion; but to be balanced, it must be taught. It is just as much a part of the inspired record; to preach the whole counsel of God (Acts 20:27) no truth can be ignored. No wonder the apostle Paul urged the Romans, "Behold therefore *the goodness* and *severity* of God ..." (Rom. 11:22).

It is possible to provoke the Lord to anger; not a very popular thought. It was the Lord Himself who asked Moses, "... How long will this people provoke me ..." (Num. 14:11). Jeremiah added God's words, "Do they provoke me to anger ..." (Jer. 7:19). God does not deal with His redeemed children in wrath, but do not lightly regard the chastening of the Lord, neither despair when rebuked by Him. "For whom the Lord loveth he chasteneth, and scourgeth every son whom he receiveth" (Heb. 12:6).

Thought For Today

God is angry with the wicked every day; we must share His feelings!

November 14

N. T. Bible Reading: Hebrews 10:24-39　　　　**Our Focus: Hebrews 10:24**

CONSIDER

"Consider" is a verb, and is a first cousin of "meditate." The dictionary says that to consider is to think carefully about, and to meditate is to reflect on or to contemplate. Obviously, that is a very close relationship, and it would be very difficult to do the one without involving the other.

We are urged to "… consider one another to provoke unto love and to good works" (Heb. 10:24). It is feared that too many may have read only the first part of this admonition, and then rushed off to carry out the orders to provoke. Actually, this seems to be medical terminology; it is used in that profession for the halting of a fever, when the raging effects of it cause the body to tremble and the bed to shake. It is used here to show the aggressive and urgent manner in which we are to attend to our fellow believers, to stem any infection or disturbance, and in its place produce peace and tranquility. It is difficult to find such zealous crusaders for harmony and unity. It seems at times there are more to produce the fever then there are of those to arrest it. Perhaps this may be included in what Paul told the Galatians, "But it is good to be zealously affected always in a good thing …" (Gal. 4:18). Thank God for those brave and loyal souls whom the Bible calls peacemakers, "Blessed are the peacemakers: for they shall be called the children of God" (Matt. 5:9).

Three consecutive verses begin with "Let us …" (Heb. 10:22, 23, 24), and each represents a duty:

1.　"Let us draw near …" (Heb. 10:22); this speaks of our duty of spiritual exercise and worship, and addresses the evil of lethargy and indifference. Health, growth, and strength are all elements of preventive spiritual endeavor; the exercising of prayer, worship, and praise prevent stagnation and deterioration.

2.　"Let us hold fast the profession of our faith …" (Heb. 10:23); the duty of a positive witness and tenacity to the Gospel is in focus here. We are not to shrink from, nor are we to shirk the responsibility of being a witness. It is another symptom of spiritual vigor and good health.

3.　"And let us consider one another …" (Heb. 10:24); those who reach out with feeling and purpose to minister to and help, relieve the burdens of others, avoid the pitfalls of self-centered grasping, and discover the sweet and fulfilling release of meeting the needs of others. This also is a duty, and a very blessed privilege.

Thought For Today

Those who have embraced the Gospel must always consider others!

November 15

O. T. Bible Reading: Ezekiel 10-12   **Our Focus: Ezekiel 12:2**

SEE NOT

God sees what men do not see; those who know and walk with God see what carnal people cannot see; those who walk in rebellion to God and His Word are blinded by the deceitfulness of sin (I John 2:11). This sad condition is further defined as blindness of heart (Eph. 4:18) which causes the *understanding* to become *darkened*. It is the presence of darkness, which clouds the inner eye of the soul, and results in the loss of inward vision, the eyes being blinded "... because that darkness hath blinded his eyes" (I John. 2:11). This great principle and truth is not often spoken of in our time, and is seldom clearly seen by those who minister.

The vivid picture which Paul paints in Romans, for the depths of depravity found in humanity, focuses on this principle: "Because that, when they knew God, they glorified him not as God, neither were thankful; but *became* vain in their imaginations, and their foolish *heart was darkened*" (Rom. 1:21). The vehicle of faith is a good conscience, and when the conscience is defiled, the consciousness of spiritual things is diminished. The results are confusion and uncertainty, in direction and purpose "Holding faith, and a good conscience; which some having put away concerning faith have made shipwreck" (I Tim. 1:19). Fog is the primary cause of shipwrecks.

The Psalmist gave us the formula for clear vision, "For with thee is the fountain of life; *in thy light* shall we see light" (Ps. 36:9). Where the fountain flows, the light shines: the clearer the flow of Divine life, the brighter the light of spiritual comprehension. John also explained this principle, "But *if* we *walk in* the light, as he is in the light, we have fellowship one with another, and the blood of Jesus Christ his Son cleanseth us from all sin" (I John 1:7). There is a progressive relationship clearly emphasized in this verse. To walk is to continue to take steps; when you stop taking steps you stop walking. It is in this forward progress *in*, or in the direction of the light, that we experience continuous cleansing; cleansing also involves clarifying, and clarifying makes clear. No wonder Jesus distinctly said, "... blessed are your eyes, for they see ..." (Matt. 13:16).

Thought For Today

The eyes of faith are the happy portion of the faithful!

November 15

N. T. Bible Reading: Hebrews 11:1-19   **Our Focus: Hebrews 11:1**

FAITH IS

Hebrews chapter 11 is certainly the faith chapter; the word is used 23 times in just this one single chapter. This fact is even the more amazing when you realize that the word "faith" is used only twice in the entire Old Testament (Deut. 32:20; Hab. 2:4). Faith is many things to many people. A young boy when asked by his teacher to explain what faith was, said very innocently, "well, faith is believing what you know ain't so." That may be about what many people feel, but probably would never dare to say. They think of faith as a venture into an unexplored area; it is like jumping with your eyes closed … it is a leap into the dark. That is not faith at all; it is fate, and that is fatal.

Only the Scriptures give us the final and accurate meaning to life's perplexing problems and baffling mysteries. They also give clear definition to the enigmas which evade the minds of the unregenerate. *Faith is* (Heb. 11:1), these are words of wealth and of wisdom; they end the search for meaning and value. They are the Divine answer to the human problem of the existence of God, and how to find Him and come to know Him.

"Now faith is the *substance* of things hoped for …" (Heb. 11:1); that is, it is a reality, and not a fancy or figment of the imagination. It is the fulfillment of your dreams; it is heaven's answer to the longings and desires of earth. The original word for substance is a "hupostasis" which is the very opposite of hypothesis or theory. It is that which is a sure foundation, and rests upon facts. Faith is the ingredient which enables the trusting heart to act upon the promises as though they were fulfillment; it translates the uncertain future into the certain now; it transforms the invisible into what can be seen and known.

"Now faith is … the *evidence* of things not seen" (Heb. 11:1); that is, it is the facts established by the court, upon which a final decision may be fairly and confidently made. It is that which is taken into court, and admitted as legitimate proof, with which to establish your case. Faith is more than desire; it is the fulfillment of desire. The foundation of faith is the Word of God. Faith rests confidently in that which God declares. To believe, therefore, that God will do exactly what He has promised is by no means presumption; it is faith in the integrity of God and His Word.

Thought For Today

Faith is the most fulfilling portion of those who trust Him!

November 16

O. T. Bible Reading: Ezekiel 13-15   **Our Focus: Ezekiel 15:2**

THE VINE

The land of Palestine was known as a land of vineyards and the producer of huge quantities of grapes, long before the nation of Israel entered the land. When the spies were sent into the land, they returned with samples of the abundant fruit consisting of grapes, pomegranates, and figs (Num. 13:23). Moses assured the congregation that Canaan was a land of "... vineyards and olive trees, which thou plantedst not ..." (Deut. 6:11). All who lived in that area were well aware of the vineyard and because of this familiarity, the symbolic significance of the vineyard is used 22 times in the Gospels.

The vineyard is used symbolically of the nation of Israel, as well as of the New Testament church; it is also used typically for the harvest of the good fruit and for the final harvest of evil (Rev. 14:14-20) at the end of the age. It is clear, however, that the prophet is speaking of the whole house of Israel (Isa. 5:7). They are compared to three trees in the Old Testament:

1.   The *fig tree* seems to be symbolic of Israel's national privileges.
2.   The *olive tree* would represent their religious privileges.
3.   *The vine* speaks of their spiritual privileges.

It is clear that Ezekiel refers to the nation of Israel. Jesus used this familiar symbol of the vine and gave it a broader application to Himself and to His followers. He said, "I am the vine, ye are the branches ..." (John 15:5), "*Abide* in me, and I in you. As the branch cannot bear fruit of itself, except it *abide* in the vine; no more can ye, except ye *abide* in me" (John 15:4). The key word is "*abide*" which is repeated 9 times in the 10 verses. He is the *true* vine (Ezek. 15:1); the old vine (Israel) had failed.

The conditions for an abiding fruitful relationship are clear and personal:

1.   There must be an ongoing process of *purging* or cleansing, and that through the personal application of His words to our lives (John 15:3).
2.   There must be an abiding relationship of nearness and communion with Him which is unbroken and undisturbed.
3.   The third condition is obedience (John 15:10). Obedience is the artery through which flows the life-blood which gives life and vitality. Any failure to *walk in the light* (obey His Word) can clog an artery and restrict the flow of life (I John 1:7).

Those who follow the plan will enjoy the results; much fruit (John 15:8)!

Thought For Today

The pruning of the vine is the key to an abundant harvest!

November 16

N. T. Bible Reading: Hebrews 11:20-40　　　　**Our Focus: Hebrews 11:34**

OUT OF WEAKNESS

The roll-call of Hebrews chapter 11 chronicles some of the greatest exploits ever accomplished in the Old Testament era. We are prone to think of these individuals as super-saints; rare people with rare gifts and abilities far beyond the normal, and certainly far beyond us personally. This passage of Scripture has been called the Westminster Abbey of the Bible. This is a gallery of greats; they are in an elite class of people who tower over the ordinary, and dwarf the average, at least so we are likely to imagine. The phrase, "... out of weakness were made strong ..." (Heb. 11:34), should put these who, like John the Baptist, were "... great in the sight of the Lord ..." (Luke 1:15), into a true focus. They were ordinary people who accomplished extra-ordinary things for God.

Their strength and prowess was not in themselves, they were weak and limited, just like every other human being. The difference was that they were *made strong*. That is, they became strong by virtue of something entirely apart from themselves. They were "... strong in faith ..." (Rom. 4:20), and therefore, were "... strong in the Lord, and in the power of his might" (Eph. 6:10). Their unusual exploits came from the measure of their yieldedness to the Lord, and not from the vastness of their own resources. The element of resistance was removed, and the depths of their surrender to the will of God made possible the flow of His great power through a clean and totally yielded vessel.

It is when He owns all that we are and have, that He can empower the human (*out of* weakness) with the supernatural. God asked Moses, who questioned his own credentials, "... What is that in thine hand ..." (Ex. 4:2). The vital element which is in our hand is our own will. When that is yielded to Him, mighty miracles will always happen. When that despised and impotent shepherd's rod is yielded to the Word of the Lord, it is transformed and becomes forever the symbol of the miraculous. We hand it over to Him for His use, when we yield it to His Word and to His command.

Thought For Today

Our awareness of weakness may be the measure of our usefulness!

November 17

O. T. Bible Reading: Ezekiel 16   **Our Focus: Ezekiel 16:6**

LIVE

The Lord spoke to Ezekiel about Jerusalem (which stands here for the nation of Israel) that she was as an illegitimate and abandoned new-born baby. She was as an unattended orphan baby lying helplessly in the filth and defilement of her own birth. It was in that pathetic condition that God found her and said unto her "… Live" (Ezek. 16:6). This symbolic language may also be applied to every son of Adam. We were born in sin and shapen in iniquity, sinful and polluted, wallowing in our own depraved and corrupted condition (Ps. 51:5). Then Jesus came; all glory and praise to His Holy name for His mercy and compassion. He issued the command to live; the Divine command is accompanied by the Divine enablement. His was the creative Word, His is the imparted life, ours is the new creation; it is a Divine miracle and a marvel to both men and angels.

Life is both the substance and the subject of the Gospel of John; the expressions "life" or "eternal life" will be found about 80 times. The key to all is found early in the book; "*In him was life*; and the life was the *light* of men" (John 1:4). Our first approach to Him as the only source of spiritual life is through His light-giving power. He does not give life until He has first given light. The thing which determines whether we receive the life is whether we follow the light. He desires to impart His life if only we will open our heart to the incoming illumination of His Word (light).

It is not a question of profession; it is a question of possession. It is not an issue of liturgy; it is an issue of liberty. It is not a matter of rituals and religious dogmas; it is a matter of a living vital and personal impartation of life. It is quite a revelation to know that the Christian experience is very simply the possession of *a life*. Spiritual life is not inherited, it is not earned, it is not humanly imparted; it is only Divinely imputed. The only source of spiritual life is the risen Lord Himself. He and He alone, can speak life into the human heart.

Thought For Today

In Him we live, for apart from Him is only death!

November 17

N. T. Bible Reading: Hebrews 12　　　　　　　**Our Focus: Hebrews 12:2**

LOOKING UNTO JESUS

Many problems and difficulties in the Christian life result from losing focus. Life is filled with distractions, discouragements, disruptions, and distress; all of which can lead to distrust when and if we lose our sense of direction. The master key to consistency is to keep our eyes steadfastly focused on the Lord Jesus. We are creatures of but a single focus; we are equipped to concentrate our vision on only one object at a time.

The high-tech culture in which we live, demands our time and attention, more so than at any other interval of man's existence. The entire spectrum of the human story has never witnessed distractions of louder and more glamorous gaieties; more sophisticated and subtle appeals of temptations, keeping life at frightening levels of tension and stress, on an immense level hitherto unknown. Life is no longer simple and solitary; it is very complex, complicated, and confusing. Ours is an age of extreme mental and nervous pressures, international crisis and nuclear paranoia, and individual dimensions of demand and involvement, both frightening and frustrating. The simple admonition of Hebrews 12:2 "Looking unto Jesus ..." was never more needed, and certainly never more appropriate.

The word used here for *looking* is not used in any other New Testament Scripture; it might as well have been written for, and reserved for our very age. The force of the original word is, "looking *off* unto Jesus." We must, by an act of enlightened intelligent determination, focus our gaze upon Him, by consciously taking our eyes *off* of or away from all else (Heb. 12:1). Literally, we are exhorted to, with *patient endurance*, keep on the track and press forward toward the goal. Jesus set the pace for us; He patiently endured the cross (Heb. 12:2), and also patiently endured the rejection of this world (Heb. 12:3). He is the "file-leader" (or author) of our faith; we must keep our eyes on Him and patiently plod on to the eternal reward.

Thought For Today

The focus of the eye produces the staying power of the will!

November 18

O. T. Bible Reading: Ezekiel 17-19   **Our Focus: Ezekiel 17:3**

A GREAT EAGLE

The prophet Ezekiel is directed to put forth a riddle, and to speak a parable to the nation of Israel (Ezek. 17:2). A riddle is a dark saying which demands thorough consideration and a little insight to fathom the meaning, and apply the message. Basically, a parable is the same thing and the double mention is meant to give it even greater emphasis. The great Eagle of Ezekiel 17:2 is the Babylonian empire of King Nebuchadnezzar (Ezek. 17:12); and the other great Eagle was the kingdom of Egypt (Ezek. 17:15, 17). There are eight species of Eagles in the area of Palestine, and the people there were well aware of the kingly nature and dominance of this fascinating "king of flight."

The Eagle is also used as a challenge to God's people; Isaiah says, "But they that wait upon the Lord shall renew their strength; they shall mount up with wings as eagles; they shall run, and not be weary; and they shall walk, and not faint" (Isa. 40:31). It seems clear that the application of this Scripture is not to three different categories or stages of growth. The very same person will experience all three of these events; he will walk, he will run, and at other times he will soar to the very heights like the mighty eagle. He will not always be on the wing, but he will enjoy the great thrill of rising above the storm; he can *look down* upon the dark clouds and the fierce winds, and *look up* into the clear blue sky and the smiling approval of God. His perspective has changed; he does not now attempt to see God through the clouds, but is able triumphantly to see the clouds from God's view-point. This is no idle dream; it is a blessed reality, and it can be truly said, "... this honour have all his saints. Praise ye the Lord" (Ps. 149:9).

The mind-set determines the foot-steps. The goal of God's people should not be the highest we can reach; it must be *the very highest*. This is the attitude of faith, and cancels the limitations of fear. The key is not "I will", but a blessed and triumphant "He can." We are not specimens on display in God's show-room; "For we are his workmanship ..." (Eph. 2:10) and it is our business to exalt Him, and to see that He gets all of the praise.

Thought For Today

God's eagles are a rare species of Divine enablement!

November 18

N. T. Bible Reading: Hebrews 13   **Our Focus: Hebrews 13:6**

WE ... BOLDLY SAY

We are timid and hesitant when we are fearful and apprehensive; we are bold when we are confident and re-assured. The word "bold" in one form or another is used 9 times in the book of Acts, and only 20 times in the rest of the New Testament. There must be a definite significance to this fact, and indeed there is. The early church basked in the refreshing, renewing, and rewarding reality of His resurrection. Their message was not "He was", but a powerful and persuasive "*He is*." His promise was recent and resonant, "... lo, *I am with you* always, even unto the end of the world (age). Amen" (Matt. 28:20). But His presence was promised, provided, and proven for we read, "And they went forth, and preached everywhere, the Lord working with them, and confirming the word with signs following. Amen" (Mark 16:20).

Our confidence will be directly proportionate to our awareness of His presence and the assurance of His promises. The Scripture for today gives the sequence, "... for *he* hath said, I will never leave thee, nor forsake thee. So that *we* may boldly say, The Lord is my helper, and I will not fear ..." (Heb. 13:5-6). If we look to ourselves, we will despair; if we look at circumstances, we will tremble; if we look at people, we will probably quit altogether; but if we *look away* to Him, pay attention to His Words, and reckon on His presence we *boldly say*, the Lord *is* my helper. We should speak and act only after we have heard what He has to say.

We must maintain this clear focus or we will be like Peter of old, "But when *he saw* the wind boisterous, he was afraid; and beginning to sink ..." (Matt. 14:30). When we realize our own feebleness, the obstacles and difficulties loom like the giants of Anak, we shrink to the level of grasshoppers, and God disappears altogether. We must not sing the blues in cadence with the thunder; we must sing the songs of faith inspired by His never-failing promises. It is then that we mount up with wings as eagles, and triumph victoriously, as we rest in His great faithfulness (Isa. 40:31).

Thought For Today

The promise glows like diamonds when we see Him who promised!

November 19

O. T. Bible Reading: Ezekiel 20-21　　　　　　**Our Focus: Ezekiel 20:9**

MY NAME'S SAKE

Four times in Ezekiel chapter 20 the words, "… wrought for my name's sake …" are repeated (Ezek. 20:9, 14, 22, 44). God is very jealous that *His Name* should be exalted, manifested, and vindicated by those who claim it. The nation of Israel had been chosen as a special instrument in the earth to extol His name among the heathen, idol worshipping nations of the world. The priests were expressly directed to "… *put my name* upon the children of Israel, and I will bless them" (Num. 6:27). He clearly stated later in the book of Ezekiel: "Therefore thus saith the Lord God; Now will I bring again the captivity of Jacob … and will be jealous for *my holy name*" (Ezek. 39:25). It was for His name's sake that He had delivered them from Egypt, had disciplined them in the wilderness, had shown mercy to their children, and was now dealing with them in judgment.

The righteousness of God is vindicated in their punishment, in view of the nature of their sin. The deepest note in their rebellious ways was not that of the actual deeds of evil, terrible as they were, but that by such deeds they were blaspheming *the Name* which they were intended to magnify. To extend their identity as a Divinely chosen nation among the nations would have been to perpetuate a misrepresentation of God. This, a righteous God could not and would not do. Therefore, now He is warning them of the impending judgments; and reminding them once more that it is to vindicate *His holy Name*.

The New Testament message was also clear and explicit: "… God at the first did visit the Gentiles, to take out of them a people *for his name*" (Acts 15:14). Those who have been called upon to bear His name have a solemn responsibility to uphold that Name and to adorn the truth of God by their exemplary behavior (Tit. 2:10). "… The Lord knoweth them are his. And, let everyone that nameth the name of Christ depart from iniquity" (II Tim. 2:19). The righteous and godly conduct and character of the people of God, in their daily behavior, is a reflection on the Name of the Lord; this makes it of solemn importance.

Thought For Today

To take His name in vain is also to dishonor it!

November 19

N. T. Bible Reading: James 1   **Our Focus: James 1:22**

DOERS OF THE WORD

An empty profession is an open deception, and a public reproach to the Gospel.

The book of James is concise, forceful, and immensely practical. The theme is obvious; it is *the proofs of the true faith*; something very timely and appropriate for us today. There are more references to the Sermon on the Mount in James, than in all the other letters of the New Testament. This fact becomes significant when we realize that this James (the name "James" occurs 40 times in the New Testament) who wrote this epistle was a brother of the Lord. He had lived with Jesus in all of His earthly years in the city of Nazareth. The record seems to indicate that he did not join himself to the disciples until after the resurrection. However, it seems also to suggest that looking back and recalling all of those years, he was gripped by the harmony which consistently manifested itself between what Jesus taught and how He lived. For this reason he argues, and rightly so, that a profession of faith which is not expressed in consistent behavior, is of no value at all.

It is the dynamic of the "… engrafted word (implanted) …" (Jam. 1:21) in the heart, which will manifest itself in godly conduct. He refers not merely to any written word, nor even in this case, to the Lord Jesus as the Incarnate Word. It is the *inborn word* which comes about through the miraculous process of salvation. The ear must hear the written Word; the heart must receive that Word as the expression of the Living Word (the Lord Jesus Himself). The will must act decisively, specifically, and obediently to that Word; it is then, and only then, that it is fused into the very person of the obedient child of God making it for him *the engrafted Word*. It is this process which leads to the salvation of the soul, and the inevitable expression of that miracle is the further miracle of an obedient heart "*doing*" the will of God. The proofs of this faith are the "works" (repeated 12 times) or the true fruits of the good seed of the Word of God.

Thought For Today

Doing the will of God is the true faith in daily practice!

November 20

O. T. Bible Reading: Ezekiel 22-23   **Our Focus: Ezekiel 22:30**

I SOUGHT A MAN

Men seek for methods, formulas, and means; God seeks for men; they are His method. The Psalmist said twice: "I sought the Lord ..." (Ps. 34:4, 77:2). The prophet Samuel told King Saul: "... the Lord hath sought him a man after his own heart ..." (I Sam. 13:14). The statements emphasize two outstanding truths:

1.   It is the responsibility of the human family to seek the Lord; surely the need is obvious, but tragically there are many more who "... forget the Lord ..." (Deut. 6:12, 8:14, 19) than there are those who "seek Him" (used more than 10 times).
2.   It is a blessed reality, and a very sobering thought, that God is still seeking for a man. This brings into sharp focus the significance of the human will in the economy of God.

There were many men, but God earnestly and diligently sought for a particular caliber of a man. His search was for a man, a man of sterling character, clear vision, pure life, strong convictions, and a godly attitude. There was no such a man to be found. The corruption and decay of the nation was so complete that even individual exceptions did not exist. The man needed was one who would interpose himself against the tide of iniquity, halt the nation in its downward path, and direct the people back to God and to His righteous ways. At such a time of decadence and corruption, the appeals of mercy and of Divine patience were utterly rejected; only the fiery furnace could consume and purge the dross in order that the corrupted precious metal may be recovered in the end.

There are only three kinds of people anywhere in this world; those who are movable, those who are immovable, and those who move both of them. These movers of men are those whom God seeks. They are likely to be those who have no desire or ambition to lead, but are pressed into such a position both by the inward impulses of the Holy Spirit and the inescapable circumstances which pin them to it. God is searching still, not for men, but for *a man*; not for a group, but for a single individual. It is only thus that we get to know God, and learn to walk with Him.

Thought For Today

Carnal ambition is really canvassing for promotion!

November 20

N. T. Bible Reading: James 2   **Our Focus: James 2:12**

THE LAW OF LIBERTY

The human heart rebels against restraints. Restraint implies control, and it is not natural for human beings to want to be controlled by someone else. Patrick Henry articulated it best in his speech to the Virginia convention on March 23rd, 1775: "... but as for me, give me liberty, or give me death."

The word "law" will be found nearly 500 times in the Bible; about 200 times in the New Testament. The word "liberty" occurs 17 times in the New Testament. The only freedom which is secure is that liberty which is bounded by and preserved by law. The motto of the displaced and persecuted Vaudois, seeking to return to their native home in the Cottian Alps, was: "eternal vigilance is the price of liberty", and so it ever will be. It was the eternal God Himself who spoke the immortal words: "... Let my people go, that they may serve me ..." (Ex. 7:16). The Divine plan was not a band of lawless nomads recklessly roaming at will, but a well defined nation functioning harmoniously, and under the banner of eternal and fruitful principles, and serving God as designed.

James refers to the "... law of liberty ..." twice (Jam. 1:25, 2:12). That law, or perhaps more accurately principle, is the key essence of true liberty. It is a functioning element in the imparted righteousness of Christ, which issues in loyalty. Loyalty is the first-born attribute of genuine love, and it expresses itself in unyielding devotion and commitment. There is as much difference between loyalty and faithfulness as there is between a son and a servant. The one may perform all the duties of the other, but never with the same warmth and feeling.

A little earlier (Jam. 2:8) James spoke of "... the royal law ..." which is "... thou shalt love thy neighbour as thyself ..." (Lev. 19:18) words quoted from the Law of Moses, and emphasized repeatedly by the Lord Jesus. This royal law can only be experienced when first we come to "... love the Lord thy God ..." (used 9 times); our new and living relationship to God and to men is love-inspired, love-mastered, and love-expressed. Love is not blind, as is commonly claimed, it is the most vigilant keen-eyed and severe sentinel ever known. When love masters and is obeyed, the law of liberty is experienced, when disobeyed only bondage prevails.

Thought For Today

Those who are led by the Spirit will always obey spiritual principles!

November 21

O. T. Bible Reading: Ezekiel 24-26   **Our Focus: Ezekiel 26:3**

TYRE

Three chapters in Ezekiel (26-28) are almost entirely devoted to the subject of Tyre (also called Tyrus). There are prophecies in Ezekiel chapters 25-32 concerning seven specific nations which had been adversaries of Israel: Ammon, Moab, Edam, Philistia, Tyre, Zidon, and Egypt. There is a principle which is unveiled in these Divine judgments. Those who fail to find God through the light of His revelation of Himself in His Word will taste His judgments that by and through them they might come to know Him.

Tyre was a great port city built on the island rock by the same name, it was a great and proud city made famous by the abundance of her commerce and industries. It is mentioned approximately 60 times in the Bible, and frequently in the New Testament. It was the capital of the powerful Phoenician nation, which imported tin from Britain, built a colony in North Africa, founded Tarshish in Spain, and plied the waters of the Mediterranean and beyond. Hiram was the king of Tyre who was friendly with King David, supplying him with building materials. It was also the center of Baal worship, and became a by-word for false religion and idolatry.

The news of the fall of Jerusalem had quickly reached Tyre, and they jubilantly exclaimed, "... Aha, she is broken that was the gates of the people: she is turned unto me: I shall be replenished ..." (Ezek. 26:2). The nation of Israel occupied the territory through which the merchants from Egypt and the southland travelled by land to Tyre. Without doubt this fact imposed limitations and restrictions on the flow of commerce. Now the impediment is removed, and therefore, Tyre rejoiced. It was this selfish and material obsession which caused the Lord to declare: "... Behold, I am against thee, O Tyrus ..." (Ezek. 26:3), and it is forever so. God is against any nation or individual who has become so material minded as to rejoice over calamities or misfortunes of others, when those calamities tend to increase opportunities for their personal benefit. Those who gauge their relationships by what they may contribute or benefit, incur the judgment of the Lord. God is a God of righteousness, and He rewards those who maintain His principles of righteous behavior.

Thought For Today

Those who line up with God's principles always enjoy His blessings!

287

November 21

N. T. Bible Reading: James 3   **Our Focus: James 3:18**

THE FRUIT

A true pearl is simply a fresh victory over irritation. Peace is the fruit of righteousness; and the basic fact is that there must first be righteousness in order that there may then be peace. Research for world peace is a multi-billion dollar effort of futility and failure. The outward conflicts are but an amplification of the uncontrolled and rebellious lusts which war in the soul. "From whence come wars and fightings among you? come they not hence, even of your lusts that war in your members?" (Jam. 4:1). The Word of God is conclusive: "There is no peace, saith the Lord, unto the wicked" (Isa. 48:22, 57:21). True peace is a fruit; it is not a product of machinery, treaties, or military conquest. It is a property of an imparted Divine life, and is owned and experienced only by those who know the Prince of Peace.

The thought expressed by James is that the fruit of true wisdom is righteous behavior _by_ those who have and therefore make peace. This is the law of propagation; every seed bears fruit "after its kind" (repeated 10 times in Genesis chapter 1). Righteousness also bears fruit after its kind, and that fruit is peace. The peace-makers are those who have personally been partakers of the heavenly wisdom, which is first pure and then peaceable (Jam. 3:17), and is explained by virtue of righteousness which is the inherent element. The pure (undiluted and unmixed) original wisdom is from above only, and is an unknown quantity by those who live on the natural level. Those who propagate peace are those who first experience the supernatural infusion of Divine life in their own personal experience.

Peace _at any_ price is too dear a price. To attempt to create peace by compromise is to gender confusion and create utter frustration. Martin Luther once warned: "it is better to be divided by truth than to be united by error." To compromise with wrong, and to seek to produce tranquility by the sacrifice of righteousness, is not to discover peace, but rather to make it utterly impossible. On the other hand, to take a brave stand for righteousness, even though there must of necessity be conflict and suffering, is to sow the life-producing seed from which the eventual fruit of peace will come. To do right at the cost of comfort, is to make peace.

Thought For Today

Only the seeds of righteousness will ever yield the harvest of peace!

November 22

O. T. Bible Reading: Ezekiel 27-28   **Our Focus: Ezekiel 28:21**

SIDON

Tyre and Sidon (also called Zidon) belong together like butter and honey, or biscuits and gravy: "… Tyrus, and Zidon, though it be very wise" (Zech. 9:2). The city was 20 miles north of Tyre, built on a promontory (a high ridge jutting out into the water), and was connected with the mainland by a bridge. The modern name is Saida, which is included in the nation of Lebanon. It was the most ancient capital of the Phoenicians, later outclassed by the city of Tyre. It plays a significant role in the Scriptures. Solomon was influenced by Sidonian idolatry; "For Solomon went after Ashtoreth the goddess of the Zidonians …" (I Ki. 11:5). The Sidonians also were worshipers of Baal. Solomon hired expert timber cutters from Sidon, and Jezebel, the daughter of Ethbaal king of Sidon, married King Ahab (I Ki. 16:30-31). Much later, Jesus visited the general area, and made reference to the wickedness of the inhabitants: "And from thence he arose, and went into the borders of Tyre and Sidon …" (Mark 7:24, 31), "… for if the mighty works, which were done in you (Chorazin and Bethsaida), had been done in Tyre and Sidon, they would have repented long ago in sackcloth and ashes" (Matt. 11:21-24).

When Israel entered Canaan, and took possession of the land, the Sidonians were among those whom they failed to drive out of the land (Jud. 3:3). The five men of valor from the tribe of Dan who were sent to spy out a particular portion of their inheritance found that the people in the area "… dwelt careless, after the manner of the Zidonians, quiet and secure; and there was no magistrate in the land …" (Jud. 18:7). They come to represent the careless and the indifferent people of this world who are a law unto themselves and live indifferent lives absorbed only in the affairs of everyday life, and the pursuit of natural pleasures and material luxury. They were a snare to Israel, and their kind are always a dangerous trap to God's people.

Paul addressed this thorny problem: "Who gave himself for our sins, that he might deliver us from this present evil world …" (Gal. 1:4). His missionary companion in the ministry, Demas, forsook him and departed to Thessalonica because of this ever-present danger "For Demas hath forsaken me, having loved this present world, and is departed unto Thessalonica …" (II Tim. 4:10). Let us beware of the deceptive lure of those who appear to dwell "careless … quiet and secure …" (Jud. 18:7). It only appears that way; their lawless living is not a true picture of their troubled and imprisoned hearts.

Thought For Today

The careless are also among the prayerless who have no peace!

November 22

N. T. Bible Reading: James 4   **Our Focus: James 4:8**

DRAW NIGH

Jesus told the 70, whom He sent forth two by two, to tell those who were needy that "… The kingdom of God is come *nigh* unto you" (Luke 10:9, 11). The Apostle Paul, quoting from Deuteronomy 30:14, showed that God was not remote and inaccessible in the distant heavens, but that "… *The word* is nigh thee …" (Rom. 10:8). Most people in the world imagine God, if there is a God at all, is very distant, very aloof, and very unapproachable. Contrary to this notion, God represents Himself as so near, so compassionate, and so solicitous that He stands at the very door of the heart knocking and waiting to be invited in (Rev. 3:20). James seems to attempt to dissolve this prevalent human concept by urging his readers to take the personal action necessary to experience the reality of the presence and power of the seeking Savior: "Draw nigh to God, and he will draw nigh to you …" (Jam. 4:8).

The invitation is His, "Come unto me, all ye that labour and are heavy laden, and I will give you rest" (Matt. 11:28); *the promise* is inclusive and powerful, "Wherefore he is able also to save them to the uttermost that come unto God by him …" (Heb. 7:25); *the responsibility* is ours, and demands action on our part, "Draw nigh to God …" (Jam. 4:8). The paralysis of inaction leaves a man where he was before, deepens his guilt and doubles his bondage, for now he has refused and rejected the Divine invitation to come. It is the deliberate-*action*, which seals the *trans-action*, which connects the needy soul to the Almighty power of God. This is a miracle of Divine grace and mercy; the action has linked you to the outstretched hand of omnipotence and all is instantly changed by the infusion of redemptive power.

The principle of acting on truth is a very critical element in spiritual growth. As an individual we must "… walk in the light …" (I John 1:7). That is, we must continue to take the necessary steps to remain in the ever-progressive unfolding of truth. It is not just an initial *crisis*; it is a crisis which leads to a *process*. Those who continue to act on the truth, continue to grow and mature. Let us keep on drawing nigh to God and He will continue drawing nigh to us (Jam. 4:8).

Thought For Today

To respond to the upward call is to gain new heights in God!

November 23

O. T. Bible Reading: Ezekiel 29-31　　　　　　**Our Focus: Ezekiel 29:6**

EGYPT

Egypt is prominently mentioned in the Bible, over 650 times, by either the name of Egypt or Egyptian. It is the first of the seven heads of the beast of Revelation, and the oldest Gentile world power. Some historians date Egyptian history to 8,000 BC; although, of course, this is open to question; there are serious problems with this date; the fact is that it is one of the most ancient civilizations. Cruden's' Concordance gives the meaning of the word as, "that which troubles or oppresses, also anguish." In the Scriptures, Egypt symbolizes the world, and the unsaved condition of mankind outside of Christ.

The recovered images of ancient Egyptian rulers depicts' them holding the scepter in their hand; the scepter was a symbol of rulership, authority, and power. Ezekiel represents Egypt as being both great and mighty, and indeed it was; very possibly, the dominant world power for over two millenniums of time. The Word of God is sure, dependable, and accurate; and the prophecies concerning Egypt have been exactly fulfilled. The prophecy was brief, terse, and shocking; from the dominance of world powers over centuries of time, God said, "... and they shall be there a base kingdom. It shall be the basest of the kingdoms; neither shall it exalt itself anymore above the nations: for I will diminish them, that they shall no more rule over the nations" (Ezek. 29:14-15). How unlikely this prophecy seemed at the time it was given; but it, like all other prophecies in the Word of God, has been or will be completely fulfilled. This specific prophecy was fulfilled 17 years later when Nebuchadnezzar, king of Babylon, conquered Egypt and carried them into captivity.

Egypt typifies the world, of which everyone is a part, by their natural birth. To reach the promised land of Canaan, the children of Israel had to leave Egypt, cross the Red Sea, and proceed to their inheritance. This fact graphically illustrates God's plan in salvation. We too must leave Egypt, the unsaved world, before we can ever claim our spiritual possession. The first step out of Egypt is applying the blood of the slain Lamb, as did the Israelites on the night of the Passover. Then we too must go "... three days' journey into the wilderness (the full length of the cross), that we may sacrifice to the Lord our God" (Ex. 3:18, 5:3, 8:27, 15:22).

Thought For Today

We cannot claim Canaan while still living in Egypt!

November 23

N. T. Bible Reading: James 5   ***Our Focus: James 5:7***

BE PATIENT

> Patience is a virtue: possess it if you can,
> Seldom in a woman: never in any man.

The most effective method of teaching is to "show and tell"; give me an example or illustration of what you are saying. James first says, "Be patient ..." (Jam. 5:7), and then in the very next verse he adds, "Be ye *also* patient ..." (Jam. 5:8). He has given us the example, it is God Himself who is the ultimate manifestation of patience which we are exhorted to possess.

One dictionary definition of "patient" is, "capable of *calmly awaiting an outcome*; not hasty or impulsive." This is the key to what James is saying, and the master key to capturing and manifesting this most rare attribute. The day of redress, when all wrongs will be righted; all oppression will cease; the poor will get a good, right, and honest deal for the very first time in the history of the world. Righteousness will rule and reign universally, when *The Righteous One* comes again to set up His kingdom. This is an established fact, and a primary teaching of the Word of God. Knowing this, and exercising faith in what He has promised; we are to await that day, and in our waiting to be long-suffering and patient even toward those who oppress us. God is our example; the reason for His patient restraint is that He is expectantly waiting for the precious fruit of the earth. He is neither nervous nor anxious in calm and settled certainty of the ultimate outcome. Even thus are we to be so absolutely certain of the final Divine intervention and correction of all wrong, that we will with serenity, self-restraint, and settled resolve endure afflictions, and smile through the storm.

Twice in the concluding book of the Bible, Revelation, we are told "Here is *the patience* of the saints ..." (Rev. 14:12, 13:10); and once he adds "... and *the faith* of the saints." To the very end of time, patience is always faith in action. Faith in God to sustain us in every circumstance; faith in the Word of God, that what He has promised He will certainly perform; and faith in the final righteous conclusion of it all. The character quality of patience is not listed as a fruit of the Spirit; it is the fruit of tried and tested faith ... the product of tribulation and trials.

Thought For Today

It is through faith, when tested, that we develop patience!

November 24

O. T. Bible Reading: Ezekiel 32-33   **Our Focus: Ezekiel 33:7**

A WATCHMAN

God had told Ezekiel early on that He "... made thee a watchman ..." (Ezek. 3:17), and now He reminds him once again of this vital prophetic responsibility (Ezek. 33:7). Isaiah told the nation of Israel that their faithful God had, "... set watchmen upon thy walls ..." (Isa. 62:6). Jeremiah echoed those very same words, "Also I set watchmen over you, saying, Hearken to the sound of the trumpet ..." (Jer. 6:17).

The picture was very clear to the nation of Israel, and to the people of that time. The cities of those days were walled for their safety and protection, and the gates of entrance into the city were shut and locked at the time of nightfall. A responsible individual, who was keen and alert, called a watchman, ascended the wall to begin the demanding task of careful vigilance through the long, dark night. His task was of great importance to the entire slumbering community. He was trained for this most responsible position; his eyes were trained to peer into the darkness and pick up any approaching danger which might appear on the horizon; his ears were tested and proven to be sensitive to any unusual sound which would signal the approach of danger or the presence of some enemy. In the Hebrew tradition there were three shifts or watches in which the watchmen were to function; the first watch began at nightfall, and continued to about midnight; the second shift went from midnight until just before dawn; and the final watch was the morning shift when the watchman announced the dawn, and the beginning of a new day. The Romans divided the night into four watches of three hours each.

It must be clearly understood that God made the office of a watchman a very definite part of the ministry of the prophet. It was his responsibility *to warn* the people of approaching danger. This is not a pleasant task, because it always involves disturbing those who rest or slumber, and no one enjoys being disturbed. The Word of God certainly embodies the glad and good news of the Gospel, but it also includes grave warnings both to the individuals and to the nations. A true prophet must be able to see into the darkness, and must have the fidelity to warn of approaching danger.

Thought For Today

A watchman must be able to see, and must be willing to warn!

November 24

N. T. Bible Reading: I Peter 1   **Our Focus: I Peter 1:16**

BE HOLY

The study of the specific things which the Word of God instructs us to _be_ is both instructive and profitable. Here we are exhorted to "… _Be ye holy_ …" (I Pet. 1:16). The words "holy" and "holiness" are used over 600 times in the Word of God; about 150 times in the book of Leviticus alone. When the Bible says, "Be patient …" (Jam. 5:7), it is because we are not, by nature, a patient people. Just so, when it says, "be ye holy" (I Pet. 1:15-16; Lev. 20:7), the disturbing fact is that, by nature, we are not. This is not an option; it is, rather, an obligation. God is holy, and we are repeatedly reminded of this great fact; He is described as, "the Holy One" 19 times; He is also defined as "the Holy one of Israel" 31 times. Those who have part in the first resurrection are said to be both _blessed_ and _holy_: "Blessed and holy is he that hath part in the first resurrection: on such the second death hath no power, but they shall be priests of God and of Christ, and shall reign with him a thousand years" (Rev. 20:6). They are called _saints_ (hagioi), which means _sanctified_ or _holy ones_. He is a holy God, and we, His people, are to be godly or God-like in our conduct and behavior.

Our primary purpose in life is not happiness, health, prosperity, nor position and power; it is God-likeness; it is holiness (I Thess. 4:7; Luke 1:75). This is certainly our calling, and we are to become mature enough in Christ that we do not tolerate, in ourselves or in others, through carnal sympathy, any practice that is not in keeping with a Holy God. Holiness means unstained and unimpaired communion with the Lord in a consistent walk with God. It is not just what God gives me, but it is also what I _manifest_ that He has given me.

God is not an infinite blessing-machine; He is a saint-producing God of might and miracle. It is His declared purpose, "… bringing many sons unto glory, to … Make you perfect in every good work to do his will, working in (or into) you that which is wellpleasing in his sight …" (Heb. 2:10, 13:21). He did not come to save men out of pity and sympathy; He came to save men because He originally created them to be holy and thus to serve Him. If our vision does not include His _pro_vision (for our holiness) it is in need of _re_vision.

Thought For Today

The call to be holy also includes the Divine enabling!

November 25

O. T. Bible Reading: Ezekiel 34-35   **Our Focus: Ezekiel 34:15**

MY FLOCK

The words "my flock" occur nine times in Ezekiel chapter 34. In this case, "the flock" refers to the nation of Israel as the concluding words of this section clearly states: "... *This land* that was desolate is become like the garden of Eden ..." (Ezek. 36:35). Today the land is still desolate, but just as prophecy declared, it would be a land forsaken and desolate, so also this yet future prophecy of Israel and the land will be fulfilled. "As the holy flock, as the flock of Jerusalem in her solemn feasts; so shall the waste cities be filled with flocks of men: and they shall know that I am Lord" (Ezek. 36:38). The land today does not, in any way, resemble the Garden of Eden; as surely as God has uttered this promise, just as surely it will one day be literally fulfilled. When God visits the restored remnant and puts His "... spirit within you ..." (Ezek. 36:27, 26). The nation of Israel is unique among the nations, because of God's peculiar design on their behalf. To get the full picture there are three aspects of their existence which must be studied and understood:

1.   Their past history.
2.   Their present plight.
3.   Their future prospect.

Jesus declared Himself to be the Good Shepherd, the True Shepherd (John 10:14); He is later defined as the Great Shepherd (Heb. 13:20), and the Chief Shepherd (I Pet. 5:4). However, the flock He tends is not a nation, but individuals who have entered the sheep-fold through *The Door*, which is a genuine and a personal experience of the new birth (John 10:7, 9). "Fear not, *little flock* (a mere handful of 120 on the day of Pentecost); for it is your Father's good pleasure to give you the kingdom (in its present hidden aspect)" (Luke 12:32) (Rom. 14:17; I Cor. 4:20).

Paul also identified this church-age-flock when he exhorted the Ephesians elders to, "Take heed therefore unto yourselves, and to all the flock (that is all that were in Ephesus), over the which the Holy Ghost hath made you overseers (shepherds), to feed the church of God, which he hath purchased with his own blood" (Acts 20:28). It is not now a *natural*, nor is it a *national* birth which puts you into the kingdom of God; it is a supernatural *new birth* which translates us out of darkness and places us into the kingdom of His dear Son (Col. 1:13). Let us carefully and faithfully follow our Shepherd this very day.

Thought For Today

The Shepherd provides for the sheep that obediently follow Him!

November 25

N. T. Bible Reading: I Peter 2   **Our Focus: I Peter 2:7**

HE IS PRECIOUS

Peter repeats the word "precious" seven times in these two epistles. The meaning of the word is costly, very dear, of great value, very expensive, and of unique value. In the previous chapter, I Peter 1, he states that we were not redeemed with things of great earthly value, "But with the *precious* blood of Christ, as of a lamb without blemish and without spot" (I Pet. 1:19). There was only One who was holy, harmless, undefiled, separate from sinners (not one of them), and made higher than the heavens (Heb. 7:26). His pure offering was singular and therefore the price is beyond the boundaries of earthly value. It is *very precious* in the sight of God, and on behalf of man.

Another version (the revised) renders I Peter 2:7 as "For you therefore that believe is the preciousness." The real meaning then seems to be that not only do the believers know and experience the preciousness of Christ, which they certainly do; but that they actually *share it*. It is theirs; they possess it. The root word is very important here, and it has to do with *honor*. The idea is the honor and dignity of the new, rare, and costly possession. It refers also to the qualities which are worthy of honor in the lives and conduct of those who have been redeemed.

The Lord has already been described as precious (I Pet. 2:4, 6); and in both cases they are a declaration of God's estimate of the Lord Jesus. He came unto His own (the Jewish nation) and His own received Him not (John 1:11); He was rejected of men, but was in the eyes of God, elect and precious. It is obvious that the attributes in Christ which made Him precious in the sight of God were His purity, His flawless behavior, His unparalleled love, and His total conformity to all of the perfect will of His Father. Here then, is the wonder and miracle of redemption; all of these exceedingly rare and very costly qualities are miraculously communicated to those who believe in Him. His very life and nature are imparted to His children, and then by the miraculous transforming power of their in-working, cause every transformed life to also be precious with His preciousness. He is the chief cornerstone, *the* living stone (I Pet. 2:4), and those who experience His dynamic power, receive those very qualities of His life, and thus become *lively stones* (I Pet. 2:5). It is as His habitation and peculiar possession that they radiate forth His Excellencies (I Pet. 2:9).

Thought For Today

Heaven's most precious gift transforms a mortal into His preciousness!

November 26

O. T. Bible Reading: Ezekiel 36-37   **Our Focus: Ezekiel 37:4**

DRY BONES

Ezekiel was clearly Divinely appointed as a prophet to the nation of Israel: "... Son of man, I send thee to the children of Israel, to a rebellious nation that hath rebelled against me ..." (Ezek. 2:3). He was a pure seer, who had visions from God; the words "vision" and "visions" are repeated 15 times in the book. Many helpful applications can be made from these visions, but it must always be carefully remembered that the first and primary interpretation relates to the nation of Israel. The two sticks of Ezekiel 37:16 were certainly not literally Judah and Israel; they were *symbols* only. God explained this by saying, "... *For* Judah ..." and again, "... *for* the children of Israel ... *For* Joseph ... *for* all the house of Israel ..." (Ezek. 37:16). They were to *represent them* and not literally to be them. Just so also, the valley of dry bones is a symbol of the nation of Israel and represents them in vision form (Ezek. 37:4). These are not to be taken as the literal bones of Israel's dead. God gave the interpretation Himself, and we would do well to accept that as final: "... these bones are (or represent) the whole house of Israel: behold, they say, Our bones are dried, and our hope is lost ..." (Ezek. 37:11).

The vision is of *national* restoration, and not of any individual resurrection; that is another subject entirely. Ezekiel 37:12 underscores this fact: "... Behold, O my people, *I will* open your graves ... and bring you into *the land* of Israel." Ezekiel 37:21 continues to emphasize their national resuscitation, reunion, and renewal: "... Behold, *I will* take the children of Israel from among the heathen (where they are now scattered) ... and bring them into *their own land*." Certainly they may be accurately described as, "... prisoners of hope ..." (Zech. 9:12). These prophecies are yet future, they have not yet been fulfilled, but these glowing passages of Israel's ultimate destiny are certain and sure.

The miracle of the bones coming to life was accomplished by the *Word of God*, and by the four winds, the *Spirit of God*. We may make a universal and a personal application for all of this. The whole world, through sin and rebellion, has become a valley of dry bones. The only hope for any individual is a Divine miracle of imparted life through the Word of God and by the resurrection power of the Holy Spirit. These dry bones can also live! The crowning diadem of the city of promise and prophecy is: Jehovah-Shammah "... *The Lord is there*" (Ezek. 48:35). Where He is, there is *resurrection*, and there is *life*!

Thought For Today

The drier the bones, the greater the miracle of their restoration!

November 26

N. T. Bible Reading: I Peter 3   **Our Focus: I Peter 3:15**

SANCTIFY THE LORD

The meaning of the word "sanctify" is to *set apart* or to *separate* for a particular purpose. The heart of the believer is to be uniquely set apart and separated from all else, to be a sanctuary for the indwelling Christ. This is an appeal for the practical and personal realization of the *Lordship* of Christ in our daily living. We must, and only we as individuals can, exalt Him to a position of absolute control in our heart of hearts.

The injunction is clear, at the very core (the heart of the matter) of every life there is to be one Lord and Master and that is to be the risen, living, reigning Savior. If and when this is done, the whole life comes together and there is a beautiful and transforming singleness of purpose and desire. There is a unified meaning to life, consistency in conduct and behavior, and fulfillment of purpose. Apart from this vital transaction, the life is splintered and divided, inconsistent in relationships, and ineffective in service because there is divided loyalty at the center of the life.

Isaiah prophesied that one day, when Israel has been restored to their calling, the song will echo throughout the land of Israel; and in retrospect they will be able both to see and to sing, "O Lord our God, *other lords* beside thee have had dominion over us ..." (Isa. 26:13). Every honest-hearted saint of God can and will say the very same thing. Herein lies the key to personal consistency and daily victorious Christian experience. If He is on the throne of the heart, and reigns supreme, there will be peace, righteousness, and joy in the Holy Ghost (Rom. 14:17).

Any other person or influence which dominates the life and governs or controls us makes us a prisoner. We are in bondage to every false thing which occupies the throne which belongs only to the blessed Savior. To become a voluntary bond-slave to Jesus Christ, releases us from every other dominion and captivity. We must choose to be free by crowning Him both Lord and Master of our lives. Each choice exalts Him just that much more, and brings just that much more fulfillment. Today let each of us "crown Him Lord of all!"

Thought For Today

Those who crown Him King, enjoy the riches of His throne!

November 27

O. T. Bible Reading: Ezekiel 38-39   **Our Focus: Ezekiel 39:29**

HIDE

God says emphatically concerning Israel and the captivity of Jacob, "Neither will I *hide* my face any more from them ..." (Ezek. 39:29). This is a beautiful prospect, and it will be fulfilled in the future when He has "... poured out my spirit upon the house of Israel, saith the Lord God" (Ezek. 39:29). There also is a very frightening aspect of the truth revealed; there was a time when *He did hide* his face from them. How tragic is this condition, and how futile the lot of those involved. If God hides Himself, let no mortal man imagine that he could ever find what God has hidden.

The Word of God is its own best commentary. It was the Psalmist who anxiously inquired, "How long, Lord? wilt thou hide thyself for ever ..." (Ps. 89:46). The answer is distinctly written in the plainest of language: "But your iniquities have separated between you and your God, and your sins have hid his face from you, that he will not hear" (Isa. 59:2). In brief staccato-like phrases God pin-points the real problem, "... your iniquities ... your sins ... your hands ... your fingers ... your lips ... your tongue ..." (Isa. 59:2-3). This gives the conclusive answer for all time to the human puzzle for Divine delays and apparent inaction. God works by eternal laws and principles; there is never any failure on the part of God. It is men who fail; and when they fail, it will always have consequences. One of these consequences is that His face of approval and blessing is hidden. It might also be more easily explained by natural phenomena. If thick dark clouds fill the sky, the sun is hidden, perhaps for many days at a time. You will not see the sun again until the clouds have been removed.

The problem was never with the sun; it is ever in its place, and continues to shine. There is always an element "under the sun" (used over and over in Ecclesiastes), if it does not appear to us to be shining. Roll the clouds away, and behold the sun shines in its full radiance. The most human thing is to blame another for our own predicament. Or originally it was, "... The woman whom thou gavest to be with me ..." (Gen. 3:12); this is called "she-did-it-itis", and it is a universal infection. Those who look into the mirror, get the true picture of the real problem.

Thought For Today

If God seems hidden, He has neither moved nor changed; we have!

November 27

N. T. Bible Reading: I Peter 4   **Our Focus: I Peter 4:16**

CHRISTIAN

The word "Christian" is loosely and commonly used in our culture, and we are forced to wonder, "In our time, does it have any meaning at all?" There are very few references to it in the New Testament; there are exactly three.

The first, of course, is Acts 11:26 where we are told that the word originated: "… the disciples were called Christians first in Antioch." Most likely, this was not used as a reproach, but simply to identify a certain group as followers of Christ.

The second is also in the book of Acts, Acts 26:28, when King Agrippa interrupted the Apostle Paul by saying: "… Almost thou persuadest me to be a Christian." This comment would seem to indicate that by this time it had become a general term, and was also in common use.

The historian Tacitus, writing near the end of the first century, commented, "The vulgar call them Christians." The author, or origin of this denomination, Christus, had, in the reign of Tiberius, been executed by the procurator, Pontius Pilate (W. E. Vine, Expository Dictionary, page 191). It is clearly indicated by early church records that by the second century the term was accepted by believers as a title of honor.

The third and final time the word is used is in I Peter 4:16, our focus for today. It is inferred that, unlike the meaningless application in our time, in that time it often brought suffering to be numbered as a Christian. Peter makes it abundantly clear that no shame whatever is to be attached to any such suffering. We can be very sure that he remembered most graphically when he and his fellow apostles departed from the Jewish Council, still bleeding and in physical pain from the stripes which fell upon their backs "… rejoicing that they were counted worthy to suffer shame for his name" (Acts 5:41). He also added, "… let him glorify God …" (I Pet. 4:16). That is, to so conduct himself, in daily behavior, as to live worthily, of all that is involved in glorifying God. We are responsible to live responsibly.

Thought For Today

Those who claim His name must also proclaim His nature!

November 28

O. T. Bible Reading: Ezekiel 40　　　　　　　　　**Our Focus: Ezekiel 40:3**

A MEASURING REED

The two words "measure" and "measured" are repeated 20 times in the 49 verses of Ezekiel chapter 40. It must be kept in mind that:

1.　　This entire experience is the content of what Ezekiel describes as, "In *the visions* of God brought he me into the land of Israel ..." (Ezek. 40:2).
2.　　Ezekiel was *a prophet* and the book of Ezekiel is a book of prophecy; signs and symbols abound in such a setting, and they must be so understood. They cannot be taken literally, but must be seen *spiritually*.

As an evident proof of their spiritual nature, take some of these measurements literally. Let us consider the dimensions of the temple as measured in this vision (Ezek. 42:15-20, 45:2). The outer court was 500 reeds long and 500 reeds wide; a reed is about 10 feet. This is a huge area, almost one square mile. The "sacred area" or oblation is given as 25,000 reeds square; this is about 47 miles, covering an area greater than the distance from the Jordan River to the Mediterranean Sea, which in some places is barely 40 miles. If this is the temple only, what would be the size of the city of Jerusalem which houses it? It seems much more simple and plausible to give it a spiritual application.

It is strikingly obvious that amazing care is taken to emphasize the minute details and their exact measurements. The vastness of the dimensions seems to magnify the awesome and transcendent nature of Israel's millennial restoration. The minute and detailed reed and cube measurements appear to emphasize Divine perfection, and the description of the sacrificial details reveal the absolute purity of the worship in that time.

The lesson we may draw from all of this is that the work of the Holy Spirit is thorough and exact; and great care must be taken to correct our careless tendencies. Carelessness, disorder, confusion, and irresponsibility belong to the *street* where they abound and thrive. Everything must change as we enter the *sanctuary*. There is a behavior which is becoming to and required by the *House of God* (I Tim. 3:15). This too may be given a much broader application; our entire conversation (manner of conduct) must be changed or transformed to become both godly and holy (II Pet. 3:11).

Thought For Today

Our vision of tomorrow must transform our conduct today!

November 28

N. T. Bible Reading: I Peter 5   **Our Focus: I Peter 5:7**

HE CARETH

The common and careless comment of the world is "So what, who cares?" Obviously, the answer is generally and in most cases, there is no one who really cares. This represents a very cold and cruel world, and certainly it is. Proverbs 12:10 says, "... the tender mercies of the wicked are cruel." That is the condition of things "out there"; they are completely changed "in Him."

There are three themes emphasized in I Peter:

1.   I Peter 1:3 through 2:10 he emphasizes the living hope, and what it produces.
2.   I Peter 2:11 through 4:11 he outlines the Pilgrim life, and how to live it.
3.   The final theme is the fiery trial, and how to bear it: I Peter 4:12 to the end. In this context, we are reminded that "... *he* careth *for you*" (I Pet. 5:7).

Two different kinds of care are explained in I Peter 5:7:

1.   There is *anxious care*, described by the words, "Casting all your care upon him ..."; anxiety is debilitating and crippling. It is a state of uneasiness, and apprehensive worry; it also is intense fear caused by the anticipation of threatening events; finally, it is eager and agitated desire. That is a huge load to carry, but we need not suffer and struggle under the burden. We are told to *cast* the whole load on Him, because *He does care*!
2.   The other type of care illustrated here is *loving care*. This is TLC (tender loving care) at its very best.

Nothing is excluded; He will shoulder it *all*. That is, the heavy and light, the natural and the spiritual, the abstract or general and the exact or the very specific; we are to unload it *all* upon Him. Weymouth translates it graphically, "Throw the whole weight of your anxiety upon Him." That is stress relief for the present and for the future. An illustration from yester-year may help. An elderly woman, with great effort, walked slowly and wearily along a country road carrying a very heavy bundle. A kind and thoughtful farmer came by in his wagon and gave her a ride. After a short distance, he turned and asked her why she still held the bundle in her arms, instead of putting it down in the wagon. She responded, "It is asking too much from you, to carry my bundle as well as to carry me." He has taken us on board, so let us lay our burdens, cares, and anxieties on Him, for He cares for you. Do not hug your bundle; cast it away and *upon Him*.

Thought For Today

He died because He cares, and He lives to relieve our anxieties!

November 29

O. T. Bible Reading: Ezekiel 41-42   **Our Focus: Ezekiel 42:20**

A SEPARATION

The symbolic and figurative description of the vision continues with the temple, and now in Ezekiel chapter 42 the buildings surrounding it. All were within the sacred precincts, and were for the priests use while engaged in temple service. Last of all, there is the description and measurement of the great wall which surrounded the entire temple area. It is with respect to that wall that it is defined as intended to make a separation between the sanctuary and the unsanctified area around it; this symbolic picture pin-points a very vital and eternal principle. God designs, that there must be a distinction between worship and social relationships.

The distinction made here is not that of a separation between the holy and the unholy or evil. That should be abundantly clear, and is specifically dealt with in other Scriptures. Neither is it the distinction between the holy (spiritual) and the common (carnal). That too is obvious and clearly explained elsewhere. What is in focus here is the eternal and Divine purpose (one of His ways), in the exercise of worship at the *human level*. There must be *a wall* to separate the exercise of worship in relation to God, and the exercise of worship incorporating the atmosphere and culture of that which is purely human and natural. This is the point which must be made. It is the difference between true worship, which is also described as "... in spirit and in truth ..." (John 4:23, 24), and counterfeit worship (unacceptable), which incorporates and encourages the culture and spirit of the world. A great wall (it is symbolic, but a reality) will be maintained to effect this separation in the final order, and we must carefully observe it *now*. The emphasis is on the sanctity and reverence of *true worship*.

It is not necessary for us in any way to erect some man-made wall or walls for the church. God has already done that to protect His property. Isaiah declares, "... but thou shalt call thy walls Salvation, and thy gates Praise" (Isa. 60:18). Genuine salvation sets apart those who follow the Lamb, from those who continue to have their names "... written in the earth ..." (Jer. 17:13). The *Berlin Wall* is like a castle of sand by comparison. The exercise of true worship and praise separates those who yet walk in the flesh, from those who soar into the heavenlies and touch God as they do so. These are the walls which separate.

Thought For Today

Spiritual life and worship are exercised by citizens of another country!

November 29

N. T. Bible Reading: II Peter 1   **Our Focus: II Peter 1:5**

ADD

The first and most simple step in the science of mathematics is to learn to add. To add is to combine or to join together. There must first be faith, but faith must not stand alone. We are to strengthen, reinforce, and supplement that faith. One of the great joys of my childhood was to spend a day just tramping through the forest with my dog. It was fascinating, intriguing, and invigorating; and it still is. There are two obvious processes going on continuously in that environment. First there is growth, luxurious foliage, and beauty in the healthy vegetation which is living; and then there is decay, deterioration, and decomposition in that which is dead. Nothing is static, there is a process going on at all times and in every element.

Peter states that we "… escaped the *pollutions* of the world through the knowledge of the Lord and Saviour Jesus Christ …" (II Pet. 2:20). The pollutions of the world are the gross evils, the apparent and distastefully vile expressions of an unregenerate heart. These are the dead leaves, the rotten and decayed wood, which carpets the floor of the forest. He also clearly states that we have "… escaped the *corruption* that is in the world through lust" (II Pet. 1:4). The corrupting is within, and it is the insidious process which leads to decay. There are only two alternatives; either we add to our vital faith in Christ and enhance the foliage; or by neglecting to do so, we actually contribute to the slow but inevitable process of decay.

II Peter 1:9 gives us the anatomy of the decay. *The problem* is near-sightedness, which he describes as blindness. *The reason* for the existing condition is failure of recognition, which is the stupefying paralysis of forgetting. Seeing the things that are near, is to see the *things of time*, the lure of the immediate, the mirage of the material, and the focus on self, secular, and sensuous. He has forgotten, that is, to treat with inattention. What you do not review, you will soon forget. The freshness and vigor of that "… first love" (Rev. 2:4) must be cherished and nourished. It also meant the sharp and clear view of that which is *eternal* (the very opposite of seeing only what is *near* and *now*). *The result* is the precious reality of God revealed to us in a personal transforming way. *It issued* in the flow and thrill of a new-found communion and fellowship. *It resulted* in an illuminating insight into Calvary, the awful agony, the triumphant meaning of "… It is finished …" (John 19:30), and the beauty and excitement of His resurrection and ours. Let us linger longer at the place of these first things, refresh our minds and thirsty souls at the over-flowing fountain, and add the blessed virtues and luxuriant growth and fruit for which He is seeking.

Thought For Today

To fail to add, leads inevitably to the decay of subtraction!

November 30

O. T. Bible Reading: Ezekiel 43-44   **Our Focus: Ezekiel 44:3**

THE PRINCE

We must keep in mind that we are reading prophecy which is very symbolic and figurative in expression. There is no clear agreement among Bible scholars as to whom this Prince may be. It seems reasonable that since this is symbolic language, and is at least a picture of final things in a restored theocracy, that we can use it to make an application to the Lord Jesus Christ, and to His place in the church, as well as in our individual lives.

The Prince is pre-eminently an heir to a throne. There can be no Prince until and unless there is a throne; he is the heir-apparent. Isaiah prophesied that His name would be "... The *Prince* of Peace" (Isa. 9:6). Daniel called Him, "... Messiah *the Prince* ..." (Dan. 9:25). The apostles taught that, "The God of our fathers raised up Jesus ... Him hath God exalted with his right hand to be *a Prince* and a Saviour ..." (Acts 5:30-31). Another aspect of the designation "prince" has to do with authority and rulership. That is why *the throne* and *the Lamb* are finally united in one and there, in the final wrap-up, we view in the last book of the Bible: "And I beheld, and, lo, in the midst of the throne (used 27 times in Revelation) and of the four beasts, and in the midst of the elders, stood a Lamb (used 24 times in Revelation) ..." (Rev. 5:6). He is now *Prince of Peace*, He shall then be crowned "... King Of Kings, And Lord Of Lords" (Rev. 19:16, 17:14). The conclusive declaration of the Scriptures is: "... and he shall reign for ever and ever" (Rev. 11:15); He does reign even *now* in the hearts and lives of those who welcome Him as Lord and Master.

It is this hidden mystery, the indwelling and reigning Savior; who transforms the life and revolutionizes the conduct. There is no miracle where there is a reasonable explanation. We control and manage what we can explain. To have a master, and to be mastered are two very different things. Many of the most vital things in life are not from conscious effort; they are there, and they transpire in the normal flow of life. Conscious effort comes in the area of what is mechanical. What comes with the infusion of Divine life is beyond explanation, because it is a miracle. The outflow of that blessed inward reality is not conscious effort; it is a genuine flow of a true life and love. It is never a burden to serve someone you love; it is a delight. Herein lies the difference between possession and a mere profession. Our heart is His throne, and He rules from a blessed and glorious relationship of love.

Thought For Today

He rules supreme only where there is no rival to the throne!

November 30

N. T. Bible Reading: II Peter 2   **Our Focus: II Peter 2:19**

BONDAGE

Bondage is not a popular word; it has a very negative connotation, and we instinctively avoid it. It involves servitude, and servitude involves slavery, and no one wants to get involved in either one. The root word is "bond" and that involves something which binds, confines, and limits. Why would anyone even consider this ugly word as a subject for an inspirational study? It is a Biblical word, and occurs 15 times in the New Testament.

"... of whom a man is overcome, of the same is he brought into bondage" (II Pet. 2:19). "Know ye not, that to whom ye yield yourselves servants to obey, his servants ye are to whom ye obey; whether of sin unto death, or of obedience unto righteousness?" (Rom. 6:16). This is a principle which is insisted upon in all Biblical revelation. Humanity resents this, and what we resent, we also reject. This is surely one of the "... bitter herbs ..." (Ex. 12:8; Num. 9:11), but so the Lamb must be eaten.

Everyone thinks of themselves as "in control" they are "their own man", independent, ingenious, and intelligent. The real truth is somewhat different. We are free to choose our master, but once the choice is made, we are free no longer. We are now a servant of that master. It is in your power to choose to yield to sin, but in so doing, you become the servant of that sin. No one wants to believe that. Everyone says and thinks that they can quit anytime they want to. Yielding is yielding, and that involves submission. The catch is we never intended to get this involved: "Sin will take you farther than you wanted to go, keep you longer than you wanted to stay, and cost you more than you wanted to pay."

The only way to have freedom from the mastery of evil appetites and lusts, is that of escape from it through submission to the Lordship of Christ. This involves infinitely more than a single act, choice, or decision; it is *an attitude* which must be maintained, reinforced, strengthened, and fortified. This is a daily and continuous process; it is the present tense aspect of salvation. It is the working out of that which He has placed within. The shackles of bondage are broken and kept under, as we continue to yield to the Lordship of Christ in the uttermost abandonment. Glorious freedom!!

Thought For Today

Absolute freedom is the ability to choose His will absolutely!

December 1

O. T. Bible Reading: Ezekiel 45-46　　　　　　**Our Focus: Ezekiel 45:1**

YE SHALL

The expression and prophetic promise "ye shall" is repeated about 40 times in Ezekiel chapters 45-46: it is preceded by the words of the Lord "I will" over 200 times up to the end of chapter 44. The prophet Ezekiel uses the emphatic words, "Thus saith the Lord" about 120 times. The eye of faith must focus on the sure Word of the Lord. It is because He has spoken that we have the foundation upon which all true faith must rest.

Foolish presumption ventures upon that which is assumed: excited emotion lunges forward on the impulse of the moment, but genuine faith steps forward in absolute confidence in Him, in His Word, and in His unfailing faithfulness. The Scriptures describe Abraham as "... faithful Abraham" (Gal. 3:9). The reason this positive attribute could justifiably be attached to this great man was because "He staggered not (fainted not when tested) at the promise ... being fully persuaded that, what he had promised, he was able also to perform" (Rom. 4:20-21). This is why the victorious nation of Israel went forth into their promised land and conclusively declared, "There failed not ought (not a single one) of any good thing which the Lord had spoken unto the house of Israel; *all* came to pass" (Josh. 21:45). He did not fail; He has not failed; He will not fail, because He cannot fail!

Thought For Today

Human certainty is possible because of Divine certification!

December 1

N. T. Bible Reading: II Peter 3   **Our Focus: II Peter 3:13**

OUR FOCUS

The most costly binoculars, out of focus, will distort the view and deceive the viewer. In "Hamlet" Shakespeare described his day by saying, "The times are out of joint." The Apostle Peter in his great sermon, on the day of Pentecost, urged his Jewish audience to "... Save yourselves from this untoward generation" (Acts 2:40). The original word means morally crooked or perverse ... swerving from an intended goal.

Peter admonishes his readers to keep a clear focus as he uses the words, "looking/look for" three times in three verses (II Pet. 3:12, 13, 14). First, "Looking for and hasting unto the coming of the day of God ..." (II Pet. 3:12). There must be a clear agreement between God's purposes and His peoples' responses. Secondly, "... we ... look for new heavens and a new earth ..." (II Pet. 3:13), that is, we eagerly and confidently anticipate. The settled fact grips our hearts and shapes our lives, and joins with glad anticipation the last prayer recorded in the Bible, "... Even so, come, Lord Jesus" (Rev. 22:20). Thirdly and finally, "... seeing that ye look for such things, be diligent ..." (II Pet. 3:14), that is, now that you have this blessed insight, diligently and earnestly guard yourselves. By His supernatural enablement, keep your focus clear, your perceptions well-defined, and your priorities carefully and prayerfully in Divine order.

The jolts and jars of life, the constant pull of the world, and the keen disappointments of human failures, will cause us to lose focus. We need, and must have, the precious renewings of our thinking by the Holy Ghost (Rom. 12:2; Tit. 3:5).

Thought For Today

The mind and life that drifts, has lost focus and force!

December 2

O. T. Bible Reading: Ezekiel 47-48   **Our Focus: Ezekiel 47:1**

AFTERWARD

The great book of Ezekiel ends with an amazing vision of the healing waters, and of the ultimate portions of the 12 tribes of Israel; it ends abruptly with the words: *Jehovah- Shammah*, "… The Lord is there" (Ezek. 48:35). What could be greater? From this rich portion of prophetic Scripture let us make some very practical and personal applications.

One of the most reassuring facts to every tested, tried, and tempest tossed saint is that because there is a great Master-Designer in control, there must always be an "Afterward …" (Ezek. 47:1) to every experience of life. This great key to personal triumph in tragedy was given to Israel by Jeremiah. There would be 70 years of captivity, anguish, and heartache, but God had a plan. His plan was the primary purpose in the apparent tragedy, and the missing element in the formula "… to give you an expected end" (Jer. 29:11). So it is also and always for God's people.

Where there is no vision there is no "afterward." It is our assured confidence in the great plan of God, for us personally and for His people, which gives faith a firm foundation and enables us to sing triumphantly, "It shall, it shall be done!"

When we lose sight of tomorrow, we lose hope for today. Circumstances are not wild uncontrolled strokes of fate, they are the tools of an all-wise God, patiently but certainly, crafting the events of time to fulfill His designs for us and for eternity.

Thought For Today

Behind a frowning providence I see a smiling face!

December 2

N. T. Bible Reading: I John 1   **Our Focus: I John 1:6**

IF

The biggest little word in the English language is "if." The last 5 verses of I John chapter 1 contain this powerful and defining little word 5 times. If the entries in Strong's exhaustive concordance are accurate the "mighty mite" occurs over 1,400 times in the Bible. John used it 24 times in these short epistles, and the Apostle Paul employs it approximately 100 times in the Corinthian epistles alone.

It will be quickly recognized by any careful reader that it is never used when speaking of God's design, His resources, nor of His desire or intent. It always relates to men; to his choices, to his will, and to his commitment. These are the vital elements in the grand formula for personal victory over which we have control. No one will and no one can force me to make a determined choice, to exercise my own willful option, nor to make a life-changing commitment to any person or to any cause. It is left to me to respond positively or to reject the offer made by pretending to be neutral (which is a technical rejection of a positive course of action) or to overtly veto the entire proposition. How vital then are our many daily choices.

It is always proven personally helpful and challenging to me to insert the word "when" instead of "if." It really doesn't change the statement, but it emphasizes the two elements of time and condition. The measure of my experience in God is determined, not by the scope of Divine promise, but by the degree of my response to it.

Thought For Today

We inherit the blessing, when we obey the command!

December 3

O. T. Bible Reading: Daniel 1-2   **Our Focus: Daniel 1:8**

BUT DANIEL

A young man is taken prisoner of war. He is deported to a heathen nation, and placed within the chambers of an evil and ungodly King. He is carefully groomed and prepared to fit into an administration of luxury and indulgence. His place of dwelling is changed, his surroundings are changed, his friends and associates are changed, the language he spoke was changed, and even his name was changed. But Daniel did not change, His life glowingly radiates through sixty nine years under four different rulers, and through these 2,500 years of time. It triumphantly signals to every young person that you can be true to God, loyal to godly principles, and faithful in behavior under the most adverse conditions.

Daniel purposed in his heart, that is, he made a commitment not to compromise his convictions, nor his principles. It cost him a great deal to remain steadfast to his godly way of life. Indeed, at the age of 70, it caused him to be viciously cast into a den of lions. This grand character of unwavering godliness had so much steel in his soul that no lion could crush nor even bite into it, even if they had tried. He was thoroughly delivered from every fiber of compromise; and God did deliver him from certain death. Little wonder that this great man of God is called "… greatly beloved …" of God three times (Dan. 9:23, 10:11, 19).

The word "but" occurs 71 times in the book of Daniel. It always marks a contrast and points out a vital and significant difference. It would be interesting to know how many times the same word could be applied to your life and mine. We can make a difference if we dare to be different!

Thought For Today

A sterling character ends with a golden crown!

December 3

N. T. Bible Reading: I John 2   **Our Focus: I John 2:3**

WE KNOW

Most authorities agree that this epistle of I John 2 is probably the last apostolic message to the whole church. The key verse to the Gospel of John is John 20:31 and the key verse to the epistle is I John 5:13. The Gospel was written that men might have life; the epistle was written that believers might "know" they have life; 35 times in five chapters, and 8 times in chapter 5 alone the word "know" is used. The Gospel declares the way of life through the incarnate Son; the epistle unveils the nature of that life as possessed by and lived out in daily experience by the children of God.

Heresy had filtered into the church in the form of Gnosticism. Those who promoted it claimed to have a superior knowledge. It is well to remember that Christianity was not in danger of being destroyed; it was and is in danger of being changed. Then, the attempt was being made to improve it, to give it a flair of intellectual respectability, and make it contemporary in terms of the popular philosophy. Now it is being promoted as easily adapted to all that is contemporary and in popular vogue. John forcefully argues that with the true Gospel "... we do know ..." (I John 2:3). This knowledge is not "... heady ..." but life changing (II Tim. 3:4).

There are seven successive contrasts used in this epistle which serve as vital highway markers, which clearly point us to our ultimate goal. If there is no sharp contrast in a person's behavior after conversion, they have taken the wrong road. John declares "hereby we know" seven times, that we have passed from death to life, from darkness into His marvelous light, from the chains of sin into the glorious liberty of a new life, and from the power of evil and vice into deliverance, and a whole new *highway* (Prov. 16:17) of victory over the world and all that is in it. The greatest miracle of all times is a transformed life. It is as real today as it was then.

Thought For Today

Only the Spirit-illuminated eye can clearly see the upward path!

December 4

O. T. Bible Reading: Daniel 3-4   **Our Focus: Daniel 3:18**

BUT IF NOT

This is one of the finest examples of unconditional commitment to the Lord that we find in the Word of God. It is the epitome of triumphant faith. It is the declaration of an all-out human instrument of absolute dependence upon the character of God, the way of God, and the principles which govern His actions. These young men with one voice clearly define the actions of anyone who knows God, and, therefore, can trust Him implicitly and without hesitation.

The bold and even daring statement had immediate results. The proud heathen King was furious at such defiance as he interpreted it. However, unknown to him, this was devotion at its very best. Little did he know that anyone who possesses such unbending resolve, is the rare person who can be absolutely trusted under all circumstances. These men were by no means traitors: they were, by the very standards of heaven itself, men who did know their God, were Divinely strengthened, and would do exploits for their faithful Master (Dan. 11:32). The fierce wrath of the king, and the fury of a furnace, heated seven times hotter than normal, were the inevitable experience on the human level.

There was no "If the Lord will deliver me, I will serve Him" in these heroes of faith. They were not bargaining with God: they were serving Him! It is no surprise that heaven moved immediately. The Lord Himself joined the trio in the furnace, and the unique quartet sang the song of Moses and of the Lamb to a shocked King and to an unbelieving world. They literally walked with God. The inevitable result was that their fetters were melted, and their liberated spirits proclaimed to the world the faithfulness of Almighty God.

Thought For Today

The only "if" in real devotion is "but if not!"

December 4

N. T. Bible Reading: I John 3   **Our Focus: I John 3:19, 24**

HEREBY WE KNOW

The message is clean-cut and intelligible, the contrast is clear and indelible, and the appeal is inevitable. No dim or fuzzy view, no pious parleying, and no vague and uncertain conclusions here. This aged seer demonstrates beyond question that here also he is *in the Spirit*. The Spirit-quickened mind and the Spirit-illuminated eyes see vital moral distinctions immediately, and the glorious result is convictions, not just inclinations. It is this vital missing link which is desperately needed today. Only this Divine ingredient can transform a squirming jellyfish character into a pillar of strength and consistency. The operation of the Spirit is a Divine transplant, which implants a saw log for a backbone and columns of steel for a rib cage.

The significant little phrase "hereby we know" or "by this we know" is repeated 7 times. The express purpose for writing this epistle is that we may "know" and distinguish, in their most vital aspects, Christian truth from error, light from darkness, the real world of spiritual values from the present world of phantom and deceit, and the spirit of truth from the spirit of error. The judgment is not for us to make. The Word of God has spoken, God has declared the decree, and it is for us not to reason and rationalize, but rather to recite and recognize the beautiful plan of God for the life-style of His children.

In reality, the seven contrasts provide a genuine Biblical test for every experience. These are the acid tests of profession, of desire, of doctrine, of conduct, of discernment, of motive, and of experience. May the Lord help each of us to pass the test, because we *do know our God*!

Thought For Today

The light shines clearest where the oil is purest!

December 5

O. T. Bible Reading: Daniel 5-6   **Our Focus: Daniel 6:3**

AN EXCELLENT SPIRIT

The single most memorable faculty of any person is the spirit which they manifest. Their words will be long forgotten, the theme of their message will fade away with time, but the kind of spirit they have manifested, remains both vivid and haunting. The Bible gives a very extensive list of the kind of spirit various individuals have portrayed. Who has ever heard a message preached on this most vital element of human behavior? The list which we find in the Word of God is interesting and challenging.

Real salvation reaches and transforms every phase and aspect of the life of an individual. Paul prayed for the Thessalonians that their whole spirit and soul and body might be Divinely preserved and blameless (I Thess. 5:23). This does not seem to leave anything out. It is an all-inclusive laundry list. This and other Scriptures clearly assert that the entire person and every inch of him/her is corrupted, polluted, and in great need of salvation. It also teaches as plainly that every nook and cranny of our being is capable of being regenerated. All of this is scheduled for surgery here and now.

Any surgical performance requires that the patient agree with the prognosis, recognize the urgent need for remedial action, and unreservedly submit to the surgical procedure. All of this has a beautiful application ... "See you in the operating room next Sunday!"

Thought For Today

May our spirit be a true mirror of the Spirit of Christ!

December 5

N. T. Bible Reading: I John 4   **Our Focus: I John 4:8**

GOD IS LOVE

John gives us three unique definitions of God in this brief little epistle:

1.   "... God is light ..." (I John 1:5), which is the theme from 1:1 to 2:2.
2.   "... God is love" (I John 4:8, 16), which is the very heart of the book from 2:3 to 4:21.
3.   "God is life", which is the subject of chapter 5.

It is an interesting fact that we do not have a definition of "love" in the entire Bible. In fact, in my own opinion, we have no adequate definition of love in any dictionary or thesaurus. It is one of those attempts which when you read it you simply smile and say, "Nice try."

The truth is that there are times when any definition is destruction. There is no one anywhere who ever questioned the captivating beauty of the sunset, but who would be so presumptuous as to attempt to define it? The astronomer can scientifically explain the mathematics of it ... but the splendor and beauty are not even included in the formula.

God is love and therefore God must love. His love, the only true and absolutely genuine love in existence, was manifested in the sending of His Son that we might have life through His death. Genuine love is impossible apart from sacrifice. No one in the world ever knew that *God is love* until it was revealed at Calvary and recorded in the Word of God (I John 4:8, 16). It is there and nowhere else. It is not found in all the literature of ancient times.

Thought For Today

To claim love without sacrifice, is to claim life without breathing!

December 6

O. T. Bible Reading: Daniel 7-8   **Our Focus: Daniel 7:14**

HIS DOMINION

The two primary elements of dominion are Lordship and Sovereignty. The basic thought of Lordship is authority, and Sovereignty speaks of supreme power.

We know for certain that there is yet a future day coming when "… he shall reign for ever and ever" (Rev. 11:15). This will be a literal kingdom and will be everlasting, and will extend from sea to sea. Then it shall be that "… the earth shall be full of the knowledge of the Lord, as the waters cover the sea" (Isa. 11:9). What a hope! What a glorious day that will be! The reason for this most blessed condition is the person and presence of the King of Kings and Lord of Lords "… and HE shall reign …" (Rev. 11:15). When and where He reigns supreme there is heaven on earth.

The Scriptures clearly predict that He "… shall reign in mount Zion …" (Isa. 24:23). We may make a spiritual application of this for the church and for the saints of God. There is a wonderful _now_ and an assuring _therefore_ for every child of God (Eph. 2:19). If and when we truly give Him authority as Lord of our lives, we also experience here and now, on a personal basis, the benefits of His mighty power. This simple key unlocks the door which opens to His banqueting house. We feast on the riches of His boundless provisions; we have tasted the heavenly manna; and have personally experienced the powers of that coming kingdom (Heb. 6:4-5).

Thought For Today

The measure of His reign is also the measure of His Kingdom!

December 6

N. T. Bible Reading: I John 5   **Our Focus: I John 5:21**

KEEP YOURSELVES FROM IDOLS

An idol is a false god. It is an object of excessive devotion. It is that which is most precious; that for which we will make the greatest sacrifices, that which draws our warmest love, that which, when lost, would leave us most desolate, and that which brings to us the greatest satisfaction. An idol, then, is anything which takes the place which God has intended for Himself in our minds and in our hearts. We are told distinctly that covetousness is idolatry (Col. 3:5). We are also told that stubborn resistance to God's Word and to His ways is as idolatry (I Sam. 15:23). In summary, it may be accurately said that an idol is anything which prevents a man from seeking and finding his *ALL* in God.

We cannot dismiss this Scripture as ... being inappropriate to our culture and to our time. The application of this last verse of I John is universal and timeless. The basic evil in idolatry is substituting the visible for the invisible. This is no small problem. It is a root cause of many evils in religion. The carnal mind is forever grasping for some tangible object which satisfies one or more of the physical senses, and to which it may cling for security and insurance. This strikes at the very taproot of genuine Christianity. The foundation of our salvation is in saving faith and not any element which anchors to anything natural or human. By grace we are saved through faith and that apart from anything in or of ourselves. We are not saved by emotion, nor by feeling. We are saved by the risen, living and victorious Christ and by Him alone.

Thought For Today

An idol claims the loyalty which only Christ deserves!

December 7

O. T. Bible Reading: Daniel 9-10   **Our Focus: Daniel 10:11, 19**

GREATLY BELOVED

What God calls great and beloved of God, let not man call insignificant and average. Three times God called Daniel "... greatly beloved ..." (Dan. 9:23, 10:11, 19). There are sterling qualities and sparkling attributes of character on its highest level in this great man. His personal grandeur was no incidental element in his towering influence and ministry. It was the very fabric of which his unblemished biography consists. The man is his message. The Divine approval on this giant of a character should forever tell the world the quality of person that God highly regards and confidently uses.

It has been observed that Daniel's life may be characterized by three words: purpose, prayer, and prophecy. I have always used a slightly different view of this mighty specimen of moral values: integrity, intercession, and insight. This combination may reveal the Divine formula for any fruitful child of God. To drop or exclude anyone would render the equation void and useless. The Divine approval on any life is no arbitrary act. God works and moves by and within certain fixed and eternal principles. Some of these laws are very complex and involved; some of them are very simple indeed; "... for them that honour me I will honour, and they that despise me shall be lightly esteemed" (I Sam. 2:30).

Our misguided and perverted world needs a mighty infusion of moral fiber. This must at least begin with a sense of values. When we do not hold the moral virtues of honesty, integrity, and trustworthiness in the highest esteem, we can neglect them without concern and conviction.

Thought For Today

The godly man is also "the man of God!"

December 7

N. T. Bible Reading: II John   **Our Focus: II John 1:4**

WALKING IN TRUTH

The obvious and tragic lack, and the apparent apathy among God's people, cannot be traced to the obscurity of God's Word. We have all seen and heard many who with great zeal contend for the faith. What I personally long for, are some who will with equal zeal contend for the *WALK*. It seems clear that what we need today are more Christians who are fundamentalists in obeying the Bible they so eagerly defend. To walk in truth, is to walk in the light. To walk in the light, is to have genuine fellowship with God's people.

Our vision is framed by the truth which we have been given. No one can ever be the same after the unveiling of a Divine truth. Any measure of disobedience to the heavenly vision, results in slavery to an attitude, which conflicts with God's will and plan for your life. We must advance obediently into the land of promise and abundance, or we will automatically turn back as a deserter.

The spiritual battle is won or lost in the secret depths of our own will. The will only acts upon the persuasion and conviction of the mind. The real battle is the battle *FOR THE MIND*. Any neutral attitude or frame of mind which fails to move forward, leads to spiritual paralysis. You cannot walk and stand still at the same time.

There is a world of difference between walking in the light of my conscience and walking in the light of God's truth. To walk in His light is to move away from all darkness, and to move ever closer to all that is in keeping with God's holiness.

Thought For Today

Walking in truth is advancing into Christ-likeness!

December 8

O. T. Bible Reading: Daniel 11-12   **Our Focus: Daniel 12:10**

THE WISE

On the list of those who possess complete and absolute wisdom there is but one name: it is the name of Jehovah … The Almighty God. Paul said of Him, "… to God who alone is wise …" (Rom. 16:27, New English Bible); Jude added, "To the only wise God our Saviour …" (Jude 1:25); and we say that He is <u>Omniscient</u>. This means that He possesses infinite knowledge, and certainly <u>ONLY</u> He does.

It is a rare but a special compliment when anyone is given credit for having great wisdom. In the truest sense it can be said that wisdom is a Divine gift. The natural mind will give credit to an individual for possessing and exercising an unusual degree of wisdom. The spiritual and better informed will discern the true source; they will honor the Lord and recognize the Divine guidance and direction which He has communicated to a human instrument. This is a rare quality, because few are childlike and foolish enough to trust God's wisdom and His supernatural provision. Perhaps the greatest obstacle we face is the forever tendency to lean upon our own ability and understanding (Prov. 3:5).

James said, "If any of you lack wisdom, let him ask of God, that giveth to all men liberally, and upbraideth not; and it shall be given him" (Jam. 1:5). I have inserted my own conclusion in the margin of my Bible, "Since all men lack wisdom!" Not everyone is prepared to file mental bankruptcy. It is a humbling thing to accept the depravity of the natural mind. Everyone agrees that the heart is deceitful (Jer. 17:9), but very few will accept God's estimate of the human mind. It is a space-age orbit removed from God's thoughts (Isa. 55:9), and is at enmity against God (Rom. 8:7).

Thought For Today

Those have the mind of Christ who disavow their own!

December 8

N. T. Bible Reading: III John

Our Focus: III John 1:9

DIOTREPHES

Diotrephes was an example of heterodoxy of spirit and attitude. He was an orthodox heretic. There is no hint that he taught or believed any false doctrine. His problem was not theology: his problem was theatrics! He loved to have the preeminence (III John 1:9). He was a showman who wanted to be in the limelight. He must be in the spotlight. He will put on quite a show ... a real actor! He is ruled by vanity and arrogance. He is the peacock of the people. I have met several of his kin.

The great (and last) Apostle John brings five serious charges against him:

1. He clamors for the attention of the church.
2. He disrespectfully refused to honor the apostle of Christ.
3. He spoke carelessly and maliciously against the ministers of the Lord.
4. He refused to entertain or provide for the Lord's servants.
5. He spoke reproachfully and acted belligerently toward those who supported the servants of the Lord.

He was a royal problem and a genuine pain in the neck for any pastor. Just as Eutychus has his sleeping kin in every church (Acts 20:9), so also has Diotrephes his genealogy of offspring who strut and stampede their sterility.

It is refreshing and reassuring that there are two very positive and profitable saints and only one spot in their feast of charity. Gaius and Demetrius were good, godly, and gallant for God. The highest praise and very possibly the greatest rewards are reserved for the humble, consistent, and dependable. They are the true and faithful followers of their crucified Savior. Their greatest fulfillment is in ministering to God's people and honoring the Lord by their godly lives. May their tribe increase and abound!

Thought For Today

Those who seek the spotlight only blur the true Light!

<u>December 9</u>

O. T. Bible Reading: Hosea 1-4   **Our Focus: Hosea 3:5**

HIS GOODNESS

God sustains four primary relationships to the human family:

1.   Creator.
2.   King.
3.   Judge.
4.   Father.

His purpose in creating humanity was not for the purpose of possession, sovereignty and control, nor for judgment. The basic motive was as a Father who created man to have fellowship with Himself. There was something of a yearning sadness in the voice of the Lord when he said to Adam and Eve, "… Where art thou?" (Gen. 3:9). In the deepest sense, it can be said that sin is not merely breaking the law of God; it also, if understood correctly, breaks the heart of God. It offends His holiness, wounds His perfect love, and resists and rejects His goodness and mercy.

The Lord told Moses that He would make all His goodness to pass before him (Ex. 33:19). The very thankful David said, "Surely goodness and mercy shall follow me all the days of my life: and (only as a direct result of His abundant goodness) I will (be enabled to) dwell in the house of the Lord for ever" (Ps. 23:6). Paul admonished the saints not to lightly esteem "… the riches of his goodness … not knowing that the goodness of God leadeth thee to repentance" (Rom. 2:4). He also prayed for the Thessalonians that they might fulfill all the good pleasure of His goodness (II Thess. 1:11).

"God is good" and "the Lord is good" are phrases repeated over and over in the Scriptures. The hearts of God's people have been encouraged and refreshed many times as they sing joyfully, "God is good … all the time!!"

<u>Thought For Today</u>

To extol His goodness is to explore His greatness!

December 9

N. T. Bible Reading: Jude   **Our Focus: Jude 1:3**

THE COMMON SALVATION

Jude warns that the common salvation, which he and those to whom he wrote held as a mutual trust and reality, was in grave danger of becoming a very uncommon phenomenon. He sounds the alarm: a thief has entered the building, and is intent on robbing the building of its most valuable treasures.

The most subtle aspect of the departure he so graphically describes is that of turning the grace of God into *lasciviousness* (Jude 1:4). This word has variously been defined by Bible commentaries as: excess, absence of restraint, wantonness, and shameful conduct. The dictionary says it means "loose", "lewd", and "unrestrained lust." It would seem accurate to simply say that it means license for loose living. How unthinkable that salvation, which means deliverance, should be warped and twisted into a permissive passivity. Jude sternly warned against this great evil. If his age revealed the seeds of this insidious plague, then our day is witnessing the awful harvest.

Any doctrine or teaching which does not produce godliness is false, and is not to be entertained (I Tim. 6:3-5). Those who have distorted Biblical obedience and dubbed it "legalism" fall very clearly into the apostasy of which Jude speaks.

We are also warned that the time would come when people would not tolerate "… sound doctrine …" (II Tim. 4:3), that is, teaching which produces sound and healthy (spiritually strong) believers. Now more than ever it can be said, "Blessed are they which do hunger and thirst after righteousness …" (Matt. 5:6).

Thought For Today

Careless living is produced by cozy preaching!

December 10

O. T. Bible Reading: Hosea 5-8   **Our Focus: Hosea 5:1**

HEAR – HEARKEN

The words Hosea, Hoshea, Joshua, and Jesus are the same in their derivation: they mean salvation. Great lessons may be learned and some very profitable applications made from the prophet's appeal to wayward Israel. He uses the word "return" no less than 15 times in his weighty treatise on repentance. To the millions of weary pilgrims, all of whom cry out for restoration and renewal from time to time, there is help and hope from the Word of God.

The prophet calls upon Israel to hear the word of the Lord. Jesus warned His listeners to take heed how they hear (Luke 8:18). He also told His disciples, "Having eyes, see ye not? and having ears, hear ye not? and do ye not remember?" (Mark 8:18). The problem then, is the same problem now. They heard sounds, recognized words, and the combined tones of sentences reached their natural ears, but they utterly failed to grasp the meaning of the words and the message they carried. Any number of factors can contribute to this common problem. It is always fitting and appropriate for all of us to pray, "Lord, anoint my ears that they may hear Thy voice."

To hearken conveys the same truth. It has the basic idea of answering a knock at the door, of responding to an appeal, and of taking some form of action. The most simple counsel is that of the mother of Jesus to the servants at the marriage in Cana of Galilee; "… Whatsoever he saith unto you, do it" (John 2:5). This always results in a new and refreshing flow of joy and victory.

Thought For Today

To hear clearly is to respond unconditionally!

December 10

N. T. Bible Reading: Revelation 1   **Our Focus: Revelation 1:1**

THE REVELATION

The Book of Revelation is, without question, one of the greatest books in the entire Bible. It is well to keep in mind that the word is in the singular number; *THE* Revelation ... not the revelations. The word "revelation" is derived from the Latin, which means "disclosure", and from the Greek "apocalypse", which means "unveiling" or "uncovering."

The book is unique in many ways. It promises a very special blessing to those who read it, and keep its sayings (Rev. 1:3). It gives a solemn warning to those who tamper with its content, "And if any man shall take away from the words of the book of this prophecy, God shall take away his part out of the book of life ..." (Rev. 22:19). It is safe to say that it is, like any other Divine revelation, contingent upon a prepared and purified human instrument, a Divine quickening of that vessel, and a unique impartation by the precious Holy Spirit of the deep things of God. It is not "common ground" for carnal minds, but "holy ground" for careful, humble, and sincere seekers after God.

It is the book of consummation ... the "grand finale!" It is the book of the unveiling of Jesus Christ. He is the theme ... He is and has the key. There are some 25 names and titles given to the Lord in the book of Revelation. One key which easily fits here is the key of repeated words. The word "throne" occurs 27 times, the word "lamb" is repeated 24 times, and combined they provide a great insight: chapters 1-5 unveil the enthronement of Christ *IN HEAVEN*, chapters 6-20 cover the enthronement of Christ *ON EARTH*, and the final chapters 21-22 speak of the enthronement of Christ in the *NEW CREATION*.

Thought For Today

The enthronement of Christ ... key to the old and new creation!

December 11

O. T. Bible Reading: Hosea 9-11   **Our Focus: Hosea 9:17**

WANDERERS

It is very doubtful that anyone would characterize himself as a "wanderer." We reserve such an appellation for other individuals or groups. Yet, in a very real sense, it is to be feared that many of God's people fall into this category.

The dictionary defines the word "wander" as follows: to ramble here and there (sounds like some speakers we have heard about) without any certain goal or object in view; to travel or move from place to place without any fixed purpose or destination; to go to a place by any way or at any pace that suits the fancy; to turn aside from or to go astray; and to drift away from or to turn direction.

The Psalmist prayed, "With my whole heart have I sought thee: O let me not wander from thy commandments" (Ps. 119:10). It is said of the children of Zebulun, they "... could keep rank: they were not of double heart" (I Chron. 12:33). It is the drift which must be avoided and overcome. The very subtle pull of the current is all that is needed to experience the unconscious departure from the channel.

The challenge is to an unbroken vigil. We must consistently check our bearings, heed the markers and the carefully prepared map, stay in touch with our experienced guide, and with purpose of heart press on to our intended goal. When the whole heart is involved in seeking after God, it leaves no room for any unguarded frontier left open to attack. Unguarded strength is double weakness. It is the forgotten frontier of many lives. We must remember that it is the little foxes which spoil the tender vines (Song of Sol. 2:15).

Thought For Today

We will not wander when our hearts are fixed!

December 11

N. T. Bible Reading: Revelation 2   **Our Focus: Revelation 2:8**

AND UNTO

The amazement which should grip the heart of every individual is that not only is the invitation extended to all, but it is specifically presented to each. The mighty experience of the launching of the New Testament church on the day of Pentecost declares that they were _all_ filled with the Holy Ghost (Acts 2:4), but it is most encouraging that it also says, it sat upon _each_ of them (Acts 2:3).

The direct message of the risen Lord to the seven churches of Asia Minor was a clear and direct appeal to each corporate local fellowship. Each one, however, concludes with a very personal appeal: "_He_ that hath an ear, let _him_ hear ..." (Rev. 2:7, 11, 17, 29, 3:6, 13, 22). What a thrill to know that not only does God speak today, but also to know that He speaks to me as an individual. The only thrill that can possibly be greater occurs when I respond to Him as an individual and say, "... Speak; for thy servant heareth" (I Sam. 3:10). It is precisely at this crisis point that we begin to get to know God (a very long and involved process) and to learn the unspeakable joy of walking with God.

The majestic glory of God and His unlimited and Almighty power all combine into two simple words "And unto ..." (Rev. 2:8). He is never finished until His very last words have been spoken to that lone, solitary individual waiting to hear God's voice. It is His voice which can speak peace to the troubled soul; the soul that waits to feel the exciting dynamic of contact with the power of His resurrection life; the soul that waits to experience the glow and flow of the rivers of living water (John 7:38).

Thought For Today

God's thoughts are never vague, and always personal!

December 12

O. T. Bible Reading: Hosea 12-14   **Our Focus: Hosea 12:1**

FEEDING ON WIND

Winds are unpredictable, undependable, unreliable, and unseasonable. They are an essential part of life, but a very poor element in which to rest or trust. There are many kinds of winds: steady winds, periodic winds, variable winds, and stormy winds. The standard for measuring winds is the Beauford scale. It specifies 12 types of air activity: from calm at number 1 (3 mph or less), to number 6 which is a strong breeze (34 mph or less), to number 12 which is a hurricane force wind (90 mph).

So also there are many types and many varieties of winds which blow in the life of every individual. There are winds of promise, winds of fortune, winds of popularity, prosperity, adversity, sorrow, sickness and on and on. Pity the person who gets inspiration, sustenance, and satisfaction from any such fickle element. Isaiah spoke of those who "... feedeth on ashes: a deceived heart hath turned him aside ..." (Isa. 44:20). Whether we attempt to place our hope and confidence in the ashes of yesterday, or in the winds of fantasy, they are phantoms which can only mock and fail.

Reality is found only in the person of our Lord Jesus Christ. We are encouraged to feast on the riches of His glory (Rom. 9:23), to plumb the depths of His wisdom and knowledge, to view the vastness of our inheritance in Christ (Eph. 1:18), and to proclaim the unsearchable riches of Christ (Eph. 3:8). There is a banquet-house where the saints of God are fed, where their hungry souls are nourished, and where the people of God enjoy the times of refreshing from the presence of the Lord. Why should anyone feed on wind or ashes?

Thought For Today

To be carnal is to be starved spiritually!

December 12

N. T. Bible Reading: Revelation 3   **Our Focus: Revelation 3:22**

AN EAR TO HEAR

Seven times the same injunction is repeated to each of the seven churches as the very last words from the risen Lord to that particular fellowship, and to us (Rev. 2:7, 11, 17, 29, 3:6, 13, 22). Hence, they assume a seven-fold importance. There must be great spiritual significance in the Levitical instructions for the cleansing of the leper (Lev. 14). Leprosy speaks of the corruption caused by sin, especially as to its activity and progress. We are told that the individual thus afflicted must have the blood of the trespass offering applied directly to "... the tip of the right ear ... and upon the thumb of his right hand, and upon the great toe of his right foot" (Lev. 14:14). Following this "And of the rest of the oil ... shall the priest put upon the tip of the right ear ... and upon the thumb of his right hand, and upon the great toe of his right foot ..." (Lev. 14:17). This can only teach clearly the necessity for personal cleansing and for personal anointing.

Every individual must experience the personal application and cleansing through the atoning blood of Christ (I Pet. 1:19). Only then can it be said that he has *an ear to hear* (Rev. 2:7, 11, 17, 29, 3:6, 13, 22). The unsaved, the unregenerate, are deaf spiritually. They are like the disconnected radio set. It cannot pick up, nor report the sound-waves of the broadcasting station. The really tragic part is that not even those who have ears will hear.

It seems abundantly clear to me that we need "... the rest of the oil ..." applied to our ears (Lev. 14:17). We must also be quickened in order for us to be able to hear (John 6:63). This is not just a one-time experience, but it is to be both continuous and constant. The risen Lord keeps on giving the Holy Ghost (in ever increasing measure) to those, and only to those, who keep on obeying Him (Acts 5:32).

Thought For Today

The quickened Word can only be heard by the quickened ear!

December 13

O. T. Bible Reading: Joel 1-3   **Our Focus: Joel 2:1**

BLOW THE TRUMPET

This is a very Jewish setting. The shophar (ram or ram's horn) was a vital part of Jewish life. It was used to give signals for war, to announce the year of Jubilee, to warn of approaching danger, and to herald the appearance of the new moon and of the full moon. It can safely be said that the single blast was to sound an alarm, while the second blast of the trumpet would summon the people for some special instruction. The sounding of the trumpet has a significant symbolic value as the proclamation of a special Divine message. However, any such event will include the vital element of an alarm or warning, but must also include the giving of instruction and the providing of clear directions.

God does not allow His people to remain at ease when there is an approaching and imminent danger. Neither will He leave them trembling and confused by the sounding of an alarm only. He will certainly inform them of the approaching danger, and will also instruct them clearly and carefully on the course of action to be taken. He will not leave Himself without a witness (Acts 14:17). "Surely the Lord God will do nothing, but he revealeth his secret unto his servants the prophets" (Amos 3:7). How reassuring for God's people when their faithful messengers provide them with these two vital ingredients!

It is at this point that the key elements of personal responsibility and accountability kick in. It is possible to hear the alarm, listen to the instructions, and simply do nothing about it. This spells tragedy. Inaction is in fact rebellion. To refuse to act when God is calling for a clear and strong response, is in the sight of God as evil as witchcraft and idol worship (I Sam. 15:23).

Thought For Today

Lo, the trumpet sounds ... blessed are those who hearken!

December 13

N. T. Bible Reading: Revelation 4   **Our Focus: Revelation 4:2**

A THRONE WAS SET

In the book of Hebrews we are invited to "… come boldly unto the throne of grace, that we may obtain mercy, and find grace to help in time of need" (Heb. 4:16). A throne is a sign and symbol of God's universal government and it proclaims a message loud and clear: "there is indeed a kingdom and a mighty ruling King, and there is a people over whom he rules as Lord of Lords and King of Kings." What a joy and privilege to be a part of this pilgrim band whose citizenship is in heaven (Phil. 3:20; Heb. 10:34)!

The throne of God comes into clear focus in Revelation chapter 4, from this point on it becomes "the book of the throne." The word "throne" occurs 27 times in the book of Revelation. The stage is now set for the beginning of His kingdom of universal government and control among the nations of the world. It is of utmost importance, even at this phase of God's prophetic plan, that we see (by faith) and know that there is a day coming when "… every knee should bow … every tongue should confess that Jesus Christ is Lord, to the glory of God the Father" (Phil. 2:10-11), and finally; "… the earth shall be full of the knowledge of the Lord, as the waters cover the sea" (Isa. 11:9).

There is a throne and it is set, fixed, and firm. God is on that throne, and He is in control of every circumstance and situation. Every human element which assumes control and authority must eventually give way as He begins to rule the nations with a rod of iron (Rev. 2:26-27). It is now no less a throne because it is a throne of grace. Let us enjoy our throne-rights!

Thought For Today

Those who truly bow now will also rule then!

December 14

O. T. Bible Reading: Amos 1-3   **Our Focus: Amos 1:1**

AMOS ... THE COUNTRY PREACHER

Not very many people know very much about the prophet Amos. The worst guess of the uninformed is that: "he is the one who worked with Andy": a reference to a popular radio program of a past generation: "Amos and Andy." Amos means "burden bearer"; Tekoa means "trumpet." God needed a voice; He found a poor, humble, country boy who was willing to take on the burden, and he became the trumpet in hand of the Lord. How many times has that testimony been repeated throughout church history? The office and art of the seer is not cultivated in the crowds.

The ministry of Amos took place during the reign of Jeroboam II, king of Israel, and Uzziah, king of Judah. He was contemporary with Jonah and Hosea, prophets in the northern kingdom, and with Isaiah and Micah, prophets in the southern kingdom.

Amos was an insignificant hayseed who was called to the big city. He was a simple person, a man with a single purpose, and a rustic, unspoiled, unpolished, down to earth man of God. His only claim to fame was that *God called him*. His credentials were framed for history, not as a gold-edged authorized certificate, diploma, or degree. The unmistakable stamp of Divine authority set him apart then, as it still does today: "And the Lord took me ... the Lord said unto me, Go, prophesy unto my people Israel" (Amos 7:15).

He was able to minister amid opposition and criticism and say, "Now therefore hear thou the word of the Lord ..." (Amos 7:16). It is the certainty of this Divine calling and commission which gives authority and boldness to God's messengers.

Thought For Today

Amos was not famous, but he was God's messenger!

December 14

N. T. Bible Reading: Revelation 5   **Our Focus: Revelation 5:5**

THE LION OF JUDAH

It is interesting and arresting that the Lord Jesus is characterized as a Lion and as a Lamb in two successive verses of scripture (Rev. 5:5, 6). The contrast could hardly be greater. A lamb is among the weakest and most vulnerable to any predator. The lion by contrast is "king of the beasts", and feared by every animal. Jesus is both.

He was a Lamb in the special aspect of His sacrificial sufferings in His first coming. He was as a conquering Lion in His resurrection. He displayed majesty and weakness, sovereignty and suffering, severity and tenderness, all in one matchless character which was holy, harmless, undefiled, separate from sinners, and made higher than the heavens (Heb. 7:26).

The figure of the Lion applied to the meek and lowly Jesus is indeed a forceful one. Noblest and most majestic among animals, the lion has been called "king of the forest." The ensign of the tribe of Judah was the lion, and Jesus sprang from that tribe: hence, He is the Lion of the tribe of Judah. Applied to Jesus, the Lion is symbolic of His prowess, His majestic dignity, and of His mighty strength. Let all know that when He comes again it is not to suffer, bleed, and die: He is coming in power and great glory to assume His throne to rule and reign as King of Kings. He is the only one who has the right and title to this earth. He has gloriously redeemed you and me, but He has also redeemed the earth. He also holds the right to rule, as He is the fulfillment of the Old Testament prophecies relative to the future of the world. And "... he shall reign for ever and ever" (Rev. 11:15). Bless His name!

Thought For Today

All who know the Lamb shall also meet the Lion!

December 15

O. T. Bible Reading: Amos 4-6   **Our Focus: Amos 4:12**

PREPARED

To prepare is to make ready. Amos urges upon the nation of Israel to prepare to meet God (Amos 4:12). God does not specifically tell them what He is about to do. It will come as a surprise. We know now, of course, that it was the Assyrians who came down upon them suddenly and took them into captivity. Many others were slain in the process. It is to these, as well as to all of us, that the wise counsel is given, "... prepare to meet thy God ..." (Amos 4:12). Secret sin on earth is open scandal in heaven. There is no option and no alternative. This is an appointment every person will keep.

Jesus promised His disciples that He would go to prepare a place for them and for us (John 14:2). Paul informed the Corinthians that "... Eye hath not seen, nor ear heard, neither have entered into the heart of man, the things which God hath prepared for them that love him" (I Cor. 2:9). We are assured in Hebrews 11:16 that the heroes of faith from Old Testament days desired "... a better country, that is, an heavenly: wherefore God is not ashamed to be called their God: for he hath prepared for them a city." We are also told that the Bride hath made herself ready ... she has completed her preparation (Rev. 19:7).

A very interesting detail regarding Lydia is given in Acts 16:14 "... whose heart the Lord opened, that she attended unto the things which were spoken of Paul." This gives two sides to the subject of preparation. God prepares the heart, and then we in cooperation with the Lord, prepare ourselves to fit into God's plan. This is a time to prepare or to make ourselves ready. There is no preparation after this life is over.

Thought For Today

Those who faithfully prepare now will be ready then!

December 15

N. T. Bible Reading: Revelation 6   **Our Focus: Revelation 6:1**

COME AND SEE

The strongest possible evidence is not what you hear, but what you actually see. The wise invitation to the two disciples of John by the Lord Himself was simply, "… Come and see …" (John 1:39). When Nathanael was hesitant and cautious, Philip extended the most convincing invitation, "… Come and see" (John 1:46). The powerful and reassuring words of the angel to the fearful and confused women on the first resurrection morning were, "… Come, see …" (Matt. 28:6). John is bidden by his heavenly escort to, "… Come and see" (Rev. 6:1) a great panoramic preview of end-time events unfolded before him.

The single most effective tool we have as the people of God is a confident invitation to "Come and see." There is such a vast field of glowing evidence to the miracle-working power of God in the lives of His people! Perhaps it would frame the issue in a more challenging way if each one of the redeemed family of God would open their lives to a skeptical world; to invite one and all to "Come, behold, what God hath wrought!" See the transformation in my relationships, and see the overflowing abundance of blessing in my life, which had been barren and bound.

It is also an open invitation by the Lord Himself to His people, "Come and see." There are vast continents of spiritual riches yet to be enjoyed, there are depths of truth and understanding waiting to be explored, and there are keys and insights to unfold to the honest seeker after God. Let us press on to inherit all that in Jesus is stored.

Thought For Today

To come is but to begin … to see is to enjoy!

December 16

O. T. Bible Reading: Amos 7-9   **Our Focus: Amos 8:11**

A FAMINE

Amaziah was the priest of the northern kingdom of Israel at Bethel. He, no doubt, was a smooth operator, a very cultured and polished compromiser who told the king exactly what he wanted to hear. He must have had great charisma and was an expert at backslapping. He deliberately lied to the king about Amos. Every true Divine messenger will be misquoted and represented as saying or doing something they never did or said at all. He did not say that Jeroboam would perish with the sword. Amos did say, "… and I will rise against the house of Jeroboam with the sword" (Amos 7:9). War would come, and indeed it did; Israel went into captivity to Assyria.

The word of the Lord was officially and individually ignored and rejected. Amos is invited to go back to his farm where he belonged. As a result, Amos assured the rebellious people that the day would come when God would send no prophet, heaven would be shut up, and no alarm would sound in the land.

There are more Bibles sold in the world today than at any other time in the entire history of the world. There is a Gideon Bible in nearly every motel or hotel room in the country. Nearly every home has a dusty Bible somewhere in the house, and many households have from 3 to 5 Bibles or more. How many read and study it? How many believe and obey it? It can be accurately said of our day also that there is "… a famine … of hearing the words of the Lord" (Amos 8:11). Gospel preaching churches have removed the ancient landmarks and have become theaters of religious entertainment.

Thought For Today

A famine follows the forsaking of the Word of God!

December 16

N. T. Bible Reading: Revelation 7   **Our Focus: Revelation 7:17**

TEARS WIPED AWAY

One of the great joys and exciting prospects, which the pictures of heaven paint for the weary pilgrim, is not only what is there, but what absolutely and categorically will not be there. "And there shall be no more curse … And there shall be no night there; and they need no candle, neither light of the sun …" (Rev. 22:3, 5); "And God shall wipe away all tears from their eyes; and there shall be no more death, neither sorrow, nor crying, neither shall there be any more pain: for the former things are passed away" (Rev. 21:4). We walk here in a vale of tears; our constant companions are sorrow, grief, heartache, and pain. The very thought of there being a place where none of these exist is enough to make it heaven, and indeed a place to be much desired.

There can be no rainbow without clouds and a storm. It is the substance of our tears which makes clear and vivid the colors of God's rainbow of promises. It is one of the brightest rays of hope, which tells us that one day through the redeeming love and saving grace of the Lord Jesus Christ all tears shall be forever wiped away. What a day … what a glorious day that will be!!

As for now, we must not waste our tears. From the cradle to the grave they will flow like overflowing rivers from broken and bleeding hearts. Most of the beatitudes have the sorrows of earth for their subject, but the joys of heaven for their completion. The bitter waters of Marah (Ex. 15:23) may be transformed into the sweet portion of His richest blessing, and the valley of Achor can miraculously become a doorway of hope (Hos. 2:15). It is when we allow these times of stress and strain to draw us closer to our blessed Shepherd and Saviour that we discover the key to their meaning and message.

Thought For Today

It is hope which enables us to smile through our tears!

December 17

O. T. Bible Reading: Obadiah   **Our Focus: Obadiah 1:6**

ESAU

The very mention of the name "Esau" brings with it feelings of disgust, and disappointment. He serves as a good illustration of the natural man of the earth, and a picture of the machinations of the flesh. The biography of this man is one of the sad and tragic chapters in the Biblical record. The Scriptures briefly sketched him as "... Esau, who is Edom" (Gen. 36:1). Had he taken a different course of action it might very well otherwise read, "Esau, who is Israel."

The Scriptures conclude in the book of Hebrews that Esau was a profane person (Heb. 12:16). This does not mean that he engaged in profanity, nor does it mean that he was a vulgar individual. It simply means that he was a man of the earth who lived for worldly things and for nothing else. He swapped a bowl of soup for a birthright, which could have included him in the genealogy of the Messianic line. The record says that he *despised* it (Gen. 25:34). That is, he did not hold it in high esteem, but regarded it with little respect. It was not high on his priority list.

There is not a single time, in the entire Genesis record, that Esau ever mentions the name of God. When Esau repented (or sought to) it was only to his father Jacob; "... bless me, even me also, O my father ..." (Gen. 27:38). He sought restitution, not pardon; he was sorry for his bargain, not for his sin. This identifies the difference between relentance and repentance. To relent is to admit a wrong course of action only due to the pressures of circumstances, and to seek relief only from the consequences of wrong doing. To repent is to deeply mourn the offense toward God, and to genuinely determine to change not only our mind, but also the entire lifestyle. Like many, Esau stands only as a red light to all generations; a warning not to make the same tragic mistakes, and not to repeat the choices which lead to tragedy, which the "... men of the earth ..." will always make (Rev. 18:23).

Thought For Today

The choices of Esau actually revealed his true character!

December 17

N. T. Bible Reading: Revelation 8   **Our Focus: Revelation 8:2**

I SAW

It is of vital importance what we see. Some see nothing, others see but dimly. Some see in a fog, men as trees walking; but others "... endured, as seeing him who is invisible" (Heb. 11:27). What we see will determine what we do, how we act and react, and it will largely frame our vision and mind-set. It is simple logic to state that your priority list will not consist of a single thing which you cannot see. This alone will limit us to a materialistic and mundane focus. Only if God touches our inner eye and enables us to see by the eye of faith, the glorious bright realities and glowing evidences of a better country, will we radically change our behavior, and aim for higher ground.

"The hearing ear, and the seeing eye, the Lord hath made even both of them" (Prov. 20:12). One of the first acts of the Philistines after they captured the weakened Samson was to put out his eyes, and to bring him to Gaza (stronghold) (Jud. 16:21). There he was bound with fetters and made to grind in the prison house. What helpful applications can be made from this tragic event! The anatomy of the process of sin: it blinds, it binds, and its victims are made to grind in a dark prison of bondage.

Thank God, we have found the One who is the Light of the world! Any measure of light brings with it the ability to see. The very first recorded event after Jesus declared Himself to be the light of the world (John 8:12), was to heal a man who was born blind, the blind man he "... washed, and came seeing" (John 9:7). It is most interesting that the Scriptures refer not to the word which the prophets heard, but rather, and more accurately, to "The word that (they) ... *saw* ..." (Isa. 2:1). Any time that anyone makes direct contact with God, there will always be the thrilling experience of both sight and insight.

Thought For Today

Our spiritual insight is no greater than our personal experience!

December 18

O. T. Bible Reading: Jonah 1-4   **Our Focus: Jonah 1:1**

JONAH

The book of Jonah … a total of 48 verses and 1,328 words in our English authorized version … is not really a prophecy, but rather the history of a prophet. Liberals and skeptics have relegated it to the same category as "Aesop's Fables." The English literary critic and author, Charles Reade, said of this book: "it is the most beautiful story ever written in so small a compass." Another worthy author describes it as "the high-water mark of Old Testament revelation."

One helpful key in grasping the core message of any book in the Bible is the need to distinguish between the essentials and the incidentals. In this case the incidentals of the book of Jonah are the fish, the gourd, the east wind, the boat, and even the city of Nineveh. The essentials here are Jehovah and Jonah; The Almighty God and a mortal man. It is a clear picture of the mighty sovereign God of the universe who is as slow to punish as He is quick to pardon where and when there is genuine repentance.

Jesus told the Scribes and Pharisees of His day that "… there shall no sign be given to it, but the sign of the prophet Jonas (Jonah)" (Matt. 12:39). The last three notable prophets, who came in quick succession, during the final period before the destruction of the ten-tribed kingdom, were all signs or types. Elisha dies and is buried, but in his death gives life to another, as did Jesus by His vicarious death. Jonah, symbolically at least, arose from his watery grave to live again, as did Jesus and as will all who are in Christ Jesus. Elijah was taken up by a whirlwind and his mantel was sent down to be passed on, as was Jesus taken away to send back His life giving Holy Spirit. Our God is mighty, His mercy is everlasting, and His love reaches to the ends of the earth.

Thought For Today

Jonah preached the shortest message ever ... eight words!

December 18

N. T. Bible Reading: Revelation 8-9   **Our Focus: Revelation 8:13**

WOE, WOE, WOE

The word "woe" is defined by the dictionary as heavy calamity, overwhelming affliction, and sustained grief and sorrow. It occurs approximately 100 times throughout the Scriptures, but only once is it given a threefold emphasis. It is used to introduce the sounding of the three last trumpets; they are separated from the other four, and are each "woe" trumpets. They signal the beginning of a period of time which will be of a very peculiar intensity and dreadful in nature. It is why those on the earth will call "… to the mountains and rocks, Fall on us, and hide us from the face of him that sitteth on the throne, and from the wrath of the Lamb: For the great day of his wrath is come …" (Rev. 6:16-17).

This is certainly not the "… blessed hope …" of the children of God (Tit. 2:13); it is rather the "… appointed time …" (Hab. 2:3) for a Christ-rejecting world whose cup of iniquity has been filled to overflowing. Knowing therefore the terror of the Lord and knowing also the time and certainty of this day of reckoning, we have fled for refuge to lay hold of the hope set before us; which hope we have as an anchor of the soul, both sure and steadfast (Matt. 3:7; Heb. 6:18-19). "For God hath not appointed _US_ to wrath (therefore, clearly, some are so appointed), but to obtain salvation by our Lord Jesus Christ" (I Thess. 5:9).

This is "… the time of Jacob's trouble …" (Jer. 30:7) not the time for the purifying of the church. The preparation of the Bride will have already been accomplished. The risen Lord will have bidden her to "… Come up hither …" (Rev. 4:1, 11:12) and to "Come, my people, enter thou into thy chambers, and shut thy doors about thee: hide thyself as it were for a little moment, until the indignation be overpast" (Isa. 26:20). "Seeing then that all these things shall be dissolved, what manner of persons ought ye to be in all holy conversation and godliness … Wherefore, beloved, seeing that ye look for such things, be diligent that ye may be found of him in peace, without spot, and blameless" (II Pet. 3:11, 14).

Thought For Today

There is no "WOE" for those who truly "KNOW!"

December 19

O. T. Bible Reading: Micah 1-3   **Our Focus: Micah 1:6**

THEREFORE

The word *therefore* occurs over 1,100 times in the Scriptures; 11 times in the book of Micah. It quite simply means "as a consequence of"; it is a verbal picture of the law of cause and effect.

The first time the word occurs is in Genesis 2:24: "Therefore shall a man leave his father and his mother, and shall cleave unto his wife: and they shall be one flesh." The 2004 Almanac of the encyclopedia Britannica states that there were approximately 2.5 million weddings in America last year. As a consequence of God creating a woman (Eve) and presenting her to Adam as a help meet, the law of marriage and procreation is fixed and sure. God's laws are absolute and final; His principles are firm and forever, and His Word is sure and steadfast.

This law has both a positive and a negative application. The Psalmist used it both ways in Psalms chapter 119. In Psalms 119:104 he said, "... therefore I hate every false way." That is, as a consequence of loving God's law, of meditating upon it all day long, and of being truly taught of God, His mature judgment causes Him to hate evil. That's pretty basic. It is just as true and sure today as it was when it was first written.

In Psalms 119:119 the Psalmist also rejoicingly said, "... therefore I love thy testimonies." That is, as a consequence of the Lord being his hiding place and shield, he has found a safe harbor in the storms of life and has come to truly love the Word of God. How many millions of God's people through the centuries could say the very same thing?

Thought For Today

We love the Lord because the Lord first loved us!

December 19

N. T. Bible Reading: Revelation 10   **Our Focus: Revelation 10:9**

EAT THE BOOK

The Book of Revelation contains 25 different names and titles of the Lord Jesus Christ. It also contains many symbols. What is symbolically stated must also be symbolically but consistently interpreted.

John is required to do a very strange thing, one which has a very typical meaning. He is told to eat the book (Rev. 10:9). To eat the book means to receive the Word of God with faith and confidence. It is sweet because the message is clear, the promise is sure, and the future is certain. It is very sweet to know what God is doing, and what He is going to do: it is bitter when we realize that there is judgment to come. That is a bitter pill. It is the reason crowds of people will flock to hear about the "antichrist" while only the "faithful few" gather to hear about "the Christ."

This same language is used by the prophet Jeremiah: "Thy words were found, and I did eat them; and thy *WORD* was unto me the joy and rejoicing of mine heart ..." (Jer. 15:16). Ezekiel echoes the very same message: "Moreover he said unto me, Son of man, eat that thou findest; eat this roll ... So I opened my mouth, and he caused me to eat that roll ... Then did I eat it; and it was in my mouth as honey for sweetness" (Ezek. 3:1-3).

There is also a very helpful and instructive application which we can make not only to the subject of Bible prophecy, but also to the entire body of Bible truth. Many people have "... itching ears" (II Tim. 4:3) to hear some new thing or some factual Bible teaching, but they quickly contract "the hotfoot" when anyone applies it to their lives and conduct. This is why the Bible is spoken of as *milk*, *bread*, *honey* and *strong meat*, but also as *a fire*, *a hammer*, and *a sword*. It speaks to us where we are, reveals the problem and the personal need, and gloriously focuses on the miraculous cure.

Thought For Today

The Bible is to be "taken in", and then to be "lived out!"

December 20

O. T. Bible Reading: Micah 4-5   **Our Focus: Micah 5:2**

BETHLEHEM

We are in the season of the year when the world celebrates the birth of Jesus in Bethlehem. That event is the pivotal point of world history. The exact time at which He was born is of very little importance; the fact that He came is the central truth of the Christian faith.

The city of Bethlehem is about 5 miles south of Jerusalem; it is elevated 2,550 feet above sea level, or 100 feet higher than Jerusalem itself. David was born in Bethlehem, and here he was anointed as the future king of Israel by the prophet Samuel (I Sam. 16:1). It was the birthplace of the Messiah. Micah and Isaiah give us the clearest predictions concerning the miraculous virgin birth of Jesus. Isaiah foretells His virgin birth, and Micah pinpoints the place of His birth as in Bethlehem of Judea (Isa. 7:14; Mic. 5:2).

The greatest announcement of all time was not made to the high priest; it was not made in the sacred temple, nor was it made in the capital city of Jerusalem. It was made, rather, to the lowly shepherds as they tended their flocks on the Judean hills. The announcement did not come from the priests, who should have known; it did not come from the slumbering "chosen people"; it came directly from heaven, and was delivered by the Angels. It was brief, crystal clear, and profoundly significant to the entire human family: "For unto you is born this day in the city of David a Saviour, which is Christ the Lord" (Luke 2:11).

No heavenly messenger was ever dispatched to announce the birth of the greatest and the most famous people who have ever lived on this earth. This is of gigantic proportions; it is the single greatest event of all time. It is this one event planned and provided by the *God of hope* which establishes the sure foundation upon which our faith is anchored (Heb. 6:19-20).

Thought For Today

Bethlehem is the House of bread, for Jesus is the bread of Life!

December 20

N. T. Bible Reading: Revelation 11   **Our Focus: Revelation 11:1**

MEASURE

Anything that is of the earth can be measured. It can be measured by time, by sphere of influence, by degree, by number of days, or simply by dimension. It is a point of Divine wisdom for us to reckon with life and its environment as measured and therefore limited. Only the Bible introduces us to those realities which are boundless, infinite, and beyond measure. We are informed of immortality, eternal life, everlasting life, and of the love of God which is *measureless*, and exceeds the boundaries of finite understanding. All of these are entities of another world, and include the great revelation of the infinite God and of everything about Him, which is beyond definition and measure. God is Almighty, His power is measureless. He is full of glory and might; there is no limit to His Majesty. He is a Holy God, and there is nothing about Him which is less than absolutely perfect.

Daniel Webster was asked, "What is the greatest thought that has ever entered your mind?" Without hesitation he gave a very brief answer, "My accountability to Almighty God." The quality of our faith in God is directly proportionate to the clarity of our concept of God and His infinite greatness. The modern concept of God is so decadent (as to be utterly beneath the dignity of the most high God) and is a stench in His nostrils. It constitutes nothing less than a moral calamity and it is a very real spiritual crisis in the Christian community. We must discover the Bible revelation of a Holy God if we are ever to recover from the powerless pretense of professionalism. Men can theorize, dogmatize, and dramatize; but only God can energize. Every person gravitates, by a secret law of the soul, to our mental image of God. A right concept of God is as important to worship as the foundation was to the temple.

Thought For Today

We know God in the measure in which we experience His power!

December 21

O. T. Bible Reading: Micah 6-7   **Our Focus: Micah 7:18**

MERCY

The word "mercy" occurs approximately 350 times in the Word of God. It is no surprise that it is used more often in relation to God than in any other way: we will never be overwhelmed by mercy from human sources … it generally comes in pretty small doses. Mercy, as a Divine attribute, is not easy to define. It is the practical expression or exhibition of loving consideration for man whose need is great and manifold. In a more general sense it is the outward manifestation of pity; it assumes need on the part of the one who receives it; it also assumes adequate resources and supply to meet the need on the part of the one who shows it.

We are told that God is "… the Father of mercies …" (II Cor. 1:3), and that He "… is rich in mercy …" (Eph. 2:4). When the words mercy and peace are combined in the same sentence they occur in that order. Mercy, then, is the act of God; peace is the consequent experience in the heart of man. Grace speaks of God's attitude toward the law-breaker and the rebel; mercy expresses His attitude toward those who are hurting and in distress.

The Psalmist uses the expression, "for his mercy endureth for ever" 26 times in Psalms chapter 136. He also speaks of "… the multitude of thy mercy …" (Ps. 5:7), and in great exultation exclaims, "For great is thy mercy toward me …" (Ps. 86:13).

The Lord is now fitting us for eternity; "… the vessels of mercy, which he had afore prepared unto glory" (Rom. 9:23). A vessel fitted for hospital and medical purposes will find itself in a hospital or some other medical facility. We have been shown great mercy by the Lord, and we should be merciful to others. It is required of us that we "Put on therefore … holy and beloved, bowels of mercies …" (Col. 3:12).

Thought For Today

Mercy is an attribute of God and of the godly!

December 21

N. T. Bible Reading: Revelation 12   **Our Focus: Revelation 12:1, 3**

A WONDER

The word <u>wonder</u>, as a noun, is not a word in common usage, and is seldom heard in everyday conversation. It is most commonly used in Scripture in the plural number, and usually follows the word "signs." Even the dictionary tacks on at the very end of the definition: "miracle." It is not surprising that we find this word 9 times in the book of Acts.

It is peculiarly reserved for the Scriptures, and for the saints of God. It is not uncommon for us to hear someone say: "God is a wonder!" Which is just another way of saying: "He is wonderful!" The prophet Isaiah clearly stated of the Lord Jesus that "... his name shall be called *Wonderful* ..." (Isa. 9:6) that is, truly amazing and genuinely miraculous; that which fills us with wonder, love, and praise. It is important to notice that this is not an adjective; it is a noun: it is <u>*His name*</u>. In Judges 13:18 He appears as the captain of the host of the Lord who declared that His name was <u>*secret*</u> (margin = wonderful). It speaks of a source of power which is supernatural.

Surely we can say of Him that He is truly and totally "<u>*Wonderful*</u>." He was wonderful in His coming to Bethlehem: He was wonderful in His life work and ministry: He was wonderful in His vicarious death on the cross: He was wonderful in His triumphant resurrection, and in His glorious ascension. He is certainly wonderful, even now, in His miraculous power to redeem and transform the life and character of those who know Him as Lord and Savior. He will be wonderful when He descends "... from heaven with a shout ... we ... shall be caught up ... to meet the Lord in the air ..." (I Thess. 4:16-17). Oh, what a wonder!

Thought For Today

Where there is no wonder, there is no Divine presence!

December 22

O. T. Bible Reading: Nahum 1-3   **Our Focus: Nahum 1:1**

NINEVEH

The city of Nineveh was the capital of Assyria, and at the time of Nahum, it was the world's greatest city. Recent discoveries indicate that it was really a complex of four cities in one. Based on a trigonometric survey, the full area has been computed as 350 square miles. The city lay on the eastern side of the Tigris River. It had 1,200 towers on its walls, each 200 feet high; the wall itself was 100 feet tall, and wide enough at the top that three chariots could drive on it, side by side. In the midst of the city was a magnificent palace, the courts and walls of which covered more than 100 acres; all built by foreign slaves. No wonder God called it a great city (Jon. 1:2). The awful and hideous cruelty and torture recorded by historians is nauseating and repulsive. It was a wicked city.

The prophet Jonah was sent to Nineveh, which at the time repented, to show the mercy of God. Now, 150 years later, the prophet Nahum pronounces the sentence of Divine judgment to show the justice of God, and to illustrate the law of retribution. They had resorted to their evil ways and the prophet said they would be "… empty, and void, and waste …" (Nah. 2:10), 86 years later they were sacked, ruined, and destroyed (606 BC) by the confederate armies of Medes, Persians, Egyptians, and Armenians. So total and complete was the destruction, that centuries later Alexander the Great marched his armies over the site of the ruins and never knew that a world empire laid buried under his feet.

The lesson is clear, and the message is very obvious: any power or kingdom based on fraud, force, and fury will fail. We are taught by the Scriptures that God will eventually shake everything (and everyone) that can be shaken, that what cannot be shaken may remain (Heb. 12:26; Hag. 2:6-7). Only what is done righteously, wrought in truth and honesty, and done in the name of the Lord will survive.

Thought For Today

Today's palaces may become tomorrow's landfill!

December 22

N. T. Bible Reading: Revelation 13   **Our Focus: Revelation 13:13, 10**

PATIENCE AND FAITH

Patience is a New Testament word: it occurs 33 times and only in the New Testament. Hebrews 6:12 reads: "That ye be not slothful, but followers of them who through faith and patience inherit the promises." This order is the reverse of our focus, Revelation 13:10. One reason perhaps is that the emphasis in Hebrews is on faith, while the most pressing issue in Revelation chapter 13 would obviously be the need for patience.

The word used for patience, if literally interpreted, would be: "to abide under." This is very suggestive and alerts us immediately to a key and vital truth. Paul clearly declares that the Mighty God we serve is: "... the God of patience and consolation ..." (Rom. 15:5), "... the God of hope ..." (Rom. 15:13), and "... the God of peace ..." (Rom. 15:33) all in one chapter. The Psalmist gives us a surer foundation for both faith and patience: "Be still, and know that I am God ..." (Ps. 46:10). A vision of God imparts a clarity and a certainty to the quickened heart, and infuses the dynamic of a steadfast tenacity, knowing that God is in control and His plan is sure to succeed. What a blessed place to abide. We are told that Moses endured because he had a vision of God (Heb. 11:27). The God of patience is also the God of hope. The acid test and proof of our vision is that we are reaching out for more than we have grasped. Complacency is the graveyard of endeavor. Any genuine vision of God brings with it an infinite vastness, which it will take all eternity to explore.

Patience is more than endurance: it is "... all joy and peace in believing, that ye may abound in hope, through the power of the Holy Ghost" (Rom. 15:13). It is the sure confidence of the clay in the hands of the skillful Potter. The clay cannot know what the master craftsman sees as the finished product. This is where a vibrant faith comes into play: we abide under the shadow of the Almighty (Ps. 91:1) knowing that He has a plan and a purpose. We cannot see just now; we are not able to understand or explain our present plight; we are buffeted, but never baffled because we know Him, and we trust Him. He cannot fail!

Thought For Today

Patience is the only rope which can grip the anchor!

350

December 23

O. T. Bible reading: Habakkuk 1-3　　　　**Our Focus: Habakkuk 2:3**

WAIT FOR IT

The Lord answers the prophet by assuring him that though the promise tarries until the appointed time, it will not tarry a moment beyond that time. Every promise in the Divine library is dated with an invisible ink which can be read only by the eye of faith. The apparent delays which we experience are really only the fulfillment of His unfailing purposes. God's will, we come to realize, is inseparable from God's time.

The believers at Thessalonica had demonstrated their turning to God by turning away "… from idols to serve the living and true God; And to wait for his Son from heaven …" (I Thess. 1:9-10). They did not wait for death, for that will come without waiting for it. They did not wait for the Spirit of God, but for the Son of God. They did not wait for Titus' legions to come from Rome, but they waited for God's Son to come from heaven.

The sure promise of His second coming, and the long time span between promise and fulfillment, constitute the single most vital aspect of waiting. This waiting is not to fold the arms and sit in a rocking chair: it is to eagerly expect. It is to occupy until He comes (Luke 19:13), that is, to throw everything we have into the conflict; to aggressively pursue His interests without reservations, and to unselfishly "… seek ye first the kingdom of God, and his righteousness …" (Matt. 6:33). The greatest single incentive to sacrificial service, and to godly living, is the purifying hope of His second coming (I John 3:3). The vision is yet for an appointed time; let us wait for it (Hab. 2:3).

Thought For Today

Those who most certainly wait, most earnestly labor!

December 23

N. T. Bible Reading: Revelation 14   **Our Focus: Revelation 14:3**

A NEW SONG

Song is the language of the soul. To those who are redeemed, it is the overflow of praise for the glorious reality of salvation. Singing and chanting are part of all heathen rituals, and modern music is designed to stir the sensuous emotions. Singers are mentioned over 50 times in the Bible, and singing more than 100 times. The word sing in all of its variation is used 74 times in the book of Psalms alone. David, "… the sweet psalmist of Israel …" (II Sam. 23:1), had an orchestra of 4,000 instruments, and a choir of 288 voices (I Chron. 23:5, 25:7). Ezra had a choir of 200 singing men and women (Ezra 2:65).

The Psalmist states that, "The dead praise not the Lord …" (Ps. 115:17). After over 50 years of experience in the ministry, I can truthfully say that the congregations of the dead, praise not the Lord, and the dead in the congregation, praise not the Lord.

Moses composed a song and led the nation of Israel in the singing of it (Deut. 31:22). Miriam, Deborah, Barak, and the many other Bible characters sang unto the Lord. David sang and played skillfully, some 55 of the Psalms bear the caption "to the chief musician." Jesus and the 12 disciples sang. Paul and Silas sang, and with some very amazing results. We know that the angels of heaven sang. However, this gigantic choir (surely the largest on record) of 144,000 harmonize their voices in united rhythmic expression to sing a new song.

We are expressly told that none could sing this new song except the company of saints who were redeemed from the earth (Rev. 14:3). There is always something new and fresh in the experience of redemption. The old garments and the stale bread are only for the pretenders. Let us enjoy the newness and the freshness of daily communion and fellowship with the Lord.

Thought For Today

When the stars cease their shining, the saints will cease their singing!

December 24

O. T. Bible Reading: Zephaniah 1-3   **Our Focus: Zephaniah 2:3**

SEEK

The word seek is a verb, and one which suggests both diligence and intensity. The root meaning of the word is: to search for, to inquire after, to look for, to ask for, and to strive after. It occurs, in all forms, about 300 times in the Scriptures.

There is a threefold injunction in Zephaniah 2:3: "Seek ye the Lord ... seek righteousness, seek meekness ...." We know, of course, this was written primarily to *Judah* (Zeph. 2:4); however, the application may be made to any person or to any group of people anywhere at any time. Our primary duty and responsibility is to seek the Lord. It is our personal relationship to Him which matters most. It is an endeavor, an animated personal pursuit, and a whole-hearted reaching out after God, which is in focus here. No cheap substitute will suffice. The hungry soul must come to know Him whom to know aright is life eternal (John 17:3).

The prophet further admonishes them to also seek righteousness. Any search for God which does not lead to right and godly conduct is misdirected, powerless, or just plain futile. The conclusion of Scripture establishes some very clear and positive absolutes; one of the most basic is: "... every one that doeth righteousness is born of him" (I John 2:29), and again, "... whosoever doeth not righteousness is not of God ..." (I John 3:10). This is the litmus paper, which defines the fluid as either acidic or alkaline. All else being considered, it is still "... by their fruits ye shall know them" (Matt. 7:20).

Seek humility. There are many ways in which pride may express itself: "pride of race, pride of face, and pride of grace." We must never allow an exalted spirit or attitude to grip our lives. Every true and genuine experience which we have with God and with His Word brings with it a withering sense of our unworthiness and need.

Thought For Today

Those whose seek diligently will be rewarded abundantly!

353

December 24

N. T. Bible Reading: Revelation 15-16   **Our Focus: Revelation 16:15**

WATCH

There are three ways in which the word "watch" is used in the Word of God:

1. To watch in order to guard or to protect.
2. To watch, meaning to look for.
3. An interval of time constituting a watch: the night being divided, not into hours, but into watches. In the Old Testament there are three mentioned: the first watch, till midnight; the middle watch, till 3 AM; the morning watch, to 6 AM. In the New Testament there were four watches of three hours each, from 6 PM to 6 PM.

In the Scripture focus for today, Revelation 16:15 (one of the seven beatitudes of the book of Revelation), we are told that there is a special blessing bestowed upon those who watch so as to keep their garments from being defiled. To be watchful and alert is to be aware and informed. The meaning here includes the thought of a particular attitude of mind, of a certain condition of heart, and of a special pattern of behavior.

The words of the Lord Jesus in Mark 13 seem to put the intended focus on the word "watch": "Take ye heed, watch and pray ..." (Mark 13:33), "Watch ye therefore ..." (Mark 13:35), "And what I say unto you I say unto all, Watch" (Mark 13:37). Primarily, He is saying keep your wits about you, remain alert, and avoid the subtle spirit of slumber, by remaining prayerful. If eternal vigilance is the price of freedom, then surely eternal watchfulness remains the price of discipleship.

Jesus urged His disciples and all of us as well, to be careful, supremely careful, in the area of their personal loyalty to Him. There will be a myriad of voices each claiming top priority at this point. Take heed! Also, He summons them to be careful to maintain the attitude of courage. Do not be distracted by threats and warfare. Do not be anxious when hostility directs the attack against you. Remain powerful. That does not mean that we are forever asking for something. It has a much broader meaning. The idea is the intense longing of the pleading soul forward toward God. The Psalmist gave it immortal expression: "My soul followeth hard after thee ..." (Ps. 63:8).

Thought For Today

Those who watch most carefully, pray most fervently!

December 25

O. T. Bible Reading: Haggai 1-2   **Our Focus: Haggai 1:5, 7**

CONSIDER

The prophet Haggai requires of the discouraged remnant that they "... Consider ..." (Hag. 1:5, 7) or set their hearts on their ways. The condition was tragic. The year was 520 BC. The remnant with Zerubbabel had enthusiastically returned to the land, and in two years the foundation of the temple had been laid. Then came opposition. The work ceased, the adversaries consolidated, and the hearts of the people grew weary. Now, nearly 15 years later, Haggai, along with Zechariah and Malachi, begin to stir up the hearts of the people. There are times when to delay is treachery, to compromise is a travesty, and to ignore is nothing short of a tragedy. This young prophet ministered for four short months, gave us a very brief book of only 38 verses, and delivered only four brief messages. His words were heeded, the people responded, the Lord stirred up the people; and within four years of his challenge, the temple was completed and solemnly dedicated.

There is a message for everyone in this great historic event. It is very easy to find excuses when opposition strikes. Either it just is not the time, or perhaps it was not God's will anyway, or the Lord has something else for me to do.

The noble thing to do is to examine our hearts. This people had substituted selfish interests for spiritual responsibilities. Their vision had been obscured by a very common problem known as "I" trouble. It is always a very wise thing to give some serious thought as to why conditions are as they are. The answer may be very near at hand and the solution very simple: _build_, that is, begin to obey.

Thought For Today

To consider our ways is to walk in His ways!

December 25

N. T. Bible Reading: Revelation 16　　　　**Our Focus: Revelation 16:15**

BEHOLD, I COME

The promise of a personal, physical, second coming of Christ back to the earth echoes and re-echoes throughout the Bible; and not surprisingly, occurs seven times in the book of final things, the book of Revelation. The last chapter of the Bible declares the blessed truth three times (Rev. 22:7, 12, 20). It is significant that the word translated "quickly" here literally means "rapidly" ... not shortly, not immediately, not even soon. Paul also emphasized this same aspect of the truth when he said: "In a moment, in the twinkling of an eye ..." (I Cor. 15:52), that is a very brief period of time ... a fraction of a second ... the smallest element of time.

The subject of the second coming is very prominent in the Word of God. Those scholars, who have carefully researched and studied the theme, give us some arresting statistics:

1. Nearly one fourth of the Bible is prophetic.
2. About 300 Old Testament scriptures relate to His coming.
3. There are 318 Testament scriptures which speak of His coming.
4. Jesus spoke of the event some 21 times.

The first message given after the miraculous ascension of Christ was preached by the Angels and it was the miraculous return of Christ: it was positive, clear, and emphatic: "... this same Jesus, which is taken up from you into heaven, shall so come in like manner as ye have seen him go into heaven" (Acts 1:11). The time of His return is not related to the Almanac, not measured by human calendars, and has no bearing to an earthly time piece. It is the maturity of conditions among men which signals Divine intervention. It is the ripening of the grain which determines the time of the harvest. God waited for the iniquity of the Amorites to be filled to the full before He acted (Gen. 15:16). The promise is plain, the proof is positive, and the preparation is personal.

Thought For Today

Faithful preparation brings certain celebration!

December 26

O. T. Bible Reading: Zechariah 1-3   **Our Focus: Zechariah 1:3**

TURN UNTO ME

This is about as basic as it can get. To turn is clearly understood … it is to change direction. Men are lost, because they turn not to God: but surely none could say that they were lost because they had not the power to turn. It also includes the basic thought of return. That is, to come back again. The same power you used to turn from, you are now required to use to return to. It is the twofold power of choice and action. You made a choice to turn away, and that choice was followed by actions which led you away. Now, God asks nothing more of you than that you reverse the process. You must make a choice (followed by many choices) to change direction, and take action to put that choice into shoe leather. This is a much neglected Scriptural emphasis in the experience of salvation.

The Old Testament Hebrew word "turn" is used some 600 times: it is the equivalent of the New Testament word "repent" which occurs 57 times. As applied to man, it means to turn away from sin and to return to God and His ways; "… ye turned to God from idols to serve the living and true God" (I Thess. 1:9). The process involved is clearly expressed by David in Psalms 119:59-60 "I thought on my ways, and turned my feet unto thy testimonies. I made haste, and delayed not to keep thy commandments." It can be accurately said that repentance involves confession, contrition, and correction. All of this brings us right back to where we began. There must, and will be, a change of direction where there has been a true encounter with God.

Thought For Today

Those who turn to God find Him awaiting their return!

December 26

N. T. Bible Reading: Revelation 17　　　　**Our Focus: Revelation 17:14**

FAITHFUL

We are told seven times in the New Testament that "God is faithful"; and Jeremiah declares in the midst of his lamentations: "... great is thy faithfulness" (Lam. 3:23). The Psalmist extolled this great attribute of God by saying, "... thy faithfulness reacheth unto the clouds" (Ps. 36:5). That is, even to the very skies. He is faithful in the absolute sense (no variation from it) and, therefore, is the sure firm and unfailing source of our trust ... He cannot fail!!

There is a strong emphasis on the faithfulness of Christ in the book of Revelation where He is called: "... the faithful witness ..." (Rev. 1:5), "... he that is true ..." (Rev. 3:7), "... the faithful and true ..." (Rev. 3:14). Behind the witness of His lips was the unflinching faithfulness of His life. There was never any contradiction between His counsel and His character.

Solomon asked quite succinctly, "... but a faithful man who can find?" (Prov. 20:6). It certainly might be very difficult, but evidently not impossible. It is clearly stated that the Great and Final Judge will say to some: "... Well done, thou good and faithful servant ..." (Matt. 25:21). We are told in today's reading that those who are with the lamb are "... called, and chosen, and faithful" (Rev. 17:14).

Most translations agree that an accurate rendering of Galatians 5:22 should read "The fruit of the Spirit is ... faithfulness" (not faith). That is to say that the sterling qualities of trustworthiness, steadfastness, and faithfulness will be manifest in the lives of all truly Spirit-filled children of God. What a manifestation of the Spirit that is! Let us aspire to the highest. The very spirit and life of Him, who is faithful, can produce no less in us.

Thought For Today

Since He is faithful those that are His can be no less!

December 27

O. T. Bible Reading: Zechariah 4-6   **Our Focus: Zechariah 6:12**

THE BRANCH

The study of the Divine names and titles used in Scripture is probably a life-long project, but certainly very revealing and most rewarding. The vast magnitude of God, and the incomprehensible heights and depths of His Person, are but dimly hinted at in the long list of names and titles by which He reveals Himself. Yet each would seem to give us yet another dimension to His infinite majesty and glory.

Zechariah identifies Him (the Lord Jesus) with the prophetic title of "... The Branch ..." (Zech. 6:12). The Scriptures reveal Him thus in a four-fold way:

1. Here in Zechariah 6:12-13 He is represented as *The Man* whose name is *The Branch*. Jesus referred to Himself as "the son of man" some 85 times as recorded in the Gospels. Although He came to a peasant home, was reared in poverty and obscurity, He shall one day rule this world as King of Kings and Lord of Lords.

2. In Isaiah 4:2 He is called the Branch of Jehovah. This is the "... Immanuel" (Isa. 7:14) character of Christ: it is "... God with us" (Matt. 1:23). He is, in this context, named "the Son of God" 48 times in the Authorized Version of the Bible (King James Version).

3. In Jeremiah 23:5 He is designated as The Branch of David. That is, of course, saying that He came as "... the seed of David according to the flesh" (Rom. 1:3). This speaks of His royal nature as King.

4. In Zechariah 3:8-9 we see Him as Jehovah's servant, The Branch. This mighty conqueror of Calvary shall one day remove all iniquity, and reign in righteousness (Jer. 33:15). We are now His branches in the earth. May our fruit glorify His worthy name (John 15:5).

Thought For Today

The branch bears fruit by drawing life from the vine!

December 27

N. T. Bible Reading: Revelation 18   **Our Focus: Revelation 18:4**

MY PEOPLE

It is a surprise to many to learn that these two words "my people" occur over 150 times in the Bible, but only four times in the New Testament. This makes it quite clear that in most cases a reference is to the nation of Israel. God plainly stated that in view of His special call and covenant He would "… walk among you, and will be your God, and ye shall be my people" (Lev. 26:12).

One of the great mysteries of the New Testament is the cutting off (temporarily) of the nation of Israel, and the grafting in of the Gentiles (Rom. 11:24-25). We Gentiles were without God, and without hope, for we had no covenant promise (Eph. 2:12). Now, through the mercy of God, "… there is no difference between the Jew and the Greek (Gentile): for the same Lord over all is rich unto all that call upon him" (Rom. 10:12). Peter plainly recognized this when he said: "But ye are a chosen generation, a royal priesthood, an holy nation, a peculiar people; that ye should shew forth the praises of him who hath called you out of darkness into his marvelous light; Which in time past were not a people, but are now the people of God (my people): which had not obtained mercy, but now have obtained mercy" (I Pet. 2:9-10).

It is a great honor for us to know that we are now His people, through the blood of Christ, and His great atonement. Every privilege carries with it responsibility and accountability. It is now incumbent upon us that we conduct ourselves in a manner that clearly identifies us as His unique possession. A Divinely transformed life is the greatest single proof of Divine ownership.

Thought For Today

His people know His voice and heed His Word!

December 28

O. T. Bible Reading: Zechariah 7-9   **Our Focus: Zechariah 7:5**

UNTO ME

When God speaks, let all the earth keep silence before Him (Hab. 2:20). When God asks a question, let every soul give earnest heed and be "… swift to hear, slow to speak …" (Jam. 1:19). The very first recorded word from God to man after the fall was in the form of a question, "… Where art thou?" (Gen. 3:9). When Job had endured unexplained suffering and unjust criticism from his false comforters he heard from God: it is said, "Then the Lord answered Job …" (Job 38:1), and it was in the form of 59 unanswered questions. Many a person could testify to an encounter with the Lord when a penetrating and silencing question from the Lord led to a glorious new experience with God. "I have heard of thee by the hearing of the ear: but now mine eye seeth thee" (Job 42:5). In the Scripture reading for today, God asks whether their religious exercises were just so many mechanical and meaningless dead and dry ceremonies, or were they genuine and, therefore, as unto the Lord (Zech. 7:5).

This seems super simple, but it defines the world of difference between reality and artificiality. Paul admonishes the church at Colosse: "And whatsoever ye do, do it heartily, as to the Lord, and not unto men" (Col. 3:23). Those who seek only to please men are sure to become dejected, disappointed, disillusioned, and defeated as well as disgusted. Those who have a single eye, a single aim, and a single heart to please the Lord will be neither displeased nor disheartened; they have a higher goal, which the good or evil treatment of men will neither excite nor exalt; the opposition and criticism of men will neither deter nor deject. Only the praise and glory of God matters to such a self-less servant of the Lord.

Thought For Today

Only what we do unto Him will endure eternally!

December 28

N. T. Bible Reading: Revelation 19   **Our Focus: Revelation 19:1, 3, 4, 6**

HALLELUJAH

There are few moments of human ecstasy which can equal what is experienced when we listen to the singing of Handel's "Messiah." It was written in 1741 and first sung in Dublin on April 13th, 1742. It has been sung many thousands of times worldwide and anyone who is not profoundly moved should be seriously examined for the basic signs of life. One great religious leader said when he first listened to the inspired music: "I buried my head in my hands and sobbed, 'Even so come, Lord Jesus!'"

The Hebrew word "Hallelujah" occurs 28 times in the Scriptures. It is translated "Hallelujah" 11 times, or, according to the Greek spelling, as in today's focus, in the New Testament, "Alleluia"; and is translated 19 times, "Praise ye the Lord", which is the literal meaning. The word is associated with praise and worship, and will seldom be heard where the spontaneous overflow of both has been lost and/or ceremonially rejected. All of which only proves the accuracy of Scripture, "The *dead* praise not the Lord ..." (Ps. 115:17).

The word "Alleluia" occurs four times in the doxology at the beginning of this chapter (Rev. 19:1, 3, 4, 6). The number four is significant in Scripture as pertaining to the natural creation, and here, to the earth in particular. The heavens resound with great rejoicing for the final and sure triumph of God over the earth and every form of rebellion found in it. Let us not fear, nor hesitate to join the chorus even now "Hallelujah!"

Thought For Today

The flow of praise is a vital sign of spiritual life!

December 29

O. T. Bible Reading: Zechariah 10-12   **Our Focus: Zechariah 10:4**

THE CORNERSTONE

Most translations agree that the corner which is promised out of the house of Judah is more accurately the *cornerstone*. The Apostle Peter enlarges upon this thought in I Peter as he depicts Christ as the chief cornerstone (I Pet. 2:4), a stone of stumbling and a rock of offense (I Pet. 2:8). He seems to combine three Old Testament Scriptures in this passage. First, Isaiah had prophetically anticipated the coming Messiah as "... a foundation a stone, a tried stone, a precious corner stone, a sure foundation ..." (Isa. 28:16). Those who believe in and trust in His certain provision will not be nervous, nor hasty, but can confidently rest in Him (Isa. 28:16). The second Old Testament reference is Psalms 118:22. The Lord Jesus makes very clear that the rejected stone which the builders refused was a prophetic reference to Himself (Matt. 21:42). The third reference is to Isaiah 8:14, where God's people are admonished to sanctify the Lord of hosts in their hearts and to fear Him above all others. Cromwell was said to be one of the bravest men to ever live, and was asked how he gained such a reputation. He answered, "I have learned that when you fear *God*, you have no *man* to fear."

This is what our generation of shallow thinkers needs. There is a light, if not frivolous thinking and attitude toward God, toward His Word, and toward His people. Our behavior is simply the truest expression of our concept of God. The prophet declared, "... the Lord is in his holy temple: let all the earth keep silence before him" (Hab. 2:20). The carnal inventions which attempt to glamorize Christianity and to popularize the Gospel are intrusions into the majesty and holiness of God.

Let us be certain that the superstructure of our faith rests securely upon the person and work of the Lord Jesus Christ, and in the precious Word of God. To disturb the authority of the Scriptures unsettles the very foundation of our faith and of the church itself.

Thought For Today

Those who fall upon the rock have found a sure foundation!

December 29

N. T. Bible Reading: Revelation 20   **Our Focus: Revelation 20:6**

THEY SHALL REIGN

The grooming of the young heir and heiress of the throne began at an early age and continued for many years. It was both thorough and unique. Not only must this person of destiny be given the very highest academic preparations, they must also be professionally tutored in protocol and international etiquette. Much time and diligence must be given to vital details of life and conduct which would be of little or no interest to the average citizen. This fact is of primary importance to that most select group of saints called the Bride of Christ.

Thrones were clearly seen, and those who sat upon them "... lived and reigned with Christ a thousand years" (Rev. 20:4). Not only were these individuals thoroughly instructed and drilled in the dynamics of kingly authority and wisdom, they were also given post-graduate skills in the function and behavior of spiritual priesthood. It is said that "... they shall be priests of God and of Christ, and shall reign with him a thousand years" (Rev. 20:6). It should be abundantly clear to all that the all-wise God would not delegate such high office to any, but the most carefully prepared and the most eminently qualified.

Those who have eyes to see and grasp the vision of such a high calling are both blessed and holy (Rev. 20:6). It is significant and interesting that in this book of Revelation the words "I saw" occur no less than 36 times; each chapter begins with the same words; and the words "I beheld" are used six times. To be given a revelation is to cause one to see. Little wonder, then, that Jesus said to His immediate disciples, "But blessed are your eyes, for they see ..." (Matt. 13:16). The very same can be said today, and with at least two exclamation marks!!

Thought For Today

Those who rule and reign are called and trained!

December 30

O. T. Bible Reading: Zechariah 13-14   **Our Focus: Zechariah 13:1**

A FOUNTAIN OPENED

The Jewish commentator, Solomon Ben Jarchi, also known as "Rashi" made the following statement: "The prophecy of Zechariah is very dark, for it contains visions much like dreams, which want interpreting, and we will never succeed in finding the true meaning until the teacher of righteousness arrives." It can also be said that until God pours "… upon the house of David (Israel), and upon the inhabitants of Jerusalem, the spirit of grace and of supplications …" (Zech. 12:10) they will not understand that a fountain has already been opened at Calvary to deal with the problem of sin and of uncleanness. The very same can also be said for every individual. The work has been done; the victor has already proclaimed, "… It is finished …" (John 19:30); and the one-time offering for sin has been crowned with Divine approval by the resurrection of Christ from the dead. However, until and unless God makes these historic facts real to our own heart and mind, there can be no redemption.

"In that day", a phrase repeated 17 times in Zechariah, has reference to a yet future period of time and events for the nation of Israel. It also has a great application for every individual, because in the day that God awakens our heart, we can come to experience His mighty transforming power. Jesus promised His disciples, "And I will pray the Father, and he shall give you another Comforter …" (John 14:16), and "At that day ye shall know that I am in my Father, and ye in me, and I in you" (John 14:20). The Apostle John uses the word "now" 25 times; his focus is not the future, but the present. "But the hour cometh, and now is, when the true worshipers shall worship the Father in spirit and in truth …" (John 4:23). This is the day for us to claim and experience His Divine enduement of power that we may be His witnesses.

Thought For Today

The fountain is open for all who see and own their need!

December 30

N. T. Bible Reading: Revelation 21   **Our Focus: Revelation 21:5**

ALL THINGS NEW

The *New* Testament, or Covenant, gives us both a new and a better hope (Heb. 7:19). The word "new" occurs about 60 times in the New Testament and the word "better" is used 13 times in the book of Hebrews alone.

The new birth produces a miraculous new creature, in whom is a new nature, which enables us to walk in newness of life serving the Lord in newness of spirit (II Cor. 5:17; Rom. 6:4, 7:6). We must not be as the Athenians who "… spent their time in nothing else, but either to tell, or to hear some *new* thing" (Acts 17:21). The great truth is that it is the old-fashioned Gospel which, and only which, produces this great harvest of new fruits. This is not a tack on, not another among many, and not a new brand in a crowded market of competitive products. It is, rather, the only cure for the hopeless leper, the only bread which imparts life, and the only way which leads to life eternal. That is why Paul preached "For in Christ Jesus neither circumcision availeth any thing, nor uncircumcision, but a new creature" (Gal. 6:15). What we were, what we had, what we had done, and what we had contributed, meant absolutely nothing. Without the new birth you are without God and without hope … you are lost!

It is indeed a refreshing thought that one day *all things will be made new* (Rev. 21:5). Every trace of evil will be forever gone; all darkness and disease will be swallowed up in light and life; all sorrow and suffering will be forgotten; all debt, doubt, despair and death will pass away. What a day … what a glorious day that will be! We have, even now, the very first-fruits of this glorious reality; in Christ "… old things are passed away; behold, all things are become new" (II Cor. 5:17).

Thought For Today

The new birth imparts a new vision with new horizons!

December 31

O. T. Bible Reading: Malachi 1-4   **Our Focus: Malachi 4:2**

THE SUN OF RIGHTEOUSNESS

Many make mention of the fact that the Old Testament ends with the word "… curse" (Mal. 4:6), but few ever remind us that the last chapter of the Old Testament gives us a glorious prophetic promise of the coming of the Great Healer, "… the Sun of righteousness …" (Mal. 4:2). This One is the same person who is the Bright and Morning Star spoken of in the last chapter of the New Testament (Rev. 22:16). Christ is never called "The Sun of Righteousness" in the New Testament, and He is never called "The Bright and Morning Star" in the Old Testament. There is a very basic and profound reason for this.

The Lord himself declares, "… I am the root and the offspring of David, and the bright and morning star" (Rev. 22:16). He came, on His earthly mission, through the stock of David; and became thereby the heir to the promised Jewish throne. However, there is a new concept emphasized in this new designation, "The Bright and Morning Star." Before the sun rises in the east, about an hour sooner, the beautiful and bright morning star appears also in the east.

The "*sun*", not "son" here, is the herald of the day. There is a new day (the east) promised in the Scriptures in which He shall reign in righteousness (Isa. 32:1; Rev. 11:15). The star is distinct and separate from the sun: first the morning star, then, later, the sun. The star is the sign of the coming of Christ to take His prepared bride to His prepared place. Only after this will He return with His saints to set up His kingdom. The Apostle Peter echoed this same truth, "We have also a more sure word of prophecy; whereunto ye do well that ye take heed, as unto a light that shineth in a dark place, until the day dawn, and the *day star* arise in your hearts" (II Pet. 1:19). It is this blessed hope of The Day Star rapture of His Bride which is the purifying and sanctifying truth for all of us (I John 3:3).

Thought For Today

The day will not begin until the morning star first appears!

December 31

N. T. Bible Reading: Revelation 22   **Our Focus: Revelation 22:14**

A BLESSED FINALITY

It is the conclusion of any matter which really counts; the process is only preliminary, and the events of the process are only temporary. The road may be pleasant, the scenery may be beautiful, the view may be breathtaking, but where will it lead to? There are many "dead-end" streets and roads. The journey of life is by far and away the most serious road any of us will ever travel. "There is a way which seemeth right unto a man, but the end thereof are the ways of death" (Prov. 14:12, 16:25). How thrilling and satisfying it is for us to see the conclusion of man's days in a glorious triumph.

The altitude at which we stand will determine the extent of our vision. It is interesting and instructive that before this great panoramic scene of final blessedness is viewed by John he was carried "... away in the spirit to a great and high mountain ..." (Rev. 21:10). Only from these lofty heights could he possibly catch such a view. At sea level he saw only a beast rising out of the waters (Rev. 13:1). What a contrast in these two scenes! It is only when we stand high that we are able to see afar. It is the elevation which gives a wide vision.

The view which Noah had from the Ark was reassuring and enlightening: "... on the first day of the month, were the tops of the mountains seen" (Gen. 8:5). It was only from the Ark which rested on the mountains of Ararat that this vision was possible (Gen. 8:4). The word "Ararat" means "holy ground." Lofty mountain peaks of Divine truth are seen only by those who stand on the high ground which is also Holy Ground. Hazy vision and blurred horizons are the experience of all who dwell in the smog-filled lowlands. Also, only from the very top of the Ark (the upper window) could these shining peaks be seen (Gen. 6:16).

Thought For Today

The dazzling sunset of time becomes the glowing dawn of eternity!

Honoring the Life and Ministry of Rev. Rodney E. Whittle
His Life Verse, Daniel 11:32
"… the people that do know their God shall be strong, and do exploits."

CPSIA information can be obtained at www.ICGtesting.com
Printed in the USA
LVOW11s0745271213

367079LV00001B/22/P